New Approaches to the Study of Esotericism

Supplements to Method & Theory in the Study of Religion

Editorial Board

Aaron W. Hughes (*University of Rochester*)
Russell McCutcheon (*University of Alabama*)
Kocku von Stuckrad (*University of Groningen*)

VOLUME 17

The titles published in this series are listed at *brill.com/smtr*

New Approaches to the Study of Esotericism

Edited by

Egil Asprem
Julian Strube

BRILL

LEIDEN | BOSTON

This is an open access title distributed under the terms of the CC BY-NC-ND 4.0 license, which permits any non-commercial use, distribution, and reproduction in any medium, provided no alterations are made and the original author(s) and source are credited. Further information and the complete license text can be found at https://creativecommons.org/licenses/by-nc-nd/4.0/

The terms of the CC license apply only to the original material. The use of material from other sources (indicated by a reference) such as diagrams, illustrations, photos and text samples may require further permission from the respective copyright holder.

Funded by the Deutsche Forschungsgemeinschaft (DFG, German Research Foundation) under Germany's Excellence Strategy – EXC 2060 "Religion and Politics. Dynamics of Tradition and Innovation" – 390726036; as well as by the Open Access Fund of the Westfälische Wilhelms-Universität Münster

Funded by

Cover illustration: mycelium, copyright Taviphoto. | Dreamstime.com, https://www.dreamstime.com/taviphoto_info

Library of Congress Cataloging-in-Publication Data

Names: Asprem, Egil, editor. | Strube, Julian, editor.
Title: New approaches to the study of esotericism / edited by Egil Asprem, Julian Strube.
Description: Leiden ; Boston : Brill, 2021. | Series: Supplements to method & theory in the study of religion, 2214-3270 ; volume 17 | Includes bibliographical references and index. |
Identifiers: LCCN 2020048069 | ISBN 9789004446441 (hardback) | ISBN 9789004446458 (ebook)
Subjects: LCSH: Occultism–Research–Methodology.
Classification: LCC BF1439 .N49 2021 | DDC 130–dc23
LC record available at https://lccn.loc.gov/2020048069

Typeface for the Latin, Greek, and Cyrillic scripts: "Brill". See and download: brill.com/brill-typeface.

ISSN 2214-3270
ISBN 978-90-04-44644-1 (hardback)
ISBN 978-90-04-44645-8 (e-book)

Copyright 2021 by Egil Asprem and Julian Strube. Published by Koninklijke Brill NV, Leiden, The Netherlands.
Koninklijke Brill NV incorporates the imprints Brill, Brill Hes & De Graaf, Brill Nijhoff, Brill Rodopi, Brill Sense, Hotei Publishing, mentis Verlag, Verlag Ferdinand Schöningh and Wilhelm Fink Verlag.
Koninklijke Brill NV reserves the right to protect this publication against unauthorized use. Requests for re-use and/or translations must be addressed to Koninklijke Brill NV via brill.com or copyright.com.

This book is printed on acid-free paper and produced in a sustainable manner.

Contents

Notes on Contributors   VII

Esotericism's Expanding Horizon: Why This Book Came to Be   1
    Egil Asprem and Julian Strube

Receptions of Revelations: A Future for the Study of Esotericism and Antiquity   20
    Dylan Burns

Towards the Study of Esotericism without the "Western": Esotericism from the Perspective of a Global Religious History   45
    Julian Strube

"That I Did Love the Moor to Live with Him": Islam in/and the Study of "Western Esotericism"   67
    Liana Saif

The Occult among the Aborigines of South America? Some Remarks on Race, Coloniality, and the West in the Study of Esotericism   88
    Mariano Villalba

"Don't Take Any Wooden Nickels": Western Esotericism, Yoga, and the Discourse of Authenticity   109
    Keith Cantú

Rejected Knowledge Reconsidered: Some Methodological Notes on Esotericism and Marginality   127
    Egil Asprem

Race and (the Study of) Esotericism   147
    Justine Bakker

"What Can the Whole World Be Hiding?": Exploring *Africana* Esotericisms in the American Soul-Blues Continuum   168
    Hugh R. Page, Jr. and Stephen C. Finley

Double Toil and Gender Trouble? Performativity and Femininity in the Cauldron of Esotericism Research   182
   Manon Hedenborg White

What Do Jade Eggs Tell Us about the Category "Esotericism"? Spirituality, Neoliberalism, Secrecy, and Commodities   201
   Susannah Crockford

Interpretation Reconsidered: The Definitional Progression in the Study of Esotericism as a Case in Point for the Varifocal Theory of Interpretation   217
   Dimitry Okropiridze

Afterword: Outlines of a New Roadmap   241
   Egil Asprem and Julian Strube

Index   253

Notes on Contributors

Egil Asprem
is Associate Professor in History of Religions at Stockholm University. He is the editor-in-chief of *Aries* and has published widely on esotericism and its study, including *The Problem of Disenchantment: Scientific Naturalism and Esoteric Discourse, 1900–1939* (Brill, 2014).

Justine M. Bakker
is a postdoctoral fellow in Critical Philosophy of Race at Radboud University, Nijmegen (the Netherlands). In May 2020, she obtained her PhD in Religion from Rice University (Houston, TX) with a dissertation that aimed to rethink the categories of and relationship between "the human" and "religion."

Dylan M. Burns
is a research associate at Freie Universität Berlin. He has published several books and many articles on Gnosticism, later Greek philosophy, early Christianity, and their modern reception, recently including *New Antiquities* (Equinox, 2019) and *Did God Care?* (Brill, 2020).

Keith Cantú
is a PhD Candidate in Religious Studies at UC Santa Barbara. He is an Associate Editor for *Correspondences* and, along with his forthcoming dissertation, is the author of "Sri Sabhapati Swami: Forgotten Yogi of Western Esotericism" (Palgrave, 2021).

Susannah Crockford
is a post-doctoral researcher at Ghent University, Belgium. Her first monograph, *Ripples of the Universe: Seeking Spirituality in Sedona, Arizona*, will be published in Spring 2021 in the Class 200 list by the University of Chicago Press. With a PhD in anthropology from the London School of Economics, her research interests focus on questions of religion and ecology, science and spirituality. On Twitter: @SusCrockford.

Stephen C. Finley
is Associate Professor of Religious Studies and African & African American Studies (AAAS) and Director of AAAS, who currently studies blackness and the paranormal. He is co-editor of *Esotericism in African American Religious Experience: "There Is a Mystery"...* (Brill 2015).

Manon Hedenborg White
holds a PhD in the History of Religions from Uppsala University. She is the author of *The Eloquent Blood: The Goddess Babalon and the Construction of Femininities in Western Esotericism* (Oxford University Press, 2020).

Dimitry Okropiridze
is a research associate at Heidelberg University of Education and lecturer at the department for the Study of Religion at Heidelberg University. He has published widely on theoretical and transcultural topics in the study of religion and culture.

Hugh R. Page, Jr.
is Professor of Theology and Africana Studies and Vice President and Associate Provost for Undergraduate Affairs at Notre Dame University. He is co-editor of *Esotericism in African American Religious Experience: "There Is a Mystery"…* (Brill 2015).

Liana Saif
is a post-doctoral fellow at the Warburg Institute and Université Catholique de Louvain. Her research focuses on Islamic occult sciences and esotericism in a global context and exchanges between the Islamic world and the Latin West in medieval and early modern periods.

Julian Strube
is a Research Fellow at the University of Münster, Germany. He has published a range of monographs, edited volumes, and articles on the relationship between religion, esotericism, and politics since the nineteenth century from a global historical perspective.

Mariano Villalba
is a PhD candidate in History of Religions at the University of Lausanne and École Pratique des Hautes Études. He is editor of *Melancolia* and has published a number of articles on esotericism in the Spanish Renaissance, Argentina, and Mexico.

Esotericism's Expanding Horizon: Why This Book Came to Be

Egil Asprem and Julian Strube

The academic study of esotericism is currently undergoing a phase of expansion and diversification. This is true whether we look at the topics, geographical regions, and subject languages of new research projects in the field, at the disciplines involved in its study, or the demographic composition of its scholars. The past decade has seen monographs, anthologies, and journal special issues on topics such as African-American esotericism (Finley, Guillory and Page, eds., 2014), esotericism in South America (Bubello, 2010), esotericism in South Asia (Djurdjevic, 2014), esotericism in Scandinavia (Bogdan and Hammer, eds., 2016), global esotericism (Bogdan and Djurdjevic, 2014), contemporary esotericism (Asprem and Granholm, eds., 2013), esotericism in antiquity (Burns, ed., 2015), Islamic esotericism (Saif, 2019), cognitive approaches to esotericism (Asprem and Davidsen, 2017), ethnographic approaches to esotericism (Crockford and Asprem, 2018), feminist and queer analyses of esotericism (Hedenborg White, 2019), and so on. We see new forays into literary studies, art history, colonial and global history, history and sociology of science, the study of popular culture, and many other domains. The study of esotericism always had interdisciplinary aspirations, but recent years have accelerated this trend. With it comes an increased need for generalists in the field to read broadly across an expanding number of disciplines.

Despite this onward rush into new territories and fields of inquiry, the central assumptions, terminology, and theoretical and methodological approaches of the field do not seem to have followed suit. On the contrary: long-standing assumptions and biases about esotericism as "Western," "rejected," "oppositional," and "elite" are becoming barriers to developing the research perspectives necessary for coming to terms with esotericism's expanding horizon. Despite understanding itself as an open and interdisciplinary field, we hold that a majority of work done under the banner of "Western esotericism" displays a tendency toward internalism and isolation from bigger debates in the humanities at large. This issue was in fact raised during the definition debate in the early 2000s (cf. Okropiridze, 2021), particularly by Kocku von Stuckrad (see e.g. von Stuckrad, 2005; 2008). In a keynote lecture to the First International Conference on Contemporary Esotericism in Stockholm in 2012, with many of the leading scholars in the field present, von Stuckrad (2012) explicitly pointed to the field's lacking engagement with theoretical debates about some of its very key concepts, such as secrecy, knowledge, identity, polemics, and the West. We observe that the debate has receded over the past decade, while the field and its key terms remain as undertheorized as they were before.

The current book is conceived from what we see as an urgent need to question, rethink, and revise existing approaches in the study of esotericism. More than simply discussing explicit theorizing, however, what we call for is a deeper, critical look at the often implicit and tacit biases that are built into the field's key concepts. These, we hold, are obstacles, not only to the advance of scholarship within the field, but also to its relationship with scholars outside of it. It is only through the "tough love" of interrogating such biases that the field may flourish for another generation.

1   The Tacit Biases of "Western Esotericism": Some Examples

By way of introduction, we may briefly consider some of the most obvious implicit biases attached to the two terms that make up "Western esotericism." The term "Western" has recently attracted a lot of attention, including a plenary panel debate at the conference of the European Society for the Study of Western Esotericism (ESSWE) in Amsterdam in 2019 (for the published debate leading up to it, see especially Pasi, 2010; Granholm, 2013; Asprem, 2014; Hanegraaff, 2015; Roukema and Kilner-Johnson, 2018; Strube, 2021). The term was originally adopted as a qualifying adjective intended to cordon off the field from universalist and perennialist approaches that had assumed a timeless and essential esotericism, manifesting across history in many separate cultures. It was conceived as a marker of historical *specificity* rather than a precisely defined geographical or cultural area. This, in turn, was linked with a historicist "empirical turn" in the study of esotericism in the early 1990s; out went metaphysical notions of timeless wisdom and transcendent experience, in came a focus on primary sources trapped in the contingency of specific historical circumstances.

At least that was the idea. The newfound identity of a "Western" esotericism construed in historicist rather than essentialist terms also came to introduce a new and largely tacit form of *cultural* essentialism: whatever else esotericism might have been, it was uniquely "Western," and would retain this unique characteristic no matter where in the world "it" travelled. Tied to widespread exceptionalist assumptions about "Western civilization," the term came to obscure the differences among the material labelled "Western" (e.g. South American, as demonstrated by Villalba [2021], Scandinavian, or South Asian

"Western" esotericism) while it accentuated differences between this Western esotericism and related materials elsewhere.

It is worth pointing out that this logic has not only barred a comparative assessment of purely analogous forms of practice in "non-Western" contexts; it has also shut the door on cases where there are obvious historical links between "Western" and "non-Western" materials. For example, in the *Dictionary of Gnosis and Western Esotericism* (2005) the choice was made to exclude both Jewish and Islamic currents from "the West" (Hanegraaff, 2005, p. xii), a choice which, although defended on "pragmatic" rather than theoretical or even historical grounds, did correspond with the explicit demarcation of "the West" proposed by Antoine Faivre in the early 1990s (cf. Pasi, 2007, pp. 152–4, 164). Since then, the study of Jewish Kabbalah has thrived in parallel with, but has still not been completely integrated into, the study of esotericism, while the study of Islamic esotericism has remained all but ignored until very recently (see especially Saif, 2019; Melvin-Koushki and Gardiner, eds., 2017).

As a consequence the entire Islamic world has been treated as a "carrier civilization" of mostly Greek (and hence, one assumes, "properly Western") material that would only become Western esotericism when discovered by Latin scholars in the fifteenth century (cf. Saif, 2021), while Jews have been relegated to minor supporting acts or "influences" on the same Western actors. This is not only problematic when considering the often somewhat ahistorical approaches to esotericism in (Greek) antiquity (cf. Burns, 2021). When central currents such as kabbalah or even alchemy, which truly came into its own in a medieval Islamic context (Principe, 2012), are defined out of "Western" esotericism, it is hard to avoid the conclusion that the exclusively "Western" identity of esotericism is an artefact of how the field has been theorized. It is a product of scholarly choices.

The cultural essentialism that sneaks in with the term "Western" has also hampered a comprehensive understanding of the consequences of colonialism and colonial exchanges for esotericism. This is particularly evident in the *diffusionist* position that some scholars have recently advanced in response to criticisms of the demarcation. Acknowledging that "Western esotericism" has to be viewed as a global phenomenon, at least in the modern period, Wouter Hanegraaff has claimed that this was the result of its unilateral export into a world of passive recipients, who became part of the history of esotericism only after their "Westernization" (Hanegraaff, 2015, p. 151). Here the implicit and unreflected essentialism of Western esotericism becomes clearly tangible: "mutations" have occurred in "originally European esoteric or occultist ideas" when they have been disseminated outside the West; these have then "traveled back to the West, only to be (mis)understood there as the 'authentic' voices of non-Western spiritualities." Hence, Hanegraaff calls for the investigation of the "globalization of *Western* (!) esotericism" (Hanegraaff, 2015, p. 86, original emphasis). Apart from its (cultural) essentialist understanding (i.e., esotericism is alway Western at core, even after "mutations" occur in "non-Western" contexts), this viewpoint is shaped by implicit assumptions about "authenticity" (cf. Cantú, 2021) and actively overlooks the agency of "non-Western" actors. When disembodied ideas are seen to simply "mutate" in a different environment, no attention is given to the local minds and bodies in which such ideas existed, or the intentions and agendas through which they were adopted, adapted, and eventually disseminated further. Behind that viewpoint stands the choice to prioritize elements that are assumed, on a vaguely canonical basis, to be "Western" over the role of "non-Western" elements. Only then can it be claimed that the result of the exchange was "Western" at heart. Again, we are dealing with an artefact of the pre-theoretical assumptions built into "Western esotericism." Scholarship on the Theosophical Society is an instructive case in point, as it tends to exclusively focus on the role of "Western," white Theosophists while practically ignoring the many "non-Western" people who, like in India, actively participated in shaping Theosophy (Strube, forthcoming; 2021).

The conceptualization of "Western esotericism" has concrete ramifications, not only for the interpretation of sources, but also for how sources are selected in the first place. This directly relates to the problem that "Western," as a marker of identity, is often coded white (cf. Bakker, 2019; Bakker, 2021; Page and Finley, 2021). It is pertinent to ask how whiteness bias has structured research on esotericism, not only in its relative lack of interest in asking questions about race, but also in its very selection of material and construction of historical narratives (Bakker, 2019, p. 9; Gray, 2019, pp. 206–216). That the link between Western and whiteness has become even stronger in the identity politics of the last couple of decades only increases the urgency of reflecting on how racialist logics operate in the field, and even on how the field's own narratives stake out positions in broader political discourses on race, culture, and identity.

While the pre-theoretical baggage of the adjective Western is thus exceptionally heavy,[1] the term "esotericism" is itself loaded with a variety of assump-

---

1 On this matter our assessment is diametrically opposed to that of Hanegraaff, who claims that "the theoretical baggage of 'Western esotericism' is, in fact, quite light" (Hanegraaff, 2015, p. 28). He is only able to argue this by separating the term from "specific assumptions about the nature of 'the West,'" which we hold is impossible to do. Even if it were possible, it would not counter the problem of cultural essentialism discussed above.

tions that must be unpacked. Let us just consider two of them. First of all, scholars in the field have often pointed out that their subject is associated with the weird, unconventional, irrational, and heterodox. This feature is now seen as the product of processes of exclusion that form central parts of current theoretical models of esotericism as "rejected knowledge" (e.g. Hanegraaff, 2012). Secondly, there is also an awareness that the term has been shaped in important ways by insider, that is to say "emic," attempts at constructing tradition—spinning imaginary webs of relations and transmissions that link mystery cults, Gnostics, and Knights Templars to Rosicrucians, contemporary initiatic orders, and "wisdom schools" of all sorts.

While both features are well-known and frequently problematized in the field, there has been surprisingly little reflection about how they still inform the way scholars select, describe, categorize, and even explain the supposedly "related currents" that they study. Despite an often explicit distancing from insider constructions of tradition and an emphasis on the need to contextualize and complicate standard narratives, lists of typical "esoteric currents" produced by scholars remain predictably stable. And while admonitions to resist the temptation of conceiving esotericism as a deviant "counterculture" have been around for twenty years (e.g. Hanegraaff, 2001), we can still find the rejection of "esotericism" grandiosely described as "the most fundamental" grand narrative of "Western culture" as a whole (Hanegraaff, 2019a, pp. 149–150).

It is important to note that the two features—"deviant," "anti-Establishment" knowledge and grand tradition narratives—are frequently connected by esoteric spokespersons. It is this connection that allows occultists, new agers, and contemporary conspirituals alike to position themselves as oppositional as well as members of an enlightened elite (cf. Asprem and Dyrendal, 2015; 2018). Rather than complicating such narratives and analyzing the strategic work that they perform in a broader societal context (cf. Crockford, 2021), scholarly accounts produced in the framework of Western esotericism have tended to reinforce and perpetuate them. When emphasizing how esoteric spokespersons have *in fact* been marginalized, scholarly narratives can themselves be read as counter-canonical descriptions of "noble heretics," approximating a succession of "great men" whose relevance for the field is precisely that each stands on the shoulders of another (misunderstood or marginalized) giant (cf. Asprem, 2021). In terms of selection of sources, then, it can sometimes be difficult to distinguish an academic historical narrative from an insider construction of esoteric tradition (see for example textbook introductions such as Goodrick-Clarke, 2008; Versluis, 2007).

Critical debates pertaining to these issues are rarely taken to their logical conclusion, as the implications of the rejected knowledge narrative illustrates.

This is also the case with the "Western" demarcation, which in fact is related to insider conceptualizations of esotericism as "tradition." Although it was pointed out already a decade ago that the notion of "Western esotericism" is itself a polemical occultist construct of the late nineteenth century (Pasi, 2010; cf. Strube, 2017), this has not led to the critical reflection on its use that one might have expected. We hold that these examples illustrate a deeper contradiction at work in the scholarly discourse on esotericism. On the one hand, scholars have been careful to state that their aim is to destabilize the category itself by showing how historical actors that only appear through its prism (because they have otherwise been neglected or rejected) are in fact fully understandable in light of the prevailing discourses of their times; on the other, the term *continues* to function as a convenient way to group, categorize, and relate "esoteric currents" under an umbrella that, for all practical reasons, sets them apart from those other fields and orders them into an alternative canon of "(Western) esoteric thought." There is a widespread tendency to insist that the latter remains useful for pragmatic reasons, perhaps as a kind of "strategic essentialism" that makes the field visible and gives it a voice (cf. Roukema and Kilner-Johnson, 2018, p. 112). However, the field has already been established quite successfully for some time, and continues to produce work demonstrating that there is little or nothing *sui generis* "esoteric" about the figures and currents that feature as major representatives of "Western esotericism" (e.g. Stengel, 2011 about Swedenborg; Strube, 2016 about Éliphas Lévi). Ironically, then, the conceptualization of "Western esotericism" prevents the desired normalization of the field's subject matter; it may even function as a self-fulfilling prophecy with regard to the marginality of its subjects—and, crucially, of the field itself.

2   Preventing the Self-Marginalization of the Field

The latter point concerning the field's self-marginalization is a key reason why we have assembled this volume. The internalist ordering of relevant authors, currents, and concepts that the theoretical apparatus of "Western esotericism" constructs and enforces is creating a barrier for dialogue with scholars in other fields, who either study the same subjects from an entirely different angle (for example as classicists, experts of early modern intellectual history, or historians of colonialism), or deal with the same broader issues that esotericism scholars highlight in their own materials (e.g. heterodoxy, initiation, ancient wisdom narratives, colonial and intercultural exchanges). It is telling that scholars have been able to produce great work on "esoteric" subjects without the concept of "Western esotericism." This is obvious if we think about classics that were written long before the field even existed (e.g. Thorndike, 1923–1958; Yates, 1964). More importantly for the present context, the same holds true for a rapidly expanding literature of cutting-edge research on what esotericism scholars would consider part of their field, covering a vast spectrum from Theosophy (Viswanathan, 1998; Bevir, 2000; van der Veer, 2001), Spiritualism and occultism (Dixon, 2001; Owen, 2004; Treitel, 2004; Albanese, 2007; Wolffram, 2009; Noakes, 2019), early modernity (Clucas/Forshaw/Rees, 2011; Rampling, 2014; Copenhaver, 2015), magic and occult arts in the middle ages (Burnett, 1996; Pingree, 1997; Fanger, 2012), "esoteric" currents in antiquity (Turner, 2001; Dieleman, 2005; Bull, 2018), or within dynamic new fields such as global history (Bayly, 2004; Osterhammel, 2014; Conrad, 2018; Green, 2015).

In turn, we observe that there is a widespread tendency to only superficially engage with scholarship from outside the field, or to outright ignore it even when it is clearly relevant. The discussion of "global" esotericism is, again, a striking case in point. Neither Bogdan and Djurdjevic (2014) nor Hanegraaff (2015) have engaged with the vast literature on global, imperial, (post-)colonial, or related history. In the latter case especially, there is even a lack of engagement with scholarship or historical sources related to the respective geographical areas that serve as examples. It should be noted that this is the case despite repeated attempts to introduce a global perspective to the field (esp. Bergunder, 2010; 2014; 2016; cf. Strube, 2016).

This has become an especially pressing issue as critical arguments directed at these problems have not always been engaged with in a constructive manner. Instead, we now see polemical broadsides aimed against "those radical theorists who are so eager to deconstruct 'Western culture'" (Hanegraaff, 2019a, p. 151). A hazy "postmodernism" is framed as a dangerous "Establishment" opponent, while rallying around a problematic mix of cultural chauvinism (defending "Western") and oppositional posturing (protecting esoteric "rejected knowledge"). A particularly striking example is found in a recent polemic against what is regarded as "critical theory" and "those approaches associated" with it, published in the official ESSWE newsletter (Hanegraaff, 2019b, p. 6).

Criticism or even rejection of certain approaches or scholarly traditions can be perfectly reasonable and is a vital part of scholarly debate. The kinds of reactions we have mentioned here, however, appear less interested in engaging with concrete scholarly arguments, which are absent due to the consistent lack of citations, than in reproducing politically charged polemical narratives embedded in a perceived "culture war." This volume unambiguously rejects these kinds of politicized polarization and instead seeks to offer new, balanced approaches to broaden the scope of the study of esotericism and add substance to its theoretical-methodological toolkit. It should be noted that many of the critical discussions that our authors highlight have long been part of the debate in the humanities at large, and in religious studies specifically. In order to halt what we see as an ongoing self-marginalization of the study of esotericism in its tracks, it is high time that they are taken more seriously in our field as well.

The ambition of this book is thus to facilitate a deeper-going critical self-examination, which we deem necessary for the current push into new regions, domains, and disciplines to succeed, but also for establishing the field more widely and solidly within its existing borders. The aim, to be sure, is not to urge esotericism scholars to change their subjects or to devalue their previous work, but rather to encourage an open and serious exchange with other perspectives, both within and beyond the field. Debating, reflecting, and possibly revising or abolishing key concepts in the study of esotericism must be an integral part of that process.

3 Overview of Chapters

We have collected eleven chapters by scholars who could, by and large, be seen as belonging to an emerging new generation of esotericism specialists. All chapters address existing limitations, biases, or problems in the field, each in its own way, and each related to the scholar's area of expertise. It has also been important for us that each chapter provides constructive, forward-looking suggestions for how research practices might be improved. Several chapters deal with problems related to the Western demarcation—for this reason we have also spent some time introducing that particular problem in this introduction. Some chapters deal with problems related to how we conceptualize esotericism itself—especially in terms of rejected knowledge or diffusely defined "related currents"—while others address specific topical areas that remain undertheorized, such as issues of race and gender.

Dylan Burns' chapter addresses the old question of whether and, as the case may be, *how* esotericism might be usefully applied to the study of the ancient Mediterranean world. The religious and intellectual history of late antiquity is a field that overlaps considerably with the typical narratives of esotericism (e.g. "Renaissance esotericism" as custodian of Hermetism, theurgy, Platonist metaphysics, Gnosticism, etc.), but it has been able to flourish perfectly well *without* the use of that term. What could "esotericism" contribute to scholars of antiquity? Conversely, scholars of esotericism are frequently pointed back to late-antique materials by their very sources, but how should they talk about the link between (modern) esotericism and antiquity? In existing scholarship, this latter issue has often been handled through the mediation of fuzzy and promiscuous concepts like "gnosis" and, more recently, "Platonic orientalism." In "Receptions of Revelations: A Future for the Study of Esotericism and Antiquity," Burns provides a methodologically clear-sighted and cogently argued alternative: instead of looking for an emphasis of "gnosis" as salvific knowledge, perhaps associated with "altered states of consciousness," and using this to construct an esoteric lineage, scholars should adopt a strict form of reception history that follows the constantly changing uses of a plethora of late-antique texts into the Middle Ages, the Renaissance, and beyond. More specifically, Burns suggests that the term "esotericism" may still be useful in the ancient world if, taking a cue from Kocku von Stuckrad, we (1) see it as a "purposeful implementation of the dynamic of secrecy, concealment, and revelation," and (2) proceed to focus on how "revelatory knowledge" is legitimized in a crowded field of revelation-based claims to authority. This, Burns argues, would allow us to talk heuristically about "ancient (Mediterranean) esoteric traditions," but in a way that would necessitate expanding our relevant sources to include revelatory material that scholars of esotericism still pay little attention to, such as the Jewish apocalyptic tradition. Doing so would only be possible through a closer engagement with the thriving work by biblical scholars, who have long taken an interest in literature on secrecy, concealment, and the establishment of revelatory authority.

In the chapter "Towards the Study of Esotericism Without the 'Western,'" Julian Strube interrogates the current debate on the "Western" in Western esotericism and argues unequivocally that the qualifier should be dropped. Noting that critique of the term's ideological baggage by now has a very long history across the humanities, Strube is unsatisfied with what attempts to introduce the same questions in esotericism research have yielded so far. He diagnoses recent responses to calls for discarding "Western" as a "diffusionist reaction," which depicts esotericism as a ready-made, unchanging European "export," an approach which conceals the agency of non-European actors. He also highlights that a thorough historicization of the term itself must lead to the conclusion that the construct "Western esotericism" has always been a polemical term with a global context, which continues to carry with it a baggage from occultist-internal debates from the turn of the previous century. We can do better, however: subtitled "Esotericism from the Perspective of a Global Religious History," Strube's chapter ends up arguing that the problems with esotericism research's lingering ethnocentrism, many of which became truly explicit only during recent discussions, can be overcome if we embed the study of esotericism in the framework of global religious history. The chapter ends with an overview of what global history entails, and concrete examples of its relevance to esotericism.

Islam is, as we have seen, an outstanding example of what Liana Saif calls the "exclusionary tendencies" expressed by the "Western" demarcation. In her chapter, Saif provides a historical overview of the division between East and West in the study of esotericism, highlighting that predominant narratives within the field sanitize orientalist perspectives. The notion of "Platonic orientalism" serves as a main example of that tendency. As Saif demonstrates, it relegates Islam to a "carrier civilization" while juxtaposing it to an ideologically charged narrative of the rise of "the West." This is not only ahistorical but also fails to take into account decades of scholarship on the intricacies of orientalism, which becomes most tangible in the popularity of the concept of "positive orientalism" in the field. Moreover, Saif examines how perennialist views of Islam have determined approaches to the subject, contradicting the many attempts to distance it from "religionist" perspectives. Arguing that the current approach to Islam is not sustainable, Saif calls for questioning the ahistorical, Europeanist narratives still informing scholarship on Islamic esotericism, and finally leaving them behind.

Mariano Villalba's contribution investigates another detrimental consequence of the "Western" demarcation, namely the *de facto* exclusion of South America and the Iberian Peninsula from its scope. This is especially instructive since Hanegraaff used the colonization of the Americas to assert the "globalization of Western esotericism." Villalba forcefully demonstrates the flaws of that perspective, by arguing that esotericism should not be viewed as a Western European phenomenon that spread to the colonies. The conquest of America decisively stimulated its emergence in the first place, and hence that emergence cannot reasonably be restricted to Europe. This is particularly significant as Villalba shows how "the West" has been restricted even within Europe, effectively removing the Iberian Peninsula from its sphere. Villalba introduces a decolonial approach to correct these distortions and unravels the cultural, racist, and ideological implications of the "Western" demarcation. The ambiguous relationship between European occultist perspectives and South American aboriginal traditions serves as an impressive illustration of how racial and cultural assumptions have shaped approaches to esotericism, not only historically but even today.

Exchanges between individuals across the globe have largely unfolded within the context of colonialism, particularly in the nineteenth century. In recent years especially, scholarly and public debates have strived to take this circumstance into account and highlight the role and agency of "non-Western" actors. The tendency arose, however, to frame such exchanges predominantly in terms of oppression and appropriation, for instance with regard to yoga. Ironically, this over-emphasis eclipsed the role of "non-Western" actors in ways similar to their outright neglect. Keith Cantú offers a critical analysis on this circumstance, discussing how more or less implicit assumptions of (pre-colonial) "authenticity" tend to obscure the contributions of South Asians to the emergence of modern yoga and related practices. Putting scholarship on esotericism into dialogue with the field of yoga studies, Cantú highlights the exceptional role of Theosophists and occultists for exchanges with South Asian authors and practitioners. Demonstrating that these exchanges were by no means unidirectional, Cantú argues for the fruitfulness of taking into account both the "local" and "translocal" dimensions of esoteric movements that defy clear differentiations between "authentic" or "inauthentic."

The conceptualization of esotericism as "rejected knowledge" is, as we have seen, one of the most pressing and problematic issues for the advancement of the field today. In his chapter, Egil Asprem provides a stringent criticism of this concept and highlights a range of problems resulting from the persisting lack of systematic reflection on its implications. Asprem argues that a "strict version" of the rejected knowledge model marked an important step within the field, as it shed light on early modern historiographies that had grouped specific currents and individuals together in a category that we today refer to as esotericism. However, Asprem demonstrates that there is also an "inflated version" of that model at work today, which effectively *reproduces*, rather than historicizes, these polemical narratives. In fact, the notion of a "Grand Polemical Narrative" running throughout "Western civilization" decidedly contributes to the self-marginalization of the field by maintaining an "oppositional" identity of both the subject matter and its scholarly study. Not only, then, does the inflated rejected knowledge model obscure much more complex developments and blur the lines between insider and academic perspectives. In its most problematic manifestations, it turns into outright polemics. Asprem's chapter is not only a potent analysis of the field's unexamined theoretical baggage, but it also proposes a way out of one of its central dilemmas by offering a more sophisticated toolkit to approach aspects such as heterodoxy, deviance, opposition, and marginalization.

In the chapter "Race and the Study of Esotericism," Justine Bakker starts with an observation that should have been obvious: that race matters in and for esotericism and its study. It matters in the formation of esoteric ideas and practices, and it matters for what scholars choose to focus on and which narratives they consequently tell. These basic insights have been almost entirely absent from scholarship on (Western) esotericism. When race appears as an analytic perspective, it is usually to identify unambiguously racist ideological formations among overwhelmingly white forms of esotericism, whether in the shape of Ariosophy or white-supremacist paganisms. As long as such studies remain the only race perspectives on offer, they obscure the fact that race (and racism) is a structural issue that shapes social practices—including the practice of academic research—in a variety of ways, both more and less subtle. It also reinforces the normativity of whiteness, obscuring that whiteness is also constructed through social practices. In her chapter, Bakker uses two case studies to illustrate how an analytic focus on race can bring new insights to the study of esotericism: (1) mediumistic contact with blacks, native Americans, and "great white men" in one white and one black Spiritualist community around the America Civil War era, and (2) processes of racialization in alien abduction narratives. The examples demonstrate how a critical perspective on race allows us to see both how race relations (including whiteness) are constructed in esoteric practices, and how these relate to broader societal realities related to race, but also how the "color line" in American society has influenced the religious experiences of blacks and, consequently, shaped and often twisted their representation in scholarship and the public imagination. Importantly, Bakker shows that there already exists a rich literature on these aspects of esoteric movements, but that all of it has been produced *outside* the field of esotericism, primarily by scholars in literary and cultural studies. The chapter is a call for esotericism scholars to follow their colleagues' lead and embrace tools from black studies, whiteness studies, and critical race theory to enhance their own work.

The aspect of race in the study of esotericism is further expanded in the chapter by Hugh R. Page, Jr. and Stephen C. Finley. Together with Margarita S. Guillory, they have co-edited *Esotericism in African American Religious Experience* (2015), a milestone for the study of esotericism that delineated the new field of Africana Esoteric Studies (AES). This field advances a trans-disciplinary approach that highlights the problems of the exclusionary tendencies expressed by both the "Western" demarcation of "Western esotericism" and its prominent conceptualization as "rejected knowledge." While the former effectively functions as a form of academic closure privileging an implicitly canonical set of sources and subjects, the latter neglects those people of color within and outside "the West" who were, first and foremost, rejected because of their *bodies*. AES therefore directs attention to the idea of "rejected people" whose knowledge was cast aside precisely because of their embodiment. Page and Finley argue that their knowledge has been doubly concealed, not only academically through the conceptualization of "rejected knowledge" within "Western esotericism," but also through the historical fact that they have been *forced* to conceal and selectively disclose their knowledge to others. The chapter proposes an experimental interpretive method, *flash non-fiction*, to approach such secretly coded esoteric cultural artifacts. Page and Finley apply this method to African American Soul and Blues lyrics from the late 1960s to the early 1970s, a period marked by civic unrest. Through their analysis—and performance—Page and Finely illustrate the role of African American artists as stewards, creators, and interpreters of *esoterica*, as well as the ways in which their artifacts become generators of context–specific *Africana* esoteric worldviews.

Given the extraordinary prominence and relevance of sexuality, sex, and gender for the subject of esotericism, it is telling that the field of "Western esotericism" has long been reluctant to engage, even superficially, with fields of study that are dedicated to these very aspects. As Manon Hedenborg White points out in her chapter on "Performativity and Femininity in the Cauldron of Esotericism Research," most research that has focused on the relationship between gender and esotericism has, indeed, been conducted outside the field. Through a close analysis of four rituals from the repertoire of Thelema, Hedenborg White demonstrates the fruitfulness of a sophisticated approach informed by gender and queer studies to grasp the many ambiguities and complexities arising from the role of sex and gender in esoteric contexts. The chapter's focus rests on different, and often contradictory, performances of femininities. While it touches the heart of debates that have been unfolding in gender-related studies for decades, Hedenborg White's adoption of the insights from those debates is not only innovative but also highly instructive. It is an impressive illustration of how the role of esoteric practices for challenging hegemonic gender logics and power relations can and should be investigated within the study of esotericism.

While esotericism is often associated with the rejected, the hidden, and the oppositional, today it is commonly packaged as glossy commodities and distributed to a growing global market of consumers. In "What Do Jade Eggs Tell Us about the Category of Esotericism," Susannah Crockford addresses the striking but surprisingly under-researched economic aspects of contemporary esotericism, lifting much bigger issues about how esoteric spiritualities function in the context of neoliberal consumer culture. Crockford starts from the observation that the vast majority of esotericism research is text based, and that even the few social science oriented approaches that exist have failed to address the material products of contemporary esotericism and the economic power relations in which they are embedded. Through the example of Gwyneth Paltrow's lifestyle company, Goop, which sells a variety of luxury commodities in areas ranging from fashion to wellness to complementary medicine, Crockford analyses how common esoteric tropes such as ancient wisdom, the revelation of secrets, subtle energies, and polemics against a materialist Establishment operate as strategies of branding and marketization within a massive global wellness industry with an estimated size of $4.2 trillion in 2018. What does the perception of esotericism as "deviant," "rejected," or "secret/hidden" mean when it is mobilized in the neoliberal market economy? Crockford argues that analyses of contemporary esotericism ought to pay more attention to the economic relationships through which esotericism is developed, disseminated, and consumed today, which will force us to take a broader look at how the common rhetoric of the esoteric (e.g. about secrets, ancient wisdom, and anti-spiritual establishments) in fact functions to create and uphold unequal economic power relations.

The final chapter by Dimitry Okropiridze provides a philosophical interrogation of how scholars have defined "esotericism" over the past few decades. At the heart of Okropiridze's discussion is a philosophical paradox that he sees as unavoidable in all acts of interpretation, that is to say, whenever we connect a term to some phenomenon. In all acts of interpretation, Okropiridze argues, we have two and only two options: either we say that concepts determine the meaning of phenomena (putting epistemology before ontology), or we say that phenomena determine the meaning of concepts (putting ontology before epistemology). The latter position (which he calls onto-epistemological) is best exemplified by essentialist approaches, while the former (called epistemo-ontological) coheres closer with discursive and constructionist approaches. The paradox, as Okropiridze sees it, is that these two options (or vectors) are mutually exclusive, yet also both necessary for meaning to be successfully produced. The chapter applies these insights to reconstruct the progress of definitions of esotericism from Faivre (form of thought manifesting in discourse), through Hanegraaff (narratives and othering processes), to Bergunder (esotericism as empty signifier), to Asprem (assembly and labelling of cognitive building blocks), arguing that we see a series of pendulum switches from the onto-epistemological (Faivre) to the epistemo-ontological (Bergunder), with Hanegraaff unresolved in between, and Asprem attempting to reconcile the two through a merger of constructionist and naturalistic approaches. Due to what Okropiridze calls the antinomy of interpretation, however, such reconciliation is impossible. Instead, Okropiridze calls for a "varifocal theory of interpretation" that admits the incommensurability of onto-epistemology and epistemo-ontology, allows the two directionalities to exist side by side, and encourages scholars to become "questing commuters" between the two approaches.

Together, these chapters address some of the most pressing challenges in the study of esotericism today, and identify a few new ones to boot. They provide a diagnosis of the theoretical state of the field and prescribe remedies which, we hope, will be adopted more systematically in the years ahead. The most significant remedy, as all chapters indicate, is to make "intedisciplinarity," "theory," and "method" more than just buzzwords. To overcome its present-day impasses and deliver on the promise of a more complex understanding of, e.g. modernity, "Western culture," or the relationships between religion, magic, and science, it seems to us that scholars of esotericism first and foremost have to read much broader and engage much wider and deeper with work carried out across the humanities and the social sciences than has so far been the case.

Bibliography

Albanese, C.L. (2007) *A Republic of Mind and Spirit: A Cultural History of American Metaphysical Religion*. New Haven/London: Yale University Press.

Asprem, E. (2014) "Beyond the West: Towards a New Comparativism in the Study of Esotericism," *Correspondences*, 2(1), pp. 3–33.

Asprem, E. (2021) "Rejected Knowledge Reconsidered: Some Methodological Notes on Esotericism and Marginality," in Asprem, E. and Strube, J. (eds.) *New Approaches to the Study of Esotericism*. Leiden and Boston: Brill, pp. 127–146.

Asprem, E. and Granholm, K., (eds.) (2013) *Contemporary Esotericism*. Sheffield: Equinox Publishing Ltd.

Asprem, E. and Dyrendal, A. (2015) "Conspirituality Reconsidered: How Surprising and How New Is the Confluence of Spirituality and Conspiracy Theory?," *Journal of Contemporary Religion*, 30(3), pp. 367–382.

Asprem, E. and Davidsen, M. (2017) "Editor's Introduction: What Cognitive Science Offers the Study of Esotericism," *Aries*, 17(1), pp. 1–15.

Asprem, E. and Dyrendal, A. (2018). "Close Companions? Esotericism and Conspiracy Theories," in Dyrendal, A., Robertson, D., and Asprem, E. (eds.) *Handbook of Conspiracy Theory and Contemporary Religion*, pp. 207–233. Brill: Leiden.

Bakker, J.M. (2019) "Hidden Presence: Race and/in the History, Construct, and Study of Western Esotericism," *Religion*. DOI: 10.1080/0048721X.2019.1642262.

Bakker, J.M. (2021) "Race and (the Study of) Esotericism," in Asprem, E. and Strube, J. (eds.) *New Approaches to the Study of Esotericism*. Leiden and Boston: Brill, pp. 147–167.

Bayly, C.A. (2004) *The Birth of the Modern World, 1780–1914: Global Connections and Comparisons*. Malden/Oxford: Blackwell.

Bergunder, M. (2010) "What is Esotericism? Cultural Studies Approaches and the Problems of Definition in Religious Studies," *Method and Theory in the Study of Religion*, 22(1), pp. 9–36.

Bergunder, M. (2014) "Experiments with Theosophical Truth: Gandhi, Esotericism, and Global Religious History," *Journal of the American Academy of Religion*, 82, pp. 398–426.

Bergunder, M. (2016) "'Religion' and 'Science' Within a Global Religious History," *Aries*, 16(1), pp. 86–141.

Bevir, M. (2000) "Theosophy as a Political Movement," in Copley, A. (ed.) *Gurus and Their Followers*. Delhi: Oxford University Press, pp. 159–179.

Bogdan, H. and Djurdjevic, G. (eds.) (2014) *Occultism in a Global Perspective*. Durham: Acumen Publishing.

Bogdan, H. and Hammer, O. (eds.) (2016) *Western Esotericism in Scandinavia*. Leiden: Brill.

Bubello, J.P. (2010) *Historia del Esoterismo en Argentina*. Buenos Aires: Editorial Biblos.

Bull, C. (2018) *The Tradition of Hermes Trismegistus: The Egyptian Priestly Figure as a Teacher of Hellenized Wisdom*. Leiden: Brill.

Burnett, C. (1996) *Magic and Divination in the Middle Ages: Texts and Techniques in the Islamic and Christian Worlds*. Aldershot: Variorum.

Burns, D. (ed.) (2015) Special Issue on Antiquity, *Aries*, 15(1).

Burns, D. (2021) "Receptions of Revelations: A Future for the Study of Esotericism and Antiquity," in Asprem, E. and Strube, J. (eds.) *New Approaches to the Study of Esotericism*. Leiden and Boston: Brill, pp. 20–44.

Cantú, K. (2021) "'Don't Take Any Wooden Nickles': Western Esotericism, Yoga, and the Discourse of Authenticity," in Asprem, E. and Strube, J. (eds.) *New Approaches to the Study of Esotericism*. Leiden and Boston: Brill, pp. 109–126.

Clucas, S., Forshaw, P.J., and Rees, V. (eds.) (2011) *Laus Platonici Philosophi: Marsilio Ficino and his Influence*. Leiden: Brill.

Conrad, S. (2018) "A Cultural History of Global Transformation," in Conrad, S. and Osterhammel, J. (eds.) *A History of the World*, vol. 4: *An Emerging Modern World, 1750–1870*. Cambridge: Harvard University Press, pp. 411–659.

Copenhaver, B. (2015) *Magic in Western Culture: From Antiquity to the Enlightenment*. Cambridge: Cambridge University Press.

Crockford, S. (2021) "What Do Jade Eggs Tell Us about 'Esotericism'? Spirituality, Neoliberalism, Secrecy, and Commodities," in Asprem, E. and Strube, J. (eds.) *New Approaches to the Study of Esotericism*. Leiden and Boston: Brill, pp. 201–216.

Crockford, S. and Asprem, E. (2018) "Ethnographies of the Esoteric: Introducing Anthropological Methods and Theories to the Study of Contemporary Esotericism," *Correspondences*, 6(1), pp. 1–23.

Dieleman, J. (2005) *Priests, Tongues, and Rites: The London-Leiden Magical Manuscripts and Translation in Egyptian Ritual (100–300 CE)*. Leiden: Brill.

Dixon, J. (2001) *Divine Feminine: Theosophy and Feminism in England*. Baltimore/London: The Johns Hopkins University Press.

Djurdjevic, G. (2014) *India and the Occult: The Influence of South Asian Spirituality on Modern Western Occultism*. New York: Palgrave.

Fanger, C. (ed.) (2012) *Invoking Angels: Theurgic Ideas and Practices, Thirteenth to Sixteenth Centuries*. University Park: Pennsylvania State University Press.

Finley, S., Guillory, M., and Page, H.R., Jr. (eds.) (2014) *Esotericism in African American Religious Experience: "There Is a Mystery"...* Leiden: Brill.

Granholm, K. (2013) "Locating the West: Problematizing the Western in Western Esotericism and Occultism," in Bogden, H. and Djurdjevic, G. (eds.) *Occultism in a Global Perspective*. London: Acumen Publishing.

Gray, B. (2019) "The Traumatic Mysticism of Othered Others: Blackness, Islam, and Esotericism in the Five Percenters," *Correspondences*, 7(1), pp. 201–237.

Green, N. (2015) "The Global Occult: An Introduction," *History of Religions*, 54(4), pp. 383–393.

Hanegraaff, W.J. (2015) "The Globalization of Esotericism," *Correspondences*, 3(1), pp. 55–91.

Hanegraaff, W.J. (2019a) "Rejected Knowledge… So You Mean that Esotericists Are the Losers of History?" in Hanegraaff, W.J., Forshaw, P.J., and Pasi, M. (eds.) *Hermes Explains: Thirty Questions About Western Esotericism*, pp. 145–152. Amsterdam: Amsterdam University Press, 2019.

Hanegraaff, W.J. (2019b) Interview in the Newsletter of the European Society for the Study of Western Esotericism. Available at: https://www.esswe.org/resources/pdf/newsletter/ESSWE_Newsletter_2019_Vol_10_No_1_2_Summer_Winter_2019.pdf (Accessed: July 27, 2020).

Hedenborg White, M. (2020) *The Eloquent Blood: The Goddess Babalon & the Construction of Femininities in Western Esotericism*. Oxford: Oxford University Press.

Hedenborg White, M. (2021) "Double Toil and Gender Trouble? Performativity and Femininity in the Cauldron of Esotericism Research," in Asprem, E. and Strube, J. (eds.) *New Approaches to the Study of Esotericism*. Leiden and Boston: Brill, pp. 182–200.

Melvin-Koushki, M. and Gardiner, N. (eds.) (2017) "Islamicate Occultism: New Perspectives," Special Issue of *Arabica*, 64(3–4), pp. 287–693.

Noakes, R. (2019) *Physics and Psychics*. Cambridge: Cambridge University Press.

Okropiridze, D. (2021) "Interpretation Reconsidered: The Definitional Progression in the Study of Esotericism as a Case in Point for the Varifocal Theory of Interpretation," in Asprem, E. and Strube, J. (eds.) *New Approaches to the Study of Esotericism*. Leiden and Boston: Brill, pp. 217–240.

Osterhammel, J. (2014) *The Transformation of the World: A Global History of the Nineteenth Century*. Princeton: Princeton University Press.

Owen, A. (2004) *The Place of Enchantment: British Occultism and the Culture of the Modern*. Chicago: University of Chicago Press.

Page, H.R. Jr. and Finley, S.C. (2021) "'What Can the Whole World Be Hiding?' Exploring *Africana* Esotericisms in the American Soul–Blues Continuum," in Asprem, E. and Strube, J. (eds.) *New Approaches to the Study of Esotericism*. Leiden and Boston: Brill, pp. 168–181.

Pasi, M. (2010) "Oriental Kabbalah and the Parting of East and West in the Early Theosophical Society," in Huss, B., Pasi, M., and Stuckrad, K.v. (eds.) *Kabbalah and Modernity: Interpretations, Transformations, Adaptations*, pp. 151–166. Leiden: Brill, 2010.

Pingree, D. (1997) *From Astral Omens to Astrology: From Babylon to Bīkāner*. Rome: Istituto italiano per l'Africa et l'Oriente/Herder.

Principe, L. (2012) *The Secrets of Alchemy*. Chicago: University of Chicago Press.

Rampling, J. (2014) "A Secret Language: The Ripley Scrolls," in Kerssenbrock-Krosigk, D.v., Wismer, B., Dupré, S. and Hachmann, A. (eds.) *Art and Alchemy: The Mystery of Transformation*, pp. 38–45. Düsseldorf: Hirmer/Museum Kunstpalast.

Roukema, A. and Kilner-Johnson, A. (2018) "Editorial: Time to Drop the 'Western,'" *Correspondences*, 6(2), pp. 109–115.

Saif, L. (2019) "What is Islamic Esotericism?" *Correspondences: Journal for the Study of Esotericism*, 7(1), pp. 1–59.

Saif, L. (2021) "'That I Did Love the Moore to Live with Him': Islam in/and the Study of 'Western Esotericism,'" in Asprem, E. and Strube, J. (eds.) *New Approaches to the Study of Esotericism*. Leiden and Boston: Brill, pp. 67–87.

Stengel, F. (2011) *Aufklärung bis zum Himmel: Emanuel Swedenborg im Kontext der Theologie und Philosophie des 18. Jahrhunderts*. Tübingen: Mohr Siebeck.

Strube, J. (2016) *Sozialismus, Katholizismus und Okkultismus im Frankreich des 19. Jahrhunderts: Die Genealogie der Schriften von Eliphas Lévi*. Berlin/Boston: De Gruyter.

Strube, J. (2016) "Transgressing Boundaries: Social Reform, Theology, and the Demarcations Between Science and Religion," *Aries*, 16(1), pp. 1–11.

Strube, J. (2017) "Occultist Identity Formations Between Theosophy and Socialism in *Fin-de-Fiècle* France," *Numen*, 64(5–6), pp. 568–595.

Strube, J. (2021) "Towards the Study of Esotericism without the 'Western'": Esotericism from the Perspective of a Global Religious History," in Asprem, E. and Strube, J. (eds.) *New Approaches to the Study of Esotericism*. Leiden and Boston: Brill, pp. 45–66.

Strube, J. (forthcoming) "Theosophy, Race, and the Study of Esotericism," *Journal of the American Academy of Religion*.

Stuckrad, K.v. (2005) "Western Esotericism: Towards an Integrative Model of Interpretation," *Religion*, 34, pp. 78–97.

Stuckrad, K.v. (2008) "Esoteric Discourse and the European History of Religion: In Search of a New Interpretational Framework," in Ahlbäck, T. (ed.) *Western Esotericism: Based on Papers read at the Symposium on Western Esotericism, Held at Åbo,*

Finland on 15–17 August 2007. Åbo: Donner Institute for Research in Religious and Cultural History.

Stuckrad, K.v. (2012) "Rejected Theory in the Study of Esotericism," Keynote Lecture at the 1st International Conference on Contemporary Esotericism, Stockholm University, Sweden, August 27–29, 2012.

Thorndike, L. (1923–1958) *A History of Magic and Experimental Science*, 8 vols. New York: Columbia University Press.

Treitel, C. (2004) *A Science for the Soul: Occultism and the Genesis of the German Modern*. Baltimore: The Johns Hopkins University Press.

Turner, J.D. (2001) *Sethian Gnosticism and the Platonic Tradition*. Québec/Leuven: Université Laval/Peeters.

Veer, P.v.d. (2001) *Imperial Encounters: Religion and Modernity in India and Britain*. Princeton: Princeton University Press.

Villalba, M. (2021) "The Occult Among the Aborigines of South America? Some Remarks on Race, Coloniality, and the West in the Study of Esotericism," in Asprem, E. and Strube, J. (eds.) *New Approaches to the Study of Esotericism*. Leiden and Boston: Brill, pp. 88–108.

Viswanathan, G. (1998) *Outside the Fold: Conversion, Modernity, and Belief*. Princeton: Princeton University Press.

Wolffram, H. (2009) *The Stepchildren of Science: Psychical Research and Parapsychology in Germany*. Amsterdam/New York: Rodopi.

Yates, F. (1964) *Giordano Bruno and the Hermetic Tradition*. London: Routledge and Kegan Paul.

Receptions of Revelations: A Future for the Study of Esotericism and Antiquity

Dylan Burns

There is no study of "esotericism" (hereafter referred to without scare quotes) in which the literature and legacy of the ancient Mediterranean world do not play a primary role.[1] To take several examples, the so-called Yates paradigm derived from Frances Yates's celebrated work *Giordano Bruno and the Hermetic Tradition* may be understood as not just relating a history of a neglected Renaissance philosopher and practitioner of magic, but the reception and revival of ancient Platonism and Hermeticism in the fourteenth and fifteenth centuries (Yates, 1964). The Yates paradigm has also been formative to Wouter Hanegraaff's many studies on (Western) esotericism, a history of modern "rejected knowledge" which deals in some way with the "gnosis" experienced by ancient philosophers making claims to eastern wisdom, a phenomenon called "Platonic Orientalism" (see below). Kocku von Stuckrad, meanwhile, has employed the term esotericism to denote wider cultural discourses that deal with the mediation of secrecy, concealment, and revelation of "absolute knowledge" in both antiquity and modernity, central *topoi* of which include Neoplatonism, Gnosticism, and Jewish mysticism (von Stuckrad, 2010; esp. von Stuckrad, 2015).

"Where there's smoke, there's fire." Specialists in the study of Mediterranean antiquity have already for some time been debating the difficult status of roughly the same body of ancient evidence (Burns, 2015b, p. 103). In early twentieth-century scholarship, one reads of a kind of "occult syncretism" of the later Roman empire, exemplified in Neoplatonic theurgy, a "spineless syncretism" which was "sucking the life-blood out of Hellenism," in Eric Robertson Dodds's memorable phrasing (Dodds, 1947, pp. 58–59). John Dillon's classic textbook *The Middle Platonists* closes with an appendix on what he loosely termed the "Platonic Underworld," i.e. Gnosticism, Hermeticism, and the *Chaldean Oracles*, viz. Neoplatonic theurgy (see below).[2] Garth Fow-

---

[1] For valuable comments and emendations to the present text I thank the volume's editors, Egil Asprem and Julian Strube, as well as Nicholas Banner. All judgments and especially errors therein remain, of course, my own.
[2] Cf. Victoria Nelson's discussion of the theme of the "grotto" "as neither a garden ornament nor a chamber of horror, but a place of worship," exemplified by Hellenistic and Roman Alexandria, where Hermetic, Gnostic, and Platonic literature flourished (Nelson, 2003, p. 31).

den's groundbreaking 1986 study *The Egyptian Hermes* located the Hermetic literature in a potpourri of ancient Platonism, Graeco-Egyptian religious syncretism, and ritual and alchemical texts which he dubbed the "Pagan intellectual milieu" exemplified by writers like the alchemist Zosimus of Panopolis (Fowden, 1993, p. 114). Perhaps aware of where these ancient materials lead in their modern afterlives, some historians and philologists have in recent years even taken to casually denoting this material "esoteric," as when Coptologist Stephen Emmel surmised that the Nag Hammadi Codices were produced by a network of "philosophically and esoteric-mystically like-minded people" (Emmel, 2008, p. 48).

In short, students of esotericism cannot avoid antiquity, and students of antiquity—or at least of ancient Platonism, Gnosticism, and magic—have not been able to avoid esotericism, either. One does not get far in the study of, say, Giordano Bruno, Paracelsus, or Carl Gustav Jung without running into the ancient sources discussed in the previous paragraph (although most scholars of esotericism have generally avoided in-depth engagement with them—Tommasi, 2016 pp. 10–18). Nor can one write effectively about the modern reception of these ancient sources without arriving at the topics the term "esotericism" is supposed to cover (on reception-history viz. ancient religion and esotericism, see Burns and Renger, 2019). Yet the question of "esotericism and antiquity" remains difficult to articulate in an effective way—much less answer—not least owing to the diversity of sources involved and the sequestering of the specialists who know them into university departments where interdisciplinarity remains *verba non acta*. The present contribution seeks to outline three of the primary lines of enquiry in the study of esotericism and antiquity, highlighting their challenges as well as promises. These are, first, the issue of the Platonic character of so much of the material at hand and its importance for the history of philosophy, particularly vis-à-vis the phenomenon of "Platonic orientalism"; second, the ever-problematic status of "Gnostic" literature and the terms "Gnosis/gnosis" and "Gnosticism"; and third, the relationship of this material to wider research on revelatory literature and phenomena. The essay will argue throughout that the answer to these problems, and the most promising methodological venue for new investigations, is not to carve out new phenomenological descriptions of "gnosis" or the "gnostic, esoteric, mystical," but to examine the reception-history of the ancient sources in question, particularly with respect to their status as competing claims to revelatory authority.

1 Spelunking the "Underworld of Platonism" and the "Dark Side of Late Antiquity"

One could argue that the study of "Western esotericism" simply charts the complex reception-history and related developments, from the Renaissance through today, regarding the sources that Dillon refers to as "some loose ends" in the study of Middle Platonism: the aforementioned "Platonic Underworld" (on a similar note, Hanegraaff, 2012, p. 332). The very proximity of this "Platonic Underworld" and its reception to the subject of esotericism requires little elaboration here. It suffices to recall the example of the aforementioned E.R. Dodds, who in 1936 succeeded the great Gilbert Murray as Regius Professor of Greek at Oxford (Christ Church). An influential scholar of Greek literature, Dodds penned many famous articles and books and produced a handsome edition of the Neoplatonist Proclus's *Elements of Theology*, an epitome of dry, metaphysical scholasticism. This same man who decried the theurgy of the Neoplatonists (Marx-Wolf, 2016, p. 60) also spent a lifetime investigating paranormal phenomena in modern London, serving as president of the Society for Psychical Research from 1961 to 1967 (Hankey, 2007, pp. 508–515; also Tommasi, 2016, p. 17). The history of the study of Neoplatonism—and as we will see, the notion of "Neoplatonism" itself—are of necessity bound to interest in and investigation of magic and occultism. What is less obvious is, firstly, the question of why (or even whether) this particular body of ancient Platonic material comprises a distinctive group in its ancient context; and second, how it came to enjoy disrepute among scholars, as it did with Dodds. Put differently: is it meaningful to speak of such a thing as "esotericism in antiquity" vis-à-vis the "Platonic Underworld"? And regardless of how the first question is answered, why did such a notion appear, with pejorative connotations, in scholarship?

The characteristics of the "Platonic Underworld" were delineated by Dillon as follows: Valentinian Gnosticism, the *Corpus Hermeticum*, and the *Chaldean Oracles* all derive existence (even that of matter) from one, supreme first principle; they distinguish between this principle and a creator-deity who is "directly responsible" for the world's creation; they describe a "pervasive female principle responsible for multiplicity, differentiation, and the generation (and ultimate salvation or return) of all lower existence"; and they make consistent use of imagery drawn from the Platonic dialogues which were also central to Middle Platonism, such as "Light against Darkness, the inexhaustible Fount of Being, and the wings of the Soul" (Dillon, 1996, p. 396). Such literature testifies that "the influence of the Platonic world-view penetrated very widely into the seething mass of sects and salvation-cults that sprang up within the Greco-Roman world in the first two centuries A.D." (Dillon, 1996, p. 396). In her introduction to a critical edition of the *Chaldean Oracles*, Ruth Majercik appropriated Dillon's phrase, and revised his description into the following typology.

1. "Elaborate and often exasperating metaphysical constructions";
2. "An extreme derogation of material existence";
3. A dualism in which the soul or mind is a "spark" trapped in the material body;
4. A "method of salvation" which involves "spiritual and/or ritual ascent";
5. A "mythologizing tendency" that renders abstract hypostases in vivid terms.

Majercik noted further the important "personal function" (i.e., soteriological function) played in this literature by female mythological figures, "operating at all levels and directly responsible for material creation," such as Sophia/Pronoia/Epinoia, Nature, and Hecate (Majercik, 1989, pp. 3–5).

While these typologies are rarely invoked in the secondary literature today, their rhetoric of marginality or exclusion persists in scholarship that treats the "Underworld" Platonist literature in its antique context. Luciana Soares Santoprete, for instance, has recently employed the differentiation between "mainstream" and "marginal" Platonisms even as she has challenged it. While she rightly emphasizes how all Platonic literature shares a "common heritage" in regarding Plato as authoritative and how important (i.e., non-marginal) the "Underworld" was for the ancient Platonists themselves, she also organizes much of the research agenda for this literature under the working title *Il lato oscuro della Tarda Antichità* ("the dark side of late antiquity"—Soares Santoprete, 2016, pp. 10–11, 14–16). Chiara Tommasi, in a paper from a conference devoted to the subject of "the dark side of late antiquity," grants some "marginality" to the "Underworld" dossier, which she takes to "come close to the areas pertaining to Western esotericism" (Tommasi, 2016, pp. 15–16). Rather than describing these esoteric Platonisms with reference to Dillon or Majercik, Tommasi highlights more general features they share, such as "innovation" and a tendency to secrecy (i.e., esotericism in a basic sense), with ramifications for the later orthodoxy and orthopraxy within the Platonic tradition (Tommasi, 2016, pp. 26–29).

The "Platonic Underworld" or "dark side of late antiquity" are, at least in their ancient contexts, misnomers. Most obviously, the metaphors do not fit. None of the literature is katagogic, i.e., concerned with journeys to the underworld—as Majercik notes, it is uniformly anagogic, concerned with the ascent of the soul. Light and the sun, not darkness and the earth, are among the most predominant images this literature uses to describe the divine. Nor is there much internal coherence to the various articulations of this "Underworld literature."³ "Dualism" is a contested category, and while it may be useful in certain cosmogonic and anthropogonic contexts, it has little purchase in Dillon and Majercik's application to soteriological contexts (see e.g. Stoyanov, 2000, pp. 2–5). Heavenly ascent or anagogic soteriology are so commonplace in late ancient Mediterranean spirituality that they hardly constitute a criterion for distinction (for survey, see Segal, 1980). Nor is the theme of the divine "spark" trapped in human bodies (highlighted by Majercik) a universal to these "marginal Platonisms"; even within Gnostic sources, it is actually a rare motif (Burns, 2015b, pp. 81–82; see also *Chaldean Oracle* 44 in Majercik, 1989, p. 66). More successful is comparison of the female deities which are responsible for producing matter (for a follow-up, see Turner, 2016), and Soares Santroprete and Tommasi are right to point to the innovative character of the literature in question, so much of which seems to coalesce around the remarkable synthesis of Plotinus in the mid-third century CE. Particularly acute is the role played by Gnostic literature in the formation of the thought we see in him, Porphyry, and the anonymous *Commentary on Plato's 'Parmenides'* (Soares Santroprete, 2016, pp. 17–35; see now Mazur 2020). The interplay of Gnostics and Platonists in the third century is all the more alluring given how vociferously Plotinus and Porphyry came to denigrate their Gnostic contemporaries, exiling them from inclusion in their construction of the tradition of Plato and Hellenic philosophy more generally (see Burns, 2014; cf. also Banner, 2018, pp. 135–137).

Finally, Majercik is right to point to the predominance of both myth and ritual, but this cannot be because ancient Platonists did not employ myths or practice rituals. On the contrary, "mainstream" Platonists were deeply interested in Plato's myths and allegorical exegesis of a range of mythological sources (Lamberton, 1986). Even if one reads Plotinus and Porphyry as distant from cultic concerns (which one need not do—Burns, 2014, pp. 18–19), the Platonist tradition following them is exemplified by its hieratic turn, extending from Iamblichus at the end of the third century CE to Damascius in the mid-sixth century. The beginning of this turn is marked by the debate between Porphyry and Iamblichus about the mechanics of theurgy and ritual practice, with chief reference to magic (Marx-Wolf, 2016). Rather, the question is which myths and which cultic practices became "mainstream" among Platonists.⁴ While later Platonists regarded the *Chaldean Oracles*, Orphic lit-

---

3   I confine myself to Majercik's typology, as it is the most developed out of the analyses reviewed in the above.
4   Cf. Hanegraaff, 2012, p. 13, arguing rather that the "underworld" is a pejorative term used by historians of philosophy to decry religiously-inclined Platonic literature; similarly Hanegraaff, 2016, p. 382.

erature, and (less often) Hermetic texts as authoritative sources of revelation, biblical sources all but disappeared from serious discussion following the aforementioned Plotinus-Gnostic controversy in the 260s CE, except to be criticized or excoriated (Burns, 2014, pp. 147–154). Conversely, as Ilinca Tanaseanu-Döbler has shown, the Neoplatonists' discussions of theurgy were not merely disagreements over the mechanics of ritual, but also vehicles for competing constructions of "the Platonic tradition" (Tanaseanu-Döbler, 2013).[5] It is to these constructions of revelation and authority with regards to the Platonic tradition—and the origin of this tradition's 'marginal' character—that we now turn.

2   Seeking Platonic Orientalism in Ancient Alexandria—and Early Modern Germany

The Gnostic, Hermetic, and "Chaldean" theurgic literature encompassed by the notion of the "Platonic Underworld" has sometimes been taken as coterminous with "Platonic Orientalism" (as by Hanegraaff, 2012, pp. 12–14). This latter term was coined by James Walbridge in a study of the twelfth-century Persian Illuminationist and Neoplatonist Suhrawardī to denote the proclivity of Platonists in general to extol a primeval "wisdom of the East," a *philosophia perennis* known by pre-Hellenic civilizations superior to Greek philosophy (Walbridge, 2001). It is central to Hanegraaff's seminal claim that Western esotericism is "the polemical Other of modernity," a *philosophia perennis* identified with a "paganism" infused with "cosmotheism" and "gnosis" (Hanegraaff, 2012, pp. 370–374; see also Tommasi, 2016, pp. 21–24). In more recent work, Hanegraaff identified gnosis as the object sought by "a kind of 'transconfessional' cultic milieu that flourished particularly in Egypt, and whose adherents—whether they were pagans, Jews, or Christians—all interpreted (Middle) Platonic metaphysics in such a way as to transform it into religious worldviews," seeking "the ancient and universal spiritual wisdom…of the Orient and their legendary sages…" (Hanegraaff, 2016, p. 381). "The possibility," Hanegraaff argues, "of gaining direct access to the realms of light by means of ecstatic states was inherent in Platonic Orientalism," which was chiefly concerned with obtaining gnosis through altered states of consciousness (Hanegraaff, 2016, pp. 383, 387–388). Hanegraaff is of course correct that narratives

---

5   Acknowledging this insight does not mean one has to agree with Tanaseanu-Döbler's excessive agnosticism about whether theurgic evidence testifies to actual ritual practices among the Neoplatonists (Tanaseanu-Döbler, 2013, esp. pp. 284–285).

which identify ultimate wisdom as being both primordial and derived of some "eastern" (or better, "barbarian"—see below) provenance are central to both the notions of the "Platonic Underworld" and the greater relationship of esotericism to antiquity.

Yet our evidence about Platonic Orientalist discourse is not concerned with ecstatic experiences of "gnosis"; it is concerned with revelatory authority, namely, which authorities get privileged, and which teachings and practices associated with these authorities are thereby legitimated. This is not to say that texts that make use of Platonic Orientalist discourse say nothing about mystical experiences or altered states; rather, the questions of authority that Platonic Orientalism engages are distinct from speculations about mystical experiences. Moreover, narratives about ancient, barbarian wisdom are sometimes used to subordinate the authority of the barbarian (i.e. non-Greek) peoples. As much is obvious by looking at the most famous and widely-cited example of Platonic Orientalism, fragment 1a of the second-century CE Platonist Numenius of Apamea, which argues that the correct procedure of theological investigation is:

> to go beyond the evidence of Plato and join it with the sayings of Pythagoras. Then, one must appeal to the justifiably famous nations, addressing their rituals, doctrines, and accomplishments in agreement with Plato (*Platōni homologoumenōs*), insofar as Brahmins, Jews, Magi, and Egyptians are in accord with one another. (trans. mine, text in des Places, 1973, p. 42)

There is nothing here about "gnosis" or altered states of consciousness. More interesting is how we construe the adverbial phrase *Platōni homologoumenōs*. It modifies the accomplishments, etc. of the non-Greek nations (rightly Hanegraaff, 2012, p. 12: "which they accomplish in full accord with Plato"). Yet this does not mean that the non-Greek sources have a wisdom superior to Plato; rather, the sense is that one should make use of them only to the extent that they agree with Plato.

Numenius then practices a type of Platonic Orientalism that extols the "wisdom of the east" even as it subordinates it to more familiar Hellenic authorities, particularly Pythagoras and Plato (whom Numenius understood as a great Pythagorean; see further Banner, 2018, pp. 102–103). Such an approach typifies his exegesis of extra-Hellenic sources in his other extant fragments, which are almost exclusively concerned with Hellenic authorities, and which use a Hellenic lens to reinterpret extra-Hellenic sources. While some Platonists (such as Plutarch, or Plato himself) did regard true wisdom as belonging to peoples antecedent and superior to the Greeks, the bulk of our evidence from Greek philosophical and rhetorical literature in the Roman Empire tends towards Numenius's view of Hellenic teachers as "first among equals"—that is, first. What is so remarkable about the Orientalizing discourse of the Hermetica, the *Chaldean Oracles*, and many Gnostic sources is the way they "auto-orientalize," insofar as they present their deeply Platonic teaching in eastern dress (for survey, see Burns, 2014, pp. 20–28).

Is it worth to continue speaking of "Platonic Orientalism" at all? I do think so, despite the misgivings of Liana Saif (2021, pp. 72–74). Saif argues that the term "orientalism" is misleading, since it is lacking in our sources. Moreover, the element of colonizing, exploitative power dynamics that is integral to Edward Said's coinage of said term is not adequately dealt with in scholarship on "Platonic Orientalism." To take the second argument first, the reading of Numenius offered here highlights that Platonic Orientalist rhetoric was often exploitative and subordinating. While modern colonialism postdates antiquity, exploitation, empire, and the complications of negotiating complex ethnic identities do not (also Tommasi, 2016, pp. 21–23). The question of how power figured into the development of Platonic Orientalist—or "barbarizing philosophical," if one wills—discourses is a promising trajectory for investigation. Indeed, so many of the individuals who participated in and developed it were themselves Hellenophone elites who initially hailed from the upper strata of Roman Syrian society (see further Burns, 2014, pp. 15–16; also Tommasi, 2016, p. 24; for a stimulating if somewhat different account, see Johnson, 2013). As for Saif's first argument, it is worth noting that some scholarship on the phenomenon here denoted "Platonic Orientalism" has preferred the phrase "barbarian wisdom," which much more closely approximates the phraseology in the ancient sources. Perhaps this is for the best; one could even add that "Platonic Orientalism" is misleading insofar as the fetishization of barbarian wisdom was hardly exclusive to Platonic-Pythagorean literature (e.g. non-Platonizing writers from the Second Sophistic such as Philostratus). At the same time, such fetishization is so central to Platonic literature that to denote it as "Platonic" is hardly a red herring (cf. the suggestion of "Platonist perennialism"—Banner, 2018, pp. 91–101). Meanwhile, the term "barbarian" can be misleading as well, insofar as the Greek term *barbaros* connoted exclusion from Greek or, later, Roman identity—including, say, Hellenophone Jews and Christians living under the Roman Empire (LSJ 306b; PGL 289a). Numenius did not fetishize just any barbarians. Rather, the regions he designated as bearers of hoary barbarian teaching—those identified with the Persians, the Chaldaeans, the Indians, the Jews, and above all, the Egyptians—overlap closely with those Said identifies as the "Orient" *avant le lettre*.

In short, the mythological and cultic aspects of the "Platonic Underworld" are hardly uniform, because Gnostic, Hermetic, and Chaldean/theurgic sources all made competing claims to revelatory and cultic authority, claims that Platonists from the mid-third century on did not necessarily regard as commensurate with one another. It is not sufficient to trade the "Underworld" out for "Platonic Orientalism," because the latter category denotes a variety of approaches to eastern wisdom among Platonists, among them a subordinating, exploitative discourse that is distinct from the auto-orientalizing one finds in the "Underworld" texts, to say nothing of any connotations of gnosis or ecstatic states. What rings true in the category of the "Platonic Underworld" is its denotation of these materials as marginal in some sense. Something happened to this material that made us, and centuries of our forebears, understand it this way. Remarkably, no earlier studies on the "Underworld" or the "dark side of late antiquity" ask whence this marginal status derives (on Hanegraaff's "grand polemical narrative," cf. however Tommasi, 2016 pp. 15–18; see also Asprem, 2021).

If we want to understand where on the road these Platonisms entered the grotto, so to speak, a reception-historical approach is a good place to start. There are many leads. While they all disrupt the notion of a "Platonist Underworld" coexisting along a "mainstream" Neoplatonism, they also remind us how many early modern writers identified the sect of the Neoplatonists with that of the Gnostics, erasing the sharp line Plotinus and Porphyry tried to draw between themselves and their Gnostic interlocutors. Leo Catana has recently shown how the conceptual underpinnings of the distinction between Middle Platonism and Neoplatonism go back to the Lutheran Johann Jacob Brucker's *Historia critica philosophiae* (1742–1767), which distinguished between earlier Platonists and the systematizing "eclectics" of Alexandria such as Plotinus, possessed of an inclination towards enthusiasm and distorted by its emergence in Egypt (Catana, 2013). Julian Strube's studies of the socialist background of nineteenth-century occultism highlight how often histories of socialism and communism from the 1830–1850s identified it as an early Christian heresy with pretensions to a universal, esoteric philosophy devised by Platonists, Pythagoreans, and Gnostics in Roman Alexandria (Strube, 2016, pp. 111–121, 206, passim; Strube, 2017b). Romantics and Transcendentalists on the other side of the Atlantic seized upon Neoplatonic authors and legends of ancient Alexandrian wisdom in formulating their own, distinctively American but "universal" non-sectarian philosophy, which had a profound influence on Blavatsky's *Secret Doctrine* (Bregman, 2016, esp. pp. 311–312; more widely, Gutierrez 2014). No less influential an authority than G.W.F. Hegel identified Neoplatonism as the philosophy of Platonist Alexandria responsible also for giving us "Kabbalistic philosophy" and "Gnostics" (Perkams, 2017, pp. 4–5). The emergence and deprecatory character of the "Platonic Underworld" is thus bundled not only with historiography of magic and the occult, as the example of Dodds showed, but with the very emergence of the category of "Neoplatonism" and related terms, and the relationship of these terms to the mythic School of Alexandria and the "Gnostics."

3   Getting to Know "Gnosis" and "Gnosticism"

Among the three "Underworld Platonisms," Gnosticism—the body of evidence regarding the teachings of individuals who in antiquity reportedly called themselves "Gnostics" (*gnōstikoi*, Grk. "knowers"; Layton, 1995)—assumes special importance. One reason, remarkably underappreciated in scholarship today, is that our Gnostic sources have a very different reception-history than do the other inhabitants of the "Platonic Underworld." A second reason is the famous terminological fog around the complex of terminology related to Gnosticism. These two issues are related, and appreciation of the former helps us resolve serious problems with the latter, particularly regarding the deeply problematic employment of the term "gnosis" as an etic category in the study of philosophy and religion—a usage which, I will argue, should be abandoned.

Our ancient reports about "the Gnostics" and their literary compositions are largely limited to the second–fourth centuries CE, with some reports extending further into late antiquity until the rise of Islam. At this point sources about the Gnostics for the most part vanish, with scattered quotations, adaptations, and rumors littering our sources through the end of the first millennium (for recent survey, see Burns, 2019a). Meanwhile, Hermetic, Neoplatonic, and theurgic literature mostly went under the radar, having nearly entirely disappeared in the Latin West while being handled gingerly in Byzantium, before being reintroduced to Western Europe at the end of the fifteenth century. Now, as discussed above, these Neoplatonic and Hermetic "Underworld Platonisms" became identified with the mysterious figures of the Gnostics themselves and the greater notion of an eclectic, Alexandrian Platonism. Yet while one could read translations of Neoplatonic and Hermetic works, for any information or accounts about the Gnostics, one was left to their opponents: the "proto-orthodox" heresiologists.

Thus, our notions about Gnostics, gnosis, and Gnosticism developed over the last two millennia largely without reference to available "Gnostic" primary texts, and so the notion of the "Gnostic" has for the vast majority of its history been employed as a term of "othering," albeit with reference to a very loose body of clichés, such as elitism, anticosmism, moral licentiousness, and so forth (Hanegraaff, 2016, p. 385). The great power of this history of othering and its attendant accretions is at the heart of scholarly calls for dismissal of "Gnosticism" and "the Gnostic" as a set of historical categories used to denote the primary sources we possess today which actually do contain the compositions by, or related to, the ancient "Gnostics" (Williams 1996; King 2003): ancient Egyptian codices with texts in the Coptic language. These books were unearthed only in modernity, having spent the centuries from late antiquity until today buried in the sands of Egypt; during that time, the discursive construction about these books' contents—of the Gnostics as a kind of 'other' connected to a Platonist School of Alexandria—developed on its own. Consequently, these terms must be used with care when interpreting this ancient Coptic evidence.

Yet debate about the viability of the terms "gnosis" and "Gnosticism" have hardly addressed the status of this terminology from the vantage point of the reception-history of the Coptic Gnostic corpus itself. Here, there is much work to be done, and all of it relates directly to esotericism: Codex Askewensis (*Pistis Sophia*) and Codex Brucianus only appeared in England towards the end of the eighteenth century, and were not translated into a modern language until the last quarter of the nineteenth. The Berlin (or "Achmim") Codex (BG 8502) was not published until 1955, and the Tchacos Codex was first published in 2006. The greatest hoard of our Gnostic primary sources by far, the Nag Hammadi Codices, was not discovered until December of 1945, nor made available in mass publication until 1977, when development of its scholarly interpretation was only beginning. Many of the terms of this scholarly interpretation were set not by the Nag Hammadi texts alone, but by the initial popularization of scholarship about the Askew and Bruce Codices—led above all by the Theosophist G.R.S. Mead (Burns, 2019b; further, Winter, 2019). Other early readers of Codex Askewensis in the later nineteenth century sought to understand it chiefly with reference to the newly-published Egyptian ritual texts known today as the Papyri Graecae Magicae (P.G.M.—Burns, 2019a, pp. 16–17). We are only beginning to understand the impact of this initial, pre-Nag Hammadi wave of interpretation of the Askew and Bruce Codices on scholarship about the greater Coptic Gnostic corpus. Conversely, the reception of the P.G.M. among contemporary occultists remains tied to the language of "Gnostic(ism)" (Johnston, 2019). While it is widely understood that C.G. Jung had an enormous interest in Gnosticism (see e.g. Hanegraaff, 2012, pp. 288–289; DeConick, 2016, below), research on the great importance of Jungianism for the phenomenon of Neo-Gnosticism remains relatively primitive (Burns, 2007, pp. 267–272; now esp. Hammer, 2019). Scholarship on the peculiar history of reception of Nag

Hammadi Codex I—the purchase of which the tsar of the study of Gnosticism in the twentieth-century Netherlands, Gilles Quispel, brokered for the Jung Institute in Zürich in 1951—has scarcely begun (see now Given, 2019, esp. 94–96).

On the other hand, the fact that the Coptic Gnostic corpus sat buried and unavailable while the "Gnostic" terminology we today use to describe it was being developed in connection with other "Underworld Platonisms" in the Renaissance and Early Modern periods may be a key for understanding the "Underworld" literature in new ways. A *doyen* of Gnostic and Coptic studies alike, Bentley Layton, sensed as much in his opening remarks at the 1978 International Conference on Gnosticism at Yale University, which set an entire generation's scholarly agenda for research on Nag Hammadi and Gnosticism:

> At the time of the Renaissance, scholars thought they could rediscover a *Prisca theologia* from which had sprung the transcendental wisdom of the West. Indeed Plato himself had hinted playfully at its existence; and the Florentine humanists believed they had found it, and published it, in the writings of Mercurius Trismegistus. Only generations later was the Hermetic Corpus unmasked as the work of Gnosticizing Platonists, probably contemporary with Valentinus and the Sethians and themselves engaged in the self-same search that had so fascinated Ficino and his patrons; while the fraudulent Horapollo continued to exert an influence until Champillon's decipherment…. (Layton, 1980, pp. xi–xii)

Layton then muses upon "the possibility that earliest Christianity and therefore Christian culture developed under the influence of a Gnostic competitor or even precursor," a different enquiry which has since largely exhausted its usefulness (Layton, 1980, p. xii). Yet his insight remains: the best way we can understand the intellectual and cultural context from which the Nag Hammadi Codices came, alongside Christianity, is the "Platonist Underworld" literature of "Mercurius Trismegistus."[6] For our purposes, the inverse of this point is worth highlighting: our Coptic Gnostic manuscripts furnish us a window into the "Platonic Underworld" prior to its Renaissance and Modern-era receptions and transformations into esotericism. They give us a peek into what the "School of Alexandria," loosely construed, looked like before the tradition of it as "marginal" and "eclectic" was invented. This is a vast task that remains to be taken up—except, perhaps, where scholars have been working on Gnosticism in terms of the history of philosophy (see above), and yes, in terms of esotericism.

---

6 Tellingly, Hermetic texts are found in Nag Hammadi Codex VI, and Codex Tchacos contains, following the infamous *Gospel of Judas*, a Coptic Hermetic tractate.

It is precisely here that we meet the other terminological difficulty in the study of Gnosticism: the question of the relationship between the terms "Gnosticism" and "gnosis." I have tackled this question in some detail elsewhere (Burns, 2015a, pp. 27–29; Burns, 2019a, pp. 17–20) and so restrict myself to brief remarks here. While the modern category of "Gnosticism" as used by Layton (1995) to denote the complex of evidence around individuals reputed in antiquity to call themselves "Gnostics" has undergone extensive critique, there is precious little theorization of the category of "Gnosis/gnosis," a fact which is all the more remarkable given that the term currently enjoys a resurgence. The term "Gnosis" (capitalized) has a long history in Continental scholarship as a synonym for what Layton called "Gnosticism," but it has just as often been used to refer to something distinct from "Gnosticism," usually relating to religious currents based upon salvific knowledge (the ostensible "gnosis").

This latter usage has become pivotal to explorations of the relationship between esotericism and antiquity. In fact, it is employed more or less as a shorthand for "ancient esotericism," or even simply "esotericism" from antiquity to today. For Hanegraaff, as discussed above, "gnosis" refers to the experience of an altered state of consciousness, which was the primary interest of adherents to Platonic Orientalism—the backbone of Western esotericism. A Dutch pioneer in the study of Gnosticism and Coptic literature, Roelof van den Broek,[7] distinguishes the dualistic teachings of the Gnostics from the greater current of "gnosis": "an esoteric, that is partly secret, spiritual knowledge of God and of the divine origin and destination of the essential core of the human being which is based on revelation and inner enlightenment, the possession of which involves a liberation from the material world which holds humans captive" (van den Broek, 2012, p. 3; similarly Yates, 1964, p. 22; Shaw, 2019, pp. 70–71; Versluis, 2019). This "gnosis" is exemplified by relatively non-dualistic literature such as the Hermetica or the *Gospel of Thomas*, in contrast to the cosmological dualism common to Gnostic sources, but it is hardly limited to a distinctive social group or even to antiquity (van den Broek, 2012, pp. 8, 11). April DeConick, meanwhile, eschews the language of "gnosis" for "Gnostic spirituality," a form of transgressive, religious mentality or epiphany that transcends adherence to an established religious tradition and emphasizes one's proximity if not identity with the divine (DeConick, 2016, pp. 11–13, 68–70; also Shaw, 2019, pp. 69, 76). DeConick identifies four "Gnostic awakenings" following the suppression

---

7 On the pivotal role van den Broek played in the establishment of the Chair for the History of Hermetic Philosophy and Related Currents (GHF) at the Universiteit van Amsterdam, see van den Broek, 2009.

of Christian Gnostics in antiquity: (*a*) the medieval dualisms of the Paulicians, Bogomils, and Cathars; (*b*) the Renaissance Platonism that blossomed in the wake of Ficino's translations of ancient Platonic and Hermetic literature; (*c*) the discovery of the Bruce and Askew Codices, and their reception by the Theosophists and Carl Gustav Jung; (*d*) and the discovery, translation, and reception of the Berlin, Nag Hammadi, and Tchacos Codices (DeConick, 2016, pp. 347–350).

Hanegraaff and DeConick's respective descriptions of "gnosis" or "Gnostic spirituality" shy away from the language of a "Gnostic religion" (Hanegraaff, 2016, pp. 384–385; DeConick, 2016, p. 10; not so van den Broek, 2012, pp. 1–3, who writes freely of "Gnostic religion" as based upon "gnosis"). Yet this is old wine in new wineskins: a religious current that extends from antiquity, particularly the milieu of Roman Egypt (home to Alexandria, of course), until today. Its basis is a secret, salvific knowledge (hence the term "gnosis") obtained through revelatory or ecstatic experiences and distinct from the dualistic myths of the ancient Gnostics, who nonetheless serve in this narrative as the masters of salvific "gnosis" *par excellance*. The coincidence of this "Gnostic religion" with some notion of "ancient esotericism" is obvious: Hanegraaff's Platonic Orientalism, van den Broek's "Gnostic mentality," and DeConick's "Gnostic spirituality" all seek to tell a story about the same things that other scholars have called Western esotericism (explicitly so for Hanegraaff, as discussed above; also van den Broek, 2012, p. 10; cf. DeConick, 2016, p. 16). One difficulty of such an approach was highlighted in the previous section: by assimilating claims to universal revelatory authority to a kind of *philosophia perennis*, it erases the way in which such claims seek to exclude competing traditions and revelations. To wit, if the Hermetica, the *Gospel of Thomas*, and Renaissance Platonism are all adherents of "gnosis" in some sense, then why do they disagree so much about the sources of supposed "gnosis" and the sort of revelatory and cultic traditions which are related to it? Second, do we not invite terminological confusion by using such closely related expressions for distinct phenomena: the "Gnosticism" of the ancient, dualistic "Gnostics," versus the "gnosis" of Western esotericism or "Gnostic mentality/spirituality"? And third, do these histories of "gnosis," so sharply demarcated from the cosmological dualism of ancient Gnostic and Manichaean literature, simply give us histories of "mysticism" under another name? Is it cosmological dualism or a more general sense of a mystical affinity of human and divine which is at stake in so much of the reception-history—among Theosophists, occultists, Jungians, and Neo-Gnostics—of the notion of "Gnosticism" and the Coptic Gnostic literature (see esp. Dillon, 2019, pp. 208–210)? Are non-marginal, relatively orthodox mystical works, such as those of the Cappadocian Fathers or the *Corpus Dionysiacum*, also exemplary of "gnosis" (also Burns, 2015a, p. 24; more generally, von Stuckrad, 2013; cf. Costache 2019, for whom "Christian Gnosis" seems coterminous with "Christian mysticism")?

Finally, do these scholarly histories of "gnosis/Gnostic spirituality" distinguish themselves sharply enough from the sort of "ancient wisdom narratives" that our primary sources draw up for themselves? Hanegraaff and van den Broek, for instance, identify "gnosis" as the third, suppressed, governing epistemological category of "Western culture," next to "faith" (revealed religion) and "reason" (Hanegraaff, 2012, p. 372; similarly van den Broek, 2012, pp. 1, 5; DeConick, 2016, prefers the language of "revolutionary spirituality"—pp. 4, 12, passim). The "faith-reason-gnosis" triad was pivotal for the aforementioned Quispel (Quispel, 2008, esp. pp. 143–146; see also Faivre, 2010, pp. 102–104).[8] Curiously enough, it also appears in the introduction of the first translation (1917) into English of the untitled Gnostic treatise in the Bruce Codex, by the Vicar of Leeds, Rev. Alfred Amos Fletcher Lamplaugh (Burns, 2019b, pp. 68–69). As Hanegraaff has shown, this faith-reason-gnosis triad goes back to the seventeenth-century anti-apologetic Protestant Jacob Thomasius, as well as the aforementioned Jacob Brucker. With Jacques Matter, the first writer to refer to *ésotérisme* in French, the term "gnosis" became used in a popular way to denote the universal teaching of the Gnostics and Neoplatonists which flourished in ancient Alexandria (Hanegraaff, 2012, pp. 101–107, 148–152 passim; Hanegraaff, 2016, pp. 385–386; further, Faivre, 2010). Strube has demonstrated that the earliest historiographies of socialism explicitly denoted socialism and communism as belonging to a heretical tradition of "gnosis" from Roman Alexandria, a development directly tied to Matter's coinage of the term "esotericism" as well as emergent scholarship on "mysticism," "theosophy," and "kabbalah" (Strube, 2016, pp. 399–416, 524, 528, passim; Strube, 2017b). Through the literary mediation of a former socialist writing under the pseudonym Éliphas Lévi (Strube, 2017a), Matter's positive sense of "gnosis" floods the literature of the Theosophical Society, where gnosis, the "One Religion," a "divine science," transcends the boundaries of religious identities or traditions as well as the teachings of the philosophers and scientists.[9]

---

8 Van den Broek and Hanegraaff, meanwhile, were of course familiar with Quispel as a senior colleague in the Netherlands. DeConick worked closely with Quispel in her early career, and her *Doktorvater*, Jarl Fossum, earned his own doctorate under Quispel (DeConick, 2008).

9 For these phrases, see Mead, 1906, pp. 6–9, 359. An investigation of the notion of "Gnosis" in the literature of the Theosophical Society would be an enormous (and exhausting) task, but good places to begin would be volume two of Blavatsky's *Isis Unveiled*, or the second edition (1906) of Mead's *Fragments of a Faith Forgotten* (particularly pp. 29–32, a discussion recalling the faith-reason-gnosis triad).

Much about the road from Thomasius, Brucker, and Matter via Lévi to Blavatsky and Mead, and from them to Lamplaugh and Quispel, remains unclear. Yet it is evident that the centuries of use of "gnosis" as an emic category by theologians and theosophists alike render it a burdensome, even disqualifying, term for use in in the etic historiography of philosophy and religion.[10] If the scholar of Platonism—to say nothing of Gnosticism or esotericism—wishes to maintain any etic posture, he or she cannot proceed further with "gnosis" as such. Again, a reception-historical approach would be more methodologically viable for the professional historian, and also open up rich, new trajectories for research. It has long been recognized that the language of "gnosis" played an important role in Continental theology and philosophy of religion of the eighteenth and nineteenth centuries, but this context and its ramifications for our use of the category in theology and religious studies today has hardly been studied (see Koslowski, 1988; also Hanegraaff, 2016, pp. 386–387). Meanwhile, "gnosis" has long served as a standard term in the translation of Buddhist texts; a pioneer of twentieth-century philology of Sanskrit and Pali literature, Edward Conze, even called himself a "gnostic" (Burns, 2016, p. 9; Versluis, 2019, pp. 22–23). These and other receptions of the notion of "gnosis" do not demonstrate a "survival of Gnostic spirituality" (DeConick, 2016, p. 17). They illustrate how important the language of "gnosis" has been for people to declare, decry, and distance themselves from claims to the possession of revelations, particularly those relating to the "Platonic Underworld."

4   Receptions of Revelations and Ancient Esoteric Traditions

Scholarly theorization of the category of "gnosis" often focuses on its revelatory quality, or the direct apprehension of higher reality (Hanegraaff, 2012, p. 372; Hanegraaff, 2016, p. 381; van den Broek, 2012, pp. 2–3; DeConick, 2016, pp. 12, 15, 17 passim). What is at stake in scholarly discussion of "gnosis" (as distinct from "Gnosticism" and "Gnostics") are competing claims to authoritative revelations, and the cultic or ritual practices associated with them. Moving the conversation from "gnosis" to "revelation" may bring not only terminological clarity, but, again, open up fruitful and hitherto neglected trajectories of investigation, above all the interface of Biblical literature and scholarship

---

10   Similarly unhelpful are the calls—usually from those who have tenure—to turn attention away from historical analysis towards the study of the "subjective experience of gnosis" and the like (e.g. Shaw, 2019, pp. 68–70).

about it (see further Burns, 2015a, pp. 24, 27–29). Theoretically speaking, if we roughly follow von Stuckrad in taking esotericism to be the purposeful implementation of the dynamic of secrecy, concealment, and revelation, then any esoteric claim necessarily implies the promise of revelation, with the converse that all revelations have been withheld and concealed prior to their unveiling. A happy consequence of this move is the necessary implication of apocalyptic (i.e., revelatory) literature and phenomena, biblical and non-biblical alike, in the study of esotericism.

Meanwhile, on the socio-historical plane, developments relating to the "Platonic Underworld," Platonic orientalism, Gnosticism, and magic in antiquity were not insulated from ancient Judaism or Christianity and related biblicizing movements, such as Manichaeism and Mandaeism. This fact is so obvious that it requires no illustration here, yet scholarship conducted today under the aegis of Western esotericism has for the most part proceeded with at best limited engagement with biblical studies and its attendant (often theological) institutions. Fortunately, the self-partitioning of the study of esotericism from biblical studies has not been reciprocal. April DeConick has done a great deal to promote the study of "Gnosticism, Mysticism, and Esotericism" at meetings of the Society of Biblical Literature, and the last decade has seen important publications that tackle questions of secrecy and concealment in biblical literature and ancient Judaism (Vander Stichele and Susanne Scholz, 2014; Coblentz-Bautch, 2015; Stone, 2018). Will scholars of esotericism read them?

Even study of the emergence of our categories governing parabiblical literature and its reception-history necessarily lead us to materials of interest to scholars of esotericism. Our chief sources for ancient and medieval understandings of the all-important personage of Enoch—a central figure of reference in Renaissance and early modern divination (Asprem, 2012)—are of course the "Ethiopic," "Slavonic," and "Hebrew" apocalypses which bear the patriarch's name. These texts are central to the greater category of "Old Testament Pseudepigrapha," works that transmit so much ancient and medieval Jewish and Christian lore and that have shed so much light upon the evolution of biblically-oriented religions, including Gnostic materials. The early stages of reception of the "Old Testament Pseudepigrapha" were dominated by seventeenth and eighteenth-century anxieties about the authoritative status of revealed Scripture following the Reformation and competing, newly-uncovered and newly-translated "heretical," revelatory authorities (Reed, 2009)—a central context for the receptions and inventions of "gnosis" and the "School of Alexandria" alike. We are in a similar situation with the so-called "New Testament Apocrypha," the reception and invention of which is closely related to that of the Old Testament Pseudepigrapha (Reed, 2015). More recently,

Enochic Pseudepigrapha and the Dead Sea Scrolls discovered at Qumran in 1947 (less than two years after the discovery of the Nag Hammadi Codices) have come to acquire authoritative status among New Religious Movements closely related to New Age and esoteric milieus and practices (Kreps, 2019). The same could be said of "New Testament Apocrypha," which, together with works from the Coptic Gnostic corpus, are often packaged for New Age, Neo-Gnostic, or "esoteric" readership as revealing a lost or hidden Christianity, whose content addresses contemporary alternative religious concerns (Burns, 2007; Burns and Radulović, 2019; Kreps, 2019; Winter, 2019). And after all, it is only logical that any study of "esotericism" also include the study of "apocrypha," which in ancient usage simply meant "hidden, secret, obscure things" before it came to have the specific sense of "secret, non-canonical books" (see LSJ 204b; Reed, 2015, pp. 407–412).

Thus, while we should be wary of speaking about "gnosis and esotericism in antiquity," we cannot avoid speaking about "Gnosticism, esotericism, and the ancient Mediterranean world," which is why many scholars are doing that already. The ancient Mediterranean sources which are so important for understanding modern discourse about esotericism—the interface of the early Christian literature called "Gnostic," the Hellenistic and late ancient flowering of revelatory (i.e., apocalyptic) literature, the works of the "Platonic Underworld," and the proximity of so much of this material to the world of ancient magic—may be usefully designated with the strategic essentialism "ancient (Mediterranean) esoteric traditions" (surveyed in Burns, 2015a). The utility of the phrase lies in its emphasis on the importance of competing claims to revelatory authority via ostensible possession of secret knowledge in a plurality of ongoing, rival constructions of tradition(s) in antiquity itself, constructions of tradition that, from the Renaissance to today, have been instrumental in further constructions of traditions of philosophy, theology, and esotericism (for a similar perspective put into practice in the study of ancient Hermetism, see Bull, 2015, esp. pp. 125–130).

History of reception and critical analysis of claims to revelatory authority and the concomitant constructions of tradition—approaches which are already flourishing in the study of ancient Mediterranean cultures (Burns and Renger, 2019)—furnish ideal, elegant means for tackling the complex problems with which ancient esoteric traditions present us. Reception-history steers us clear of simply utilizing emic terminology or presentations of evidence (on both the ancient and modern discourses; cf. the genealogical approach to the "Western" in "Western esotericism," in Strube, 2021). It reminds us, for instance, that what we call the Neoplatonism of the third century CE was a rather different thing than the Neoplatonism outlined by eighteenth-century historians of philosophy, and that the latter conditions our understanding of the former. This point is an essential corrective to the at times willful ignorance of many more traditional historians or philologists to the reception-history of their categories and artefacts (such as Layton, 1995, p. 335). Secondly, the problematic of the invention and construction of tradition is especially acute when it comes to questions of esotericism, where projections of modern or contemporary ideas onto an antique past in order to authorize them are omnipresent. The claims made by the professional scholar of antiquity in analysis of the ancient sources ought not echo or be easily mistaken for the claims made by the primary sources themselves in constructing the authority of revelation and/or tradition.

It is surely no coincidence that drawing lines of investigation along the tracks of histories of reception of these "ancient esoteric traditions" leads us into what are particularly vibrant spheres of scholarly research today that are distinct from the Yates paradigm and related models of the history of Western esotericism, but which also share so many historical roots with them. The modern discovery and "invention" of "Old Testament Pseudepigrapha" and "New Testament Apocrypha" has already been discussed; one could add to this the relationship between Gnosticism and early Jewish mysticism (Luttikhuizen, 2007; Burns, 2015a, pp. 26–27), the reception and relevance of Kabbalah in contemporary philosophy and even politics (Brown, 2019), or early Islamic philosophy and the phenomenon of "Islamic Gnosticism" (Amir-Moezzi, 2016). None of these phenomena are themselves "esoteric" or "esotericism" (for the cases of early Jewish mysticism and ancient Hermetism, see Boustan, 2015; Bull, 2015). Rather, they are phenomena that are more easily understood if one also masters evidence I have here loosely termed "ancient esoteric traditions," as well as its modern reception-histories and concomitant inventions of tradition, inventions that are inextricable from modern discourse about esotericism. It is here, and not in a modern reconstruction of "the esoteric gnosis" of yore, that there is a future for a most fruitful study of esotericism and antiquity.

Bibliography

Amir-Moezzi, M. (ed.) (2016) *Esotérisme shi'ite: ses racines et ses prolongements*. Bibliothèque de l'École des Hautes Études Sciences Religieuses 177. Paris and London: Bibliothèque de l'Ecole des Hautes Etudes; Institute of Ismaili Studies.

Asprem, E. (2012) *Arguing with Angels: Enochian Magic and Modern Occulture*. Albany: State University of New York Press.

Asprem, E. (2021) "Rejected Knowledge Reconsidered: Some Methodological Notes on Esotericism and Marginality," in Asprem, E. and Strube, J. (eds.) *New Approaches to the Study of Esotericism*. Leiden and Boston: Brill, pp. 127–146.

Banner, N. (2018) *Philosophic Silence and the "One" in Plotinus*. Cambridge; New York: Cambridge University Press.

Boustan, R. (2015) "Secrets without Mystery: Esotericism in Early Jewish Mysticism," *Aries: Journal for the Study of Western Esotericism*, 15(1), pp. 10–15.

Bregman, J. (2016) "Synesius of Cyrene and the American 'Synesii,'" *Numen*, 63(2–3), pp. 299–323.

Broek, R.v.d. (2009) "The Birth of a Chair," in Hanegraaff, W. and Pijnenburg, J. (eds.) *Hermes in the Academy: Ten Years' Study of Western Esotericism at the University of Amsterdam*, Amsterdam: Amsterdam University Press, pp. 11–15.

Broek, R.v.d. (2013) *Gnostic Religion in Antiquity*. Cambridge: Cambridge University Press.

Brown, J. (2019) "'La Perversión de la Cábala Judía': Gershom Scholem and Anti-Kabbalistic Polemic in the Argentine Catholic Nationalism of Julio Meinvielle," in GhaneaBassiri, K. and Robertson, P. (eds.) *All Religion is Interreligion: Essays in Honor of Steven M. Wasserstrom*, New York: Bloomsbury, pp. 65–73, 218–223.

Bull, C. (2015) "Ancient Hermetism and Esotericism," *Aries: Journal for the Study of Western Esotericism*, 15(1), pp. 109–135.

Burns, D. (2006) "The *Chaldean Oracles of Zoroaster*, Hekate's Couch, and Platonic Orientalism in Psellos and Plethon," *Aries: Journal for the Study of Western Esotericism*, 6(2), pp. 158–179.

Burns, D. (2007) "Seeking Ancient Wisdom in the New Age: New Age and Neo-Gnostic Commentators on the *Gospel of Thomas*," in von Stuckrad, K. and Hammer, O. (eds.) *Polemical Encounters: Esoteric Discourse and its Others*, Aries Book Series 6, Leiden: Brill, pp. 252–289.

Burns, D. (2014) *Apocalypse of the Alien God: Platonism and the Exile of Sethian Gnosticism*. Divinations. Philadelphia: University of Pennsylvania Press.

Burns, D. (2015a) "Ancient Esoteric Traditions: Mystery, Revelation, Gnosis," in Partridge, C. (ed.) *The Occult World*, Routledge Worlds, London: Routledge, pp. 17–33.

Burns, D. (2015b) "μίξεώς τινι τέχνῃ κρείττονι—Alchemical Metaphor in the *Paraphrase of Shem* (NHC VII,1)," *Aries: Journal for the Study of Western Esotericism*, 15(1), pp. 79–106.

Burns, D. (2016) "Telling Nag Hammadi's Egyptian Story," *Bulletin for the Study of Religion*, 45(2), pp. 5–11.

Burns, D. (2019a) "Gnosticism, Gnostics, and Gnosis," in Trompf, G., Johnston, J., and Mikkelsen, G. (eds.) *The Gnostic World*, Routledge Worlds, Abingdon; New York: Routledge, pp. 9–25.

Burns, D. (2019b) "Weren't the Christians Up Against a Gnostic Religion? G.R.S. Mead at the Dawn of the Modern Study of Gnosticism," in Hanegraaff, W., Forshaw, P. and Pasi, M. (eds.) in *Hermes Explains: Thirty-One Questions about Western Esotericism*, Amsterdam: Amsterdam University Press, pp. 60–69.

Burns, D. and N. Radulović (2019) "(Neo-)Bogomil Legends: The Gnosticizing Bogomils of the Twentieth-Century Balkans," in Burns, D. and Renger, A.-B. (eds.) *New Antiquities: Transformations of Ancient Religion in the New Age and Beyond*, London: Equinox Press, pp. 275–303.

Burns, D. and A.-B. Renger (2019) "Introduction: What Are New Antiquities?," in Burns, D. and Renger, A.-B. (eds.) *New Antiquities: Transformations of Ancient Religion in the New Age and Beyond*, London: Equinox Press, pp. 1–13.

Catana, L. (2013) "The Origin of the Division between Middle Platonism and Neoplatonism", *Apeiron*, 46(2), pp. 166–200.

Coblentz-Bautch, K. (2015) "Concealment, Pseudepigraphy and the Study of Esotericism in Antiquity," *Aries: Journal for the Study of Western Esotericism*, 15(1), pp. 1–9.

Costache, D. (2019) "Christian Gnosis: From Clement the Alexandrian to John Damascene," in Trompf, G., Johnston, J. and Mikkelsen, G. (eds.) *The Gnostic World*, Routledge Worlds, Abingdon; New York: Routledge, pp. 259–70.

DeConick, A. (2008) "Gnostic Letters from Bilthoven," in van Oort, J. (ed.) *Gnostica, Judaica, Catholica: Collected Essays of Gilles Quispel*. Nag Hammadi and Manichaean Studies 55, Leiden; Boston, pp. xv–xxi.

DeConick, A. (2016) *The Gnostic New Age: How a Countercultural Spirituality Revolutionized Religion from Antiquity to Today*. New York: Columbia University Press.

Dillon, J. (1977) *The Middle Platonists*. London: Duckworth.

Dillon, M. (2019) "The Impact of Scholarship on Contemporary 'Gnosticism(s)': A Case Study on the Apostolic Johannite Church and Jeremy Puma," in Burns, D. and Renger, A.-B. (eds.) *New Antiquities: Transformations of Ancient Religion in the New Age and Beyond*, London: Equinox Press, pp. 199–223.

Dodds, E. (1947) "Theurgy and its Relationship to Neoplatonism," *Journal of Roman Studies*, 37(1–2), pp. 55–69.

Dodds, E. (1977) *Missing Persons: An Autobiography*. Oxford: Clarendon Press.

Emmel, S. (2008) "The Coptic Gnostic Texts as Witnesses to the Production and Transmission of Gnostic (and Other) Traditions," in Frey, J. et al. (eds.) *Das Thomasevangelium: Entstehung–Rezeption–Theologie*, BZNW 157, Berlin: De Gruyter, pp. 33–49.

Faivre, A. (2010) "Le terme et la notion de 'Gnose' dans les courants ésotériques occidentaux modernes (essai de périodisation)," in Mahé, J.-P., Poirier, P.-H., and Scopello, M. (eds.) *Les textes de Nag Hammadi: Histoire des religions et approches contemporaines*. Paris: AIBL–Diffusion De Boccard: pp. 87–112.

Fowden, G. (1993) *The Egyptian Hermes: A Historical Approach to the Late Pagan Mind*. Princeton: Princeton University Press.

Given, J. (2019) "Nag Hammadi at Eranos: Rediscovering Gnosticism among the Historians of Religion," in GhaneaBassiri, K. and Robertson, P. (eds.) *All Religion is Interreligion: Essays in Honor of Steven M. Wasserstrom*, New York: Bloomsbury, pp. 87–98, 231–237.

Gutierrez, C. (2014) *Plato's Ghost: Spiritualism in the American Renaissance*. Oxford: Oxford University Press.

Hammer, O. (2019) "The Jungian Gnosticism of the Ecclesia Gnostica," in Burns, D. and Renger, A.-B. (eds.) *New Antiquities: Transformations of Ancient Religion in the New Age and Beyond*, London: Equinox Press, pp. 175–198.

Hanegraaff, W. (2012) *Esotericism and the Academy: Rejected Knowledge in Western Culture*, Cambridge: Cambridge University Press.

Hanegraaff, W. (2016) "Gnosis," in Magee, G. (ed.) *The Cambridge Handbook of Western Mysticism and Esotericism*, Cambridge: Cambridge University, pp. 381–392.

Hankey, W. (2007) "Re-Evaluating E. R. Dodds' Platonism," *Harvard Studies in Classical Philology* 103, pp. 499–541.

Johnson, A. (2013) *Religion and Identity in Porphyry of Tyre: The Limits of Hellenism in Late Antiquity*. Cambridge: Cambridge University Press.

Johnston, J. (2019) "Binding Images: The Contemporary Use and Efficacy of Late Antique Ritual Sigils, Spirit-Beings, and Design Elements," in Burns, D. and Renger, A.-B. (eds.) *New Antiquities: Transformations of Ancient Religion in the New Age and Beyond*, London: Equinox Press, pp. 254–274.

King, K. (2003) *What is Gnosticism?* Cambridge: Harvard University Press.

Koslowski, P. (1988) *Gnosis und Mystik in der Geschichte der Philosophie*. Zürich: Artemis Verlag.

Kreps, A. (2019) "Reading History with the Essenes of Elmira," in Burns, D. and Renger, A.-B. (eds.) *New Antiquities: Transformations of Ancient Religion in the New Age and Beyond*, London: Equinox Press, pp. 149–174.

Lamberton, R. (1986) *Homer the Theologian: Neoplatonist Allegorical Reading and the Growth of the Epic Tradition*. Transformation of the Classical Heritage 9. Berkeley: University of California Press.

Layton, B. "Preface," in Layton, B. (ed.) in *The Rediscovery of Gnosticism: Proceedings of the International Conference on Gnosticism at Yale, New Haven, Connecticut, March 28–31, 1978*, Numen Book Series, Leiden: Brill, pp. 1:ix–xii.

Layton, B. (1995) "Prolegomena to the Study of Ancient Gnosticism," in White, M. and Yarbrough, L. (eds.) *The Social World of the First Christians: Essays in Honor of Wayne Meeks*, Minneapolis: Fortress Press, pp. 334–350.

Lowe, N.J. (2019) "The Rational Irrationalist: Dodds and the Paranormal," in Stray, C., Pelling, C. and Harrison, S. (eds.) *Rediscovering E. R. Dodds: Scholarship, Education, Poetry, and the Paranormal*, Oxford: Oxford University Press, pp. 88–115.

Luttikhuizen, G. (2007) "Monism and Dualism in Jewish-Mystical and Gnostic Ascent Texts," in Hilhorst, A., Puech, É. and Tigchelaar, E. (eds.) *Flores Florentino: Dead Sea Scrolls and Other Early Jewish Studies in Honour of Florentino García Martínez*, Journal for the Study of Judaism Supplement 122, Leiden; Boston: Brill, pp. 749–775.

Majercik, R. (1989) *The Chaldean Oracles: Text, Translation, and Commentary*. Studies in Greek and Roman Religion 5. Leiden: Brill.

Marx-Wolf, H. (2016) *Spiritual Taxonomies and Ritual Authority: Platonists, Priests, and Gnostics in the Third Century C.E.* Divinations. Philadelphia: University of Pennsylvania Press.

Mazur, A. J. (2020) *The Platonizing Elements of Plotinus's Mysticism*. Rev. ed. Dylan Burns, et al. Nag Hammadi and Manichaean Studies 98. Leiden: Brill.

Mead, G. (1906) *Fragments of a Faith Forgotten* [2nd ed.], London; Benares: Theosophical Publishing Society.

Nelson, V. (2003) *The Secret Life of Puppets*. Cambridge: Harvard University Press.

Perkams, M. (2017) "Einheit und Vielfalt der Philosophie von der Kaiserzeit zur ausgehenden Antike," in Riedweg, C. (ed.) *PHILOSOPHIA in der Konkurrenz von Schulen, Wissenschaften Und Religionen: Zur Pluralisierung des Philosophiebegriffs in Kaiserzeit Und Spätantike*, Philosophie der Antike 34, Berlin; Boston: De Gruyter, pp. 3–32.

Places, É.d. (1973) *Numénius: Fragments*. Collection des universités de France Série grecque 226. Paris: Les Belles Lettres.

Quispel, G. (2008) "Gnosis and Culture," in van Oort, J. (ed.) *Gnostica, Judaica, Catholica. Collected Essays of Gilles Quispel*, Nag Hammadi and Manichaean Studies 55, Leiden; Boston, pp. 141–153.

Reed, A. (2009) "The Modern Invention of 'Old Testament Pseudepigrapha,'" *Journal of Theological Studies*, 60(2), pp. 403–436.

Reed, A. (2015) "The Afterlives of New Testament Apocrypha," *Journal of Biblical Literature*, 133(2), pp. 401–425.

Saif, L. (2021) "'That I Did Love the Moor to Live with Him': Islam in/and the Study of 'Western Esotericism,'" in Asprem, E. and Strube, J. (eds.) *New Approaches to the Study of Esotericism*. Leiden and Boston: Brill, pp. 67–87.

Segal, A. (1980) "Heavenly Ascent in Hellenistic Judaism, Early Christianity and their Environment," *Aufstieg und Niedergang der Römischen Welt* II.23.2, pp. 1333–1394.

Shaw, G. (2019) "Can We Recover Gnosis Today?," *Gnosis: Journal of Gnostic Studies*, 4(1), pp. 67–80.

Soares Santoprete, L. (2016) "Tracing the Connections between 'Mainstream' Platonism (Middle- and Neo-Platonism) and 'Marginal' Platonism (Gnosticism, Hermeticism and the Chaldean Oracles) with Digital Tools: the Database, the Bibliographical Directory, and the Research Blog *The Platonisms of Late Antiquity*," in Seng, H.

and Gasparro, G.S. (eds.) *Theologische Orakel in der Spätantike*, Bibliotheca Chaldaica 5, Heidelberg: Universitätsverlag Winter, pp. 9–45.

Stone, M. (2018) *Secret Societies in Ancient Judaism*. Oxford: Oxford University Press.

Stoyanov, Y. (2000) *The Other God: Dualist Religions from Antiquity to the Cathar Heresy*. London; New Haven: Yale University Press.

Strube, J. (2016) *Sozialismus, Katholizismus und Okkultismus im Frankreich des 19. Jahrhunderts: Die Genealogie der Schriften von Eliphas Lévi*. Religionsgeschichtliche Versuche und Vorarbeiten 69. Berlin; Boston: De Gruyter.

Strube, J. (2017a) "The 'Baphomet' of Eliphas Lévi: Its Meaning and Historical Context," *Correspondences*, 4, pp. 37–79.

Strube, J. (2017b) "Revolution, Illuminismus und Theosophie: Eine Genealogie der 'häretischen' Historiographie des frühen französischen Sozialismus und Kommunismus," *Historische Zeitschrift*, 304(1), pp. 50–89.

Strube, J. (2021) "Towards the Study of Esotericism without the 'Western'": Esotericism from the Perspective of a Global Religious History," in Asprem, E. and Strube, J. (eds.) *New Approaches to the Study of Esotericism*. Leiden and Boston: Brill, pp. 45–66.

Stuckrad, K.v. (2010) *Locations of Knowledge in Medieval and Early Modern Europe: Esoteric Discourse and Western Identities*. Brill's Studies in Intellectual History 186. Leiden: Brill.

Stuckrad, K.v. (2013) "Afterword: Mysticism, Gnosticism, and Esotericism as Entangled Discourses," in DeConick, A. and Adamson, G. (eds.) *Histories of the Hidden God: Concealment and Revelation in Western Gnostic, Esoteric, and Mystical Traditions*, Durham: Acumen, pp. 312–319.

Stuckrad, K.v. (2015) "Ancient Esotericism, Problematic Assumptions, and Conceptual Trouble," *Aries: Journal for the Study of Western Esotericism*, 15(1), pp. 16–20.

Tanaseanu-Döbler, I. (2013) *Theurgy in Late Antiquity: The Invention of a Ritual Tradition*. Göttingen: Vandenhoeck & Ruprecht.

Tommasi, C.O. (2016) "Some Reflections on Antique and Late Antique Esotericism: between Mainstream and Counterculture," in Seng, H., Soares Santoprete, L.G., and Tommasi, C.O. (eds.) *Formen und Nebenformen des Platonismus in der Spätantike*, Bibliotheca Chaldaica 6, Heidelberg: Universitätsverlag Winter, pp. 9–36.

Turner, J. (2016) "The *Chaldaean Oracles*: A Pretext for the Sethian Apocalypse *Allogenes?*," in Seng, H. and Gasparro, G.S. (eds.) *Theologische Orakel in der Spätantike*, Bibliotheca Chaldaica 5, Heidelberg: Universitätsverlag Winter, pp. 89–114.

Vander Stichele, C. and Scholz, S. (eds.) (2014) *Hidden Truths from Eden: Esoteric Readings of Genesis 1–3*. Semeia Studies 76. Atlanta: Society of Biblical Literature.

Versluis, A. (2019) "What Is Gnosis? An Explanation," *Gnosis: Journal of Gnostic Studies*, 4(1), pp. 81–98.

Walbridge, J. (2001) *The Wisdom of the Mystic East: Suhrawardī and Platonic Orientalism*. Albany: State University of New York Press.

Williams, Michael (1996) *Rethinking "Gnosticism": Arguments for Dismantling a Dubious Category*. Princeton: Princeton University Press.

Winter, F. (2019) "Studying the 'Gnostic Bible': Samael Aun Weor and the *Pistis Sophia*," in Burns, D. and Renger, A.-B. (eds.) *New Antiquities: Transformations of Ancient Religion in the New Age and Beyond*, London: Equinox Press, pp. 149–174.

Yates, F. (1964) *Giordano Bruno and the Hermetic Tradition*. London: Routledge and Kegan Paul.

Towards the Study of Esotericism without the "Western": Esotericism from the Perspective of a Global Religious History

Julian Strube

This chapter holds that the demarcation "Western" is a significant shortcoming of the study of esotericism. While it has helped to draw the contours of an emerging field in its earlier stages, it has by now become an impediment to its further establishment. As most scholars would agree, "Western" is a historically contingent and highly volatile concept that is as much ideological as geographical. While the same holds true for many concepts with which scholars operate, other fields of study have long gone through a difficult and often tedious process of self-reflection and critical debate to deal with this challenge. Such debates have by no means been absent from the field of Western esotericism, but so far they have yielded limited and overall unsatisfying results.

As discussed in the introduction to this volume, Wouter Hanegraaff has recently suggested conducting research on esotericism as a corrective to "those radical theorists who are so eager to deconstruct 'Western culture.'" This research, unlike "postmodern" approaches, "is best done with a minimum of theoretical baggage, at least at the outset, because the prime objective consists in *listening* to what the sources have to tell us instead of imposing our own ideas on them" (Hanegraaff, 2019, p. 151, original emphasis). Surely one does not have to be a "radical" to recognize the need for a critical approach to notions such as "Western culture," and neither does one have to be lost in "postmodern" theory to maintain the impossibility of simply "listening" to what the sources have to tell. What Hanegraaff designates as an excess of postmodern radical theory are insights that have been established, on the basis of strong arguments and sound research, in other fields and disciplines, some of them fairly conservative, for several decades.

Instead of driving a wedge between the chimera of postmodern radical theorists and those who allegedly do empirical history by listening to the sources, the main plea of this chapter is for an open dialogue that encourages a plurality of approaches, which will transcend the confines of Western esotericism and has the potential to initiate a fruitful dialogue with other fields. This is especially relevant because, as will be seen, previous criticism of the "Western" demarcation has provoked what I refer to as the "diffusionist reaction," which depicts esotericism as a European "export" to the rest of the world.

© JULIAN STRUBE, 2021 | DOI:10.1163/9789004446458_004
This is an open access chapter distributed under the terms of the CC BY-NC-ND 4.0 license.

By conflating diverse approaches—most notably global historical perspectives and postcolonial theories—into an unspecified "postmodernism," Hanegraaff holds that scholars of esotericism should counter "postmodern" theories in order to explain the "true meaning" of "Western culture," rather than "deconstructing" it. Any engagement with concrete approaches, however, is absent from Hanegraaff's critique. It is unclear who or what he wishes to refute, especially as most global historical and postcolonial approaches are not concerned with simply deconstructing or even vilifying "Western culture." Rather, they aim at unraveling the historical conditions for (academic) knowledge production and its ramifications up to the present day, for which the "diffusionist reaction" is in itself an instructive exemplar. This underlines the need for an improvement of the theoretical-methodological repertoire of the field: it goes without saying that the microcosm of Western esotericism will not fare well among its neighbors if the insights from other fields and disciplines are not only ignored, but misconstrued.

I will begin my discussion by stressing that calls for a "strictly historical" (Hanegraaff, 2016, p. 165) approach to Western esotericism must lead to its recognition as not only a notion that emerged in a global context, but as a polemical concept that carries far-reaching implications for its use as a scholarly category and academic identity marker. After outlining previous debates within the field and the diffusionist reaction to them, I will contrast some approaches from global and postcolonial history with their diffusionist misrepresentation before, finally, introducing the program of *global religious history* to propose constructive impulses for the current debates about the "Western." The aim is to develop an understanding of esotericism that does not operate with the model of European diffusionism, a model that has convincingly been criticized by decades of scholarship. As is the case with "modernity," "the West," or concepts such as "religion," esotericism emerged, not in European isolation, and not unidirectionally as a result of European hegemony imposing itself on a passive "rest," but within a complex of multilateral exchanges that are best grasped from a global perspective.

This does not imply that there is no such thing as "the West" as a historically contingent identity marker, or that this marker is inherently "good" or "bad." The perspective suggested here is historical, aiming at a deeper and more comprehensive understanding of historical contexts of which esotericism formed an integral part. Its aim is not to suggest that everyone should study "non-Western" subjects, learn "non-European" languages, or that research moving within such confines is in any way objectionable. Rather, scholars focusing on such subjects can only benefit from an engagement with perspectives that put different meanings of "Western" concepts in their historical contexts. No scholar shall be urged to adopt approaches from, say, global history or postcolonial studies, but a field that chooses the demarcation "Western" would do well to engage with debates that are of major relevance for it, if only to refute (some of) their arguments.

Such an engagement is no threat to the study of esotericism, but arguably the greatest opportunity since its creation. Two desirable outcomes may be envisioned: either a theoretical and methodological substantiation of the "Western" demarcation, or its abolishment in favor of an open-minded, open-ended, and more sophisticated toolkit whose users and constant revisers are dedicated to the *study of esotericism*. This chapter argues for the latter option, since "Western esotericism" carries a historical baggage, the lack of effective reflection on which makes it virtually indefensible, *not as a historical object of study*, but as an analytical concept and academic identity marker. The way that "Western esotericism" is currently conceptualized not only reproduces a "religionist" narrative that excludes "non-Western" historical contexts, it also imposes on "non-Western" historical and present-day actors the necessity to either be "Westernized" before being able to participate in "esotericism," or to be of no direct relevance for it. From a historical perspective, however, esotericism *was and is* a globally entangled subject.

1   A Historical Look at the Concept "Western Esotericism"

In his ground-breaking work, Hanegraaff (2012) has developed the paradigmatic conceptualization of esotericism as "rejected knowledge in Western culture." Hanegraaff has transparently discussed the "religionist" context of emergence of Western esotericism as a field of study, stressing the need for an ongoing critical debate about the theories and methods employed within it (esp. Hanegraaff, 2012, pp. 334–361). Such a debate is traceable from Antoine Faivre's pioneering work, which is most directly responsible for the demarcation of the field as *ésotérisme occidental* (Faivre, 1986; English translation 1994). As is well known, Faivre developed his approach from an overtly "insider" or "religionist" understanding towards a critical historical method. Against that background, the new "Western" demarcation was an attempt to avoid universalist notions that esotericism denotes a perennial truth manifesting across time and space. Hanegraaff took these efforts several steps further, effectively abolishing ideal-typical definitions of esotericism in favor of the elaboration of a historical narrative culminating in esotericism as "rejected knowledge in Western culture" (for an important early step, see Hanegraaff, 1995; this paradigm receives critical scrutiny by Egil Asprem, 2021).

Early criticism of the concept "Western esotericism" revolved not so much around the notion of "Western" itself, but around what Kocku von Stuckrad has termed the neglect of the "complexities of Western culture," which had manifested in a dismissive attitude towards Jewish and Islamic contexts (Stuckrad, 2005a, pp. 82–83; Stuckrad, 2005b, pp. 3–5; for the relationship between Islam and the study of esotericism, see Saif, 2021). In 2010, however, Marco Pasi directly addressed the conceptual problems related to the "Western" demarcation, pointing out that, "if esotericism is not a universal phenomenon, but is specifically rooted in, and limited to, Western culture, then it should not be necessary to qualify it as 'Western'. The very moment it is labeled as 'Western', it becomes also possible to conceive that other, 'non-Western' forms of esotericism exist" (Pasi, 2010, p. 153). Pasi also rightly highlighted the fact that the concept "did not originate in a scholarly discourse, but in a religionist one," namely within occultism during the second half of the nineteenth century, when a polemical distinction was first made between a "Western" and an "Eastern" esotericism: "It is therefore mostly as the reaction to an idea of 'Eastern esotericism' that the idea of 'Western esotericism' could develop" (pp. 155–156). These significant arguments notwithstanding, Pasi stated in the beginning of his article that they "appear in the end to be not as strong as the necessity to emphasize—even rhetorically—the idea that esotericism belongs to a specific cultural area" (p. 153). However, it is difficult to see how Pasi substantiated this alleged necessity, especially as he arrived at quite a different conclusion in the very same article. He noted that "pragmatic reasons, understandable as they may be, are often unsatisfactory from a theoretical point of view, and make one wonder whether there is a full awareness of the conceptual problems they leave unsolved" (p. 163). And, indeed, he then concluded the text by asking: "is it legitimate to talk about 'Western' esotericism when in fact what one is talking about is only Christian and post-Christian forms of it? Eventually, one cannot help wondering if it would not be more consistent to use the latter label instead of 'Western'" (p. 164).

The reader might take away from this that the theoretical debates revolving around the "Western" were anything but straightforward. Acknowledgement of the problematic aspects of the emergence of the term "Western" has logical consequences, but doubling-down on use of the term is not one of them. It is well known that we are not dealing with a scholarly concept, but a polemical, occultist term with a concrete history. I have elsewhere investigated this history within the French context, arguing for its immediate relevance for conceptual debates within the field (Strube, 2017a): since the 1880s, a particular French understanding of *ésotérisme occidental*, with a constructed tradition of "true" theosophy in the vein of a Böhme or Saint-Martin, was juxtaposed to the "false" Theosophy of the Theosophical Society, which was perceived as a degenerate "Eastern esotericism." This French notion of *ésotérisme occidental*, with a supposedly true *théosophie* and *illuminisme* at its heart (Strube, 2017b), largely informed the work of Faivre and overlaps with the demarcation of Western esotericism as a field of study in significant ways.

The history of this signifier is evidently not detached from the history of the field. Western esotericism is not simply the *object* of the field, but an integral part of its conceptualization up to the present day. Apart from the many problems arising from the use of a polemical identity marker as both the paradigm and the name for an academic field of study, it cannot be stressed enough that the term was formulated as a response to the success of an esoteric society that had relocated its headquarters to India and had many thousands of "non-Western" members. It becomes blatantly clear that, in order to understand the emergence of "Western esotericism," it does not suffice to look at the French, British, German, or any other isolated national context, whether European or not. The historical polemics raging about "Eastern" versus "Western" esotericism were the outcome of globally entangled developments.

In order to understand the historical meanings of "esotericism," a term that emerged and was shaped throughout the nineteenth century, it is hence necessary to broaden the scope beyond what is usually delineated as "the West." This does not entail the dissolution of the boundaries of the field. The point is precisely that such a fear results from a narrow focus on the history of, and the debates within, the field of Western esotericism—it is such parochialism that poses the largest threat to the field's further development. Engagement with approaches from global history and/or postcolonial studies does not bear the danger of a "universalist" understanding of esotericism, as is often argued, or of a resurgence of "neo-perennialism." Before substantiating this point, it is necessary to understand ongoing debates within the field.

2   First Steps beyond the West

The first comprehensive effort to open a perspective on esotericism beyond "the West" was *Occultism in a Global Perspective*, edited by Henrik Bogdan and Gordan Djurdjevic in 2014. The volume's merit, and self-declared intention, was to arouse interest in looking at occultism as a phenomenon that was not restricted to geographical boundaries. It also included the first substantial problematization of the "Western" demarcation. At the same time, the volume was framed in a consistently unidirectional way, attempting to "understand how occultism changes when it 'spreads' to new environments, that is to place occultism in its cultural, political and social context" (Bogdan and Djurdjevic, 2014, p. 5). From such a viewpoint, "Western" occultism is "exported" into other parts of the world, and it is no accident that the majority of the chapters in the volume do not investigate "non-Western" actors in their own right.

This highlights a concrete methodological consequence of the conceptualization of Western esotericism, namely a focus on white Europeans (and, more rarely, North Americans or the descendants of white colonists in Australasia), not only outside of "the West," but even within its boundaries (an issue that is addressed by Justine Bakker, 2021; Stephen Finley, and Hugh Page, 2021; also see Gray, 2019, pp. 206–216). This can be observed even in the case of the Theosophical Society, beginning with the work by scholars such as Joscelyn Godwin (1994) and Hanegraaff's assertion that Theosophy "was not only rooted in western esotericism, but has remained an essentially western movement" (Hanegraaff, 1996, p. 455). Such attitudes still inform scholarship within the field, including even the comprehensive *Handbook of the Theosophical Current*, edited by Olav Hammer and Mikael Rothstein in 2013. "Non-Western" actors—and people who are not white, for that matter—are virtually absent from scholarship on Theosophy conducted under the auspices of Western esotericism.

In most cases, such limitations result from a lack of linguistic or otherwise disciplinary competence, but the methodological problem at hand manifests as the absence of a problematization of those lacunae, or even an awareness of their existence. In some cases, an outright dismissal of "non-Western" actors can be observed, for instance in Nicholas Goodrick-Clarke's claim in the *Handbook* that: "For all its Asian costume and fabulous intermediaries, modern Theosophy retains its Western Hermetic motive, logic, and end" (Goodrick-Clarke, 2013, p. 303). While there is much to unpack in this statement, it must suffice here to point out that Theosophy did not merely encounter "fabulous intermediaries" in Asia (the legendary "Mahatmas"), but thousands of Asian individuals who joined, interacted with, and *actively* transformed the Society. In the process, they were not simply "Westernized" and became part of "Western esotericism," but they shaped the very meaning of esotericism against their own diverse backgrounds (for further discussion of this aspect, see Keith Cantú, 2021). Ignorance of that fact constitutes, not only a methodological flaw but a missed opportunity, for the study of esotericism could significantly contribute to an understanding of one of the most influential, genuinely *global* societies of the nineteenth century. As Hanegraaff acknowledges, Theosophy was also "the most influential esoteric movement of the nineteenth century [...] that created essential foundations for much of twentieth-century esotericism" (Hanegraaff, 2013, pp. 130–131). If the most important esoteric movement was global, it is implausible when Hanegraaff simultaneously maintains that esotericism was "an inherently Western domain of research" (Hanegraaff, 2013, p. 15).

In his contribution to *Occultism in a Global Perspective*, Kennet Granholm leveled criticism against the lack of reflection of the field's demarcation, highlighting the amorphous and highly contingent, ideologically charged meanings of both "Western" and "European" (Granholm, 2013, pp. 18–22). Granholm's critique marks an important step, but it also differs in crucial points from the approach that I am going to propose. First, despite poignant criticism of the "Western," Granholm still sustains a steady focus on "Western" actors, for instance when the Theosophical Society appears as a monolithic organization "appropriating Indian terminology and teachings" (p. 30). This assessment still brushes over the Indian members and interlocutors of the Society who played a decisive and active role in shaping Theosophy. Related to this is, second, Granholm's use of the notion "positive orientalism" (p. 23) that serves as a distinction between more pejorative forms of orientalism. The borders between such forms, however, are anything but clear, since "positive" images of "Orientals" as spiritual bearers of ancient wisdom are inexorably intertwined with notions of being effeminate, static, child-like, degenerate, and so on (cf. Partridge, 2013, pp. 329–330). Thirdly, Granholm makes concrete methodological suggestions to approach modern esotericism in terms of modernity and globalization, transnationality, pluralism, detraditionalization, and secularization (pp. 25–28). The conceptualization of these theories stems from a sociological repertoire that has, as will be seen below, been criticized from the perspective of global history and postcolonial studies.

In 2014, Egil Asprem weighed in on the conversation by offering another, comparative approach. Asprem's article contains a concise and accurate critique of the "Western" demarcation, which emphasizes the political aspects of the establishment of the field as "boundary-work" and discusses the emergence of different research programs in the process (Asprem, 2014, pp. 4–20). Asprem eventually discards rivaling historical and typological heuristics as "largely a result of boundary-work during the professionalisation process" of the field (p. 20), instead suggesting a comparative approach that is not limited to geographical or historical delineations. We will return to the question of comparativism below. First, it is important to shed critical light on the response to the developments that have now been outlined.

3   The Diffusionist Reaction

In 2015, Hanegraaff took up the discussion in an article about "The Globalization of Esotericism," wherein he generally acknowledged the need to expand the field's scope beyond "the West." Effectively, Hanegraaff transposed his narrative of rejected knowledge into that of a "global dustbin" or "waste basket": those confronted with European expansion became included in the same polemical narratives as European esotericists (Hanegraaff, 2015, pp. 64–67). We learn that this rejection gave way, during the Romantic period, to a "fascination" resulting in the "positive orientalism" characteristic for later occultists. Hanegraaff scolds Edward Said's *Orientalism* for only being aware of the "negative" kinds of orientalism while neglecting this "positive" variant. This raises more issues than can be mustered in this chapter, but the central problem is that the text does not at all engage with Said's book, nor with the extensive scholarly debates that unfolded since its publication in 1978 (pp. 67–69; cf. e.g. Young, 2004, pp. 165–180). Instead, Hanegraaff proceeds to discuss the history of the field of Western esotericism, including a lengthy elaboration on Faivre's typology (2015, pp. 70–80).

As the fleeting reference to Said and the subsequent limitation of the discussion to the field of Western esotericism indicate, the article is deeply problematic for a range of reasons: for failing to take seriously the arguments proposed by critics of the "Western," or for not engaging with them at all; for ignoring or misrepresenting scholarship beyond the field of Western esotericism that would be crucial for a discussion of the "global"; and for an underlying lack of theoretical and methodological rigor that also manifests in an unconvincing separation of "theory" from "history."

Hanegraaff's diffusionist model of European esotericism professes that "originally European esoteric or occultist ideas and practices have now spread all over the globe." Hanegraaff notes that there had been "mutations" of those ideas that "traveled back to the West, only to be (mis)understood there as the 'authentic' voices of non-Western spiritualities," a process that he finds an "important and fascinating phenomenon." For the future, he suggests an investigation of the "globalization of *Western* (!) esotericism" (Hanegraaff, 2015, p. 86, original emphasis) that would require "intensive collaboration between Western and non-Western scholars." While Hanegraaff does recognize the need for an investigation of "Islamic, Asian, and Middle and Latin American" contexts, his engagement with efforts to conduct research along those lines is ambivalent: "To my knowledge (and profound regret), we do not yet have a study of Western esotericism on the North Pole region and Antarctica, but surely that is only a matter of time!" (pp. 61–62). This ironic statement coheres well with the often-voiced conviction that a global scope gravitates towards randomness and universalism. Not only, however, is this a misrepresentation of what the broad spectrum of global approaches is about; it also underlines Hanegraaff's exclusion of "non-Western" historical actors from his conceptualization of esotericism: those who are merely carriers for the "mutations" of Western ideas remain voiceless. The difference between Asia and the North Pole might then very well appear insignificant.

Unfortunately, Hanegraaff does not engage with the scholarship on global history, imperial history, colonial history, postcolonial studies, or any related field that would be indispensable for a discussion of the subject at hand. The result is an imprecise treatment of theories, approaches, and concepts such as global history, globalization, or comparativism; a persistent confusion of "global" with "universal"; and several other misconceptions that appear to result from *ad hoc* understandings of terminology, rather than an engagement with the relevant literature. Perhaps the most striking indication of these issues is a long list of rhetorical questions that Hanegraaff poses about the consequences of adopting a "global" approach, starting with: "If we see esotericism as something global, then does this mean that 'it' is universal and remains always the same regardless of context?" (pp. 62–63). Hanegraaff is then able to arrive at the conclusion that this "series of questions finally leads us full circle" because he has drawn it up himself, rather than considering relevant scholarship. Similarly, he has recently dismissed the approach of "entangled histories" as a "fashionable notion," because "there is no such thing as *non*-entangled history, and hence the adjective is strictly superfluous" (Hanegraaff, 2020). As we shall see later, this is hardly an accurate representation of what entangled histories are all about. The issue, then, is not disagreement with a particular approach, no matter what one might think of it, but that the point has been entirely missed.

This self-referential, circular style of argumentation also pertains to Hanegraaff's binary of "history" versus "theory." Suggesting that we should "historicize" the problem, Hanegraaff juxtaposes such an intention with "the world of theory" that is clearly distinguishable from the "empirical world" populated by "people" (2015, p. 63).[1] This juxtaposition is intended as a plea for thoroughly source-based scholarship, and it certainly is fair to level well-argued criticism against historians who neglect working with historical sources or the philological training necessary for it. In principle, then, the intentions of the "historical

---

[1] This binary seems to stem from a polemical exchange with Kocku von Stuckrad (Hanegraaff, 2012, pp. 365–366). In any case, it is hard to see how it relates to global approaches, as will be elucidated below.

method" outlined by Hanegraaff are perfectly reasonable: concrete evidence and close work with sources, instead of theoretical abstractions. In practice, however, the "historical method" portrayed by Hanegraaff fails to meet the very demands of his own plea—and this is so, ironically, not least because of a lack of theoretical reflection. This is only underscored by Hanegraaff's conviction that his own theoretical baggage is "in fact quite light" (2015, p. 82; cf. Gray, 2019, p. 211). As the introduction and several chapters of this volume demonstrate, the theoretical baggage of terms like "Western" and "esotericism" are anything but light, and few examples illustrate this circumstance as clearly as Hanegraaff's diffusionist perspective, which is largely detached, not only from the scholarship but also from the historical sources relevant to its central arguments.

The claim that Hanegraaff's "historical method" necessarily leads to the "specificity of the West" (2015, p. 82) further helps to illustrate the flaws in his argumentation. Hanegraaff's entirely different treatment of "Western" and "non-Western" actors within the history of esotericism is an instructive case in point. As Hanegraaff explains, his proposed method would consist of studying a wide range of specific and different, historically situated subjects, "the representatives of which *may or may not* happen to think of themselves as 'esotericists,' or of their perspectives as 'esoteric' (or any equivalent term, in any relevant language)" (2015, pp. 81–82, original emphasis). As Hanegraaff admits with respect to Marsilio Ficino (1433–1499), esotericism is a nineteenth-century term that can be applied retroactively, or in any context where it is semantically absent, only at the historian's discretion. Why, then, include an Italian Renaissance scholar, who did *not* think of himself as an esotericist, into research on esotericism that is based on a nineteenth-century model, while excluding "non-Western" actors who *happened* to think of themselves as esotericists and partook in the very shaping of "esotericism" *in the nineteenth century*?

At least to a significant degree, these problems arise from Hanegraaff's canonical definition of "Western" esotericism and the lack of theoretical reflection thereof. Since there is little room for "non-Westerners" taking an *active* role in the history of esotericism in Hanegraaff's model, this blind spot remains unrecognized. Hanegraaff even cautions against "yet another form of terminological imperialism" that would result from applying "esotericism" to the "traditional beliefs and practices" of "people in Africa, Japan, India, Latin America, or Antarctica" (2015, p. 86). However, "non-Western" actors have in fact used "esoteric" vocabulary to describe their practices before the historical concept of "Western esotericism" had even emerged—the Theosophical Society is an illustration of this circumstance, but by no means the earliest (for an in-depth development of that argument, see Strube, forthcoming). Hanegraaff's dismissal of "non-Westerners," or his assumption that they must have been "Westernized," exemplifies how "non-Western" actors are effectively denied agency. It also contradicts his call to "listen to the sources," as his own *selection* of sources is restricted to, and based on, the paradigm of "rejected knowledge in Western culture." Hanegraaff, then, makes sweeping and dismissive statements about "non-Western" contexts, while not working with any historical source that would belong to one. It is hard to see how such an approach could qualify as strictly historical and source-based, or as part of an "*anti-eclectic historiography*" (Hanegraaff, 2012, p. 152, original emphasis).

This development is unfortunate, since the study of esotericism has much to offer for historians and other scholars working on the complex emergence of "Western" identities and their entanglement with "non-Western" contexts. Hanegraaff does address several important aspects that could be part of such conversations, such as the categorization of "non-Western" practices as "magic" or "superstition," or the attractiveness of "non-hegemonic" forms of knowledge production that, for instance, made the Theosophical Society attractive for colonized individuals (Strube and Krämer, 2020, pp. 4–6). Hanegraaff is also aware of the fact that "the West" carries the legacy of "imperialism, colonialism, orientalism, racism, and so on" (Hanegraaff, 2015, p. 60), but his conclusions warrant criticism, as becomes further evident in light of his most recent interventions. For instance, Hanegraaff suggests that esotericism belonged in the same "series" as the "exclusion and marginalisation of women, black people and other people of colour, various alternative or non-dominant gender and sexualities, and the victims of Western colonisation worldwide" (Hanegraaff, 2019, p. 149; cf. Asprem, 2021, pp. 127–146). Hanegraaff holds that "postmodern" scholars should thus enthusiastically embrace Western esotericism, while in fact they do not: because, as Hanegraaff suspects, "female academics may be attracted by women's history, black academics by the history of racial prejudice, and so on," while academics would usually not (openly) identify as "esotericists" (Hanegraaff, 2019, p. 150). It is in that passage that Hanegraaff then reprimands "those radical theorists who are so eager to deconstruct 'Western culture.'" Instead of rebuking grand narratives, scholars of esotericism should counter those postmodernists by writing "*new and better grand narratives*" to demonstrate "the true course of Western culture" (p. 152, original emphasis). These statements once more underline the urgency for a precise engagement with actual scholars and their publications, rather than vaguely and polemically alluding to the machinations of shadowy postmodern radicals. As they stand, they read less like a scholarly argument than an identity-political intervention.

4   Approaches from Postcolonial Studies and Global History

Whoever the radical theorists are that Hanegraaff writes about, they cannot be the most prominent and influential proponents of global history and related fields, including the one that could most reasonably be labeled "postmodern," *postcolonial studies*. Critically reflecting on the "jargon of our times," Homi Bhabha stressed in 1994 that, "if the interest in postmodernism is limited to a celebration of the fragmentation of the 'grand narratives' of postenlightenment rationalism then, for all its intellectual excitement, it remains a profoundly parochial enterprise" (Bhabha, 2004, p. 6). Postcolonial studies were not concerned with eagerly deconstructing and vilifying "Western culture," but with unravelling the historical, social, and political complexities behind it. "We have to use short-hand generalizations, like 'West' and 'western,'" wrote Stuart Hall, "but we need to remember that they represent very complex ideas and have no simple or single meaning" (1992, p. 276). "Western" ideas were not regarded as inherently bad. Nor were they rejected, even as they were transmitted through colonialism. Rather, Dipesh Chakrabarty affirmed that European knowledge was "now everybody's heritage" (2000, pp. 16, 255). His famous project of "provincializing Europe [...] does not call for a simplistic, out-of-hand rejection of modernity, liberal values, universals, science, reason, grand narratives, totalizing explanations, and so on," and neither can it be "a project of cultural relativism." Instead, the idea was "to write into the history of modernity the ambivalences, contradictions, the use of force, and the tragedies and ironies that attend it" (pp. 42–43).

From its inception, postcolonial criticism was directed against the fact that the socio-political benefits of ostensibly universalistic ideas and values, such as humanity and liberty, were historically restricted to "the West," which aggressively denied others, not only the rights resulting from them, but the very status of being human (Young, 2004, pp. 158–165). This process was by no means limited to outright colonial acts of violence or the structures of colonial administration; it was inherently inscribed into European knowledge production. The histories produced in Europe "were self-contained histories complete in themselves, as if the self-fashioning of the West was something that occurred only within its self-assigned geographical boundaries" (Chakrabarty, 2000, p. 45). This idea of "first in Europe, then elsewhere" lies at the heart of the idea that "non-Western" societies must always be passive recipients, that they are "incomplete," characterized by a "lack" that necessarily excludes them from "modernity," "progress," or "development" (pp. 7–8, 12–15; Asad, 2003, pp. 13–14). These structures did not only shape the emergence of modern academic disciplines, with sociology focusing on "the West" and anthropology on "the others," but they informed scholarship, including history, where "Europe works as a silent referent in historical knowledge." As a consequence, while "third-world" historians felt a need to refer to works in European history, historians of Europe did not feel any need to reciprocate. This "inequality of ignorance" was not simply a matter of arrogance on the part of European historians and, as Chakrabarty stresses, it also does not diminish their work or achievements. Rather, it was the "result of a much more complex theoretical condition under which historical knowledge is produced" (Chakrabarty, 2000, pp. 28–29; cf. Randeria and Römhild, 2013, pp. 15–17).

In line with this argument, postcolonial scholars have rejected binary divisions within history/historiography and social experiences, between past and present, tradition and modernity. It was argued that history always *also* functions within the formation of present identities. Bhabha elaborated concepts such as *hybridity* and *cultural difference* to highlight these problems. He stressed that knowledge production never happens in a space where unitary cultures and their homogeneous traditions meet, but that knowledge is the product of *negotiation* and difference, which is always ambivalent (Bhabha, 2004, pp. 19, 37–38, 49–56). In that respect, postcolonial perspectives shared much with poststructuralist philosophies, however without simply reproducing them. Gayatri Spivak agreed with poststructuralist theorists "that the networks of power/desire/interest are so heterogeneous, that their reduction to a coherent narrative is counterproductive" and hence a persistent critique was needed. But she also denounced the failure of leftist intellectuals such as Foucault and Deleuze to adequately consider "subaltern" voices (Spivak, 1994, pp. 66–68). Such positions are generally well known among present-day scholars, but they are practically absent from the conceptualization of Western esotericism.

As is the case with every author, the writings of postcolonial scholars contained self-contradictions, inconsistencies, lacunae, and reductions. They also invited interpretations that painted the relationship between the colonizer and the colonized, for instance, along the same binary lines that they sought to destabilize. In addition to respective debates within postcolonial studies, *global history* functioned as an important corrective to such tendencies, providing some of the most valuable criticism of postcolonial approaches, especially with regard to colonialism, cultural representation, and the question of agency (Conrad, 2016, pp. 56–57; Moyn and Sartori, 2013, pp. 18–20). A particularly important point was that "positive Western exceptionalism" sometimes found its mirror image in postcolonial notions of cultural imperialism that "are essentially diffusionist and take the European origins of modernity for granted" (Conrad, 2016, pp. 74–75).

These disagreements notwithstanding, global historians subscribed to the criticism of Eurocentrism, recognizing the "birth defects of modern social sciences and humanities" and the necessity to contemplate power structures and asymmetries. The alleged diffusion of European achievements culminating in modernity stands at the center of that criticism (pp. 3–4; Conrad and Randeria, 2013, pp. 35–36). Global historians also highlight the circumstance that the spatialization and regionalization which still serve as the foundations of academic disciplines, call for recognition as historical constructs and concomitant critical self-reflection (Duara, 2013; Conrad and Randeria, 2013, pp. 33–34).

The implication of the term "global" is, in most conceptualizations, neither "universal" nor "planetary." Quite the opposite. It implies an awareness of global interconnections and structural conditions, focusing on interactions, mobility, and fluidity (Conrad, 2016, pp. 12, 64–65; cf. Moyn and Sartori, 2013, pp. 5–15). They might very well focus on micro-investigations within local and regional contexts, where developments on a global scale can become particularly tangible (e.g. Ghobrial, 2019; Fischer-Tiné, 2018). Often these methodological angles are expressed through the *relational perspective* of *entangled histories*. Again, the suggestion is not that "everything is connected," and neither to the same degree, in the same way, and at any time. An entangled history is tendentially fragmentary rather than holistic, investigating concrete problems and connections, rather than postulating world-historical totalities or attempting to write a history of the entire planet (Conrad and Randeria, 2013, p. 40; cf. Manning, 2003, pp. 270–272; Wenzlhuemer, 2017, pp. 79–84).

These assumptions imply that European identities, even within the colonial framework characterized by power asymmetries, have formed through a complex dependency on, and interactions with, the perceived Other (Conrad and Randeria, 2013, pp. 51–52; Veer, 2001, pp. 3–13). Global history is hence concerned with a "focus on the global conditions and interactions through which the modern world emerged" (Conrad, 2016, p. 76). This focus on the modern period is plausible given the importance of the nineteenth century for the processes in question, but this does by no means imply a restriction to the modern period. The chronological framework is a lively discussed subject among global historians, who stress the need for interdisciplinary dialogue and continuous self-reflection to tackle this question (Moyn and Sartori, 2013, pp. 15, 20). The wide-spread consensus is that "global connections are preceded by conditions," which means that a diachronic perspective is necessary to understand the conditions under which global connections could arise: "Exchange, in other words, may be a surface phenomenon that gives evidence of the basic structural transformations that made the exchange possible in the first place" (Conrad, 2016, pp. 69–70).

5 Global Religious History as a Way Forward

The program of global religious history (*Globale Religionsgeschichte*) combines elements from global history, a genealogical method, a critical engagement with postcolonial theories, and a poststructuralist epistemology. At the outset, its intention is to bridge divisions, including those between postcolonial and global history, and between disciplines such as religious studies, theology, history, different area studies, and fields such as Western esotericism (Strube, 2016b). Writing a global religious history means acknowledging the need to constantly contextualize and reflect continuities, ruptures, and ambivalences instead of attempting to streamline historical developments. This also pertains to the formation of "Western" identities through unstable and highly contested negotiations, polemics, and mutual exchanges that transgressed geographical, social, or political boundaries. For this reason, constant attention must be paid to the agency of those historical actors who are often neglected by other historiographies, without romanticizing the role or over-emphasizing the agency of colonized or otherwise marginalized people. An awareness of power relations and often ambiguous hierarchies, especially within a colonial context, also means avoiding simplifications and/or ideological binaries.

One key difference to related approaches is the centrality of a particular genealogical method that rejects both the search for pure origins and teleological understandings of history. A genealogy always, if only implicitly, retains a focus on the present that requires the historian to reflect on her or his own historical context, bias, and ideological assumptions (Foucault, 1984, pp. 80–81, 89–91). As Talal Asad put it, a genealogy can be seen as "a way of working back from our present to the contingencies that have come together to give us our certainties" (Asad, 2003, p. 16). Global religious history combines such a method with an epistemology that is significantly informed by the work of Ernesto Laclau, among others (Strube, 2016a, pp. 29–37; for more about this approach, see Okropiridze, 2021, pp. 220–231). This work revolves around the formation of social and political identities, but it can be effectively applied to subjects such as "religion" or "esotericism" (Bergunder, 2010, pp. 19–24; Bergunder, 2014b, pp. 259–273). From such a perspective, the discursive production of meaning operates through a logic of equivalence and difference, which can be clearly observed, for instance, in the separation between a "Western" and an "Eastern" esotericism: historical actors attributed different signifiers to each, for instance "Hermetism" and "Rosicrucianism" to the former, and "Hinduism" and "Buddhism" to the latter. While participants in such discourses are continually concerned with fixating a particular "true" meaning, such a fixation is, in reality, always impossible (Laclau, 1994, p. 168). Epistemologically, "esotericism" is hence an "empty signifier," which does not mean that it is devoid of meaning, but that this meaning is constantly re-negotiated and historically contingent. The attempts at fixating discourses are understood as historical processes and social practices (Laclau, 2000, pp. 44–59), which opens them up to scholarly scrutiny. Since scholars are part of that practice, they too must be the object of such an enquiry (Bergunder, 2010, p. 25).

One of the first consequences of such an approach is the rejection of Eurocentrism, including the model of European diffusionism which assumes that modernity, religion, or esotericism were exported into a world that was, according to the referenced scholarship in Western esotericism, populated by passive and silent Others. If the study of esotericism can teach anything to historians of the modern period, it is that the meaning of modernity, religion, science, etc., was not even stable *within* Europe, which means that such concepts were not ready-made products that could have simply been exported to the rest of the world. In Europe as elsewhere, they *were and are* subject to intense negotiations, the participants in which were and are not only "Westerners."

In the nineteenth century, esotericism had "a significant influence in a global religious discourse" that went "beyond a synchronous esoteric network and points far beyond it" (Bergunder, 2010, p. 29). Scholars of esotericism are usually eager to point out its "modernity" (e.g. Pasi, 2009), but then they also must acknowledge its relationship with imperialism and colonialism, as Mariano Villalba (2021) aptly underscores. More fundamentally, they must also acknowledge that the meaning of "esotericism" *emerged within a global context* that can only be grasped when one extends the scope of research beyond the field of Western esotericism as it has so far been conceptualized. As has become clear by now, the shortcomings of this conceptualization are an exemplar of everything that global and postcolonial historians have convincingly exposed as historiographically flawed.

As in the case of "religion," esotericism *was and is* used globally, and quarrels about its "Western specificity" can only arise when one insists on its "origins" in "Europe" and links this claim with one of ownership (the prerequisite for export). This claim of ownership, however, is unwarranted, decidedly ideological, and inherently intertwined with identity politics. A genealogical approach is capable of avoiding such ideological trappings by asking what connections exist between today's global use of esotericism and European history (Bergunder, 2014b, pp. 275–279). The efficiency of such a perspective has been demonstrated repeatedly by Michael Bergunder, who highlighted the entanglements of esotericism, not only with "non-esoteric" contexts, but also beyond the confines of Europe or "the West" (Bergunder, 2014a, pp. 401–404; Bergunder, 2016b, pp. 95–134).

As is the case with global history in general, the focus of global religious history on the nineteenth century raises the question of *diachronic* connections to "pre-modern" periods. By virtue of its focus on the self-reflexivity of the scholar and her or his present *positionality*, it is, however, ideally suited to open a forum of conversation with historians focusing on earlier periods, in order to collaborate on a more comprehensive understanding of long-term historical developments. It does not assume that things emerged out of nowhere, but it cautions against imposing modern concepts on earlier periods without considering what has transpired in-between (cf. the focus on reception-history by Burns, 2021). This generates important and innovative research questions and perspectives along the lines that have been discussed in this section. In a similar vein, it is also perfectly suited for a *comparative* approach that has been elaborated in some detail by Bergunder (2016a).

The potential of global religious history for the study of esotericism is huge, as the example of Theosophy illustrates. Major works of global history do mention the Society, but evidently without knowing much about it (Bayly, 2004, p. 365; Osterhammel, 2014, p. 813; Conrad, 2018, p. 582). Why none of those scholars would need the scholarship of Western esotericism, and why that circumstance will not change if the field does not change, should be evident by now. There can be no doubt that Theosophy, Spiritualism, occultism, etc., were extremely influential movements that shaped many relevant ideas and practices up to the present day. They were also some of the most globally entangled subjects that one could possibly imagine at the time. Fortunately, this is increasingly noted within the field, as the works of Karl Baier, Julie Chajes, Boaz Huss, Keith Cantú, or Mriganka Mukhopadhyay, among others, in addition to several of the contributors to this volume, demonstrate.[2]

As has been pointed out in the beginning of this chapter, such a change should not be viewed as a threat to the field, but as an opportunity. Global religious history makes concrete proposals for how to enter dialogue with scholars of other fields, specializing in different chronological periods, geographical spaces, or subjects that lie either beyond the confines of Western esotericism, or within those many blind spots that the "rejected knowledge in Western culture" paradigm carries even with respect to "the West." A constructive engagement of the study of esotericism with other fields will not only lead to an improvement of its theoretical and methodological toolkit, but also to improved recognition, reputation, and expansion within professional academic institutions. Finally, by investigating entangled histories that lie behind

---

2 My own operationalization of the method suggested here is currently in progress with the working title *Tantra in the Context of a Global Religious History*.

an increasingly fragmented and ideologized public discourse, it would be able to make contributions that question, rather than reinforce, identity-political polemical concepts. Not only would it help the study of esotericism prosper, but it would open up more comprehensive and open-minded perspectives on how we can make sense of the world around us.

Bibliography

Asad, T. (2003) *Formations of the Secular: Christianity, Islam, Modernity*. Stanford: Stanford University Press.

Asprem, E. (2014) "Beyond the West: Towards a New Comparativism in the Study of Esotericism," *Correspondences*, 2(1), pp. 3–33.

Asprem, E. (2021) "Rejected Knowledge Reconsidered: Some Methodological Notes on Esotericism and Marginality," in Asprem, E. and Strube, J. (eds.) *New Approaches to the Study of Esotericism*. Leiden and Boston: Brill, pp. 127–146.

Bakker, J.M. (2021) "Race and (the Study of) Esotericism," in Asprem, E. and Strube, J. (eds.) *New Approaches to the Study of Esotericism*. Leiden and Boston: Brill, pp. 147–167.

Bayly, C.A. (2004) *The Birth of the Modern World, 1780–1914: Global Connections and Comparisons*. Malden/Oxford: Blackwell.

Bergunder, M. (2010) "What is Esotericism? Cultural Studies Approaches and the Problems of Definition in Religious Studies," *Method and Theory in the Study of Religion*, 22(1), pp. 9–36.

Bergunder, M. (2014a) "Experiments with Theosophical Truth: Gandhi, Esotericism, and Global Religious History," *Journal of the American Academy of Religion*, 82, pp. 398–426.

Bergunder, M. (2014b) "What is Religion? The Unexplained Subject Matter of Religious Studies," *Method and Theory in the Study of Religion*, 26, pp. 246–286.

Bergunder, M. (2016a) "Comparison in the Maelstrom of Historicity: A Postcolonial Perspective on Comparative Religion," in Schmidt-Leukel, P. and Nehring, A. (eds.) *Interreligious Comparisons in Religious Studies and Theology*. London/New York: Bloomsbury Academic, pp. 34–52.

Bergunder, M. (2016b) "'Religion' and 'Science' Within a Global Religious History," *Aries*, 16(1), pp. 86–141.

Bhabha, H.K. (2004) *The Location of Culture*. London/New York: Routledge.

Bogdan, H. and Djurdjevic, G. (2014) "Introduction: Occultism in a Global Perspective," in Bogdan, H. and Djurdjevic, G. (eds.) *Occultism in a Global Perspective*. Abingdon: Routledge, pp. 1–15.

Burns, D. (2021) "Receptions of Revelations: A Future for the Study of Esotericism and Antiquity," in Asprem, E. and Strube, J. (eds.) *New Approaches to the Study of Esotericism*. Leiden and Boston: Brill, pp. 20–44.

Cantú, K. (2021) "'Don't Take Any Wooden Nickles': Western Esotericism, Yoga, and the Discourse of Authenticity," in Asprem, E. and Strube, J. (eds.) *New Approaches to the Study of Esotericism*. Leiden and Boston: Brill, pp. 109–126.

Chakrabarty, D. (2000) *Provincializing Europe: Postcolonial Thought and Historical Difference*. Princeton: Princeton University Press.

Conrad, S. (2016) *What is Global History?* Princeton: Princeton University Press.

Conrad, S. (2018) "A Cultural History of Global Transformation," in Conrad, S. and Osterhammel, J. (eds.) *A History of the World*, vol. 4 : *An Emerging Modern World, 1750–1870*. Cambridge: Harvard University Press, pp. 411–659.

Conrad, S. and Randeria, S. (2013) "Einleitung: Geteilte Geschichten – Europa in einer postkolonialen Welt," in Conrad, S., Randeria, S. and Römhild, R. (eds.) *Jenseits des Eurozentrismus: Postkoloniale Perspektiven in den Geschichts- und Kulturwissenschaften*. 2 ed. Frankfurt am Main/New York: Campus Verlag, pp. 32–70.

Duara, P. (2013) "Asien neu denken: Zum Verständnis einer zusammenwachsenden Region," in Conrad, S., Randeria, S. and Römhild, R. (eds.) *Jenseits des Eurozentrismus: Postkoloniale Perspektiven in den Geschichts- und Kulturwissenschaften*. 2 ed. Frankfurt am Main/New York: Campus Verlag, pp. 526–553.

Faivre, A. (1986) *Accès de l'ésotérisme occidental*. Paris: Gallimard.

Fischer-Tiné, H. (2018) "Marrying Global History with South Asian History: Potential and Limits of Global Microhistory in a Regional Inflection," *Comparativ*, 28(5), pp. 49–74.

Foucault, M. (1984) "Nietzsche, Genealogy, History," in Rabinow, P. (ed.) *The Foucault Reader*. New York: Pantheon Books, pp. 76–100.

Ghobrial, J.-P.A. (2019) "Introduction: Seeing the World like a Microhistorian," *Past & Present*, 242(14), pp. 1–22.

Godwin, J. (1994) *The Theosophical Enlightenment*. Albany: State University of New York Press.

Goodrick-Clarke, N. (2013) "Western Esoteric Traditions and Theosophy," in Hammer, O. (ed.) *Handbook of the Theosophical Current*. Leiden/Boston: Brill, pp. 261–307.

Granholm, K. (2013) "Locating the West: Problematizing the 'Western' in Western Esotericism and Occultism," in Bogdan, H. and Djurdjevic, G. (eds.) *Occultism in a Global Perspective*. London: Acumen Publishing, pp. 17–36.

Gray, B. (2019) "The Traumatic Mysticism of Othered Others: Blackness, Islam, and Esotericism in the Five Percenters," *Correspondences*, 7(1), pp. 201–237.

Hall, S. (1992) "The West and the Rest: Discourse and Power," in Hall, S. and Gieben, B. (eds.) *Formations of Modernity*. Cambridge/Oxford: Polity Press/Blackwell Publishers, pp. 275–320.

Hanegraaff, W.J. (1995) "Empirical Method in the Study of Esotericism," *Method and Theory in the Study of Religion*, 7(2), pp. 99–129.

Hanegraaff, W.J. (1996) *New Age Religion and Western Culture: Esotericism in the Mirror of Secular Thought*. Leiden/New York: State University of New York Press.

Hanegraaff, W.J. (2012) *Esotericism and the Academy: Rejected Knowledge in Western Culture*. Cambridge: Cambridge University Press.

Hanegraaff, W.J. (2013) *Western Esotericism: A Guide for the Perplexed*. London/New York: Bloomsbury Academic.

Hanegraaff, W.J. (2015) "The Globalization of Esotericism," *Correspondences*, 3(1), pp. 55–91.

Hanegraaff, W.J. (2016) "Esotericism Theorized: Major Trends and Approaches to the Study of Esotericism," in DeConick, A. (ed.) *Religion: Secret Religion*. Farmington Hills: Macmillan, pp. 155–170.

Hanegraaff, W.J. (2019) "Rejected Knowledge... So You Mean that Esotericists Are the Losers of History?," in Hanegraaff, W.J., Forshaw, P.J. and Pasi, M. (eds.) *Hermes Explains: Thirty Questions About Western Esotericism*. Amsterdam: Amsterdam University Press, pp. 145–152.

Hanegraaff, W.J. (2020) "Western Esotericism and the Orient in the First Theosophical Society," in Krämer, H.M. and Strube, J. (eds.) *Theosophy Across Boundaries: Transcultural and Interdisciplinary Perspectives on a Modern Esoteric Movement*. Albany: State University of New York Press, pp. 29–64.

Laclau, E. (1994) "Why do Empty Signifiers Matter to Politics?," in Weeks, J. (ed.) *The Lesser Evil and the Greater Good. The Theory and Politics of Social Diversity*. London: Rivers Oram Press, pp. 167–178.

Laclau, E. (2000) "Identity and Hegemony: The Role of Universality in the Constitution of Political Logics," in Butler, J., Laclau, E., and Žižek, S. (eds.) *Contingency, Hegemony, Universality: Contemporary Dialogues on the Left*. London/New York: Verso, pp. 44–89.

Manning, P. (2003) *Navigating World History: Historians Create a Global Past*. New York: Palgrave Macmillan.

Moyn, S. and Sartori, A. (2013) "Approaches to Global Intellectual History," in Moyn, S. and Sartori, A. (eds.) *Global Intellectual History*. New York: Columbia University Press, pp. 3–30.

Okropiridze, D. (2021) "Interpretation Reconsidered: The Definitional Progression in the Study of Esotericism as a Case in Point for the Varifocal Theory of Interpretation," in Asprem, E. and Strube, J. (eds.) *New Approaches to the Study of Esotericism*. Leiden and Boston: Brill, pp. 217–240.

Osterhammel, J. (2014) *The Transformation of the World: A Global History of the Nineteenth Century*. Princeton: Princeton University Press.

Page, H.R. Jr. and Finley, S.C. (2021) "'What Can the Whole World Be Hiding?' Exploring *Africana* Esotericisms in the American Soul–Blues Continuum," in Asprem, E. and Strube, J. (eds.) *New Approaches to the Study of Esotericism*. Leiden and Boston: Brill, pp. 168–181.

Partridge, C. (2013) "Lost Horizon: H.P. Blavatsky and Theosophical Orientalism," in Hammer, O. and Rothstein, M. (eds.) *Handbook of the Theosophical Current*. Leiden/Boston: Brill, pp. 309–333.

Pasi, M. (2009) "The Modernity of Occultism: Reflections on Some Crucial Aspects," in Hanegraaff, W.J. and Pijnenburg, J. (eds.) *Hermes in the Academy: Ten Years' Study of Western Esotericism at the University of Amsterdam*. Amsterdam: Amsterdam University Press, pp. 59–74.

Pasi, M. (2010) "Oriental Kabbalah and the Parting of East and West in the Early Theosophical Society," in Huss, B., Pasi, M., and Stuckrad, K.v. (eds.) *Kabbalah and Modernity. Interpretations, Transformations, Adaptations*. Leiden: Brill, pp. 151–166.

Randeria, S. and Römhild, R. (2013) "Das postkoloniale Europa: Verflochtene Genealogien der Gegenwart," in Conrad, S., Randeria, S., and Römhild, R. (eds.) *Jenseits des Eurozentrismus: Postkoloniale Perspektiven in den Geschichts- und Kulturwissenschaften*. 2 ed. Frankfurt am Main/New York: Campus Verlag, pp. 9–31.

Saif, L. (2021) "'That I Did Love the Moore to Live with Him': Islam in/and the Study of 'Western Esotericism,'" in Asprem, E. and Strube, J. (eds.) *New Approaches to the Study of Esotericism*. Leiden and Boston: Brill, pp. 67–87.

Spivak, G.C. (1994) "Can the Subaltern Speak?," in Williams, P. and Chrisman, L. (eds.) *Colonial Discourse and Post-Colonial Theory*. New York: Columbia University Press, pp. 66–111.

Strube, J. (2016a) *Sozialismus, Katholizismus und Okkultismus im Frankreich des 19. Jahrhunderts: Die Genealogie der Schriften von Eliphas Lévi. Religionsgeschichtliche Versuche und Vorarbeiten* Berlin/Boston: De Gruyter.

Strube, J. (2016b) "Transgressing Boundaries: Social Reform, Theology, and the Demarcations Between Science and Religion," *Aries*, 16(1), pp. 1–11.

Strube, J. (2017a) "Occultist Identity Formations Between Theosophy and Socialism in *Fin-de-Siècle* France," *Numen*, 64(5–6), pp. 568–595.

Strube, J. (2017b) "Revolution, Illuminismus und Theosophie: Eine Genealogie der 'häretischen' Historiographie des frühen französischen Sozialismus und Kommunismus," *Historische Zeitschrift*, 304(1), pp. 50–89.

Strube, J. and Krämer, H.M. (2020) "Introduction," *Theosophy Across Boundaries: Transcultural and Interdisciplinary Perspectives on a Modern Esoteric Movement*. Albany: State University of New York Press, 1–26.

Strube, J. (forthcoming) *Tantra in the Context of a Global Religious History* (working title).

Stuckrad, K.v. (2005a) "Western Esotericism: Towards an Integrative Model of Interpretation," *Religion*, 35, pp. 78–97.

Stuckrad, K.v. (2005b) *Western Esoterisicm: A Brief History of Secret Knowledge*. London/Oakville: Equinox.

Veer, P.v.d. (2001) *Imperial Encounters: Religion and Modernity in India and Britain*. Princeton: Princeton University Press.

Villalba, M. (2021) "The Occult Among the Aborigines of South America? Some Remarks on Race, Coloniality, and the West in the Study of Esotericism," in Asprem, E. and Strube, J. (eds.) *New Approaches to the Study of Esotericism*. Leiden and Boston: Brill, pp. 88–108.

Wenzlhuemer, R. (2017) *Globalgeschichte schreiben: Eine Einführung in 6 Episoden*. Konstanz/München: UVK Verlagsgesellschaft.

Young, R. (2004) *White Mythologies: Writing History and the West*. 2 edn. London/New York: Routledge.

"That I Did Love the Moor to Live with Him": Islam in/and the Study of "Western Esotericism"

Liana Saif

In recent years, the field of "Western esotericism" has been confronted by problems related to the cultural and regional demarcations it has adopted. This field is based on a *longue durée* narrative that underplays non-"Western" currents, including ones which, through appropriation or reactions to them, constituted major sources for it. One of the most immediate arguments against the use of the qualifier "Western" and an essentialized "West" is European entanglements with Islamdom. This article tackles the ambiguous place given to Islam in the narrative of "Western esotericism" and the wider intellectual and historical complex that feeds the exclusionary tendencies expressed by the "Western" in "Western esotericism." It begins by providing a historical background of the West versus East divide in order to grasp the genealogy of the discourse and locate the problems resulting from an esotericism labelled as "Western." Two major components of this narrative within which Islam is usually evoked are then highlighted: first, the sanitization of orientalist perspectives, and, second, the reliance on perennialist sources, especially the writings of Henry Corbin. Finally, the article recommends, on one level, a reflective global approach that takes into account the agency of non-Western actors in the globalization of values and concepts in modern and pre-modern eras, thus allowing us to engage in more suitable comparative practices in the study of esotericism. On another level, I have argued elsewhere that an Islamic esotericism (*bāṭiniyya*) has a long history dating back to the ninth century at least, based on principles, epistemological paradigms, and social orientations, conceptualized and negotiated (Saif, 2019). I demonstrated there, as I do here, that this esotericism had—and still has—connections with the currents discussed in the study of "Western esotericism," especially through the Traditionalists and Sufism.

1   Historicizing the West-East Divide

The premise upon which the argument of this chapter rests is that "West" and "East" are ever-shifting constructs based primarily on political, cultural, and economic aspirations of different groups at specific periods of time (Bonnett,

2004, p. 8). Aspiration here is understood as social, economic, and political motivations for the cultivation of group power (Appadurai, 2004, pp. 60–63). Movements of ideas, people, goods, and texts largely follow these aspirations. Therefore, the field's historical grounding is unstable from the outset, because it fails to clarify what is "Western" about it and according to whom, which also implies ambiguous ideas about what is then "Eastern." The general tendency to view Islam as limited to the East also connotes that the Islamic experience is geographically confined there, thus overlooking Islamic religious and esoteric experiences in Africa, the Americas, Asia, and Europe. Nevertheless, it is important to historicize the binary of East versus West itself, in broad lines at least, in order to demonstrate the fruitful venues for refining the study of esotericism beyond a historically and politically unreflective and monolithic "West," as well as how this binary has been constructed in the Islamic context.

A collective identity requires outsiders, cultivated through cultural transactions, necessitating friction and the creation of fiction regarding the Other (Webb, 2016, p. 11). In discussing Arabic-Islamic views of the Latin West during the Middle Ages, Daniel König stresses that there are certain "standardizing forces" based on self-identification and perception of alterity that must not be understood in terms of "Othering" only, but in terms of multiple perspectives in different times and directions: military, political, economic, intellectual, religious, personal, emotional, and other forms of relations (König, 2015, p. 23). For example, early Islamic texts from the fifth to the seventh centuries suggest that the worldview of the pre-expansionist Arabs was confined to what is now recognized as "the Middle East" (König, 2015, p. 35). Expansion to the Iberian Peninsula and central Asia transformed this perspective. The earliest description of Europe (*Urūfā*) from the ninth century presents it as "containing Andalusia, the lands of the Slavs, Byzantines, Franks, and Tangier till the borders of Egypt" (Ibn Khordābeh, 1889, p. 155). Islamic cultures of "the east" considered themselves as of the "west" in relation to South East Asia through to China when trade with these areas was heavy. Interactions with Buddhism, Hinduism, and Zoroastrianism had in turn a deep influence on Mediterranean Islamicate cultures, including their religious traditions, movements, and ideas that could be regarded as esoteric. This same political and economic aspiration created channels and pools of entanglement. Muslims of al-Andalus were viewed as part of *al-maghreb*, meaning "the west," while the Muslim-dominant regions of Iraq, Syria, Egypt, and Persia were called *al-mashriq*, "the east" (Lazáro, 2013, pp. 260–264).

The conquest of al-Andalus acquainted Arab-Muslims with the 'lands of the Franks' (*bilād al-ifranja, bilād al-firanj*) which only received an Arabic name in the course of expansion at the beginning of the eighth century. The term 'Gaul' (*ghaliyya, ghalish*) became an alternative regional toponym when the first Arabic paraphrase of Orosius's *Historiae adversus paganos* was produced at the end of the ninth century or the beginning of the tenth. Regions lying further, such as the British Isles, the Slavic world, and Scandinavia, do not appear in the earliest ninth-century accounts of westerly expansion, despite being mentioned in Arabic-Islamic works based on Ptolemaic geography (König, 2015, pp. 43–44). Nevertheless, there were no incentives to engage systematically with these regions in the early medieval period. Furthermore, the limited intellectual investment in romance languages likely contributed to the creation of a sense of cultural divide (König, 2015, p. 81). There was also a lack of ideological motivations to expand to these regions (König, 2015, p. 92). However, Constantinople, the capital of the Eastern Church remained a sore spot for Islamic rule, which ended with the fall of Constantinople in 1453 under the reign of Mehmed II, also known as Mehmed the Conqueror (König, 2015, p. 42). With a strong westward gaze, he consolidated the expansionist projects of his predecessors in Western Anatolia, the Serbian and Bosnian kingdoms, the Genoese and Venetian lands, and the Wallachian and Moldovian principalities (Kafadar, 1994, pp. 595–7).

In premodern Eurasia, it was not only imperial and dynastic projects that determined the orientation of aspirations; cultural and religious identities were often formed in multiple directions at the same time. For example, the term *Mashriqiyyūn*, the Easterners, also designated the Persian or Nestorian Church (al-Maqrīzī, 1998, 4: p. 401), and those along with the Jews of al-Andalus, Egypt, Greater Syria or Mesopotamia, some of whom converted to Islam, contributed to the intellectual transfers between eastern and western regions. They became an integral part of Arabic-Islamic societies (König, 2015, p. 44). Although, as König notes, the divide is exacerbated by the fact that Christian communities of Egypt, Greater Syria, and Mesopotamia had come into being in the vast regions of the Roman Empire; "they preserved a memory of imperial unity and the process of Christianization and occasionally kept a record of relations with the Latin West from the pre-Islamic into the Islamic period, e.g. with the Bishop of Rome" (König, 2015, p. 44).

Blocked by the Atlantic Ocean in the west, European aspirations and anxieties of self-definition could only be formulated in relation to the east initially (Wintle, 2005, pp. 63–75). This is also reflected by medieval European T-O maps with the three continents: Asia, Africa, and Europe, with Africa and Europe occupying the west, and Asia, the largest continent, occupying the east. This scheme integrated the biblical account of human population descending from the three sons of Noah: Asia–Shem, Africa–Ham, and Europe–Japeth, creating a racial template that served as a model well into the nineteenth century (Villalba, 2021). As Suzanne Akbari writes, "the purpose of all these schemes, however variable, was to impose order on the abundant heterogeneity of creation, to gain control over the world by fitting it into an intellectually coherent system." This order implies the erasure of human agency and that racial and ethnic variations are divinely decreed (Akbari, 2009, pp. 20–1). As a result, Bartholomeus Anglicus, in his thirteenth-century account of the divisions of the continents among the sons of Noah, following Isidore of Seville, states that the heat of the Sun discolors the children of Africa, causing weak humors and black faces. Contrary to these are "men of the northe londe" whose cold temperatures make men huge due to their strong humors. People of Asia, "and here first londe is by eeste," have mediocre dispositions (Akbari, 2009, pp. 41, 47).

Then, as today, Christian-European identities were, to a significant extent, formed against the most immediate geographical and ideological "neighbor," whose profile is different enough to be othered, but similar and interlinked enough to be perceived as a threat to a Euro-Christian autonomy: near eastern Muslim-dominant regions. As Akbari notes, "medieval constructions conflated categories of ethnicity and religion within a single term that served as a marker of both": the Saracen, a term rarely used to identify Christian Arabs (Akbar, 2009, p. 155). By the early modern period, with the failure of the Crusades and the fall of Byzantium to the Ottomans in 1453, military and intellectual engagement with Muslim-dominant regions became less intense. Moreover, smoother social integration of Christians and Jews contributed to the relatively quick decline of the missionary incentives of Muslim expansionism after the death of Muhammad, becoming more about the inflation of dynastic power (König, 2015, p. 60, 92).

The colonial expeditions to the Americas partially re-oriented European economic, ideological, and political objectives (Villalba, 2021). Furthermore, race was gradually being understood in terms of blood rather than climes and continents, and maps were becoming more mimetic. The Saracen is replaced by the Turk and the Moor. From there onwards, especially in the nineteenth century, a renewed imperial and colonial aspiration lead to the subjugation of regions across the globe to fuel a sense of a Western autonomous power that marches toward a modernity on the basis of rationality, industrial and technological monopoly, and "a kind of intellectual apartheid regime in which the superior West is quarantined off from the inferior East" (Ernst, 2010, p. 25). Now, there is "the West," "the East," and of course "the Rest."

Since the medieval period, then, the relationship of the "West" to Muslim-dominant regions in the "Near East" has been determined by complex oscillating dynamics. Dissociation (othering) is responsible for cementing fictional cultural boundaries; and competition is over economic—natural and human—resources and the legitimacy of one "Abrahamic" religion over the other. Finally, this shared intellectual and religious heritage simultaneously allowed for establishing connected networks between the two "worlds." The "Islamic world" is as fictional as "the West," from the medieval period till our days; however, these terms resulted to a great extent from imperial expansion and colonialism, making them containers for entrenched narratives that in turn shaped those who experienced and reacted to them. In our case, this is demonstrable by the fact that "Western esotericism" is historically a nineteenth-century polemical term adopted by esotericists and occultists in opposition to the "orientally" inspired Theosophical Society (Strube, 2017; Strube, 2021).

The neglect of Islamic materials in the study of Western esotericism reinforces the West/Islam divide, seeing them as separate and homogenous identities (Ernst, 2010, p. 23). Like nationalism, Western-centrism—which also often excludes nations and cultures from the Americas, East Europe, and the Balkans, while including some Australasian nations—has "blinded us to the possibility of connection, and historical ethnography, whether in one of its western variants of high Orientalism, or whether practised in the East, has aided and abetted this unfortunate process" (Subrahmanyam, 1997, p. 761). Despite Antoine Faivre's very brief, one-paragraph acknowledgement of "other non-Christian traditions" that include "Arabic intellectual activity," and despite his equally short discussion of "Esotericism in Medieval Thought," the accepted *longue durée* of Western esoteric currents has no substantial references to Arabic or medieval connections (Faivre, 1994, pp. 52–3; Hanegraaff, 2013, pp. 18–44; Hanegraaff, 2012; for Arabic and other medieval connections, see Saif, 2015). This is reflected in the dominating view within the field of Western esotericism that Islamic and Jewish traditions are seen to "have emerged and developed as largely self-contained and relatively autonomous traditions" (Hanegraaff, 2013, p. 15), or seeing the West as the "occident *visited* by Judaism and Islam" (Faivre, 2006, p. 208; my italics).

As I show below, even when this is directly challenged, Islam is still viewed through perennialist and Traditionalist perspectives, often reproducing orientalist tropes such as overemphasizing "sober" and "learned" Sufism as the only Islamic esoteric current, or favoring the ideas of Muslim intellectuals, such as al-Suhrawardī, whose thought was brought forward due to a perceived compatibility with *philosophia perennis* (von Stuckrad, 2010, pp. 25–26).

2 "Platonic Orientalism"

In addition to the ideology of domination that moves Orientalist discourse, the essentialized Orient has also been a romantic ideation, creating such tropes as the "wise barbarian." It is troubling to see that a "sanitized" version of this persists in the study of Western esotericism and is even defended. John Walbridge in his *Wisdom of the Mystic East* historicizes the concept of the wise barbarian, especially the "Persian sage," exemplified by Herodotus's *History of the Persian Wars*. He notes that Persian wisdom is recorded in Greek texts on occult sciences, especially in relation to Zoroaster, Hystaspes, and Ostanes. Other foreign groups were interesting to the Greeks: Egyptians, Jews, Indians, Celts, etc. (Walbridge, 2001, p. 5). As a result, Walbridge defines Platonic Orientalism as "this fascination with the exotic, and especially with the *Oriental* [which] was particularly pronounced among the philosophers of the Pythagorean and Platonic traditions, the so-called Italian school" (Walbridge, 2001, pp. 8–9). According to Dylan Burns, "Platonic Orientalism" also refers to a growing sense of a pan-Hellenic identity which melded the primordial wisdom of the East, (that is, "non-Greek") with Pythagoreanized Platonism, influenced by "pilgrimages to the Orient to obtain scientific and ritual knowledge" (Burns, 2014, p. 20; cf. Burns, 2021). According to this construction of this ancient "orientalism", "the Orient" represented an adherence to allegorical and symbolic interpretations of revelatory and experiential modes of obtaining knowledge on Being, in addition to commitments to "theurgy" and "white magic" (Walbridge, 2001, pp. 11–12). Wouter Hanegraaff adopts this notion to highlight that for Renaissance thinkers, Plato was seen, through the lens of "Platonic Orientalism," as "gnostic, hermetic, and theurgical" (Hanegraaff, 2012, p. 12). It would be "unplatonic" for Renaissance thinkers not to be adherents of *philosophia perennis* (Hanegraaff, 2012, p. 16). For Walbridge, as for Hanegraaff, al-Suhrawardī and to some degree Ibn Sīnā are awkwardly and arbitrarily placed as the conduits of symbolic and allegorical "Platonic Orientalist" philosophy to the "West" as represented by intellectuals such as Plethon, Marsilio Ficino, and even Corbin (Hanegraaff, 2012, pp. 33–34; Walbridge, 2001, p. 13). Included as a component of "cultural transfers," it perpetuates a narrative that is widely criticized; namely, "white" civilizational narratives that see Islam as a "carrier civilization": which starts in Greece and classical Rome, whose philosophical and aesthetic legacies are revived in the Renaissance with "the West" now no longer needing the mediation of Islamicate sciences; then it arrives at the "Scientific Revolution," followed by the Enlightenment; a narrative which eulogizes the successful rise of "the West," and the decline of the "Muslim world" (Asad, 2003, pp. 168–9).

In addition to the narrowness of this view of Islamic philosophy's developments in theorizing revelatory and intellectual modes of knowing, "Platonic Orientalism" is deeply problematic in many ways. None of the classical sources cited by Wallbridge, Hanegraaff, and Burns refer to the "Orient" as such, in the homogenizing sense that warrants the label "Orientalism," rendering "Platonic Orientalism" inaccurate at best (Hanegraaff, 2012, p. 15). More problematic is the deliberate avoidance of engaging with literature on Orientalism, via Edward Said or others. Hanegraaff in a footnote writes: "'Platonic Orientalism' is a new coinage, independent of the famous work of Edward Said" (Hanegraaff, 2012, p. 15n13). However, they simply cannot be separated. Orientalism is:

> A manner of regularized (or Orientalized) writing, vision, and study, dominated by imperatives, perspectives, and ideological biases ostensibly suited to the Orient. The Orient is taught, researched, administered, and pronounced upon in certain discrete ways. The Orient that appears in Orientalism, then, is a system of representations framed by a whole set of forces that brought the Orient into Western learning, Western consciousness, and later, Western empire. (Said, 1978, p. 202)

On the other hand, Burns engages with Said's conceptualization and takes advantage of the similarities; namely, that here we have the Greeks with a sense of group identity that creates an inferior Other. He also shows that "Platonic Orientalism" is not a fixed and even phenomenon among the Greeks. For example, Diogenes Laertius, Philostratus, Celsus, and others insisted that the origin of all the knowledge non-Greeks excelled at belong to the primordial Greeks. Even Porphyry and Iamblichus subordinated non-Greek wisdom to Platonic and Pythagorean traditions (Burns, 2014, pp. 22–5). Elsewhere, Burns also notes the fictional nature of many of these ideas about non-Greeks (Burns, 2006, pp. 158–9n4). Nevertheless, although the Platonic fascination with apocryphal Chaldeans, Magi, Babylonians, and Egyptians is similar to the fantasy of the Orient in Orientalist discourse, it is not identical. One of the prerequisites of a discourse centered on the term "Orientalism" is the genesis of a "Western" consciousness that contrasts with a projected East or Orient, which, as mentioned earlier, is not found in the cases used by Wallbridge, Hanegraaff, and Burns.[1] The tenacity of such a perspective is emblematic of the lack of engagement with debates on colonial and imperialistic frameworks inherited

---

1 By now, postcolonial studies have shed light on many of the issues that outdate some elements of Said's argument. One of these critical responses pertain to the essentializing of the "occident" (Baruma and Margalit, 2004, p. 10). However, as Ernst states, "It should be

from the eighteenth and nineteenth centuries; debates that are central to other major fields, as is argued in some more detail in the contribution to the present volume by Julian Strube.

In an article from 2013, Kennet Granholm posits a "positive orientalism" that stretches back to ancient times. It is contrasted with "standard orientalism" which creates an exotic other, measured against "inherent European values"; while the former is said to be a "fascination with that which is far away and exotic." Platonic Orientalism is subsumed under "positive orientalism," which Granholm seems to imply is less problematic (Granholm, 2013, pp. 22–3). However, access to the sources of the "romantic" and "positive" Orient is facilitated by the violence of colonialism. Granholm's concept is influenced by another over-emphasized arbitrary dyad; namely, administrative-political orientalism (bad) and intellectual-aesthetic orientalism (harmless) (Kaiwar and Mazumdar, 2009, p. 19). However, this type of rehabilitating "Orientalism" remains unconvincing, for in our case most "Western esoteric" currents from the nineteenth century onwards were themselves part of colonial power dynamics as is demonstrated in the case of the Theosophical Society (Strube, 2021, pp. 48–51). This esoteric Orientalism demoted the beliefs, convictions, and practices of the majority of people, often deeming them superstitious and irrational, part of an "Islam," for example, construed as a spiritually bereft "religion." It generates apocryphal histories of ancient religions that permeate the air of the Orient (Sijbrand, 2013, pp. 5–7; Masuzawa, 2005, p. 20).

3 The Corbinian Perspective within "Western Esotericism"

Even when concessions are made, Islam is viewed through a West-centric and orientalist lens. In the West, the reduction of "esoteric Islam" to Sufism resulted largely from the initial Traditionalist coining of the term "l'ésotérisme islamique" with its perennialist focus on Sufism. This view was deeply influential on the scholarship of Henry Corbin (1903–1978). Due to his perceived position as the bridge between Islamic "mystical" thought and European explorations of esotericism, his biases are transferred into much of the research that calls for the inclusion of Islam in the study of esotericism, as this section will demonstrate. At work here is the aforementioned ahistoricity of the

---

emphasized that Orientalism and Occidentalism do not exist on the same level. There is a hierarchal and asymmetrical power relation between the two. Occidentalists do not have colonies in Europe and America" (Ernst, 2010, pp. 29–30).

"West" and "East" in the field of Western esotericism demonstrated by the relationship between Corbin and the works of the philosophers Ibn Sīnā and al-Suhrawardī, who have become the Muslim favorites within "Western esotericism."

The following exemplifies this distortion and its adoption in relation to the selective understanding of the "East's" relation to the "West". Another use for the term "eastern" in the Islamicate world described the region and cultural setting of Khurasan (northeast of Iran) in relation to Iraq to the west (Gutas, 2014, p. 140n40). The lost and enigmatic work of the philosopher Ibn Sīnā, *The Easterners* (*al-Mashriqiyyūn*), juxtaposes the indigenous Aristotelian philosophical tradition of his homeland with Baghdadi Aristotelian philosophical traditions (Gutas, 2014, p. 129). Here lies an interesting case of interpretive fancy which saw in this lost work a more "esoteric" meaning, due in part to its reception by al-Suhrawardī, founder of Illuminationist philosophy (*hikmat al-ishrāq*). Along with Ibn Sīnā, he formed the nexus of Islamic esotericism in the thought of perennialists and religionists, such as Corbin.

For Corbin, the title *The Easterners* is understood as an expression of "Oriental philosophy," which expounds an ancient wisdom centering on divine emanations. Persian-Muslim philosophers revived it against the tide of the "rationalistic" and technical Aristotelian traditions of Baghdad (Arabs) (Corbin, 1960, pp. xii, 258–61; Fakhry, 1982; Nasr, 1964, pp. 60–30). This "Oriental philosophy" overemphasizes the "mystical" and (neo-)Platonic, for nothing indicates that Ibn Sīnā had substantial "mystical" or "esoteric" objectives behind this work, beyond a reinstatement of the Khuarasanian school of Aristotelian philosophy, as it was actually understood by al-Suhrawardī himself (Gutas, 2014, p. 140; Gutas, 2000; Pourjavady, 2013). In Corbin's case, *ishrāq* (illumination) and *mashriq* (east) are conflated to present Ibn Sīnā as a forerunner of the Illuminationist school, serving perennialist (Western) appropriation of Islamic philosophical and esoteric knowledge. In *Avicenna and the Visionary Recitals*, Corbin writes:

> In Iran it is customary to divide philosophers into *Mashsha'un*, Peripatetics or disciples of Aristotle, and *Ishraqiyun*, theosophists of Ishraq or of the Orient of Pure Lights [...]. Thus considered in the life of individual consciousnesses, the "Oriental philosophy" of the two masters reveals what they have in common, far better than any theoretical discussions, or hypotheses deputizing for lost works, can do. For the two canons, that of the one [al-Suhrawardī] and that of the other master [Ibn Sīnā], display this common trait: side by side with extremely solid systematic works, they both contain a cycle of brief spiritual romances, narratives of inner

initiations, marking a rupture of plane with the level on which the patencies successively acquired by theoretical expositions are interconnected. (Corbin, 1960, p. 6)

The language here clearly betrays an orientalist/colonial (re)ordering of Islamic religious history itself: "canon", "romances", and "narratives" articulated for European ends. As Harun Küçük points out, Islam understood transhistorically "led to conclusions about the very nature of religion, and of Christianity, that were as valid in the middle ages as they were in nineteenth-century Europe" (Küçük, 2011, pp. 111–112). To a large extent, Corbin's perspective has been deeply influenced by Traditionalist and perennial conceptualization of Islam and Islamic esotericism that follow such tendencies.

The first to speak of "l'ésotérisme islamique" is the French Traditionalist René Guénon (1886–1951). His construction is based on the conviction that there is a rift between the primordial tradition of the Orient and the spiritually bereft Occident. For Guénon, Islamic esotericism is a pure self-evolving tradition while being simultaneously universal in the sense that all kinds of traditions and *ṭuruq* (paths) lead to the Truth (Guénon, 1973, pp. 1–8). This view was as critical of popular Sufi practices, for example, as Wahhabi reformists were, while simultaneously elevating a "sober" variety of Sufism, largely imagined as textual and learned (van Bruinessen, 2009, passim, esp. 126–7). At the same time, Guénon was employing concepts that are indeed present in the discourse on esoteric knowledge (*al-bāṭiniyya*) since early medieval times; such as the tension between seeking Truth (*ḥaqīqa*) and abiding by Law (*sharīʿa*) (Saif, 2019, pp. 18–31).

In addition to limiting Islamic esotericism to Sufism, Traditionalist perspectives played a major role in attending to Sufi texts that are seen as "more elegant and polished," and that are of "text-induced lustre," than the "popular *taṣawwuf*" that emerges from observing the more day-to-day quotidian aspects which would mar its exoticism and mystery (Knysh, 2019, p. 59). Indeed, Sufism "serves as a meeting place of discourses and imaginations, both Muslim and Western," whether in the way the former sometimes reproduces the latter's orientalist abstractions, especially when Sufism is denounced as "heterodox" in modern times, or due to the censure of traditionalist groups that see it as deviation (Knysh, 2019, p. 58). It is true, also, that attempts at assigning authenticity to one and not the other is a fruitless distraction. However, it remains valid that in attempts to study esotericism in Islam or the study of Western esotericism, the focus on Sufism only has resulted in part from Western intellectual dismissive attitude towards local lived religions, seeing in them a corruption of a pure Islam, Hinduism, Buddhism, etc.

While Guénon applies "Islamic esotericism" to Sufism, Corbin almost exclusively intends Shīʿī esotericism, referred to as *ʿirfān*—often translated as 'gnosis'—to distinguish it from its Sunni variant, *taṣawwuf* (Sufism). The former is envisaged to be a Persian achievement (Corbin, 1991, pp. 186–218, i, xiv). Corbin rejects the identification of Islamic "spirituality" with Sunnī Islam (i.e. "orthodoxy," according to Corbin) and Sufism, for Shīʿī esotericism and spirituality outrank (*déborder*) those of Sufism (Corbin, 1991, p. iii). This is a symptom of approaches in the study of Islamic religious movements that adopt the binary of orthodoxy versus heterodoxy. For the most part, they are employing anachronistic criteria often imposed on the religious experience of the colonized. The binary has proven to be tenacious in non-Muslim as well as Muslim audiences, resulting in the over-simplification of the ideological topography of Islam, for example, pitting a scripturalist Islam, mainly Sunnism, against the hermeneutic methods of esotericists, rationalists, philosophers, and saints. According to Corbin, it is "non-Islamic," non-Arabic, and generally "Aryan" influences—Zoroastrianism, for example—that validated his own perception of Shīʿa Islam, elevated over Sufism and Sunnism, leading him to celebrate its "heterodoxy" (Adams, 2001, pp. 134–41; Knysh, 1993, pp. 48–67; Knysh, 2019, pp. 54–58; Saif, 2019, pp. 30–31). Once Islamic esotericism had become espoused with a kind of romantic Persianophilia, it came to be Shīʿi-oriented to Western eyes.

The representation of Sufism as the only esoteric current in Islam (Traditionalists) and "heterodoxy" as the criterion of inclusion into the category of "esotericism" (Corbin) has become characteristic of the limited discussion of Islam in the study of Western esotericism (Bergunder, 2010, p. 17). Nicholas Goodrick-Clarke, in *The Western Esoteric Traditions: A Historical Introduction*, very briefly nods at "East-West exchanges and shared traditions" that for him culminate in the figure of Corbin who, after spending many years in Turkey and Iran, "assimilat[ed] the esoteric imaginaries of Sufi and Persian spirituality," inspiring a generation of Arabic scholars "whose work on Islamic mysticism has entered Western academic discourse" (Goodrick-Clarke, 2008, p. 5). In addition to the terminological conflations (mysticism, esoteric, spirituality), here Corbin is seen to function as the conduit to the very study of Islamic "mysticism" and its "entry" into Western scholarship, without making mention of any of those "Arabic" scholars or the works of non-Western scholars in the twentieth century whose research was independent of Corbin. This amply shows the narrow West-centric view of Islam in the field of Western esotericism. The reliance on a Corbinian approach is also evident in Hanegraaff's *Esotericism and the Academy*, which suggests that "Ficino's own approach was closer to the one highlighted by Henry Corbin with reference to

Suhrawardī, i.e. that of the various ancient sages (and their contemporary adherents) as 'members of one spiritual family' who are connected simply by virtue of their participation in the same metaphysical worldview" (Hanegraaff, 2012, p. 49n194). Despite the field's rejection of the religionist approach characteristic of the Eranos group (Corbin, Eliade, etc.), religionism persists in the study of Western esotericism to taint the narrative by uncritical engagement with Corbin when it comes to Islam (Hanegraaff, 2012, pp. 299–302).

Criticism of the exclusion of Jewish and Islamic esoteric traditions from the grand narrative of Western esotericism was voiced by Kocku von Stuckrad, who pointed out the problematic notion of a West merely "visited" by Judaism and Islam (von Stuckrad, 2010, pp. 19–20). However, von Stuckrad's own treatment of the subject is superficial (Hanegraaff, 2012, pp. 71–2). He exemplifies the Islamic tradition with al-Suhrawardī almost exclusively, attributing to him "the establishment of a philosophical system that integrated rational modes of demonstration with experiential modes of gaining truth, the latter being itself part of a demonstrable system of interpretation" (von Stuckrad, 2010, pp. 83–88). This is not unique to al-Suhrawardī and was developed by thinkers and esotericists before him (Saif, 2017, pp. 297–345).

4   New Approaches

From the problems discussed so far, it becomes clear that the current dominant approach to Islam in the study of Western esotericism is not sustainable. Nevertheless, one of the most important contributions by the field is questioning the post-Enlightenment epistemological framework that tends to discredit esoteric movements and occult philosophies and practices for not subscribing to an idealized notion of rationality (Hanegraaff, 2012, p. 157).

However, the critique of the Enlightenment must not leave unchallenged European hegemony, its "civilizing" objectives, the privileging of the West-centric project of modernity (Seixas, 2007, pp. 24–5), and the resulting and inherited methodological chauvinism that disregards the contributions of women, people of color, sexual minorities, etc. (Legêne, 2007, pp. 188–204; van Stipriaan, 2007, pp. 205–219). Furthermore, the fruitful challenges in writing a *longue durée* are not taken up fully, such as confronting the intensification of global interconnectedness in the early modern *and* modern periods (Subrahmanyam, 1997, p. 745; Moyn and Sartori, 2013, p. 23). With distrust of religionist models and apprehension toward a more global study of esotericism turning "into a form of comparative religious studies that seeks to discover the universalia of 'inner' religion world-wide" (Hanegraaff, 2012, p. 15), the existence of other forms of esotericism is gravely underestimated, often on the basis that a comparative study is supposedly "doctrinal" and not historiographical (Hanegraaff, 2012, pp. 6, 126). This also stems from the tendency to view historical categories and typological concepts as mutually exclusive (Asprem, 2014, pp. 5, 9–11).

Western post-Enlightenment rationality is understood to privilege Kantian intellectual individualism, Cartesian notions of natural sciences, empiricism, industrialization, and the exclusion of non-Western knowledge production and non-Western agencies in globalizing "the normative values associated with 'the West' at the same time as they were challenging Western imperial hegemony" (Conrad, 2016, pp. 73–4; Cemil, 2013, pp. 73–4; Purakayastha, 2014; Pyenson, 1993). In the first place, however, the European Enlightenment cannot be thought of as something of the past only, but a process that has been generating philosophical and epistemological stances with a view of progress that destabilizes the role of "religion," favoring scientific developments instead. The resulting standards of modernity and rationality are still negotiated, so is an individual's or a group's positionality within this process. As Siep Stuurman explains:

> The Enlightenment is not a finished ideology of high modernity, but a set of critical reflections upon an emergent European modernity. It is not a neat package of ideas but a series of debates and polemics, held together by some broad common themes and axioms, but also torn apart by competing and conflicting conceptual languages and knowledge claims. (Stuurman, 2007, p. 80)

One way whereby non-Western negotiations of rationality and modernity is undermined in the narrative of "Western esotericism" is by confusing "global" with "universal" (Hanegraaff, 2015, pp. 64–66; Asprem, 2014, p. 8, 20–1; Strube, 2021, pp. 52–55). A global approach rejects traditional geographic units and calls attention toward zones of interaction which can be geographical and also chronological: where and when intellectual exchanges occurred and contributed to the (re)shaping of global trends and values. Universalism overlooks cultural variants and political contexts; global history emphasizes them and sheds light on the networks of association and reference between them (Strube, 2021, pp. 56–62). Concepts which often become the elements that make the common ground of global comparison and serve as *tertium comparationis*, are retrieved from European prototypes embedded in nineteenth-century methodologies of social sciences. However, as Dipesh Chakrabarty and later Michael Bergunder argue, it is crucial to recognize that the prototypes have become globalized; therefore, to abandon them would be to dismiss the agency of non-Western actors in this negotiation (Bergunder, 2016, pp. 37–8). As a result, interesting avenues of research are lost since an approach that acknowledges the role of non-Western agents in globalizing values and ideas opens up new sites of entanglement with "the West," with direct ramifications for esoteric currents. For example, the creedal purity of Islamist revivalists of the early twentieth century, including those who adopted Wahhabi and Salafi theology, was bolstered by expunging "heterodoxy" and "superstition" from a rationalist program of reform (Lauzière, 2016, p. 47). This rationality overtly shuns the occult sciences and dismisses Islamic esoteric currents, deemed as embarrassing and backward superstitions ('Abd al-Wahhāb, 2008, pp. 30, 34, 80–86). While such positions adopted in essence earlier criticisms, aligning in particular with traditionalist theologians such as Ibn Taymiyya (1263–1328), in the context of the twentieth century this view takes on an explicit anti-colonial and anti-imperialist dimension (Lauzière, 2016, pp. 48, 118).

Moreover, the negotiation of Western rationality led to the marginalization of esotericism in Muslim-dominant regions. However, it also caused the creation of private and public spaces where new expressions of Islamic esotericism emerged, allowing for the adoption of other strategies of rationalization. In many places of Muslim-dominant regions, the privilege of middle and upper classes secured a level of social immunity and access to Western forms of occult and esoteric currents which led to the surge of Spiritualism, occultism, even Wicca, New Age practices, and Quantum Mysticism (Türesay, 2018; ANR-DFG Neoreligitur Research project; Doostdar, 2018). The latter particularly created a modern process of rationalization that derided traditional occult sciences and esoteric currents, yet elevated those that can be expressed in what is perceived as scientific terms (energy, wavelengths, consciousness, etc.). To some level, this "westernizing" turn contributed even further to the suppression of the traditional occult sciences and esoteric movements, correlating them with the "superstition" and desperation of the lower classes. This highlights modern intrications across the globe, and the political, economic, and social power structures that are, and have been, shaping Islamic esoteric currents according to everchanging discursive constructs of "rationality."

The historical narrative of Western esotericism also reproduces the post-Enlightenment's privileging of modernity in the story of "the West," since it bypasses the middle ages, and gives prominence to European early modernity. Renaissance humanism's revival of Platonism and Neoplatonism and the discovery of the Hermetic corpus have been considered by a generation of scholars as heralding an occult and esoteric awakening with limited medieval connections (Yates, 2002, p. 18; Garin, 1992, pp. 85–86). However, the intelligibility of the universe, and therefore its "openness" to exoteric and esoteric interpretative models, was a central theme in the natural philosophy of the twelfth century, for instance in the works of Albertus Magnus (1193–1280) and Roger Bacon (1214–92). It also led to scholarship's resistance to consider medieval connected histories between Europe and Muslim-dominant regions, and the intellectual and cultural interlinks. The translation of Arabic philosophical, occult, and esoteric texts had a substantial impact on European medieval and early modern worldviews; most notably, however, their introduction of causal and semiological connections between cosmological and natural dimensions that made the universe intelligible and hidden phenomena knowable (Saif, 2015).

Studies of Western esotericism thus neatly follow the European trajectory of modernity and appeals to Europeanist civilizational narratives that begin in ancient Greece, pass momentarily through the "Islamic world," and then proceed to Western modernity. It is important to question this by delinking modernity and early modernity from this particular European trajectory, considering such legacies as those of Turco-Mongol invasions, in addition to the Counter-Reformation and its missionary drive, and the so-called "Voyages of Discovery" (Subrahmanyam, 1997, pp. 737, 749).

The same approach that utilizes globalized prototypes and local agencies can shift the appreciation of Corbin and Traditionalist authors on Islam from being deficient secondary sources on Islamic esotericism, to primary sources that show an episode of entanglement. This has the benefit of steering us away from either "Corbinophilia" or "Corbinophobia," both tendencies found in Western esotericism and Islamic studies, respectively (van den Bos, 2005, pp. 113–125; Landolt, 1999, pp. 484–490, esp. 489; Green, 2008, pp. 247–259).

Using the Europeanist paradigm of rationality against which "Western esotericism" is strictly understood, and the adherence to a European civilizational trajectory, meant that a non-inclusive *canon* has developed (from Plethon, Ficino, John Dee to Aleister Crowley and the New Age, and so on) (Asprem, 2021). As Siep Stuurman and Maria Grever define it, a canon is "a historical grand narrative, consisting of selected figures, events, story lines, ideas and values, colligated by definite plots, perspectives and explanations" frequently privileging particular political events and personalities, leaving little room for differing and competing perspectives (Stuurman and Grever, 2007, pp. 3–4).

A global contextualization of esoteric currents and the cultural and sociopolitical structures within which they are formulated enables us to identify the networks where the connection is more intense, thus warranting a special focus, as in the case between different esoteric currents. It also habituates us to question, and historically and philosophically unpack, the constructs that became essential(ized) in dominant historical interpretations, such as East, West, rationality, etc. "Global history, therefore, has a polemical and political dimension. It constitutes an assault on many forms of container-based paradigms" (Conrad, 2016, pp. 4, 12–13). It is important to ask then who the agents and mediators are that establish networks that defy any "preordained closure" (Moyn and Sartori, 2013, pp. 9, 14).

Curiosity about what is hidden and inaccessible to our immediate senses is a human impulse. Christianity, Judaism, and Islam have excited this attraction with hermeneutics characterized by a tension between revealing exoteric realities and alluding to esoteric truths. Processes of othering and relating which this paper highlights also shape what Noah Gardiner labels "the cosmological imaginary" (Gardiner, 2019, p. 737), resulting from occulto-esoteric ideations of connections and difference, which soon play out on land through ever changing rules of sympathy and antipathy to reflect competing sacral, esoteric, and occult topographies. Hence, esotericism stemming from, or reacting to, Islamic traditions cannot be understood fully without referring its various currents to this process of othering and relating.

Bibliography

ʿAbd al-Wahhāb, M. (2008) *Kitāb al-Tawḥīd*, al-Qufaylī, A.M. (ed.). Egypt: Maktabat al-ʿulūm wa al-ḥikam.

Adams, C.J. (1985) "The Hermeneutics of Henry Corbin," in Martin, R.C. (ed.) *Approaches to Islam in Religious Studies*. Oxford: One World, pp. 129–150.

Akbari, S.C. (2009) *Idols in the East: European Representations of Islam and the Orient, 1100–1450*. New York: Cornell University Press.

Allen, S.J. and Amt, E. (eds.) (2014) *The Crusades: A Reader*. Toronto: Toronto University Press.

ANR-DFG Noreligitur Research project, "New Religiosities in Turkey: Reenchantment in a Secularized Muslim Country?" https://anr.fr/Project-ANR-13-FRAL-0006. Accessed on July 27, 2020.

Appadurai, A. (2004) "The Capacity to Aspire: Culture and the Terms," in Rao, V. and Walton, M. (eds.) *Culture and Public Action*. Stanford: Stanford University Press, pp. 59–84.

Asad, T. (2003) *Formations of the Secular: Christianity, Islam, Modernity*. Stanford: Stanford University Press.

Asprem, E. (2014) "Beyond the West: Towards a New Comparativism in the Study of Esotericism," *Correspondences*, 2 (1), pp. 3–33.

Asprem, E. (2021) "Rejected Knowledge Reconsidered: Some Methodological Notes on Esotericism and Marginality," in Asprem, E. and Strube, J. (eds.) *New Approaches to the Study of Esotericism*, pp. 127–146.

Aydin, C. (2013) "Globalizing the Intellectual History of the Idea of the 'Muslim World'," in Moyn, S. and Sartori, A. (eds.) *Global Intellectual History*. New York: Columbia University Press, pp. 159–186.

Bailey, M.D. (2008) "The Age of Magicians: Periodization in the History of European Magic," *Magic, Ritual and Witchcraft*, 3, pp. 1–28.

Bergunder, M. (2016) "Comparison in the Maelstrom of Historicity: A Postcolonial Perspective on Comparative Religion," in Schmidt-Leukel, P. and Nehring, A. (eds.) *Interreligious Comparisons in Religious Studies and Theology*, London: Bloomsbury, pp. 34–52.

Bianchi, L. (2007) "Continuity and Change in the Aristotelian Tradition," in Hankins, J. (ed.) *The Cambridge Companion to Renaissance Philosophy*. Cambridge: Cambridge University Press, pp. 49–71.

Bonnett, A. (2004) *The Idea of the West: Culture, Politics, and History*. Hampshire: Palgrave Macmillan.

Bruinessen, M.v. (2009) "Sufism, 'Popular' Islam and the Encounter with Modernity," in Masud, M.K., Salvatore, A. and Bruinessen, M.v. (eds.) *Islam and Modernity: Key Issues and Debates*. Edinburgh: Edinburgh University Press, pp. 125–157.

Burns, D. (2006) "The Chaldean Oracles of Zoroaster, Hekate's Couch, and Platonic Orientalism in Psellos and Plethon," *Aries*, 6(2), pp. 158–179.

Burns, D. (2014) *Apocalypse of the Alien God: Platonism and the Exile of Sethian Gnosticism*. Philadelphia: University of Pennsylvania Press.

Cantú, K. (2019) "Islamic Esotericism in the Bengali Bāul Songs of Lālan Fakir," *Correspondences*, 7(1), pp. 109–167.

Casewit, Y. (2017) *The Mystics of al-Andalus: Ibn Barrājan and Islamic Thought in the Twelfth Century*. Cambridge: Cambridge University Press.

Conrad, S. (2016) *What is Global History?* Princeton and Oxford: Princeton University Press.

Corbin, H. (1960) *Avicenna and the Visionary Recital*. Trask, W.R. (trans.). New York: Pantheon Books.

Corbin, H. (1991) *En Islam iranien, Tome I: Le Shîisme duodécimain*. Paris: Editions Gallimard.

Doostdar, A. (2018) *The Iranian Metaphysicals: Explorations in Science, Islam, and the Uncanny*. New Jersey: Princeton University Press.

Ernst, C. (2010) "'The West and Islam?' Rethinking Orientalism and Occidentalism," Ishraq: *Islamic Philosophy Yearbook* (Moscow/Tehran), 1 (2010), pp. 23–34.

Ernst, C. and Martin, R.C. (2010), *Rethinking Islamic Studies: From Orientalism to Cosmopolitanism*. Columbia: The University of South Carolina Press.

Faivre, A. (2006) "Kocku von Stuckrad et la notion d'ésotérisme," *Aries*, 6(2), pp. 205–214.

Fakhry, M. (1982) "Al-Suhrawardi's Critique of the Muslim Peripatetics (al-Mashsha'un)," in Morewedge, P. (ed.) *Philosophies of Existence, Ancient and Modern*. New York: Fordham University Press, pp. 279–84.

Gardiner, N. (2019) "Book on Occult Sciences," in Necipoğlu, G., Kafadar, C. and Fleischer, C.H. (eds.) *Treasures of Knowledge: An Inventory of the Ottoman Palace Library (1502/3–1503/4)*, volume 1: Essays. Leiden: Brill, pp. 735–766.

Garin, E. (1992) "Magic and Astrology in the Civilisation of the Renaissance," in Levack, B.P. (ed.) *Articles on Witchcraft, Magic, and Demonology*. New York and London: Garland Publishing, pp. 83–104.

Goodrick-Clarke, N. (2008) *The Western Esoteric Traditions: A Historical Introduction*. Oxford: Oxford University Press.

Granholm, K. (2013) "Locating the West: Problematizing the Western in Western Esotericism and Occultism," in Bogdan, H. and Djurdjevic, G. (eds.) *Occultism in Global Perspectives*. London: Acumen Publishing.

Gray, B. (2019) "The Traumatic Mysticism of Othered Others: Blackness, Islam, and Esotericism in the Five Percenters," *Correspondences*, 7(1), pp. 201–238.

Green, N. (2008) "Between Heidegger and the Hidden Imam: Reflections on Henry Corbin's Approaches to Mystical Islam," in Djalili, M.-R., Monsutti, A. and Neubauer A. (eds.) *Le monde turco-iranien en question, coll. Développements*. Paris/Karthala/Genève: Institut de hautes études internationales et du développement, pp. 247–259.

Guénon, R. (1973) "Islamic Esoterism," in Fohr, S.D. (ed.) and Fohr, H.F. (trans.) *Insight into Islamic Esoterism and Taosim*. New York: Sophia Perennis, pp. 1–8.

Gutas, D. (2000) "Avicenna's Eastern ('Oriental') Philosophy: Nature, Contents, Transmission," *Arabic Sciences and Philosophy*, 10, pp. 159–180.

Gutas, D. (2014) *Avicenna and the Aristotelian Tradition: Introduction to Reading Avicenna's Philosophical Works*. Leiden: Brill.

Hanegraaff, W.J. (2012) *Esotericism and the Academy: Rejected Knowledge in Western Culture*. Cambridge: Cambridge University Press.

Hanegraaff, W.J. (2013) *Western Esotericism: A Guide for the Perplexed*. London: Bloomsbury.

Hanegraaff, W.J. (2015) "The Globalization of Esotericism," *Correspondences*, 3, pp. 55–91.

Ibn Khordābeh, Abū al-Qāsim (1889), *Kitāb al-Masālik wa al-mamālik*, ed. Goeje, M.J.d. Leiden: Brill.

Kafadar, C. (1994) "The Ottomans and Europe," in Brady, T.A., Oberman, H.A. and Tracey, J.D. (eds.) *Handbook of European History, 1400–1600, Late Middle Ages,*

Renaissance and Reformation, volume 1: Structures and Assertions. Leiden: Brill, pp. 589–636.

Kaiwar, V. and Mazumdar, S. (2009), "Coordinates of Orientalism: Reflections on the Universal and the Particular," in Mazumdar, S., Kaiwar, V. and Labica T. (eds.) *From Orientalism to Postcolonialism: Asia, Europe and the Lineages of Difference*. London and New York: Routledge, pp. 19–42.

Kaviraj, S. (2015) "Global Intellectual History: Meanings and Methods," in Moyn, S. and Sartori, A. (eds.) *Global Intellectual History*. New York: Columbia University Press.

Knight, M.M. (2019) "'I am Sorry, Mr. White Man, These are Secrets that You are Not Permitted to Learn': The Supreme Wisdom Lessons and Problem Book," *Correspondences*, 7(1), pp. 167–200.

Knysh, A. (2019) "Definitions of Sufism as a Meeting Place of Easter and Western 'Creative Imaginations,'" in Malik, J. and Zarrabi-Zadeh, S. (eds.) *Sufism East and West: Mystical Islam and Cross-Cultural Exchange in the Modern World*. Leiden: Brill, pp. 53–76.

König, D. (2015) *Arabic-Islamic Views of the Latin-West: Tracing the Emergence of Medieval Europe*. Oxford: Oxford University Press.

Kristeller, P.O. (1943) *The Philosophy of Marsilio Ficino*, trans. Conant, V. New York: Columbia University Press.

Küçük, H. (2011) "Islam, Christianity and the Conflict Thesis," in Cantor, G., Dixon, T. and Pumfrey, S. (eds.) *Science and Religion: New Historical Perspectives*. Cambridge: Cambridge University Press, pp. 111–130.

Lauzière, H. (2016) *The Making of Salafism: Islamic Reform in the Twentieth Century*. New York: Columbia University Press, 2016.

Lazáro, F.L. (2013) "The Rise and Global Significance of the First 'West': The Medieval Islamic Maghrib," *Journal of World History*, 24(2), pp. 259–307.

Martin, R.C. (1985) "Islam and Religious Studies," in Martin, R.C. (ed.) *Approaches to Islam in Religious Studies*. Oxford: Oneworld, pp. 1–18.

Masuzawa, T. (2005) *The Invention of World Religions, or, How European Universalism was Preserved in the Language of Pluralism*. Chicago: University of Chicago Press.

Moyn, S. and Sartori, A. (2013) "Approaches to Global Intellectual History," in Moyn, S. and Sartori, A. (eds.) *Global Intellectual History*. New York: Columbia University Press, pp. 3–32.

Nasr, S.H. (1964) *Three Muslim Sages: Avicenna, Suhrawardi, Ibn 'Arabi*. Cambridge, MA: Harvard University Press.

Pinto, K.C. (2016) *Medieval Islamic Maps: An Exploration*. Chicago: Chicago University Press.

Pollock, S. (2013) "Cosmopolitanism, Vernacularism, and Premodernity," in Moyn S. and Sartori, A. (eds.) *Global Intellectual History*. New York: Columbia University Press, pp. 59–80.

Pourjavady, N. (2013) *Ishraq wa 'Irfan: maqalah'ha wa naqd'ha*. Tehran: Sukhan.

Purakayastha, A.S. (2014) "After the End of Conceit and Theory: Postcolonial Critique of Western Rationality," *Postcolonial Studies*, 19(1), pp. 122–5.

Pyenson, L. (1993) "The Ideology of Western Rationality: History of Sciences and the European Civilizing Mission," *Science and Education*, 2(4), pp. 329–343.

Rutkin, H.D. (2002), "Astrology, Natural Philosophy and the History of Science c.1250–1700: Studies Toward an Interpretation of Giovanni Pico della Mirandola's Disputationes adversus astrologiam divinatricem," doctoral thesis, Indiana University.

Rutkin, H.D. (2013) "The Physics and Metaphysics of Talismans (Imagines Astronomicae) in Marsilio Ficino's De vita libri tres: A Case Study in (Neo)Platonism, Aristotelianism and the Esoteric Tradition," in Send, H. (ed.) *Platonismus und Esoterik in Byzantinischem Mittelalter und Italienischer Renaissance*. Heidelberg: Universitätsverlag Winter, pp. 149–74.

Safi, O. (2007) "I and Thou in a Fluid World: Beyond 'Islam versus the West'," in Cornell, V.J. (ed.) *Voices of Islam*, volume 1: Voices of Tradition. Connecticut, London: 2007, pp. 199–222.

Saif, L. (2015) *The Arabic Influences on Early Modern Occult Philosophy*. Hampshire: Palgrave Macmillan.

Saif, L. (2017) "From Ġāyat al-ḥakīm to Šams al-maʿārif: Ways of Knowing and Paths of Power in Medieval Islam," *Arabica*, 64 (3–4), pp. 297–345.

Saif, L. (2019) "What is Islamic Esotericism?," *Correspondences*, 7(1), pp. 1–59.

Sedgwick, M. (2004), *Against the Modern World*. Oxford: Oxford University Press.

Seixas, P. (2007) "Who Needs a Canon?," in Grever, M. and Stuurman, S. (eds.) *Beyond the Canon: History for the Twenty-First Century*. Hampshire: Palgrave Macmillan, pp. 19–30.

Sijbrand, L. (2013) "Orientalism and Sufism: An Overview," in Netton, I.R. (ed.) *Orientalism Revisited: Art, Land, and Voyage*. New York: Routledge, pp. 98–114.

Strube, J. (2017) "Occultist Identity Formations Between Theosophy and Socialism in *fin-de-siècle* France," *Numen*, 64, pp. 568–95.

Strube, J. (2021) "Towards the Study of Esotericism Without the 'Western': Esotericism from the Perspective of a Global Religious History," in Asprem, E. and Strube, J. (eds.) *New Approaches to the Study of Esotericism*, pp. 45–66.

Stuckrad, K.v. (2010) *Locations of Knowledge in Medieval and Early Modern Europe Esoteric Discourse and Western Identities*. Leiden: Brill.

Stuurman, S. and Grever, M. (2007) "Introduction: Old Canons and New Histories," in Grever, M. and Stuurman, S. (eds.) *Beyond the Canon: History for the Twenty-First Century*. Hampshire: Palgrave Macmillan, pp. 1–18.

Subrahmanyam, S. (1997) "Connected Histories: Notes towards a Reconfiguration of Early Modern Eurasia," *Modern Asian Studies*, 31(3), pp. 735–762.

Türesay, Ö. (2018) "Between Science and Religion: Spiritism in the Ottoman Empire (1850s–1910s)," *Studia Islamica*, 113, pp. 166–200.

Villalba, M. (2021) "The Occult Among the Aborigines of South America? Some Remarks on Race, Coloniality, and the West in the Study of Esotericism," in Asprem, E. and Strube, J. (eds.) *New Approaches to the Study of Esotericism*, pp. 88–108.

Webb, P. (2016) *Imagining the Arabs: Arab Identity and the Rise of Islam*. Edinburgh: Edinburgh University Press.

Wintle, M. (2005) "Looking Outwards: The Inclusivity of European Identity," in Baum-Ceisig, A. and Faber, A. (eds.) *Soziales Europa? Forschungen zur Europäischen Integration*, volume 15. VS Verlag für Sozialwissenschaften, Wiesbaden, pp. 63–75.

Yates, F. (2002) *Giordano Bruno and the Hermetic Tradition*. London: Routledge & Kegan Paul.

The Occult among the Aborigines of South America? Some Remarks on Race, Coloniality, and the West in the Study of Esotericism

Mariano Villalba

In recent discussions about its global dimensions, esotericism is conceived as a "Western European" phenomenon "spread" or "diffused" from Western Europe to the rest of the world. This can be seen in Wouter Hanegraaff's notion of a "globalization" of esotericism, by which "originally European esoteric or occultist ideas and practices have now spread all over the globe" (2015, p. 86); in Henrik Bogdan and Gordan Djurdjevic's proposal to understand how "occultism changes when it 'spreads' to new environments" (2013, p. 5); in Granholm's statement that "often 'Western culture' is used to denote a 'European culture', which has spread beyond Europe" (2013, p. 18); or in Juan Pablo Bubello's perspective on esotericism in Latin America that presents the idea of a "diffusion of Western-European esotericism in the New Continent in the sixteenth-nineteenth centuries" (2017, p. 39).

In contrast, I argue that esotericism is not a Western European phenomenon spread to the New Continent, as it did not originate exclusively in Europe. Rather, its emergence can only be fully comprehended in light of the conquest of America. While the scope of this article can hardly suffice to fully elaborate this argument, I provide examples from the conquest of the Anáhuac, later known as Mexico, shedding new light on both the nature of the phenomenon and the historical context of its emergence. In the first part of this article, I show how aborigines educated in Castilian institutions produced modern esoteric discourses grounded in Platonism to resist the colonization of their past and integrate it in a European historiography of salvation. In doing so I briefly describe the result of this in modern Mexico, what I term a racial *prisca theologia* in the cultural movement known as the "Mexican Renaissance" (1920–1925).

Second, I show how the aforementioned diffusionist perspectives are grounded in a misleading Eurocentric premise, making it difficult to address these issues in a productive manner. By denying the Iberian modernity and isolating Europe from its colonial context, this practice conceives modernity (and esotericism) as an *exclusive intra-European phenomenon* (that would later spread), giving no role to non-European "others," and most importantly to the Iberian Peninsula, in its constitution. Further exploring the context of its emergence, I highlight overlooked currents and factors in the Spanish Renaissance and show how this Eurocentric perspective is the main obstacle for correctly identifying the West.

Third, I propose, as a remedy, a decolonial approach that moves from isolated and teleological frames and understands modernity as a phenomenon that emerged in the 1500s through the Conquest. From this perspective, I provide, on one hand, a clear and historically informed definition of the West and, on the other, discuss race as the central category of modernity that legitimized the new relationships of domination that implanted the caste system in America. Finally, I discuss Martinism in Argentina by way of Henri Girgois' *L'occulte chez les aborigènes de l'Amérique du Sud* (1897, "The Occult Among the Aborigines of South America"), to show how race and colonialism operate and how this new perspective can be useful.

1 The "Occult" among the Aborigines of "South America"?

According to Serge Gruzinski (2017, p. 16), renowned Latin America specialist and pioneer of global history, the Conquest of Mexico constituted the foundation of the European historical consciousness, and the globalization of history started with the Spanish and Portuguese colonial expansions. Gruzinski shows that there was not a world history in an empirical sense until Spaniards started writing the histories of aborigines in the Americas. Prior to 1492, the planet was polycentric. Different civilizations coexisted with different ways of recording their past and conceptualizing their territory. However, all civilizations were at the center of their own origin stories. In 1492, for the first time, Europeans insisted that their story was the planetary center, and desired to homogenize the world according to its image. As Gruzinski explains (2017, p. 16), the historization of Amerindian cultures implied both the creation of a historical time and the imposition of it as a universal notion on other civilizations, a process that has not stopped since then.

When examining this issue, Walter Mignolo (1995; 1992) considers the underlying philosophy and civilizing ideology of this historiographical enterprise, by way of the introduction of Western literacy and the book as warranty of "historical truth." The *Mexicas* recorded their past not with "letters" but paintings (a function occupied by a "specialist," the *tlacuilo*) and with the "word of the elders," not the "word of the book." Oral transmission of knowledge was considered to be more important than written communication, being deposited in the living body rather than in the book or the letter. The word *Tlatollótl*, for example, meant "word-memory" or "discourse-memory," whose function was to preserve and transmit the memory of the past.

Mignolo (1992, p. 303; 1995, p. 80) remarks that European "philosophers" and "men of letters" (notions alien to the *Mexicas*) inverted the supremacy of the oral set forth in Plato's *Phaedrus*, thereby disqualifying the relevance of Amerindian non-alphabetic writings. Writing the correct history of peoples without letters or history of salvation was then a way to colonize their past, thought to be told in a thoroughly irrational manner. Moreover, the writing of thousands of grammars of Amerindian languages resulted in the colonization of their oral languages and the taming of the voice: "when the word was detached from its oral source (the body), it became attached to the invisible body and the silent voice of God, which cannot be heard but can be read in the Holy Book" (Mignolo, 1995, p. 82).

However, this enterprise did not proceed as smoothly as expected. Aboriginal historians began to negotiate the conflict between the forces of their own past and the rhetorical education they received in Castilian institutions (in Latin, Castilian, and Náhuatl), both in the content of their memories and the way of remembering them. Whereas Franciscans, preoccupied with evangelization, tried to link those memories to European religious figures, aboriginal and *mestizo* intellectuals found in "pagan" figures like Ovid or Homer the references to write their own histories.

Gruzinski (2017, p. 160) calls this process a "secularization of memory," as aborigines started "secularizing" their own memories when writing their codex, erasing all of their past that the Franciscans saw as "religion" and considered as "idolatries." Platonism functioned as a bridge between these oral memories considered as idolatries and Renaissance Hermeticism as "true ancient religion," appropriated by aborigines to resist the said imposition and integrate themselves into Christian historiography (Gruzinski and Bernand, 1992, p. 111). Natives went further and equated their own "pagan" divinities to the "religious" ones, presenting them as potentially superior. Quetzalcóatl, the main *Nahua* divinity, was equated to Moses or Thomas the Apostle, euhemerized by both Spaniards and aborigines, and was presented as a historical king of the Toltecs who had potentially Christianized those lands prior to the arrival of the Spaniards.

Among the most significant representatives in Peru is Inca Garcilaso de la Vega (1539–1616), son of a Spanish captain and an Inca princess and translator of Leon Hebreo's *Dialoghi d'amore* (1503). Defending the Incas from "idolatry," Garcilaso proposed an Andean utopia and a common redemption based on a cabalistic interpretation of the Incas' language, the "sacred science" that Plato had learned in Egypt (Bernand, 2006). Other similar cases in New Spain include the *mestizo* historians Fernando de Alva Ixtlilxóchitl (1568–1648) and Diego Muñoz Camargo (1529–1599), who evoked "Divine Plato" and the "ancient discourse of the wise" to write the history of their own nobilities, Texcoco and Tlaxcala, respectively (Gruzinski, 2010, p. 232); Francisco Hernández de Toledo (1514–1587), who advocated the "science of cabala" to explain the common origin of creation between the two worlds (Varey, Chabrán and Weiner, 2000, p. 178); there are also the numerous informers and readers of Athanasius Kircher, for example, Carlos de Sigüenza y Góngora (1645–1700), astrologer and director of the *Mexican Academy*, the treatises on alchemy of the sixteenth and seventeenth centuries or the unprecedented cases of Hermetic women, the poets Sor Juana Inés de la Cruz (1648–1695) and Sor Ana de Zayas (Trabulse, 1998, 1994).

These productions must be understood in the context of the aborigines' varied acts of resistance to the colonization of their memories and their efforts to relativize cultural differences in European historiography. The crucial aspect is that Latin and Castilian were still considered languages of Enlightenment and religion, and Hebrew the oldest language implanted by God, to which Náhuatl or Quechua could not be really compared. Although aborigines attempted to mark a difference when transmitting their past, by adopting the colonizer's language and historiography they only contributed to the penetration of Occidentalism and the negation of their own traditions (Gruzinski, 2017, p. 37). This tension can be illustrated with reference to Ixtlilxóchitl and Juan Bautista Pomar (1535–1601), two aboriginal historians writing in Castilian the history of Texcoco, the first favorable to Platonism and local memories and the second to Western literacy and historiography.

To learn about the past of New Spain, Ixtlilxóchitl used as sources of information ancient painted historical records and oral testimonies of the elders, that were in tension with Western literacy and historiography:

> The philosophers and wise men among them [the nobility of Texcoco] were entrusted with painting all the knowledge they possessed and had attained, and with teaching from memory all the chants they observed in their histories and lore; all of which time altered with the fall of the kings and the lords. (Mignolo, 1995, p. 95)

By means of Platonism, and despite writing in Castilian, Ixtlilxóchitl attempted to integrate into Christian historiography both the content and way of remembering the oral and painted memories. Ignoring this colonial context, Hanegraaff reduces Ixtlilxóchitl's mention of the "Divine Plato" to a "positive appreciation" of "non-Western beliefs":

> Some degree of positive appreciation for non-Western beliefs and practices was possible in so far as they were somewhat reminiscent of monotheist religion; for instance, the Renaissance model of a *prisca theologia*, based upon a positive idea of "pagan wisdom," could be used as an interpretative grid or "intellectual filter," as when Fernando de Alva Ixtlilxochitl described the ruler Nezahualcoyotl (1402–1472) as "a sage even wiser than the divine Plato, who alone has managed to raise himself up to the knowledge of a single 'creator of visible and invisible things.'" (2015, p. 65)

On the contrary, Ixtlilxóchitl's mention of divine Plato should be read as a way of building a legitimate genealogy of his own nobility according to Western historiographical conventions, based in the orally transmitted past recorded by the *tlacuilos*. This discourse was known as *huehuetlatolli*, "the ancient discourse-memory delivered by the elders," used to refer to the wisdom upon which social behavior was regulated and the younger generation educated, equivalent to Western philosophy (Mignolo, 1995, p. 143). By arguing that Nezahualcóyotl preceded divine Plato in this wisdom, Ixtlilxóchitl could construct a pre-idolatrous past and autonomous origin of the religious revelation in his own nobility.

In the opposite case, Juan Bautista Pomar celebrated the cultural achievements attained by the Texcoco nobility through the adoption of Western literacy, and the colonization of previous forms of transmitting the past and knowledge:

> It is clear that if they [the nobility of Texcoco] had possessed letters, they would have come to grasp many natural secrets; but as paintings are little capable of retaining in them the memory of the things painted, they did not advance, because almost as soon as the one who had made the most progress died, his knowledge died with him. (Mignolo, 1995, p. 45)

Gruzinski (2017, p. 152) calls this phenomenon an aboriginal "Renaissance," the emergence of a European historical consciousness and the construction of their own transitions from "barbarism" to "civilization" integrating their own repressed past. This "Renaissance" in colonial Mexico took the form of a racial *prisca theologia* in the "Mexican Renaissance" (1920–1925), the most famous expression of which is the movement of Mexican painters. Mexican intellectuals imagined this past in an older and, thus, superior New World antiquity or "Ancient Mexico" in respect to the European one. The aspiration, still crystallized in the National University of Mexico's motto, "Through my race the spirit will speak" (1921), was to invert Hegel's philosophy of history, in which the "spirit" (*Geist*) originated in China and moved to India, Persia, Egypt, and Greece until "the Germanic spirit (*germanische Geist*) is the spirit of the New World (*neuen Welt*)" (Dussel, 1995, p. 23).

The Mexican model of *prisca theologia* was based, like its European counterpart, upon the idea of a "pagan wisdom" potentially superior to Christianity coming from (the New World's) antiquity: beginning with its founder, Quetzalcóatl, a figure older than Hermes Trismegistus, followed by Buddha (Hegel's origin of the "spirit" moving in a second phase), Plato (European "classical" antiquity), and Bartolomé de las Casas (Spain) as the inaugural moment of modernity. If Hermes was euhemerized in late antiquity and revalorized in the European Renaissance as the potential restorer of "true ancient religion," Quetzalcóatl was euhemerized in colonial America and revalorized in the Mexican Renaissance as the potential founder of a truly New World (Villalba, 2019).

2 Diffusionist Perspectives and Eurocentrism

The sequence of world history from Greece to Germany/modern Europe is grounded in Hegel's *Philosophy of History*. The main agent of history, spirit, moved from "East" to "West" with Asia as a European prehistory and America as a likely candidate to overcome previous forms of history. What Mexican intellectuals attempted in this scenario was to render this "oriental origin" of spirit as older and place it not in Asia but in a "further orient," the "New World." As we now know, the aspiration to render Latin America a superior civilization and culmination of world history failed. For our purposes, this shows that the sequence "Ancient Greece"–Rome–Christianity–modern Europe is an ideological construct only designed, as Hanegraaff (2015, p. 85) noted, to present those that control it (or attempt to) as superior and the very summit of world history itself.

Dussel (2000; 1998; 1995) and Bernal (1987) showed how this was an ideological construct of eighteenth-century German romantics, a discourse about modernity's own origins that appropriated Greek culture as exclusively Western European and posited both the Greek and Roman cultures as the center of world history. Thus, modernity was presented as a self-sufficient, auto-realization of Europe, made possible by its own rationality without any contact with other cultures, and the conquest of "America" as an *Entdeckung* ("discovery"). This Eurocentric version of modernity is a Kantian "way out" (*Ausgang*) that usually runs from Italy (fifteenth century), Germany (sixteenth–eighteenth century), England (seventeenth century) to

France (eighteenth century) and would later "diffuse" to the rest of the world. It is important to understand that Eurocentrism does not simply mean placing Europe in the center but placing a *certain* Europe in the center while excluding a supposedly peripheral one. In this canonical version, 1492 and the Spanish and Portuguese colonial expansions are considered as having nothing to do with modernity but rather with the end of the Middle Ages.

Gruzinski (2008, p. 54) and Bernand (2009, p. 111) consider the denial of the Iberian modernity as Eurocentric and argue that modernity did not start exclusively in Europe, as other modernities emerged in Colonial America that differed from the canonical Eurocentric one. Dussel (1998, p. 4) and Bhambra (2007) remark upon the academic and ethical problems that this created with regard to non-European "others," whose humanity was negated and who are still considered in predominant sociology as having nothing to do with the constitution of modernity (or esotericism). Dussel shows how Hegel intentionally occluded the Iberian Peninsula and, by extension, the Conquest of America, in canonical narratives of modernity: the "culmination of the spirit" was an auto-realization of Germany, France, Denmark and the Scandinavian countries, "the heart of Europe" (*das Herz Europas*). This was different from a "Europe from the south of the Pyrenees" where, according to Hegel: "Here one meets the lands of Morocco, Fez, Algeria, Tunis, Tripoli. One can say that this part does not properly belong to Africa, but more to Spain, with which it forms a common basis" (1995, p. 26).

In the field of esotericism, this Eurocentrism is most evident when one observes that Spain and Portugal are virtually absent in the *Dictionary of Gnosis and Western Esotericism* (Hanegraaff, Faivre, van den Broek and Brach, 2005), and several currents are overlooked. For instance, as I indicated elsewhere (2018b; 2016; 2015), Castilian humanist Enrique de Villena (1384–1434) built an "ancient wisdom narrative" and appropriated Jewish kabbalah in the 1420s and 1430s, several years prior to Marsilio Ficino and Pico della Mirandola. Villena pioneered a literature on the evil eye about the powers of "imagination" to cause harm and kabbalistic and astrological practices to prevent this. As unique features of the Spanish and Portuguese Renaissance, this valid object was not observed (Villalba, 2016, p. 37). The *alumbrados* ("illuminated") movement, initiated by the Erasmist Juan de Valdés (1499–1541) in Guadalajara (1525–1559) and also present in New Spain, is not reflected in the *Dictionary* either (Márquez, 1980).

Although a part of what today is considered Western Europe or "Western culture," the Iberian Peninsula is also excluded from any discussion about the historical context of the emergence of esotericism. For instance, Hanegraaff (2012, p. 5) begins the first chapter of his *Esotericism and the Academy* with the canonical Eurocentric starting point (fifteenth-century Italy) that omits the Iberian modernity: "The history of human thought emerged as a topic of intellectual fascination among Italian humanists in the fifteenth century, and the historiography of what we now call Western esotericism was born along with it." From this perspective, it may seem that the Spanish historiographical enterprise and the philosophical conclusions that took place in the Iberian Peninsula about the nature of the "Indians" had *nothing* to do with the rest of the polemical historiographies studied and "rejected knowledge" in "Western culture."

This Eurocentrism impedes to observe a relevant factor. Since its imperial expansion at the beginning of the fifteenth century, the Castilian Crown started constructing the historiographical concept of *prisci hispani*, the origins of the ethnic nation that carried a more glorious past in opposition to Rome. This past was forged by Antonio de Nebrija (1441–1522), author of the first Castilian grammar (1492), who established the origin of Castilian as the language of Enlightenment and religion to unify the territories of the vast imperial Castilian dream together with the expansion of Christianity (Mignolo, 1995, pp. 29–67). The spread of Western literacy and historization of Amerindian cultures produced a discontinuity with the classical tradition, expressed in the tensions between the Renaissance philosophy underlying this historiographical enterprise and the Amerindian resistance to its assimilation based in their own traditions and languages (Gruzinski, 2017; Mignolo, 1995, p. 203; 1992). This historiographical construction and the Conquest, I argue, was a fundamental factor in the emergence of the "ancient wisdom narrative," more precisely, the need to absorb the silence created by the colonization of the Amerindian past and knowledge and to frame Europe's self-colonized past as its own "tradition" (Mignolo, 2011, p. 172). As Hanegraaff concluded, this narrative emerged to integrate the pagan "Other" in some sort of "grammar of encompassment," where it could be constructed "as really 'belonging to us' (that is, Christianity)" (2012, p. 274).

In his article about globalization, Hanegraaff acknowledges that the core of the problem lies in 1492, stating that "when explorers and missionaries arrived in Mexico, Peru [...] they brought their Western models of 'paganism' and 'idolatry' with them." Therefore, esotericism became global when they "discovered that pagan, idolatrous or irrational forms of belief and practice reigned all over the globe" (2015, p. 66). This is an illustration of Dussel and Bhambra's remark, as it neglects that aborigines also "discovered" European culture, making, for instance, Platonic interpretations of their own "idolatry." As Julian Strube (2021, p. 53) rightly points out, Hanegraaff does not engage the relevant literature regarding the aforementioned colonial contexts, resulting in a self-referential line of argumentation and isolating Europe from the power relationships established in colonial expansion. This is why Hanegraaff (2015, p. 85) remains firmly in the abstract realm of "mentality" or the intellectual ("positive and negative appreciations," "intellectual filters," a "struggle between the forces of light and darkness," a "dramatic notion of two monolithic 'worlds' or mentalities") and arrives at idiosyncratic conclusions.

According to him, the "way of thinking" of "people in Africa, Japan, India, Latin America, or Antarctica" is based in "participation" and is equivalent to "esotericism" as a "form of thought" (also proposing a cognitive science of religion that would allow us to address this), with rationality as an "anomaly" that "appeared just very recently, in a relatively small part of the world, although it has been spreading like a virus ever since" (2015, pp. 84–86). Quijano (2007), Sousa Santos (2016) and Dussel (1995) remark that techno-scientific rationality is the determining factor in the generation and expansion of European colonialism. Therefore, it is not simply an "anomaly" that "rejected" knowledge exclusively in Europe; it also rejected other forms of life and produced new knowledge outside of Europe, leading, as seen, to a profuse appearance of "esoteric currents" in the Americas.

From the perspective of specialists in native languages and cultures, Hanegraaff's assumption appears misguided and ethnocentric. It is based in an evolutionary technological determinism, according to which the absence of the alphabet would have imposed an insuperable limitation on analytic thought and reflection to other societies (Houston, 2004, p. 32). Mignolo (1995, p. 45) remarks that "writing grammars of Amerindian languages was a complex process with more at stake than just a cognitive issue." Kusch (2010) shows that indigenous thought is also rational, but in accordance with the tributary economic systems in Mesoamerica or the Andes, not a capitalist economy such as that associated with Enlightenment rationality. Gruzinski (2002) described the emergence of what he called the "Mestizo Mind" as a result of the planetary "miscegenation" (*métissage*), seriously questioning the binary and monolithic oppositions that assume stable and coherent totalities that would condition cognition and behavior. I suggest, then, situating the dichotomies in language and imperial difference, not "cognition" or "mentality."

These aspects should be further explored both in the Iberian Peninsula and in Mexican libraries of the sixteenth century. I will limit this analysis to presenting a decolonial perspective that permits us to better address this vast neglected part of "Western culture," as it moves from isolated and Eurocentric frames and underlines a spatial articulation of power within the Americas. In addition, it offers conceptual tools for understanding race as the central category of modernity that pervades its specific rationality, Eurocentrism, to which esotericism and/or occultism would be no exception.

3 A Decolonial Approach

The collective known as Modernity/Coloniality (MC) is a group of decolonial thinkers that has been active since the nineties, originating in the aftermath of U.S. programs of "modernization" and installation of military dictatorships in Latin America during the Cold War (Escobar, 2007). These studies focus on the relationships between power and knowledge established during the conquest of America, and hence they are distinguished from postcolonial studies, which are generally dominated by authors coming from former English or French colonies in Asia, Oceania, and the Middle East. Belonging to different geographical origins, imperial interlocutors, and disciplinary boundaries, the two currently hold a productive dialogue. Their differences are outlined by Gurminder Bhambra:

> Postcolonialism emerged as an intellectual movement around the ideas of Edward W Said, Homi K Bhabha, and Gayatri C Spivak. While much work in the area of postcolonial studies has directly addressed issues of the material, of the socio-economic, there has also been a tendency for it to remain firmly in the realm of the cultural. In contrast, the modernity/coloniality school emerged from the work of, among others, sociologists Aníbal Quijano and María Lugones, and the philosopher and semiotician Walter W Mignolo. It was strongly linked to world-systems theory from the outset as well as to scholarly work in development and underdevelopment theory and the Frankfurt School critical social theory tradition. (2014, p. 115)

MC's central difference with postcolonial studies was Aníbal Quijano's distinction of "coloniality" from "colonialism." The decolonial concept was formulated at the closing of the Cold War following discussions on decolonization after the Bandung Conference (1955) and struggles for liberation in Asia and Africa. In usual interpretations, colonialism appears to be an issue that occurs outside of Europe, or a by-product of modernity, an unhappy situation that modern visions and ideals would end. Quijano showed that coloniality was the overall dimension of modernity, certainly a European phenomenon, but forged through the emergence of the Atlantic slave triangle and the "modern world-system" in the 1500s.

The central thesis of MC is thus that coloniality is constitutive of, and inseparable from modernity; in other words, modernity/coloniality are two sides of the same coin. As Mignolo claims, coloniality is the "hidden side" of modernity and the underlying logic common to all Western colonialisms from the Renaissance to today, even after the end of colonial administrations and processes of decolonization. From one side, the "rhetoric of modernity" tells the triumphant narratives of Western civilization and, from the other, the "logic of coloniality" is the hidden and darker side since the Renaissance and the Enlightenment. Based either on the word of salvation through conversion in the colonial era (1500–1750), salvation by civilization (1750–1945) or modernization (1945–2000) in the contemporary one, the "rhetoric of modernity" marginalizes all other epistemes that do not fit with the principles that aspire to build a "totality of knowledge" where everyone would be included (Mignolo, 2011; Mignolo and Walsh, 2018, pp. 194–210).

4   Relocating the West in the Study of Esotericism

Eurocentrism is the reason that there are so many difficulties in delimiting "the West" in the field of esotericism. In his article, "Locating the West," Granholm (2013, p. 22) discusses the appearance of the ideas of "the West" and "Europe," moving from the tripartite division of the world in late antiquity according to the sons of Noah (Japheth/Europe, Ham/Africa, Shem/Asia) to the U.S. formation of NATO in 1949. The missing factor is the addition of "America" to Isidoro de Sevilla's maps and the extension of the old tripartite division of the world in the 1500s. When "the Other" came into the picture, it was too late for Noah to have a fourth son; therefore, the "Western Indies" (the name that was synonymous, for three hundred years, with "America") were invented from the very beginning as an extension of Japheth/Europe, as predicted in biblical narratives (Mignolo, 2011, p. 195).

The first fictional East/West division, which later became ontological, began with the Treaty of Tordesillas (1494), when Pope Alexander VI created an imaginary line that divided the Atlantic Ocean from north to south and settled the dispute between Spain and Portugal for the possession of *Indias Occidentales*, and with the Treaty of Saragosa (1529), which created its respective *Indias Orientales* among the same emerging empires (Mignolo, 2011, p. 78; Gruzinski, 2010, p. 85; Sousa Santos, 2007, p. 3). The other important but usually ignored fact, is the appearance of "Latin America" as a new geopolitical concept in the middle of the nineteenth century, a crucial piece in the redistribution of power that made Orientalism possible in the second stage of modernity with England and France expanding toward Asia and Africa (Mignolo, 2011, pp. 55–57; 2008).

According to Coronil (1996) and Mignolo (2011), "Occidentalism" or *Westernization* is not the reverse of Orientalism but its condition of possibility. Occidentalism is "inseparable from Western hegemony not only because as a form of knowledge it expresses Western power, but because it establishes a specific bond between knowledge and power in the West" (Mignolo, 2011, p. 56). What constitutes the West, more than geography or a cultural sphere, is an epistemology constituted by the six modern European imperial languages that since the Renaissance established this bond: in the first phase of modernity, Castilian, Portuguese and Italian, eventually relegated as not well suited for scientific and philosophical discourse in the second phase, when Amsterdam replaced Seville in the management of the "centrality" of the modern world and English, French, and German were posited as the main languages of scientific discourse. Therefore, there is no "Western civilization" before the 1500s (Mignolo, 2011, p. 19; 1995, p. 8).

An important aspect for inquiring into the boundaries of "Western" esotericism is then whether there is an "exteriority" to this process of *Westernization*, largely discussed by Dussel (2000; 1998; 1995). Beginning with his doctoral research on esotericism in Argentina (2010), Bubello argued that the various autochthonous cultural practices prior to the colonization should be understood as a "cultural other totally alien," but "what is only historizable is the reappropriation/resignification of that universe by the colonizers" (2017, p. 43). I demonstrated that the inverse situation—the appropriation of European culture by aborigines—is not only historizable, but that it is imperative to do so. In no manner should this exteriority or "universe" be considered pure outside, untouched by the modern; rather, it should be considered a *negated* alterity that is constituted as difference by a hegemonic discourse (Dussel, 1995, p. 66). The crucial aspect is that this negation of humanity is structured in racial terms with the first global racial classification that took place at the beginning of the process of invention of the Western Indies/America.

5 "Race" in the Study of Esotericism

The words "race" (*raza*) and "lineage" (*linaje*) became linked to biological ideas about horse breeding and reproduction in Spain in the first half of the fifteenth century (Greer, Mignolo, and Quilligan, 2008, pp. 75–79). Legal, religious, and racial categories were first structured in Spain with the genealogical notion that Christians who descended from Jewish converts were "New Christians," essentially different from "Old Christians" or "Christians by nature," who were considered "clean." The ideological underpinning of those discriminations is most evident in the doctrine and statutes of "blood purity" (*limpieza de sangre*) that structured the Western Indies' caste system, which argued that Jewish and Muslim blood was inferior to Christian and had no rights to be in the Americas (Mignolo, 2011, pp. 17–19).

According to Quijano (2007, p. 171; 2000), race was the first category of modernity which produced the three "main" social identities that imposed the colonial order in the Indies, "White," "Indian," and "Black," with a sophisticated pyramid of thirty-six new sub-identities regulated by statutes (*mestizo, mulato, zambo, criollo*, etc.). Race was applied in the first place to the peoples that became Indians, not to the peoples that became blacks, meaning that race appeared much earlier than "color" in the history of the social classification of world populations. In addition, the much older principle of gender domination was encroached upon by the inferior/superior racial classifications in the system. For example, a *criolla* woman (born in America from Spanish *whites*) was superior to a *mestizo* man (born of a Spanish *white* and an *Indian* woman); a *mestiza* woman was superior to a *mulato* man (born of a *white* and a *black*), with the *black* woman being at the bottom of the pyramid (Quijano, 2000, p. 535).

The first global racial mapping of the world took place at the Valladolid Debate (1550) about the "nature of the Indians" (*polémica de los naturales*) and the "right of the peoples" (*derecho indiano*). The orthodox perspective was represented by Juan Ginés de Sepúlveda, for whom reason and religious revelation were not something that natives could find in their own past. In that sense, they were "irrational" and "pagan," thus incapable of accepting religious truth and deserving the conquest by means of violence. His opponent, Bartolomé de las Casas, discussed in his *Apologetica Historia Sumaria* (1552) the story that attributed the foundation of magic to Zoroaster, to argue that the Indians, like the Europeans, were deceived by the devil when using magic; thus, their religion was not pagan but rational, and therefore compatible with Christian truths, justifying their evangelization and education (1992, p. 709).

Besides inventing "Amerindian religions," Bartolomé de las Casas pioneered our modern idea of humanity, by showing that certain groups of natives potentially had the same rational nature as Europeans, unlike blacks who had no "soul" and were not "human/rational" (Álvarez-Uría, 2015, p. 11). Racism then, does not have to do with one's blood type, or with the color of one's skin, but with the potential of sharing one's genealogy with a European ancestor based on this religious difference (Mignolo, 2011, p. 8). As I will show below, occultists argued that these particular Indian races had indeed arrived by their own means to the monotheistic idea of God (according to the Missionaries' conception of a non-European "human/rational" being), but what that proved was the appearance of "occult" phenomena prior to the arrival of the Spaniards.

6   The Occult among the Aborigines of South America

Henri Girgois was the first General Delegate of Martinism in South America, and director of the Latin American branch of the Groupe indépendant d'études ésotériques in Buenos Aires. As a French official and medical doctor in the Argentinian army, he participated in the "Conquest of the Desert" (1878–1885), a genocide of aborigines in the Pampas and Patagonia that "brought them to light" and appropriated their lands and resources with the goal of consolidating the nation state. In *The Occult Among the Aborigines of South America*, aboriginal cultures recently "discovered" are thus presented as a privileged source of knowledge for the esoteric or occult tradition: "the study of the occult in South America was not worth more than one journal article, but new data from new points of view had increased our duty" (Girgois, 1897, p. 5) and "studying seriously the occult tradition in the aborigines means studying all of their main races" (p. 14).

Girgois' study consists of an analysis of what he considers the three "main races" present in the Pampas, the *Araucanos*, *Guaraníes*, and *Quechuas*, with a list of their respective "sub races." The nature of the "occult" in the different races depends, in Girgois' study, on their position in the complex social classifications created by the colonial order. As mentioned, "race" was applied first to Indians, and preceded and structured all other social classifications: gender, color of people, and, in this case, the color of "magic" as well. For example, one of the actors that attracted Girgois' attention was the *machi*, an Indian woman and traditional healer of the Mapuche culture:

> Is it not admirable for the thinker to see, in the middle of the desert, the transmission of a centuries-old occult scientific initiation by the savages? Is she not sublime this machi from the Pampas who, captive, surrounded by enemies, not even surrendering to the priests and the threats, does not unveil the secrets acquired by this occult initiation? (1897, p. 236)

However, sometimes the *machi* invoked the *Hualicho*, a term originally imported by black slaves from Africa, which all the other social actors (whites, *criollos*, *mestizos*, etc.) believed to be an evil "spirit" or "demon." In this case, the "occult scientific initiation" of the *machi* not only turned "black" but also could be a part of a counter "black initiation" parallel to the white one:

> If we consider the tree consecrated to Hualicho in the island of Guaminí, certainly centuries old, from everywhere in the Pampas come the machis several times a year to repeat their consecrations [...] certain practices of black magic that we can find a little bit everywhere, in the savages or the civilized, the ancients or the moderns, would make believe in a black initiation parallel to the [*white*] science of the mages. (1897, p. 214)

To thoroughly analyze the historical relationship between race and esotericism, it is useful to observe Girgois' study of *Huiracocha*, the main Inca divinity. Ultimately, of the three major Indian races residing in the Pampas, the one that kept "the great lines of religion" (1897, p. 87) were the *Quechuas*. Huiracocha was historically represented by Spanish missionaries with Trinitarian features, with the purpose of demonstrating that, by their "reason" (narrative opened, as seen, by de las Casas), the *Quechuas* had potentially understood the Christian message prior to the arrival of the Spaniards. Following these narratives, in Girgois' occultist historiography, the *Quechuas* or *Pirhua* race originated in Atlantis (in the Atlantic Ocean) and developed "esotericism" (which refers here rather to "initiation") at some stage of the historical development of the Inca civilization prior to the arrival of the Spaniards, when the *Quechuas* arrived by their own means to the monotheistic understanding of God:

> The idea of this supreme God [Huiracocha] had two very different forms: on one hand, a monotheistic idealism, a God pure spirit, capable of incarnating himself in an independent nature and creating himself outside himself; on the other, pantheism, the divination of nature's living forces whose activity is always exercised without being able to raise to the state of a pure spirit, independent from nature [...]. The alteration from Huira-Kocha to Illa-Tiksi Huira-Kocha, spiritual light of the abyss, indicates an intellectual progress or a manifestation of the priests' esotericism, when the [Inca] people, by a higher degree of civilization, was capable of understanding something else than symbols. (1897, p. 74)

This decentering of esotericism from either its European or oriental origins took a further step with the second delegate of Martinism in South America, the German occultist Arnold Krumm-Heller (1879–1949), who would take on the name of "Huiracocha." In this case, as I have shown elsewhere (2018a, p. 248), a "Hermetic reaction" can be observed in a South American context, which claimed that "Western esotericism" did not originate in Europe, India, or Atlantis, but among the "Ancient Mayas" in America. Julian Strube (2017) has demonstrated how "Western esotericism" is a historical designation developed in the nineteenth century that dissociated India or "the East" from this concept, thus subject to geopolitical reorientations. Precisely, the replacement of Girgois (French military) by Krumm-Heller (German military) in 1908 as head of Martinism coincided with a reorientation in the geopolitics of knowledge in Latin America, represented by the decline of the French intellectual influence and the increasing presence of Germany. Following Marco Pasi's remark, I showed (2018a, p. 247) how Krumm-Heller's understanding of kabbalah played a relevant role in this partition that situated "Latin America" in "Western esotericism." Whereas in 1908, kabbalah had a Jewish origin and was synonymous with "Western esotericism," in 1930, the "true" kabbalah became the "Nordic" one that appeared among the "Ancient Mayas," with the Jewish kabbalah no longer part of "Western esotericism." This conceptualization, therefore, can only be fully grasped in relation to the diverse imperial powers and geopolitical interests, in a more complex way than its adoption as a present academic context might suggest.

7 Conclusions

It can be concluded that the absence of the Iberian Peninsula in the *Dictionary* is not simply a lacuna but rather the expression of a more general occlusion in Eurocentric narratives of modernity. Dussel (1995, p. 18), Sousa Santos (2008, p. 29), Bernand (2009) and Gruzinski (2017) emphasize the need to re-include the Iberian Peninsula, and I argue the same for the field of esotericism. Bringing back potentially occluded currents in Spain and Portugal would represent an important step toward a better understanding of the global dimensions of esotericism and the historical context of its emergence. Future research should consider that these currents were deliberately written out of history by Spanish Enlightened thinkers and modern intellectual proponents of a Catholic Spain, such as Benito Jerónimo Feijoo y Montenegro (1676–1764) or Marcelino Menéndez Pelayo (1856–1912) (Byrne, 2015, p. 11).

I hope to have convinced the reader that esotericism is not simply a Western European phenomenon spread to the rest of the world. Western culture is not synonymous with a European culture that later spread to the rest of the globe, as is commonly assumed in the literature summarized by Granholm (2013, p. 18). Rather, people in the Americas produced, and still produce "Western culture" without being a European culture, such as Inca Garcilaso de la

Vega, a modern and Western *Americano*. The West, as I showed, has little to do with a geographical location or a specific culture but rather with a locus of enunciation defined by the European imperial languages. Although not yet acknowledged in the field, modern "esoteric currents" were an integral part of the intellectual discourse of colonial America so that the "globalization of esotericism" was definitely not a "discovery" of "Christian missionaries and explorers" (Hanegraaff, 2015, p. 66). Arguably, it is also not strictly a "Western European" phenomenon—"diffused" to the New Continent, as it has been considered so far (Bubello, 2017)—but global from the outset. Moving from Eurocentric frames and adopting a decolonial or global history approach, one should not be surprised to find indigenous people talking about the Egyptian Hermes or kabbalah in the Spanish Philippines or in any other location of the vast *Indies*.

The absence of the Iberian Peninsula and the Americas in the *Dictionary* may also be an important reason why the notion of race which, as I have shown, emerged with the Conquest, is largely absent from current discussions. The present case shows that, when encountering indigenous cultures, modern occultism reproduces hierarchical structures and classifications of race that are constitutive of modernity. In Girgois' occultist historiography, the *pirhua* race may constitute a "positive Other" (Granholm, 2013, p. 22), but the fact is that this "other" is continually negated, subjected to racial classifications subtended by a religious difference since the narrative pioneered by de las Casas. This allows us to affirm that, if occultism is modern (Pasi, 2009), it is inherently intertwined with colonialism. The "modernity/coloniality of occultism" is most evident in Krumm-Heller's Fraternitas Rosacruciana Antiqua in Latin America, an important chapter of the German politics of racial and cultural expansion (Villalba, 2019, p. 61).

If we continue to assume that esotericism was simply a phenomenon globalized or spread from the West or Europe, this will only contribute to rendering these others invisible. In this sense, we should be conscious not only of the logical or theoretical contradictions of the East/West division but rather of what remains hidden by the geopolitics of knowledge in this division: coloniality. In fact, why was esotericism labeled "Western" in academic discourse, but not "religion," if this is, as Hanegraaff (2016) argued, a *tertium comparationis* that emerged as result of the crisis of comparison caused by the colonialist expansion and confrontation with "the Other"? Why would esotericism be an *exclusively* intra-European phenomenon based in the rejection of an *exclusively* intra-European "Pagan Other"? We conclude by foregrounding the emergence of esotericism through the interaction with a negated Other in America in a constant struggle of power, domination and resistance, aspects that further research on colonial America and the Iberian Peninsula can significantly contribute to illuminate.

Bibliography

Álvarez-Uría, F. (2015) *El reconocimiento de la humanidad: España, Portugal y América Latina en la génesis de la modernidad*. Madrid: Morata.

Bernal, M. (1987) *Black Athena: The Afroasiatic Roots of Classical Civilization*, volume 1: The Fabrication of Ancient Greece, 1785–1985. New Brunswick: Rutgers University Press.

Bernand, C. (2006) *Un Inca platonicien: Garcilaso de la Vega, 1539–1616*. Paris: Fayard.

Bernand, C. (2009) "La marginación de Hispanoamérica por la Historia universal europea (siglos XVIII-XIX)," *Co-herencia*, 6(11), pp. 107–122.

Bhambra, G.K. (2007) *Rethinking Modernity: Postcolonialism and the Sociological Imagination*. Basingstoke: Palgrave Macmillan.

Bhambra, G.K. (2014) "Postcolonial and Decolonial Dialogues," *Postcolonial Studies*, 17(2), pp. 115–121. [Online] DOI: 10.1080/13688790.2014.966414.

Bogdan, H. and Djurdjevic, G. (eds.) (2013) *Occultism in Global Perspective*. London and New York: Routledge.

Bubello, J.P. (2010) *Historia del Esoterismo en Argentina*. Buenos Aires: Editorial Biblos.

Bubello, J.P. (2017) "Difusión del esoterismo europeo-occidental en el Nuevo Continente (siglos XVI-XX)," in Bubello, J.P., Chaves, J.R., and De Mendonca Junior, F. (eds.) *Estudios sobre la historia del Esoterismo Occidental en América Latina: Enfoques, aportes, problemas y debates*. Buenos Aires: Editorial de la Facultad de Filosofía y Letras, pp. 39–96.

Byrne, S. (2015) *Ficino in Spain*. Toronto: University of Toronto Press.

Coronil, F. (1996) "Beyond Occidentalism: Toward Nonimperial Geohistorical Categories," *Cultural Anthropology*, 11, pp. 51–87. [Online] DOI: 10.1525/can.1996.11.1.02a00030.

De las Casas, B. (1992) *Obras completas 6–8, Apologética historia sumaria*. Castelló, V.A. (ed.). Madrid: Alianza Editorial.

Dussel, E. (1995) *The Invention of the Americas: Eclipse of "the Other" and the Myth of Modernity*. New York: Continuum.

Dussel, E. (1998) "Beyond Eurocentrism: The World-System and the Limits of Modernity," in Jameson, F. and Miyoshi, M. (eds.) *The Cultures of Globalization*. Durham: Duke University Press, pp. 3–31.

Dussel, E. (2000) "Europe, Modernity, and Eurocentrism," *Nepantla: Views from the South*, 1.3, pp. 465–478.

Escobar, A. (2007) "Worlds and Knowledges Otherwise: The Latin American Modernity/Coloniality Research Program," *Cultural Studies*, 21(2–3), pp. 179–210. [Online] DOI: 10.1080/09502380601162506.

Girgois, H. (1897) *L'occulte chez les aborigènes de l'Amérique du Sud*. Paris: Chamuel éditeur.

Granholm, K. (2013) "Locating the West: Problematizing the Western in Western Esotericism and Occultism," in Bogdan, H. and Djurdjevic, G. (eds.) *Occultism in Global Perspective*. London and New York: Routledge, pp. 17–36.

Greer, M.R., Mignolo, W., and Quilligan, M. (eds.) (2008) *Rereading the Black Legend: The Discourses of Religious and Racial Difference in the Renaissance Empires*. Chicago: University of Chicago Press.

Gruzinski, S. (2002) *The Mestizo Mind: The Intellectual Dynamics of Colonization and Globalization*. New York: Routledge.

Gruzinski, S. (2008) *Quelle heure est-il là bas ? Amérique et Islam à l'orée des temps modernes*. Paris: Éditions du Seuil.

Gruzinski, S. (2010) *Las cuatro partes del mundo: Historia de una mundialización*. México: Fondo de Cultura Económica.

Gruzinski, S. (2017) *La machine à remonter le temps: Quand l'Europe s'est mise à écrire l'histoire du monde*. Paris: Fayard.

Gruzinski, S. and Bernand, C. (1992) *De la idolatría: Una arqueología de las ciencias religiosas*. México: Fondo de Cultura Económica.

Hanegraaff, W.J. (2012) *Esotericism and the Academy: Rejected Knowledge in Western Culture*. Cambridge: Cambridge University Press.

Hanegraaff, W.J. (2015) "The Globalization of Esotericism," *Correspondences*, 3, pp. 55–91.

Hanegraaff, W.J. (2016) "Reconstructing 'Religion' from the Bottom Up," *Numen*, 63, pp. 576–605.

Hanegraaff, W.J., Faivre, A., Broek, R.v.d., and Brach, J.-P. (eds.) (2005) *Dictionary of Gnosis and Western Esotericism*. Leiden-Boston: Brill.

Houston, S. (2004) "Literacy among the Pre-Columbian Maya: A Comparative Perspective," in Boone, E.H. and Mignolo, W. (eds.) *Writing without Words: Alternative Literacies in Mesoamerica and the Andes*. Durham: Duke University Press, pp. 27–49.

Kusch, R. (2010) *Indigenous and Popular Thinking in America*. Durham: Duke University Press.

Márquez, A. (1980) *Los alumbrados: Orígenes y filosofía, 1525–1559*. Madrid: Taurus.

Mignolo, W. (1992) "On the Colonization of Amerindian Languages and Memories: Renaissance Theories of Writing and the Discontinuity of the Classical Tradition," *Comparative Studies in Society and History*, 34(2), pp. 301–330. [Online] DOI: 10.1017/S0010417500017709.

Mignolo, W. (1995) *The Darker Side of the Renaissance: Literacy, Territoriality, and Colonization*. Ann Arbor: University of Michigan Press.

Mignolo, W. (2008) *The Idea of Latin America*. Malden: Blackwell.

Mignolo, W. (2011) *The Darker Side of Western Modernity: Global Futures, Decolonial options*. Durham: Duke University Press.

Mignolo, W. and Walsh, C.E. (2018) *On Decoloniality: Concepts, Analytics, and Praxis*. Durham and London: Duke University Press.

Pasi, M. (2009) "The Modernity of Occultism: Reflections on some Crucial Aspects," in Hanegraaff, W.J. and Pijnenburg, J. (eds.) *Hermes in the Academy*. Amsterdam: Amsterdam University Press, pp. 59–75.

Quijano, A. (2000) "Coloniality of Power, Eurocentrism, and Latin America," *Nepentla: Views from South*, 1(3), pp. 533–80.

Quijano, A. (2007) "Coloniality and Modernity/Rationality," *Cultural Studies*, 21(2–3), pp. 168–178. [Online] DOI: 10.1080/09502380601164353.

Santos, B.S. (2007) "Beyond Abyssal Thinking: From Global Lines to Ecologies of Knowledges', *Revista Crítica de Ciências Sociais*, 78, pp. 3–46.

Santos, B.S. (2008) "A filosofia à venda, a douta ignorância e a aposta de Pascal," *Revista Crítica de Ciências Sociais*, 80, pp. 11–43. [Online] DOI: 10.4000/rccs.691.

Santos, B.S. (2016) *Epistemologies of the South: Justice against Epistemicide*. Abingdon: Routledge.

Strube, J. (2017) "Occultist Identity Formations Between Theosophy and Socialism in fin-de-siècle France," *Numen*, 64, pp. 568–595.

Strube, J. (2021) "Towards the Study of Esotericism Without the 'Western': Esotericism from the Perspective of a Global Religious History," in Asprem, E. and Strube, J. (eds.) *New Approaches to the Study of Esotericism*, pp. 45–66.

Trabulse, E. (1994) *Ciencia y tecnología en el Nuevo Mundo*. México: Colegio de Mexico.

Trabulse, E. (1998) "El tránsito del hermetismo a la ciencia moderna: Alejandro Fabián, sor Juana Inès de la Cruz y Carlos de Sigüenza y Góngora," *Calíope: Journal of the Society for Renaissance and Baroque Hispanic Society*, 4(1–2), pp. 56–71.

Varey, S., Chabrán, R., and Weiner, D. (2000) *Searching for the Secrets of Nature: The Life and Works of Dr. Francisco Hernández*. Stanford: Stanford University Press.

Villalba, M. (2015) "El Tratado de Astrología atribuido a Enrique de Villena: Esoterismo en la corte de Juan II de Castilla," *Magallánica: Revista de historia moderna*, 2(3), pp. 186–216.

Villalba, M. (2016) "Cábala y aojamiento en el Tratado de la Fascinación de Enrique de Villena," *Melancolia*, 1, pp. 30–50.

Villalba, M. (2018a) "Arnold Krumm-Heller, la Revolución Mexicana y el esoterismo en América Latina," REHMLAC+, 10(2), pp. 227–258. [Online] DOI: 10.15517/rehmlac.v10i2.33355.

Villalba, M. (2018b) "Enrique de Villena," in Burns, W. (ed.) *Astrology through History. Interpreting the Stars from Ancient Mesopotamia to the Present.* Santa Barbara: ABC-CLIO, pp. 342–343.

Villalba, M. (2019) "Mission de la race ibéro-américaine: Arnold Krumm-Heller et l'Empire allemand pendent la Révolution Mexicaine (1910–1920)," *Politica Hermetica*, 33. Lausanne: L'Age d'Homme, pp. 51–66.

"Don't Take Any Wooden Nickels": Western Esotericism, Yoga, and the Discourse of Authenticity

Keith Cantú

Hardly anyone would doubt that history is full of charlatans. However, the situation becomes much trickier when dichotomies like "real" vs. "fake," "genuine" vs. "fraudulent," or "authentic" vs. "inauthentic" become applied not just to individuals or institutions but wholesale to entire objects of study, such as musical genres, regional cuisines, or in our case modern occultists who have engaged with the literatures and traditions of Asia. It is a scholar's job to analyze, and in the process we often discover bogus representations that necessitate a good, solid debunking. Such critical assessments can serve as an etic "check" on over-enthusiastic emic perspectives or exaggerated idealizations of charismatic personalities. However, there is always an important corollary to keep in mind: to postulate something as "inauthentic" requires by dialectical reasoning to assume that there is an "authentic" something (unless, of course, everything is "inauthentic," but then the descriptor becomes categorically meaningless).

In this chapter I examine how this "discourse of authenticity" both differs and overlaps in two growing academic fields, that of Western esotericism and yoga studies, and how the preoccupation with preserving an authentic, premodern "East" often overlooks the innovative contributions of native South Asians who adapted their teachings to fit new audiences, both pan-Indian and outside of India. This discourse is especially relevant to post-Orientalist scholarship that treats on Western occultist movements in the nineteenth and early twentieth centuries, such as for example the early Theosophical Society founded by H.P. Blavatsky (1831–1891) and Henry Olcott (1832–1907) as well as the Thelema of Aleister Crowley (1875–1947), all of whom integrated, albeit in different ways, not just Indian teachings but also ideas from Buddhism, Daoism, Sufism, and so on into published occult literature and oral teachings (cf. Sand and Rudbøg, 2020; Krämer and Strube, 2020; Baier, 2016; Djurdjevic, 2014; Bogdan and Djurdjevic, 2013). It is also relevant to the study of lesser-known personalities, such as Theodor Reuss (1855–1923) and Franz Hartmann (1838–1912), both of whom likewise expanded their views on occultism to also encompass yogic teachings. To be sure, these Western occultists modified and adjusted religious teachings to fit their own agendas, curriculums, and worldviews, which is certainly a phenomenon that should be considered with a critical eye. However, what I wish to emphasize in this chapter is that there were also colonial-era Indian authors who made recourse to theories of Western scientists and philosophers to reinterpret Indian teachings, especially on Early Modern Yoga.[1] Upon further examination of both sides of the exchange, a narrative emerges that shows a great deal of agency on the part of Indian authors; these processes were far from unidirectional from West to East.

To make the above points clear I will first explain how the discourse of authenticity is operative in the fields of Western esotericism and yoga studies, especially where they intersect. I will then contextualize this preoccupation with authenticity itself and problematize its participation in a much more specific and ethically normative discourse, that of "cultural authenticity," and highlight the problems with the normative assumptions of "authentic culture," whether Western or not. As an example I will refer to a Bengali vernacular-language translation that utilizes European scientific and philosophical terminology to help facilitate a reader's understanding of yogic teachings on a Tamil regional form of Rajayoga (Tamil: *rājayōkam*). At the conclusion of the chapter I will argue that it is more productive to frame esoteric movements more neutrally as having "local" and "translocal" dimensions, using a slightly modified definition of "translocalization" as postulated by Ros (2012). My overall aim is to encourage scholars to be open to critically examining the historical contingencies of any given movement's interaction with outside theories or practices, regardless of their perceived (in)authenticity.

Before proceeding, first a note on geographical terminology: in this chapter I use the adjectives "Western" and "Eastern" only for convenience, especially with regard to occultism, which I would argue has been translocal in scope since at least the nineteenth century. The same goes for the related terms Orientalism and its corollary Occidentalism. As Makdisi (2014) has pointed out, Occidentalism, the opposite pole of Said's *Orientalism* (1978), also has a historical genealogy that is inextricably intertwined with the genealogy of Orientalism, pointing to the problems with addressing what is Western unless one also addresses what is Eastern. Indeed, when these words are stripped of discursive baggage, Occidentalism and Orientalism only etymologically refer to Latin present participles that denote the directions of the sun's rise (*oriens*, "rising")

---

1   I have elected to keep both Early Modern Yoga (which I generally date to the eighteenth to late nineteenth century) and Modern Yoga (following De Michelis, starting around 1896 with the publication of Vivekananda's *Rāja Yoga*) capitalized since this defines a fairly discrete trajectory of yoga's engagement with modernity. At the same time, I have preferred to keep "yoga" lowercase when speaking about it in more general terms.

and fall (*occidens*, "falling down," "setting"), which are also inextricable from each other—except perhaps at the earth's poles. My point is that to postulate a Western esotericism also implies the postulation of an "Eastern esotericism," which even if left unstated or unanalyzed creates a category that has no intrinsic existence apart from various disconnected movements, whether Islamic, Hindu, Buddhist, Daoist, or non-sectarian (e.g. the Bāul Fakirs of Bengal, see Cantú, 2019) that could be justifiably said to participate in a kind of esotericism.

1 The Problem of Authenticity at the Intersection of Western Esotericism and Yoga Studies

The fields of Western esotericism and yoga studies[2] currently have differing approaches to the discourse of authenticity based on the research priorities of their respective scholars. Even a cursory survey of subsequent scholarship on Western esotericism will show that a preoccupation with authenticity does not currently figure highly into the discourse of the field, in which ritual innovations and creative adaptations to a disenchanted modernity are ever-present themes (cf. Pasi, 2009 for a good thematic summary of occultists' engagement with modernity). Faivre (1994, p. 7, cf. p. 58) locates a late fifteenth-century CE formation of modern Western esotericism in the Italian Renaissance harmonization of disparate philosophical "links in a chain," represented by various personalities (e.g. Moses, Zoroaster, Hermes Trismegistus, and so on), while Hanegraaff (2015, p. 64) locates such a formation in the "virulent polemics of early modern Protestant thinkers." Such historical frameworks rarely if ever dismiss the contributions of nineteenth- to twentieth-century occultists as outright inauthentic by comparison, although sometimes these occultists' adaptations to post-Enlightenment modernity are framed as reinterpretations of, or changes from, an "original" (i.e. authentic) esoteric worldview as informed by Faivre's six characteristics of esotericism as a "form of thought" (Faivre, 1994, pp. 10–15).

For instance, Hanegraaff elsewhere praises—as a methodological example—a hypothetical research project on occultism that would "demonstrate how the original contents and associations of an idea complex that originated

---

2 While there are earlier foundations for these fields, for the sake of simplicity I locate the beginning of Western esotericism in Antoine Faivre's *Access to Western Esotericism* (1994, a translation from two volumes in French published in 1986) and the beginning of yoga studies in Eliade's seminal publication *Yoga: Immortality and Freedom* (1958).

in the Renaissance are *changed* under the broad cultural impact of Enlightenment values and the rise of mechanistic science" (1995, p. 121, emphasis as in original). It does not appear that this example was intended to promote a discourse of authenticity, however, but rather to show the critical importance of historical context in the study of esotericism at a time in which the field was finding its theoretical *raison d'être*. At the same time, in later discourse on esotericism there is an understandable impetus to show how post-Enlightenment, "disenchanted" modernity (Hanegraaff, 2003), and especially philosophers of science (cf. Asprem, 2018, pp. 444–533; Faivre, 1994, p. 88) shaped these same occultists' perspectives and social interactions and altered their relationship with the past.

By contrast, several prominent scholars in the growing field of yoga studies have been trying to excavate what in a recent book (Mallinson and Singleton, 2017) has been perhaps most aptly framed as the "roots of yoga," that is, source texts of Hathayoga (Sanskrit: *haṭhayoga*), Rajayoga (*rājayoga*), and precursors to postural and meditative practice that are presented not just for philologically-minded scholars but also for the interested public at large. These as well as books published on Modern Yoga in the past decades (De Michelis, 2008; Singleton, 2010) are valuable studies, and present the genealogies of yoga in a comprehensive and relatively neutral manner with regard to authenticity claims. At the same time, such scholarship in yoga studies constantly has to negotiate with a popular concern both in and outside of academia about whether or not this or that tradition or author of Modern Yoga has or has not departed from the original traditions of the past. This is precisely where the discourse of authenticity steps in, and it becomes necessary to make an argument about what constitutes an authentic practice of yoga or to sidestep the question altogether and remain neutral.

For a good example of this popular concern from a yoga studies perspective, consider Chris Wallis (2016), who writes in a blog post on the "real story" of the chakras (Sanskrit: *cakra*), or "wheels" in the yogic body that are meditated on, that "the West (barring a handful of scholars) has almost totally failed to come to grips with what the chakra-concept meant in its original context and how one is supposed to practice with them." Phrases like "original context" and "how one is supposed to practice" are, of course, authenticity claims, to which Wallis juxtaposes the perceived inauthenticity of John Woodroffe (1865–1936) and C.W. Leadbeater (1854–1934). Of course, Wallis correctly notes that these authors did modify and emphasize certain teachings on the chakras that were simply not present in the sources they consulted. However, in the hunt for authenticity Wallis also paints "the West" in broad strokes and in-so-doing omits consideration of other occultists, such as Aleister Crowley, who was apparently unfamiliar with Woodroffe's work and recorded teachings on the chakras in an unpublished diary at least as early as 1901 during a trip to Sri Lanka. Occultists like Crowley, Reuss, and even Carl Kellner (1851–1905, cf. Baier, 2018) derived teachings on them based on a translation by Srish Chandra Basu (a.k.a. Sris Chandra Vasu, 1861–1918) of the *Shiva Samhita* (*Śiva Saṃhitā*), and in Crowley's case also the published works of Sri Sabhapati Swami (b. 1828).

These and other interesting stories of occultist engagement with yoga are often elided in the pursuit of authenticity, which is less interested in analyzing the historical intersections of ideas than delineating a culturally authentic "yoga" that is rooted in premodern, pre-colonial India. The main theory is that yoga, as a culturally authentic invention of pre-colonial India, has been constantly appropriated and modified by cultural or ethnic outsiders. Yet the occultists known to Western esotericism are problematic in this regard, since their roles are usually much more ambivalent than the missionaries and government administrators of the period.

Some scholars like De Michelis (2008, p. 10) have also noted this elision and expressed such engagement in terms of "modern re-elaborations." Others use similar terminology such as "hybrid," "syncretic," "innovative," "neo-," and even "colonial-era." To be clear, I think these are all fair ways of framing yoga's encounter with modernity. At the same time, I wish to point out how such phrases can be distorted so as to assume a normative lens of cultural authenticity. In this case, "re-elaboration" entails that there was a pre-modern (and non-Western) elaboration of Hinduism—or any religion for that matter—prior to its re-elaboration. This may very well be objectively and historically true, in that certain religious currents later described as Hindu did of course develop in the classical and medieval periods independently of Western "influence" as defined in general terms. It may also understandably be the difficult task of the scholar, whether Indian or foreign, to excavate what these pre-modern views really were, as unmediated as possible by the gloss of the present; such a task is important and should not be minimized. However, to take this analysis a step further and dismiss any Western-inspired re-elaborations as "inauthentic" and instead idealize original Hindu elaborations as "authentic" is to freefall head-first—and to be fair, often unwittingly—into the discursive labyrinth of authenticity with its competing claims of power structures and hegemonies, cultural and racial identity politics, and commercialization.

It is where the fields of yoga studies and Western esotericism intersect that one often finds the most explicit scholarly preoccupation with authenticity. The works of De Michelis (2008) and Djurdjevic (2014) largely sidestep such a concern to focus on various historical actors and/or phenomenological comparisons, although Djurdjevic does briefly indicate (ibid., p. 12) the problems associated with an imbalanced scholarly focus on "the issue of legitimacy and the supremacy of origins." Other prominent treatments on this intersection (Urban, 2008; Partridge, 2013), however, as well as popular media (Ratchford, 2015), have more or less directly framed Western interest in yoga—whether on the part of occultists or by practitioners of the "modern postural yoga" of the for-profit studio—in the context of a commodification or exoticization of culturally authentic traditions, the original substance of which has been lost in the process. It is clear that the points raised by Urban and Partridge pose the most serious challenges to the authenticity of occultist mediators of yoga, which I will focus on here, and therefore their critiques will be directly addressed.

Urban (2008) examines the Bavarian occultist Theodor Reuss in his chapter "The Yoga of Sex." The chapter is part of a broader phenomenon that Urban terms *magia sexualis*, which is the title of a French translation of a work by Paschal Beverly Randolph (1825–1875; Randolph, 1931) as well as a clever modification of the Foucauldian dichotomy of *scientia sexualis* and *ars erotica* (Foucault, 1976, pp. 53–73). Foucault (p. 57) was already dismissive of the idea that there could be any kind of *ars erotica* or cultivation of the art of pleasure in sex in Western society, at least on the surface, noting instead that China, Japan, India, Rome, "Arabo-Muslim," and numerous other societies had endowed themselves with such an art. Urban seems to follow this line of reasoning, framing Reuss's complex in the Western concept of transgression as rooted in the framework of confession and its punishment (Foucault, 1976, pp. 84–85). After selectively quoting sources that describe the initiations of Reuss's Ordo Templi Orientis (O.T.O.) at Monte Verità as a menagerie of orgiastic rites, he concludes (2008, p. 428):

> But in this regard, Reuss was perhaps only fulfilling his role as founder of the secret order of "Oriental Templars." An eclectic blend of Eastern exotica and Western erotica, the O.T.O. was from its inception less an embodiment of any actual Indian tradition than a product of Orientalist fantasy, nineteenth-century sexual obsession, and an ideal of radical liberation through sexual transgression.

Note the distinction between "actual Indian tradition" and "Orientalist fantasy," which appears to be predicated on a discourse of authenticity. This line of reasoning seems intuitive and even superficially attractive, and similar discourses form a recurrent theme in Urban's extensive body of work (cf. especially Urban, 2004, 2003, and 2001 for similar dismissals of Western esotericism as inauthentic appropriations of tantra). Yet there is more here than just novel Orientalist interpretations: an examination of Reuss's sources reveals that the layers of textual strata are more complicated. For the "actual Indian tradition" in this case, Urban upholds the ca. sixteenth-century *Brihat Tantrasara* (*Bṛhat Tantrasāra*, "Great Essence of the Tantras") as an exemplary model for both tantra and yoga. This Sanskrit text, attributed to one Krishnananda Agamavagisha and composed in a Bengali milieu, was primarily designed for ritual practice (*sādhana*) and included seed-syllable formulae (*mantras*) and diagrams (*yantras*) used to invoke various deities. While *Brihat Tantrasara* is undoubtedly an historically important tantric text of Indian origin, Urban sets it up as a de facto standard to which Reuss's own writing should adhere to in order to pass an authenticity test. In other words, he seems to juxtapose what he perceives as an actual exemplar of tantric literature as the lens through which to expose Reuss's phony imitation, a comparison that is made clear at the very beginning of the chapter, which is opened with apparently incompatible quotes by both Krishnananda and Theodor Reuss. Although Urban admits that he refers only to the *Brihat Tantrasara* and not to other tantric texts for "the sake of simplicity," his selection ends up obscuring the fact that Reuss himself did consult other Sanskrit source texts that include teachings on yoga, albeit in translation or as mediated by his associate Carl Kellner (Baier, 2018, p. 405), for his writing on yoga and tantra. These Sanskrit texts, particularly the ca. fifteenth-century *Shiva Samhita* and to a lesser extent the *Shiva Svarodaya* (*Śivasvarodaya*, portions of which may date from the twelfth century CE), were translated and published by highly literate Indian colonial-era Sanskrit pandits and authors,[3] and are the ultimate source for much of the Indic material in Reuss's pseudonymous essay, "Mystic Anatomy," a primary source—neglected by Urban—that includes some of Reuss's same teachings on sexual magic that he dismisses as an "Orientalist fantasy" (cf. Bogdan, 2006 for a reprint of "Mystic Anatomy" and an insightful counterpoint to the common scholarly conflation of sexual magic with tantra).

Partridge frames his critique of the Theosophical Society in the context of late twentieth-century theoretical discourses on Orientalism (Said, 1978). While admitting the presence of "sweeping generalizations" in Said's work, Partridge (2013, p. 312) notes at the same time that it is difficult to deny "his thesis that, by and large, the history of Western attitudes towards 'the East' is a history of the formation of a powerful European ideology constructed to

---

3 The first translation of the *Shiva Samhita* was made by Srish Chandra Basu, as mentioned above, and published serially in *The Arya* journal between 1884 and 1885 as well as separately in 1887 and 1893. A partial translation of the *Shiva Svarodaya* was first published by Rama Prasad in 1890.

deal with the 'otherness' of Oriental cultures." He then goes on to apply this rubric to all kinds of esoteric wisdom of an Eastern character that entered Theosophy, from Egyptosophy to the *Book of Dzyan*. Although Partridge does not directly treat Theosophical attitudes towards yoga, they are implicated in his critique since they are explicitly framed by Theosophists as a source of Eastern knowledge. In his concluding remarks, Partridge notes (p. 330) that, as the "unwitting" example of Blavatsky suggests, one can detect a Western style for dominating the Orient "simply in the attitudes of those belonging to a colonial power." Hanegraaff (2015, p. 70), citing Partridge, similarly notes that the discourse on what separated Western from Eastern "just happened to be dominated by European and American occultists." However, the claim that one must have an Orientalist attitude simply by virtue of belonging to a colonial power, or by osmosis so to speak, is however precisely what post-Saidian scholars like Makdisi have been at pains to nuance by bringing up problematic exceptions to the typical Orientalist model, such as the poet and abolitionist William Blake (1757–1827). Partridge furthermore concludes (ibid.) that the hidden Tibetan wisdom of Theosophy was not an Indian teaching but "a product of Western Romantic and esoteric occulture, informed by earlier Orientalist interpretations of Indian and Egyptian texts." While this very well may be true, Partridge frames this transformed "product" as not authentically Eastern (whether Indian or otherwise), which, of course, brings us right back to the problems associated with the discourse of authenticity (cf. also a similar use of "authentic" in Hanegraaff, 2015, p. 86).

The criticisms of Urban and Partridge depart from an earlier generation of scholars, who sometimes introduced criticisms of Western esotericism or related currents on other grounds. As De Michelis points out (2008, pp. 10–11), the seeds for dismissive attitudes as far as modern Western esotericism goes are traceable in the earlier scholarship of Raymond Schwab (1884–1956) and Mircea Eliade (1907–1986), the latter of whom penned a highly influential monograph on the study of yoga that, as his former personal secretary David White records in his introduction to a recent reprinting, was "the first truly mature and comprehensive study of yoga ever written," despite its shortcomings (Eliade, 2009, p. xxv). Eliade is especially worth considering since his book *Occultism, Witchcraft, and Cultural Fashions* (1976) treats on the so-called "occult explosion" that was happening in the late 1960s and 1970s, in which there was a renewed interest among American and European youth in everything from astrology to yoga and tantra. Interestingly, Eliade (1976, p. 66) puts forward the voice of René Guenon (1886–1951) as an insider critic of occultism whose critique of Theosophy on the grounds of inauthenticity continued to resonate even amid the current occult explosion: "Considering himself a *real* initiate and speaking in the name of the *veritable* esoteric tradition, Guénon denied not only the authenticity of modern Western so-called occultism but also the ability of any Western individual to contact a valid esoteric organization" (italics as in original). In other words, the Traditionalism of Guénon (cf. Sedgwick, 2004 for his role in this movement, also Faivre, 1994, pp. 100–102) was Eliade's counter-pole to the youthful, overweening enthusiasm for the occult that he perceived in his day. Guénon, therefore, represents an even earlier foundation of the discourse of authenticity as a Traditionalist critic *par excellence* of the perceived inauthenticity of occult interest in yoga. Of course, when we bring these poles in conversation with Hanegraaff's observations on disenchantment, it becomes clear that the Guénonian dismissal of occultist authenticity cannot be separated from his wholesale dismissal of modernity, which was so extensive that "one wonders what would be left of their concept of 'Tradition' if modernity did not exist" (Hanegraaff, 2003, p. 377n37). As a result, I would argue that the critiques of Urban and Partridge on occultists' engagement with Asia, founded primarily on post-Orientalist, Foucauldian, or Marxist arguments, depart from Guénon's Traditionalist rejection of modernity despite their similar assumptions as to the *a priori* inauthenticity of Western occultists who attempted to engage Eastern teachings.

Regardless of whether post-Orientalism or Traditionalism is the premise, I wish to emphasize another major substantive issue that arises in both the above treatments of occultists' engagement with South Asia. The issue is that, while both authors attempt to deconstruct the dominant lens of the Western gaze on yoga and/or esotericism, the result is an analysis of this material almost entirely from the perspective of Western authors. In other words, instead of considering the biographical and publication data of the actual mediating Indic sources that occultists like Reuss, Crowley, and/or Blavatsky consulted, instead all we get is a scathing critique of these very same Western occultists. While infamous occultists can certainly take the criticism (as they did in their lifetimes!), in such treatments the agency of certain important Indian vernacular and English-language authors (e.g. Sri Sabhapati Swami, Srish Chandra Basu, Baman Das Basu, Ram Prasad Keshyap, T. Subba Row) and publishers (R.C. Bary & Sons) in these colonial-era occult milieus is unfortunately all but ignored. Yet they are critically important in this context since these are precisely the same authors who informed occultists on matters of yoga, whether accurately or not, and they had their own agendas and historical contexts that are nevertheless relevant to the field of Western esotericism as well as to yoga studies.

De Michelis's informed focus primarily on celebrated personalities especially points to the need for a closer examination of some of these more tangential figures in the early formulation of Modern Yoga, such as Sri Sabhapati Swami and his editor Srish Chandra Basu, also mentioned in the list above. I would argue that the reception history of their works, while perhaps idiosyncratic and strange to a scholar of pre-modern yoga, should be thoroughly analyzed before making claims as to the authenticity or inauthenticity of a given occultist's teaching on yoga. Such authors have a two-fold legacy: on the one hand, they have one foot in colonial modernity with its Victorian trappings and biases against the perceived degeneracy of Hinduism, but on the other hand they dug deep into the historical and textual traditions of the premodern past. Some engaged living teachers on yoga and collected oral instructions, while others supplied the first available translations of a wide variety of medieval Sanskrit works (e.g. *Shiva Samhita*, *Shiva Svarodaya*, and *Hatha Pradipika* [*Haṭhapradīpikā*]), works that have only in recent decades attracted the critical attention of philologically trained scholars. Although there are deficiencies in these translations due to either an inadequate number of manuscript exemplars or colonial-era biases on Hathayoga, the legacy of their contributions should still at least be properly contextualized before making sweeping claims as to the complete inauthenticity of their perspectives.

Now that it should be clear how the discourse of authenticity is operative in the fields of yoga studies and Western esotericism, and especially where the two fields intersect, I want to examine the term "authenticity" itself and stress how it is usually inextricably intertwined with the concept of "cultural authenticity" today. An analysis of the word's etymology brings to light two of the most salient features of what it means for something to be "authentic" in contemporary English: 1) it must be "original," or 2) it must be "authoritative," meanings that both overlap and contrast. While a genealogy of the term "authentic" in philosophical discourse would widen our overall semantic view, by the twentieth century the term also became intertwined with culture (cf. Lindholm, 2008). As Frosh (2001, pp. 541–542) has argued, the concept of "culture" evolved from a distinction between sophisticated elites and the vulgar masses into a distinction between "inauthenticity" and an artist-like "truth-to-oneself." Beginning from around the late-1960s and 1970s onward, however, a broader, more collective ideal of "cultural authenticity" arose simultaneously (such as in Iran in the lead up to the Iranian Revolution of 1979; cf. Nabavi, 2015, p. 175), and was later expressed in the Nara Document on Authenticity (1994). Today, similar collective ideals of cultural authenticity are behind treatments of the "cultural appropriation" or "cultural borrowing" of Modern Postural Yoga (Appiah, 2018), today a multi-billion-dollar global industry (Jain, 2015; Foxen, 2017). The discourse of authenticity has especially emerged in popular debates in which yoga is considered a Hindu cultural practice that should not be modified by meddling foreigners, such as the Take Back Yoga campaign launched in 2010 by Aseem Shukla (Vitello, 2010). Although reasonable criticism could be levelled against commercialized forms of yoga and their surface-level, aesthetic marketing of stereotypical Indian tropes, I would nevertheless argue that the ethical normativity attached to popular concepts like cultural appropriation or borrowing obscures their shifting foundations in this broader discourse of cultural authenticity.

2 Yoga and Western Philosophy and Science

A final topic of relevance is the application of science and philosophy (or even "philosophy of science") in the discourse of authenticity when applied to Modern Yoga. Joseph Alter has presented perhaps the most comprehensive study of this interplay, and observes (2004, p. 33) that "…the term 'science' is an eminently modern concept that is saturated with power implications and linked as much to a hierarchy of knowledge as it is simply to the rational techniques and procedures of knowing, and the nature of reality so known." He goes on to note how yoga, especially Hathayoga, needed to distance itself from religious beliefs and ally itself with an objective, verifiable practice, and introduces the experiments of Swami Kuvalayananda in 1924 as a useful starting point for this synthesis. Alter's overall analysis of yoga's embrace of science and the tension between its universality and cultural relativity is, in my view, fair and certainly on point. However, like De Michelis's use of "re-elaborations" above, I think it is important to expand on Alter's above definition of science by emphasizing that pre-modern understandings of the yogic body were also saturated with power implications between guru, students, and devotees (e.g. the popular Indian saying "Guru is God"), as well as in the broader social climate in which they operated. In this respect Western science and philosophy only introduced new authorities and methods into the mix that could be resorted to, while at the same time offering yet another foundation for the discourse of authenticity (i.e., whatever is scientifically verifiable is authentic). Even similar attitudes to Western scientific materialism were not entirely new on Indian soil; we know for example that there were philosophical schools such as the Charvaka (Sanskrit: *cārvāka*) and Lokayata (*lokāyāta*) prevalent in the pre-modern period that made truth claims based on what was materially verifiable rather than based on hearsay or inference (*anumāna*) (cf. Bhaṭṭācārya, 2011).

In any event, the early modern period offers a critical transition period in which indigenous systems of yoga begin to be justified, in Indian vernacular languages no less, with recourse to the science of the times rather than earlier proofs or authorities (*pramāṇa*s). For example, consider the case of Sri Sabhapati Swami (b. 1828), whose practice of yoga called "Rajayoga for Shiva" (Tamil: *civarājayōkam*) is the subject of my dissertation (see also Cantú, forthcoming). His works were published in a variety of Indian vernacular languages such as Tamil, Hindi, and Bengali in addition to English and German, and he was known to both Blavatsky and Olcott as well as Hartmann and Crowley (although there is no evidence that the latter two ever met him personally). Sabhapati had two gurus, at least one of whom (Chidambara Periya Swamigal) was directly linked to the Tamil Virashaiva (Sanskrit: *vīraśaiva*) movement, which is a radical caste-rejecting Shaiva movement with origins in Karnataka and Andhra Pradesh that spread to Tamil Nadu around the seventeenth century CE via the efforts of figures like Perur Santhalinga Swamigal and his disciple Kumara Devar (Steinschneider, 2016, pp. 20–21). Subsequent Tamil Virashaiva figures in their lineage-based tradition (*parampara*), like Sabhapati's aforementioned guru, also incorporated Brahmanical teachings on the Upanishads, Vedanta and so on into their discourses, accounting for the presence of Vedanta in Sabhapati's works, which therefore has a different origin from the Vedanta of later authors like Swami Vivekananda (1863–1902). Sabhapati's teachings on yoga more broadly reflect a local colonial-era Tamil synthesis of these Virashaiva practices with, on the one hand, the teachings of the Siddhars (Tamil: *cittarkaḷ*), that is, regional Tamil alchemists and yogins, that he obtained from his other guru, Shivajnanabodha Rishi of the Pothigai Hills in the south of Tamil Nadu, near the border with Kerala.

Sabhapati only superficially engaged Western scientific or philosophical discourse in his works, and was mostly content to express his own interpretations of the teachings of the gurus mentioned above as well as his own doctrines. However, some of his followers, called both "admirers" and "students" depending on the work and its context, did engage Western discourses. In a translation of one of his works into Bengali, the translator Ambikacharan Bandyopadhyay supplied (1885) an additional prologue that makes recourse to the opinions of Immanuel Kant (1724–1804), Herbert Spencer (1820–1903), William Hamilton (1788–1856), and Henry Longueville Mansel (1820–1871) in the context of such topics as "contraction and expansion," the "relative realities" of time and space, the "negation of conceivability," the "unconditioned consciousness," the "inconceivable and imperceptible," and "mechanical motion." These are figures related to the worldview of what Egil Asprem (2018, pp. 67–72) has called Victorian scientific naturalism. This worldview had such a prominence that Crowley, who engaged Sabhapati's works, also used the theories of some of these authors—independently of Sabhapati's Bengali translator—to justify his own theoretical teachings on modern ceremonial magic.[4] Examples like these highlight the fact that Western authors were not alone in subjecting indigenous cosmological theories and practices to scientific speculation, but rather Indian authors also participated in this project, using many of the same authoritative voices that their Western occultist counterparts did. The appeal to authorities of course has a long history in the Indian context as well, with its vast Sanskrit commentarial tradition and inclusion of certain voices at the expense of others. These early modern Indian authors' own unique perspectives on science and philosophy therefore deserve proper treatment beyond what the discourse of authenticity, as reflected in the writings of Urban and Partridge, as well as in the works of much earlier "authenticators" like Guénon, currently allows for.

3 Conclusion: Authenticity or (Trans)Locality?

The above issues have been raised to provide a counterpoint to the perspective that authors of Western esotericism, both within and outside of India, were promoting or selling inauthentic interpretations of yoga for any number of reasons, and that as a result these views should be unequivocally dismantled and/or corrected in favor of restoring the pre-modern or indigenous "real thing" that predates any Western alteration of yoga in the context of colonial modernity. While not dismissing the importance of subaltern studies and sincere efforts to "decolonize" the academy, I think that a more comprehensive historical perspective emerges when occult interest in South Asia is treated in more neutral terminology that avoids an idealization of pre-colonial "authenticity" in the context of yoga. One example of an insightful and nuanced use of such neutral terminology is the phrase "intercultural transfers" employed by Baier in the context of Theosophical appropriations of the Tantric chakras. Baier (2016, p. 310) describes these transfers as "not simply an encounter between Western Theosophy and South Asian tradition... but a complex reciprocal process of transculturation within the Theosophical Society itself." Citing Fernando Ortiz and Mary Louise Pratt, he notes (ibid.) that such a concept as transculturation provides "an alternative to the concept of mono-directional assimilation" and "emphasizes the multi-laterality of intercultural processes within colonial settings."

Indeed, if we strip away the ethical and normative aspects of "cultural authenticity," I think what we are primarily left with is a raw tension between

---

4 I am grateful to Bill Breeze for this insight.

local and translocal cultural perspectives, very similar to Baier's mention of "transculturation" above. The flow from local to translocal has also been referred to as "translocalization," by which I mean that practices—in this case of yoga—were circulated through networks that gradually separated them from their original local religious contexts but at the same time never fully eliminated certain distinctive traces of localized content. This is a slightly modified definition from that given by Alejandra Aguilar Ros (2012), to whom I am indebted for this concept. The flow from translocal to local, on the other hand, is called "localization," and describes the reverse process of translocal content becoming localized or even "re-localized." This is similar to what Michael Bergunder (2014, p. 401) notes is "the primary focus of postcolonial studies," namely the appropriation of Western knowledge by the colonized, although I would add that in the case of yoga and occultism such knowledge also often includes pan-Indic content that is re-localized in vernacular-language sources, as we saw in the example of Sabhapati's Bengali translation above. Translocalization additionally resembles the now-famous "pizza effect" that Agehananda Bharati (1923–1991) first described, except that the presence of the translocal necessitates a common medium, in the case of Early Modern Yoga the dissemination of books published in English (and to some extent also German and French), accessible in a variety of geographical contexts—both among educated elites in India and abroad—rather than a "mono-directional assimilation" from one regional milieu to another.

The interplay between local and translocal could also inform debates as to whether or not Western esotericism should drop the geographical and cultural qualifier "Western" (cf. Roukema and Kilner-Johnson, 2018; Asprem, 2014). The dichotomy forces the following question in particular: for something to be translocal, must it necessarily be Western as well, and thus in the modern Indian context a colonial imposition? The presence of Indian authors on yoga who were the primary mediators for Western occultists complicates such a rigid adherence to the qualifier Western, even if at times they wrote in a Western language (English), often came from Brahman and/or other elite caste backgrounds with exposure to the West, and made recourse to Western philosophy. Indeed, even such general assumptions about the social and economic status of individual identities start to blur when one looks at the historical contexts in which each author operated as well as their broader family, teachers, and associates, or when one analyzes differences between the personalities that various occultists consulted or rejected. I think that it makes more sense in cases like these, therefore, to use categories like "translocal esotericism" and "local esotericism" to describe the ways in which Indian teachers and authors on esotericism have transformed and adapted to a variety of translocal and local audiences. While I don't think this necessitates a full departure from the adjective "Western" in every case, I think it is at least important to avoid debates over whether or not this or that esotericism is an *authentic* form of Western esotericism, thus falling right back into the discourse of authenticity as analyzed in the context of an "authentic yoga" in the above sections.

In concluding, I leave the reader with three general suggestions for tackling these issues that I think may facilitate further scholarly understanding of these flows between the local and translocal. First, while it may be tempting to automatically judge the translocal as inauthentic since it departs from the perceived authenticity of a local perspective, I think it makes more sense to suspend such a judgment and only levy it as a secondary step in the event that it is the explicit wish of a given scholar or author. Second, if one really wants to pursue a judgment of inauthenticity on the grounds of localized authenticity then I am also of the persuasion that this first necessitates a rigorous appraisal of the translocal primary source material and its context. Thirdly, while recognizing that all translocal literature must be localized to some extent and *vice-versa*, I think that a useful if not necessary practice is to conduct a rigorous examination of local perspectives in conversation or comparison with the translocal literature, either through ethnography, textual study, or preferably a combination of both, together with a command of the relevant languages necessary. Only then can a full perspective emerge that more comprehensively engages both local perspectives and translocal literature without risking the dismissal of one as limited in scope or the other as culturally inauthentic.

Bibliography

Alter, J.S. (2004) *Yoga in Modern India: The Body between Science and Philosophy*. Princeton, NJ: Princeton University Press.

Appiah, K.A. (2018) "Cultural Borrowing is Great, The Problem is Disrespect," *The Wall Street Journal*. Available at: https://www.wsj.com/articles/cultural-borrowing-is-great-the-problem-is-disrespect-1535639194 (Accessed: July 28, 2020).

Asprem, E. (2014) "Beyond the West: Towards a New Comparativism in the Study of Esotericism," *Correspondences*, 2(1), pp. 3–33.

Asprem, E. (2018) *The Problem of Disenchantment: Scientific Naturalism and Esoteric Discourse, 1900–1939*, Albany, NY: State University of New York Press.

Baier, K. (2016) "Theosophical Orientalism and the Structures of Intercultural Transfer: Annotations on the Appropriations of the Cakras in Early Theosophy," in Chajes, J. and Huss, B. (eds.) *Theosophical Appropriations: Esotericism, Kabbalah and* the Transformation of Traditions. Be'er Sheva, Israel: Ben-Gurion University of the Negev Press, pp. 309–354.

Baier, K. (2018) "Yoga within Viennese Occultism: Carl Kellner and Co.," in Baier, K., Maas, P.A. and Preisendanz, K. (eds.) *Yoga in Transformation: Historical and Contemporary Perspectives*. Vienna: Vienna University Press, pp. 183–222.

Bhaṭṭācārya, R. (2011) *Studies on the Cārvāka/Lokāyata*. London: Anthem Press.

Bogdan, H. (2006) "Challenging the Morals of Western Society: The Use of Ritualized Sex in Contemporary Occultism," *Pomegranate: The International Journal of Pagan Studies*, 8, pp. 211–246.

Bogdan, H. and Djurdjevic, G. (eds.) (2013) *Occultism in a Global Perspective*. London: Routledge.

Cantú, K. (2019) "Islamic Esotericism in the Bengali Bāul Songs of Lālan Fakir," *Correspondences*, 7(1), 109–165.

Cantú, K. (forthcoming) "Sri Sabhapati Swami: Forgotten Yogi of Western Esotericism," in Pokorny, L. and Winter, F. (eds.) *The Occult Nineteenth Century: Roots, Developments, and Impact on the Modern World*.

De Michelis, E. (2008) *A History of Modern Yoga: Patañjali and Western Esotericism*. London: Continuum.

Djurdjevic, G. (2014) *India and the Occult: The Influence of South Asian Spirituality on Modern Western Occultism*. New York: Palgrave Macmillan.

Eliade, M. (1995) *Occultism, Witchcraft, and Cultural Fashions: Essays in Comparative Religions*. Chicago: University of Chicago Press. First published 1978.

Eliade, M. (2009) *Yoga: Immortality and Freedom*. Princeton, NJ: Princeton University Press. First published 1958.

Faivre, A. (1994) *Access to Western Esotericism*. Albany, NY: State University of New York Press.

Foxen, A.P. (2017) *Biography of a Yogi: Paramahansa Yogananda and the Origins of Modern yoga*. New York: Oxford University Press.

Frosh, P. (2001) "To Thine Own Self be True: The Discourse of Authenticity in Mass Cultural Production," *The Communication Review*, 4(4), pp. 541–557.

Hanegraaff, W.J. (1995) "Empirical Method in the Study of Esotericism," *Method & Theory in the Study of Religion*, 7(2), pp. 99–129.

Hanegraaff, W.J. (2003) "How Magic Survived the Disenchantment of the World," *Religion*, 33, pp. 357–380.

Hanegraaff, W.J. (2015) "The Globalization of Esotericism," *Correspondences* 3, pp. 55–91.

Jain, A.R. (2015) *Selling Yoga: From Counterculture to Pop Culture*. Oxford: Oxford University Press.

Krämer, M. and Strube, J. (2020) *Theosophy Across Boundaries: Transcultural and Interdisciplinary Perspectives on a Modern Esoteric Movement*. Albany, NY: State University of New York Press.

Lindholm, C. (2008) *Culture and Authenticity*. Malden, MA: Blackwell Publishing.

Makdisi, S. (2014) *Making England Western: Occidentalism, Race, and Imperial Culture*. Chicago: The University of Chicago Press.

Mallinson, J. and Singleton, M. (eds.) (2017) *Roots of Yoga*. London: Penguin Books.

Nabavi, N. (ed.) (2015) *Modern Iran: A History in Documents*. Princeton, NJ: Markus Wiener Publishers.

Nara Document on Authenticity, The (1994) Published by the International Council of Monuments and Sites (ICOMOS). Available at: https://www.icomos.org/charters/nara-e.pdf.

Partridge, C. (2013) "Lost Horizon: H.P. Blavatsky and Theosophical Orientalism," in Hammer, O. and Rothstein, M. (eds.) *Handbook of the Theosophical Current*. Leiden: Brill.

Pasi, M. (2009) "The Modernity of Occultism: Some Crucial Aspects," in: Hanegraaff, W.J. and Pijnenburg, J. (eds.) *Hermes in the Academy: Ten Years' Study of Western Esotericism at the University of Amsterdam*. Amsterdam: Amsterdam University Press, pp. 59–74.

Pasi, M. (2014) *Aleister Crowley and the Temptation of Politics*. Durham: Acumen.

Randolph, P.B. (1931) *Magia Sexualis*. Paris: Robert Télin au Lys Rouge.

Ratchford, S. (2015) "Is Western Yoga Cultural Appropriation? Yes, but That Doesn't Mean White People Can't Practice It," *Vice*. Available at: https://www.vice.com/en_us/article/jmakbx/is-western-yoga-cultural-appropriation-obviously-but-that-doesnt-mean-you-cant-practice-it (Accessed: July 28, 2020).

Ros, A. (2012). "Translocalization," in: Juergensmeyer, M. and Clark Roof, W. (eds.) *Encyclopedia of Global Religion*, vol. 1. Thousand Oaks, CA: SAGE Publications, pp. 1301–1302.

Roukema, A. and Kilner-Johnson, A. (2018) "Editorial: Time to Drop the 'Western'," *Correspondences*, 6, pp. 109–115.

Said, E.W. (1978) *Orientalism*. London: Routledge and Kegan Paul.

Sand, E. and Rudbøg, T. (eds.) (2020) *Imagining the East: The Early Theosophical Society*. Oxford: Oxford University Press.

Sedgwick, M.J. (2004) *Against the Modern World: Traditionalism and the Secret Intellectual History of the Twentieth Century*. Oxford: Oxford University Press.

Singleton, M. (2010) *Yoga Body: The Origins of Modern Posture Practice*. Oxford: Oxford University Press.

Steinschneider, E. (2016) *Beyond the Warring Sects: Universalism, Dissent, and Canon in Tamil Śaivism, ca. 1675–1994*. Unpublished PhD thesis. University of Toronto.

Urban, H. (2001) "The Omnipotent Oom: Tantra and Its Impact on Modern Western Esotericism," *Esoterica*, 3, pp. 218–259.

Urban, H. (2003) "The Power of the Impure: Transgression, Violence and Secrecy in Bengali Śākta Tantra and Modern Western Magic," *Numen*, 50, pp. 269–308.

Urban, H. (2004) "Magia Sexualis: Sex, Secrecy, and Liberation in Modern Western Esotericism," *Journal of the American Academy of Religion*, 72, pp. 695–731.

Urban, H. (2006) *Magia Sexualis: Sex, Magic, and Liberation in Modern Western Esotericism*. Berkeley, CA: University of California Press.

Urban, H. (2008) "The Yoga of Sex: Tantra, Orientalism, and Sex Magic in the Ordo Templi Orientis," in: Hanegraaff, W.J. and Kripal, J.J. (eds.) *Hidden Intercourse: Eros and Sexuality in the History of Western Esotericism*, Leiden: Brill, pp. 401–443.

Vitello, P. (2010) "Hindu Group Stirs a Debate Over Yoga's Soul," *The New York Times*.

Wallis, C. (2015) "The Real Story on the Chakras," Tantrik Studies Blog. Available at: https://hareesh.org/blog/2016/2/5/the-real-story-on-the-chakras (Accessed: July 28, 2020).

Rejected Knowledge Reconsidered: Some Methodological Notes on Esotericism and Marginality

Egil Asprem

The notion that esotericism is a form of rejected knowledge has come back in style since the publication of Wouter J. Hanegraaff's *Esotericism and the Academy* in 2012. The association of esotericism with heterodoxy, deviance, opposition, and marginalization is itself old news: it has been a standard trope in insider discourses at least since the nineteenth century, and has also featured in earlier scholarly approaches to the field. In its strictest formulation, the new rejected knowledge model differs from these earlier approaches in important ways. Its central claim is that the *historiographical category* of "esotericism" emerged from heresiological writings in the seventeenth and eighteenth centuries, which for the first time imagined a diverse set of "heterodoxies" that we now associate with the category as "related currents." However, I will argue that the new rejected knowledge model also comes in an *inflated* version, in which the distinction between the historiographic concept ("esotericism") and its subject matter becomes blurred. The strict version represents an important contribution to the conceptual history of "esotericism." The inflated version, by contrast, introduces a host of problems that range from how groups and individuals are represented, to how we analyze and explain the data, to how esotericism is legitimized as a relevant field of study in the academy.

1   On Old and New Rejected Knowledge Narratives

The association of esotericism with the rejected, marginal, and repressed has a long history. Modern esoteric insiders have embraced it since the nineteenth century, often sublimating a self-perceived repressed status into the image of a secret tradition of radical opposition to establishment and orthodoxy. Models pitting esotericism against establishment have also been influential in academic takes on the subject. Frances Yates' (1964) presentation of the Renaissance "Hermetic tradition" as an autonomous, progressive counterculture, pointing the way from the "dark middle ages" to an enlightened modernity of science and humanism is an early example, which, presumably because of the counter-canonical view of modernity it provided, was also well received outside of academia in the 1960s (cf. Hanegraaff, 2001).[1] James Webb's influential characterization of nineteenth- and twentieth-century occultism as an "underground" of rejected knowledge is another example, this time associating the esoteric (or "occult") with the "irrational," pitting it against a post-Enlightenment establishment valorizing "reason." Similarly, the 1970s "sociology of the occult," associated with sociologists such as Edward Tiryakian and Marcello Truzzi, sought to understand the occult explosion of the postwar period in terms of deviance and tension with accepted opinions, devising a number of theoretical perspectives for understanding the significance of such "rejected knowledge" and its associated practices (see e.g. Tiryakian, ed., 1974).

These earlier approaches were questioned and sometimes subjected to polemics when a handful of scholars sought to establish the historical study of esotericism as a valid subfield in the history of religions in the 1990s (see e.g. Faivre and Hanegraaff, 1998). There is, therefore, a certain irony in the fact that, after a short period of trying to define what the study of esotericism is all about in *positive* terms, most notably through Antoine Faivre's later works (e.g. Faivre, 1994), the negative conceptualization of esotericism as "rejected knowledge" has once again sailed up as a leading approach through the works of Wouter J. Hanegraaff (2005, 2010, 2012). This appears all the more surprising when we consider that Hanegraaff has been the most vocal critic of the abovementioned approaches, dismissing them either as producing too simplistic narratives (2001), for being too "reductionist" (1995, pp. 119–120), or for being outright "anti-esoteric" (1998, pp. 40–41).

This turn of events becomes less surprising when we recognize that the new rejected knowledge model differs in at least one important respect from the earlier ones. The Yates paradigm held that hermetically inclined Renaissance scholars *really were* an oppositional counterforce to the scholastic establishment: the worldview of Hermes Trismegistus and the other *prisci theologi* was pitted against the worldview of Aquinas and late-medieval Aristotelianism. Eventually, at least by the time of the counter-reformation, the establishment stakeholders of the latter would go after the former with inquisitorial methods, culminating in the martyring of one irreverent "Hermeticist," Giordano Bruno, in 1600. Webb, too, held that the nineteenth-century occult *really was* "rejected

---

[1] Note, however, that Yates never talked about "esotericism," nor of "rejected knowledge" explicitly. Her hermetic tradition thesis is included here due to its later status as part of esotericism's research tradition. Similarly, it can be appraised as an early rejected knowledge model due to the portrayal of main protagonists as comprising a more or less consistent progressive "counterculture."

knowledge;" it was explicitly ridiculed and condemned by polite society, and was moreover organized socially in an oppositional underground that would at times seek to *overturn* the establishment (with horrid consequences when it temporarily succeeded: Webb saw the rise of the "occult" in the early twentieth century as part of a general growth in political irrationalism associated with the rise of anti-Semitism, Fascism, and National Socialism; Webb, 1974). Finally, at least one of the sociologists of the occult (Truzzi) also took as a given that "the occult" is deviant from the perspective of authorized systems of knowledge, whether in the fields of science, medicine, history, or religion. The task was to analyze how such deviance comes about, who is drawn to it, and what social consequences and functions it might have (see Asprem, forthcoming).

2   A New Narrative: The Strict Version

What the old models have in common is an emphasis on currents that are in some way marginalized or oppositional *in their own immediate context*. This is precisely where the new narrative, in its most developed formulation, differs. Its main point is *historiographical* rather than historical: it concerns itself with how history is written, and the role that the *category* of esotericism plays within the writing of history—not, as the previous approaches did, with how we should characterize the various individuals, groups, practices, or ideas that might be lumped into the category. The statement that esotericism *as a historiographical category* emerged as rejected knowledge is, quite simply, a statement about how historians have treated certain historical phenomena (or, rather, ignored them). Hanegraaff's *Esotericism in the Academy* is an attempt to explain why and how that happened.

To simplify the book's complex argument, it all boils down to a perceived problem with paganism that culminated in the seventeenth- and eighteenth centuries. In the seventeenth century, a series of German-speaking Protestant scholars (most notably Jacob Thomasius and Ehregott Daniel Colberg) started formulating explicit heresiological criteria that would allow the scholar to separate pious doctrines from those tainted by paganism. On the one hand, this led to the exclusion of Platonic and Hermetic aspects of Christianity; on the other, it allowed these scholars to construct a view of a whole range of "related currents" which would include, *inter alia*, Gnosticism, Hermetism, Neoplatonism, Paracelsism, Rosicrucianism, and Christian theosophy. Then, in the eighteenth century, the early historian of philosophy, Johann Jacob Brucker (1696–1770), would base himself on the heresiologists when devising criteria for his project of writing a *Historia critica philosophia* (1742–1744)—that is to say, a critical history of philosophy that selects only that which is good and excludes all the old follies. The result was two parallel narratives: one of true, and one of false philosophy. The story of false philosophy was, once again, made up of currents that would now be seen as "esotericism."

The core argument in *Esotericism and the Academy* is that these distinctions constituted the first attempts to see such currents as somehow related to each other. The resulting narratives were adopted wholesale by the *philosophes* of the Enlightenment period, most notably through the extensive plagiarism of Brucker's work by Diderot, d'Alembert, and the authors of the *Encyclopédie*. This, then, is the point of origin for the rejection of a wide group of currents—which, *nota bene*, were not necessarily marginal, rejected, or particularly "related" currents in their own time—from serious academic consideration.

3 Return of the "Grand Polemical Narrative": The Inflated Version

In practice, however, the crucial distinction between the metalevel of category formation and the status of individual historical cases has not always been so clearly upheld, giving way to an *inflated* version of rejected knowledge. The strict model tends to be inflated for two related reasons. On the one hand, the rejection episode featuring Protestant heresiologists and Enlightenment historiographers is (often implicitly) put in a broader explanatory context that is best characterized as *structural*. On the other, this structural explanatory frame casts members of the esoteric family as *always implicitly* at odds with, and therefore at least potentially discriminated or repressed by, the "dominant culture." This explanatory framework was most explicitly put forth in the article "Forbidden Knowledge: Anti-Esoteric Polemics and Academic Research" (Hanegraaff, 2005), which framed esotericism as the product of a "Grand Polemical Narrative," "the dynamics of which can be traced all the way back to the beginnings of monotheism" (ibid., p. 226). On this story, esotericism is the product of a several millennia long series of polemical formations (specifically: monotheism vs. idolatry, Christianity vs. Gnosticism, Christianity vs. magic and demon-worship, Protestantism vs. ["pagan"] Roman Catholicism, and the Enlightenment vs. the irrational), each of which produced practices of exclusion, silencing, repression, and even extermination of deviant voices. The Grand Polemical Narrative is presented as a persistent structural injustice at the heart of "Western culture." Moreover, "the academic study of Western esotericism" is provided with an emancipatory mission to counter and correct this structural injustice, since it "is clearly the natural enemy of the Grand Polemical Narrative" (2005, p. 248).

It is notable that sweeping references to a Grand Polemical Narrative were excised from the 2012 version of the rejected knowledge model. Nevertheless, the notion of a deep, even hidden structural injustice underlying any particular instance of "rejection" remains very much present in practice, even in post-2012 deployments of the model. For example, in a 2019 explanation of what rejected knowledge entails, the treatment of currents now sorted under "esotericism" is explicitly compared to "the traditional exclusion and marginalisation of women, black people and other people of colour, various alternative or non-dominant genders and sexualities, and the victims of Western colonization worldwide" (Hanegraaff, 2019, p. 149). In fact, the injustices committed against "esotericism" are portrayed as *deeper* than these obvious cases of structural violence, as we read that "the most fundamental grand narratives of Western culture have been constructed on the very basis of 'Othering' and rejecting precisely everything that is studied under the 'esotericism' label today!"—followed by a list of the same disjunctions mentioned in 2005 (Hanegraaff, 2019, pp. 149–150). That critical scholars have so far failed to realize the operations of this anti-esoteric structure is cast as evidence of just how powerful and hegemonic it is:

> the pervasive power of that same Western "anti-esoteric" discourse ... is far more dominant and pervasive than most academics realize. Like those fish who wonder "what the hell is water?," even radical critics of Western hegemonic narratives tend to be unaware that this discourse even exists, let alone how it structures their very own assumptions about acceptable and non-acceptable (rejected or discredited) forms of knowledge or methods of inquiry. In short, esotericism is the blind spot *par excellence* among those radical theorists who are so eager to deconstruct "Western culture". (ibid., pp. 150–151)

These broader implications of the rejected knowledge model—which not only go far beyond the core argument of *Esotericism in the Academy*, but are now also frequently couched in ideologically loaded language about "identity politics," "no-platforming," and taking the "red pill" (Hanegraaff, 2019; Hanegraaff, Pasi, and Forshaw, 2019)—are deeply problematic. As I will argue in the following, the inflated rejected knowledge model poses problems both for the practical scholarly task of analyzing and explaining historical sources, and for the continued status and relevance of the field in academia.

4 Practical Problems with the (Inflated) Rejected Knowledge Model

The problems posed by the inflated version for practical research purposes can be listed in five concrete issues:
1) The problem of defining the field;
2) the reinforcement of counter-canonical narratives;
3) the affirmation of insider self-understandings;
4) an undifferentiated view of "rejection processes";
5) a failure to address and explain "elected marginality."

The three first problems have a direct bearing on longstanding discussions in the historical study of esotericism. The final two, while also clearly relevant to historical research, become all the more pressing when we look to social science perspectives and to modern and contemporary esotericism. All of these concerns also point us towards the bigger issue of how the field relates to the rest of academia. The following sections will therefore lead us directly to a concluding discussion on what I see as a credible risk of *self-marginalization* if we fail to refine our approach to rejection and stigmatization processes and relegate these to one issue among many in the field's battery of research questions.

5 The Problem of Defining an Object of Study

The main rationale for the rejected knowledge model in its strict formulation is precisely to provide grounds for delimiting an object of study: Esotericism refers to a historically contingent "wastebasket" of currents seen to conflict with "proper" religion, philosophy, and science. Although the argument in *Esotericism and the Academy* makes clear that what was rejected was not chosen arbitrarily, but was rather grounded in specific epistemological and worldview positions,[2] giving the rejection process itself the pride of place does leave us with a purely negative definition of the field. This problem was already identified by Marco Pasi (2013), Michael Stausberg (2013), and Olav Hammer (2013) during a book symposium in the journal *Religion*. For all its contributions to our understanding of how a concept of esotericism took shape historically, Pasi noted, the rejected knowledge model in fact "renounces engaging in a

---

2 Rooted in a so-called "Platonic Orientalism"—itself a far from clear concept—and elsewhere defined as "cosmotheism" and "gnosis" (see Hanegraaff, 2012, pp. 370–373, 377). For a discussion of this concept, see Liana Saif (2021) and Dylan Burns (2021).

more 'positive' (in the sense of 'position-taking') theoretical work of etic conceptualization" (Pasi, 2013, p. 210). For that reason, it fails to provide a direction for scholars to operationalize the concept. We lack, as Hammer (2013, p. 249) similarly pointed out, a discussion of "the relationship between a *genealogical* account of how a term is used, and its potential *theoretical* use."

Stausberg brought up two related problems. First, as we have seen in a number of quotations in the previous section, the model is often phrased as covering *everything* that has been rejected by the "Enlightenment establishment." Yet, as Stausberg (2013, p. 223–224) points out, the "esoteric repository was only part of a larger picture and not even its most significant specimen." Ignoring everything else that was marginalized, such as "folk" religion and "popular systems of healing," means overshooting the mark. To Stausberg's list may be added a whole range of other ideas, practices, and even categories of people that were, in various ways and to various extents, "rejected" in this period, from political systems such as monarchism, to scientific theories such as phlogiston theory, to entire groups of people such as women or blacks, whose stigmatization were amplified on the grounds of at least *some* "enlightened" philosophy and science.[3] Yet, this has not made women's history, the history of monarchy, or theories of heat essential elements of a study of "esotericism." Put differently, "esotericism" is *underdetermined* by rejection processes (cf. also Hammer, 2013, p. 248).

Stausberg also made the point that it is not entirely obvious why "anti-esoteric" authors like Thomasius, Colberg, and Brucker should be given priority as "defining the field" when, as Hanegraaff's own narrative shows, similar clustering is also found by "pro-esoteric" authors like Gottfried Arnold's *Unparteyische Kirchen- und Ketzer-Historie* (1699–1700) or even the much earlier Catholic perennialist Agustino Steuco's (1497–1548) *De perenni philosophia* (1540), both of which, like the heresiologists' works, include much of what we would now consider belonging to "esotericism." In a response, Hanegraaff (2013b, p. 263) has explained that the difference is that these works are based on a theological "theoretical framework" that is utterly ahistorical and therefore unusable today. This however seems to miss the point. We are clearly not looking for a fully-fledged scholarly perspective among our sources that we can simply adopt wholesale (that is not what Hanegraaff does with Colberg or Brucker), but simply for works marking a *terminus ante quem* for emic understandings of "related currents" that we might today call "esotericism."

---

3 See e.g. the relevant entries in Diderot and d'Alembert, *L'encyclopédie*.

The rejected knowledge model has excavated some important twists and turns in scholarly perception of what we would now call "esotericism," but it dodges the question of how to delimit the field. What is more, since earlier historiographical (or mnemohistorical) models *did* exist, the insistence on giving the polemical category pride of place appears to be grounded in (pre-)theoretical assumptions. One can only suspect that these assumptions were more explicitly stated in 2005, as the Grand Polemical Narrative. The solution to these problems seems to me fairly simple: we must separate the study of rejection processes (a valuable sub-track in research on "esotericism" and its conceptual history) from the vexed question of how to define and operationalize the concept itself for scholarly research. While I will not engage the definition debate here, it suffices to note that a number of different alternatives are on the table, from stipulating new "positive" definitions (including along neo-Faivrean lines), to taking a systematically genealogical approach to esotericism as an "empty signifier" (Bergunder, 2010), or even "fractionating" the concept into more fine-grained analytical concepts that inevitably dissolves "its" status as a separate, semi-autonomous entity, but opens up new vistas of comparison (Asprem, 2016; on the definition debate, see Okropiridze, 2021).

6 The Reinforcement of Counter-Canonical Readings

These considerations lead us to the second problem: the elevation of rejected knowledge as *the* model for understanding esotericism *reinforces* the notion of esotericism as a "counter-canonic" current of heterodox thinkers and noble heretics. This is an unintended consequence; the stated goal of the model is, after all, to write "new and better grand narratives" that include and integrate "rejected thinkers" such as Ficino, Lazzarelli, Agrippa, or Paracelsus as "perfectly normal and legitimate" contributors to "Western culture" (Hanegraaff, 2019, pp. 151–152). Yet, when these "perfectly normal and legitimate" figures are circumscribed in terms of their assumed heterodox, rejected status, we have, as it seems to me, two problems: on the one hand, the persons of interest of such narratives remain exactly the same "usual suspects" as would previously have been included as members of "the Esoteric Tradition"; on the other, as this inclusion is now justified on the basis of its members having been "rejected" by historical actors cast as representative of "the Establishment," it remains unclear on what—or rather *whose*—grounds they should now be seen as perfectly legitimate and normal. It must also be noted that simply *insisting* that figures like the ones mentioned above have been universally rejected by scholars comes with the danger of imposing a language of marginality on subjects that have already for a long time been treated as "normal." As Hammer (2013, pp. 249–250) has noted about the Swedish scholarly context, intellectual historians in Sweden agreed already in the early twentieth century that Swedenborg's mystical side was part of a wider trend in the Enlightenment period, and works on the role of alchemy in early-modern Swedish history entered the scholarly mainstream, without ridicule or judgment, in the 1940s (see Lamm, 1911; Lamm, 1918–1920; Lindroth, 1943). These advances were made without recourse to a broader category of "esotericism"; insisting on subsuming them under an umbrella of rejected knowledge would represent a step backwards if the aim is to demonstrate the normality of such currents.

Again, all of this is easily solved if we accept only the *strict* form of the rejected knowledge model, and see the seventeenth- to eighteenth-century rejection process simply as one particular episode of interest in the conceptual history of "esotericism." On those grounds, the "normality and legitimacy" of *some* members of the category at some times and places could be studied in relation to other voices in their immediate society, that is to say, by analyzing their position within their local systems of privilege and hegemony. The post-Enlightenment view of an influential humanist philosopher such as Marsilio Ficino (1433–1499) under the powerbroker Cosimo de' Medici's patronage as one of the marginal "irrationals" could then simply be explained as an anachronistic projection. More importantly, since normality and legitimacy are never stable terms, our objective can hardly be to demonstrate that *all* esotericism was always considered "legitimate," but rather to determine when, by whom, and in what contexts, a certain thinker, current, or practice was variously normalized or contested. Pico della Mirandola (1463–1494) is a good case in point: clearly privileged in terms of his social and economic status (hailing from nobility), his 900 theses also ended up on the index of the Roman Catholic Church. Regimes of power are rarely singular, and the same goes for normativity.

These complexities get lost if "rejected knowledge" is made the *defining characteristic* of the category that organizes our study, and anti-paganism presumed as a persistent hegemonic structure in *all* periods of "Western culture." Against the backdrop of such invisible structures, even the esotericism of privileged elites, whether we think of the multitudes of alchemists and magicians at the court of emperor Rudolph II in Prague in the seventeenth century, the magical experiments at the court of king Gustav III in Stockholm in the late 1700s, or even the mass-marketized esotericism of multi-billion industries such as the contemporary "wellness sector" (Crockford, 2021), can, despite being obviously favored with power, be cast as implicitly "marginalized."

7 The Affirmation of Esotericist Self-Understandings

The above issue is intimately connected with a third problem, namely the risk of reproducing and propping up contemporary esotericist self-understandings that do not necessarily have much to do with reality. The rhetoric of an oppressive establishment pitted against esoteric underdogs has been central to esotericism ever since the term first started to be used as a self-designation among nineteenth-century occultists (cf. Strube, 2017a). A typical characteristic of this ubiquitous narrative is to portray existing establishments, notably in religion and the sciences, as not only repressive, but also dogmatic and simpleminded, while at the same time casting the esoteric underdog as not only repressed, but also in possession of a supreme knowledge that far outmatches that of the establishment. While "the other" is repressive and also wrong, "the self" is marginalized and also part of a superior, underground elite that will, eventually, win out.

We see versions of this narrative time and again, from Theosophy to Traditionalism to parts of contemporary paganism to the so-called New Age movement and contemporary commercialized spirituality. Wherever it is articulated, it functions to create an oppositional us-them binary that not only validates the esoteric "higher knowledge" of the in-group and grounds it in pseudo-historical myths about repressed noble heretics; it also creates a protective barrier around the esoteric knowledge system by *explaining away* any contradictions by contemporary knowledge specialists (whether scientists, doctors, or academic historians) as part of a repressive rejection strategy.

It is worth noting here that this narrative structure is also usually present when contemporary esotericists articulate *conspiracy theories* (see Asprem and Dyrendal, 2015; Asprem and Dyrendal, 2019). Public criticism, conflicting views of the past by professional historians or archaeologists, state regulations on complementary medicine or food supplements, or the failure of a new harmonic age to emerge can be dismissed as the machinations of a conspiracy that seeks to *suppress* the truth and keep the unenlightened sheeple in the dark (cf. Robertson, 2016, pp. 205–210).

Of course, neither the strict nor the inflated version of the rejected knowledge model holds that what is rejected must also be *true*. Hanegraaff has been clear to specify that the aim of presenting the rejected as "normal" should be pursued irrespective of whatever one might personally think of its value and veracity (Hanegraaff, 2019, pp. 151–152). Yet, casting the whole field as characterized first and foremost by rejection does reinforce the oppositional establishment vs. underground structure.

This issue gets more serious when the emic view is turned into a normative project by which the field's very rationale is to *emancipate* the victims of "the establishment." In fact, I see the rejected knowledge paradigm as engaging in two separate emancipation projects, which mirror the strict and inflated versions of the model. The first is to counter the rejection of esotericism *in the academy*, that is to say, to make the academic *study* of esotericism a legitimate pursuit in the eyes of other academics. This is a reasonable pursuit, and one that has by now largely succeeded. A quite separate emancipation project, which does not follow from the first, is to liberate the *subject matter* from its assumed "rejected status" in society at large.

Whenever the social emancipation agenda enters the picture, the risk of (re)producing simplified, partisan, and even soft conspiratorial explanations for esotericists' perceived plight, increases. We see this tendency when polemically charged simplifications, such as "reductionism," "materialism," and more recently "postmodernism," are adopted to identify "anti-esoteric" scholarship, and the scholarly traditions attached to these labels are implicated in "no-platforming" esotericism from the stage of history (Hanegraaff, 2019, p. 149). Singling out "neo-Marxism" and "the Frankfurt School" as central culprits is another example (e.g. Hanegraaff, 2012, pp. 312–314), which has sometimes been carried out in ways that border on the conspiratorial insider discourses of Traditionalism that see a (Jewish coded) "cultural Marxism" as the enemy of "true" spirituality (for an example, see Hakl, 2012, in an article translated from German by the noted Radical Traditionalist Michael Moynihan). While I doubt that such language reflects genuine beliefs of a nefarious conspiracy trying to suppress esoteric spokespersons, it enters an ambiguous discursive field that certainly affords and emboldens such convictions. All of this has consequences for the field's place within the academy, which I will return to in the conclusion.

8   An Undifferentiated View of Rejection Processes

An underlying problem that has been running through the discussion so far is the imprecise usage of rejected knowledge in the inflated sense, which leads to confusions regarding *who*, *when*, and *for what reasons* a certain piece of knowledge assumes the status of "rejected." As we have already seen, this problem is clear enough from a historical point of view, where we need to separate between the actors that we are studying, other actors in their environments, the judgments of the scholar, and general academic "tacit knowledge." The problem, however, gets even more pressing when we look at how assumedly "rejected knowledge" is negotiated in the modern and contemporary periods, *after* the processes covered by the strict model had taken place.

First of all, we must recognize that there is more than one way in which some piece of knowledge can fail to find favor with some establishment. Knowledge can be directly rejected and polemicized against by authorities (as the strict model has it with regards to an assorted set of religio-philosophical ideas and traditions), but it can also, as Michael Barkun (2002) argues in his discussion of "stigmatized knowledge," be *superseded, ignored*, or simply *forgotten*. In fact, a lot of what scholars might categorize as rejected knowledge is better characterized as *superseded knowledge*: knowledge which used to be authoritatively recognized, but has since lost that status in competition with new knowledge. Alchemy, astrology, and natural magic could all be framed this way. While the processes through which they were superseded can, of course, be fruitfully analyzed in terms of the polemical discourses operating in the early modern period, we miss crucial nuances if we ignore the fact that they were also *replaced* and instead lump them together with, e.g., "heretical" religious beliefs, as part of one big category of "rejected knowledge."

Other "non-hegemonic" knowledge claims are simply *ignored*, not taken seriously enough to critique or engage with and thus not explicitly "rejected." This arguably makes up a huge and understudied segment of the field, especially where esotericism intersects with "low-prestige" knowledge, from popular culture to lived religion. Ironically, due to its focus on counter-canonical narratives dominated by white male literati, the field itself continues the tendency of ignoring low-prestige and "peripheral" knowledge. It is illustrative that we do not even have a proper debate yet about, for example, the practices and knowledges of village cunning folk, or the divination services provided by travelling Romani families in Europe since the fifteenth century, as part of esotericism. The case of the Roma is particularly interesting: not only have they played a role in esoteric invented traditions imagining a lineage from Egypt (see e.g. Farley, 2006, pp. 22–26), but they have also been explicitly rejected for doing "sorcery" by some of the very same "establishment" voices cited as inventors of esotericism as rejected knowledge. In fact, Jacob Thomasius wrote a dissertation on "the philosophy of the gypsies" (*Dissertatio philosophica de Cingaris*, 1652), which became a foundational work of European antiziganism (Saul, 2007, pp. 2–4).

Another way in which the study of "rejected knowledge" should be made more precise is by distinguishing clearly between three things: 1) *empirically verifiable* campaigns to reject or marginalize some knowledge, 2) *subjective perceptions* of having been marginalized, and 3) claims about *the goals and intentions* of those who (allegedly) do the marginalization or rejection. As we have already seen, this is necessary because the claim that one's own position is (dogmatically) rejected performs important identity protecting work in esoteric discourses that needs to be analyzed regardless of whether the claim holds empirically.

Even in cases where we are dealing with authorities explicitly countering some knowledge claim it is important for the scholar to ask *on what grounds* this happens. In the context of contemporary liberal states, there is for example a huge difference between the rejection of something like neopagan religious groups as not being "real religions," and the rejection of homeopathy as not "real medicine." When a Norwegian Asatru group called Det Norske Åsatrosamfunn tried to get official recognition as a religion according to Norwegian law in 1996, the Ministry of Justice intervened to reject the group for not having an official creed, for endorsing the practice of "magic," and for being a threat to "public morals" through alleged "Satanic rituals" (see Asprem, 2008, pp. 57–58). This could with some justification be considered a case of religious suppression based in an old anti-pagan polemic enforced by the state. By contrast, when homeopathy is rejected as not real medicine, it is typically with reference to countless scientific studies failing to find effects beyond placebo, on the one hand, and by pointing out that the mechanisms by which it is claimed by proponents to work ("potentization" through dilutions, the "memory of water") contradict basic, well-established physics and chemistry, on the other (see e.g. Goldacre, 2008; Singh and Ernst, 2008). Yet, proponents of homeopathy have been known to claim that this is in fact *suppression* of something that *does* work (and that Big Pharma knows it!). There have even been attempts, most notably in the UK, by proponents of alternative and complementary medicines to silence scientific critique by suing scientists for libel—a fact which shows just how complicated and distributed the dynamics of suppression by using established legal powers really is.[4]

Surprisingly, perhaps, I find that the older literature on the sociology of the occult, dismissed by esotericism scholars in the 1990s, had better tools for differentiating between the who, what, when, and why of rejected knowledge than the present model provides. One example suffices to make this point. Marcello Truzzi (1971) has been criticized for viewing "the occult" as "anomalous knowledge," defined in terms of its deviance from various epistemic norms, and thereby, as the criticism goes, creating a concept that is normative, ahistorical, and anti-esoteric (see Hanegraaff, 1995, for the first formulation of this criticism). This criticism ignores the methodological imperatives

---

4   See e.g. *The Guardian*, April 1, 2010.

that most occupied Truzzi. In fact, he developed an intricate framework for studying how various types of "anomalies" are produced and perceived. One of these, which he calls "theoretical anomalies," are indeed defined in relation to some scientific discipline, but as Truzzi wrote, they "appear unusual only to one with special knowledge or training." In other words, the very practice of singling out deviations from a particular scientific system is entirely dependent on, and relative to, the existence of some expert system. In addition, Truzzi stressed the importance of thorough historicization. Researchers must ask *"who* is labelling the beliefs as occult [i.e. anomalous], *where* the labelling is being done (the social context), and *at what time* the designation is made (the historical period)" (Truzzi, 1971, 637). That the status of a particular piece of knowledge is not fixed, but constantly negotiated by situated social actors was, in fact, a central tenet in the sociology of the occult's research program.[5]

9   Elected Marginality: Heterodoxy as Hegemonic Value

One final and crucial aspect that the rejected knowledge model tends to overlook is this: to the extent that associating oneself with esotericism leads to a degree of marginalization, the marginality tends to be *elected* rather than *imposed*. While we lack systematic studies on how people are socialized into esoteric movements, the anecdotal view is that very few are born into esotericism. Much more commonly, involvement in esoteric currents results from active seekership in what Colin Campbell (1972) calls the "cultic milieu," characterized precisely by circulation of more or less "deviant," non- or counter-hegemonic ideas and practices. The elected nature of esoteric involvement underscores just how unwise it is to compare any resulting marginality with the "traditional exclusion" (Hanegraaff, 2019, p. 149) of less mobile identities, such as socio-economic class, gender, sexual orientation, or ethnicity. An otherwise well-positioned, middle class person choosing to adhere to rejected knowledge is a different thing altogether from being marginalized for who you are. But it also points to an important set of research questions that are not really being asked by scholars of esotericism: what *motivates* involvement in rejected knowledge? Is the associated marginality simply a liability, to be balanced against perceived benefits, or may it in fact be seen as an asset?

---

5   For a thorough reassessment of the sociology of the occult, see Asprem, forthcoming.

Again, we lack studies of what motivates social actors drawn to esoteric movements and what they think about esotericism's presumed rejected status. But we do know that taking a heterodox stance can in many circumstances be highly desirable. Being "anti-Establishment" is a winning recipe in populist politics as much as in a business culture that rewards norm-breaking startups that "disrupt" the system. At a time when "political correctness" has become perhaps the most widely used political boo-word, aligning with heterodox, assumedly "rejected" or marginal ideas can take on the function of virtue signaling: "I don't go with the consensus!" In everyday contexts, this may just as well lead to social rewards as to stigma, depending on the circles in which one moves and the audiences from which one seeks attention. In contexts such as the cultic milieu, it is far from obvious that actors would want to seek normalization or mainstream acceptance. The opposite may well be true: mainstreaming is often countered by the "amplification of deviance," doubling down on radical expressions in ways that reestablish one's transgressive subcultural capital (Asprem, forthcoming; cf. Kahn-Harris, 2006). Historically, we find precisely this sort of self-conscious embrace of the "heretical," standing proudly against the corrupt alliance of church and state, when the notion of "occultism" emerged in French socialist circles in the early nineteenth century (Strube, 2017a, 2017b).

We also know that, at least since the 1960s, the oppositional and deviant *sells*. As Thomas Frank noted in his work on "hip consumerism," "[c]ommercial fantasies of rebellion, liberation, and outright 'revolution' against the stultifying demands of mass society are commonplace almost to the point of invisibility in advertising, movies, and television programming" (Frank, 1997, p. 4–5). Elected marginality is mainstream, everyday, even commercialized. It is tied to the production of identities that play on tropes such as the underdog, the noble heretic, the authentic non-conformist, or the rebellious freethinker; yet, it plays to thoroughly hegemonic cultural values of individualism, autonomy, and self-dependence.

Against this background, it is not hard to imagine that making rejected knowledge one's own might be attractive to many. It makes the emergence of "popular occulture" (Partridge, 2014) seem entirely unsurprising, and the embrace of the aesthetics of the occult as a language of resistance (e.g., the witch as feminist icon, the labeling of criticism as "witch hunts," or the use of Satan and "dark occultism" as rebellious expression on both the left and the right) quite predictable. Since the logic of such uses are entirely in line with late modern hegemonic notions of individualism and self-expression, it indicates that embracing esoteric rejected knowledge may lead to a sense of empowerment rather than to marginalization in any socially meaningful sense.

10 Rejected Theory and the Risk of Self-Marginalization

As I hope to have demonstrated, overemphasizing the construction of the category esotericism as rejected knowledge comes at the expense of obscuring the complicated, but much more important questions of how deviance and hegemony are produced, negotiated, and enforced in concrete socio-historical contexts. A sophisticated study of such negotiations must, as I have highlighted above, differentiate between emic and etic explanatory models, elected and enforced marginality, and the benefits and drawbacks of claiming the underdog role. In order to do so, I have argued that esotericism scholarship still has a lot to learn from the social sciences.

There is, however, a danger that the very inflation of the rejected knowledge model is only separating the field further from those approaches that could help refine it. As we have seen, the emancipatory agenda of countering "rejected knowledge" appears to have moved much beyond historicizing how the category was initially shaped in a polemical context, to now also identify an increasing number of contemporary academic approaches, schools, and theoretical traditions as inherently "anti-esoteric." From the early polemic against "reductionist" approaches, recent publications show a worrying fixation with labels such as "neo-Marxism," "Critical Theory," "the Frankfurt school," and "postmodernism," sometimes apotheosized into an attack on "theory" *as such* (see Strube, 2021, pp. 53–54). "Neo-Marxist" critical theory tends to be implicated directly in a continued rejection of esotericism, often by quoting Adorno's famous "Theses against Occultism" (e.g. Hakl, 2012; cf. Hanegraaff, 2012, pp. 312–314). This, however, tends to come at the expense both of a more nuanced historical understanding of how early critical theory in fact related to "esotericism" (the case of Walter Benjamin's esoteric fascinations being the most obvious counterpoint; cf. Josephson-Storm, 2017, pp. 209–239), and by underplaying the real concerns of "Frankfurt School" critics' diagnoses of modern capitalist society (see e.g. Kilcher, 2019 for a closer reading of Adorno's theses). The problem is that the historical analysis of how certain scholars influenced the conceptual history of esotericism becomes conflated with a polemic against contemporary perspectives on, for example, critical theory. This is particularly unfortunate seeing how important critical theory is for a whole range of approaches that the study of esotericism sorely needs to engage with in order to refine its perspectives, from gender studies and critical race studies to postcolonial and decolonial theory and issues of class (see e.g. Bakker, 2021; Hedenborg White, 2021; Strube, 2021; Villalba, 2021). Excluding those perspectives and dismissing colleagues who work with them can only lead to further theoretical isolation of the field itself.

In this light, the rejection of "theory" itself by juxtaposition with "history," a peculiarity in some of Hanegraaff's recent work (2012, pp. 366–367; 2013, pp. 266–267), is perhaps the most puzzling of all. The argument is again intimately tied to the emancipatory agenda of the rejected knowledge model: the worry is that coming to, or even selecting, the material with an explicit theoretical framework in mind will end up looking only for specific things with the end result that sources not considered relevant will once again "disappear." The problem with this argument is that there is only one alternative to departing from explicit theorizations, namely, departing from implicit, hidden, or even unrecognized ones. One does not have to be a "radical theorist" (Hanegraaff, 2019, p. 151) to make the point that all scholars, no matter how big the pretention of meeting the world with a "theory-free" open mind, carry with them assumptions about what is relevant and what is not prior to even selecting one's sources. It is a basic epistemological point recognized from the hermeneutics of Gadamer in the humanities to the post-positivism of Popper, Quine, or Kuhn in the natural sciences. The rejected knowledge model, as I have argued, appears to come with heavy layers of unexamined theoretical baggage about what "esotericism" is (what are its sources), which versions of it are relevant in the first place (who speaks for it), and how it ought or ought not to be studied (methods, research questions, analyses). If those unreflective assumptions lead to a suspicion of theoretical reflection in general, and a rejection of certain lines of theorizing in particular, we are at risk of creating an insular field. While the rejected knowledge model had sought to strengthen the legitimacy of the field, it is precisely that wider legitimacy that is at stake if the inflated version of the model takes hold. We should not reject theory to save our sources from oppression; what we need is more sophisticated and systematic theories in order to select and understand them better.

Bibliography

Asprem, E. (2008) "Heathens up North: Politics, Polemics, and Contemporary Norse Paganism in Norway," *The Pomegranate*, 10(1), pp. 41–69.

Asprem, E. (2016) "Reverse-Engineering 'Esotericism': How to Prepare a Complex Cultural Concept for the Cognitive Science of Religion," *Religion*, 46(2), pp. 158–185.

Asprem, E. (forthcoming) "On the Social Organization of Rejected Knowledge: Reassessing the Sociology of the Occult," in Rudbøg, T. and Hedenborg White, M. (eds.) *Esotericism and Deviance*. Leiden: Brill.

Asprem, E. and Dyrendal, A. (2015) "Conspirituality Reconsidered: How Surprising and How New is the Confluence of Spirituality and Conspiracy Theory?" *Journal of Contemporary Religion*, 30(3), pp. 367–382.

Asprem, E. and Dyrendal, A. (2019), "Close Companions? Esotericism and Conspiray Theories," in Dyrendal, A., Robertson, D., and Asprem, E. (eds.) *Handbook of Conspiracy Theory and Contemporary Religion*, Leiden: Brill, pp. 207–233.

Bakker, J. (2019) "Hidden Presence: Race and/in the History, Construct, and Study of Western Esotericism," *Religion*. [Online] DOI 10.1080/0048721X.2019.1642262.

Bakker, J. (2021) "Hidden Presence: Race and the Study of Esotericism," in Asprem, E. and Strube, J. (eds.) *New Approaches to the Study of Esotericism*. Leiden and Boston: Brill, pp. 147–167.

Barkun, M. (2003) *A Culture of Conspiracy: Apocalyptic Visions in Contemporary America*. Berkeley: University of California Press.

Bergunder, M. (2010) "What Is Esotericism? Cultural Studies Approaches and the Problems of Definition in Religious Studies," *Method & Theory in the Study of Religion*, 22(1), pp. 9–36.

Campbell, C. (1972). "The Cult, the Cultic Milieu, and Secularisation," *A Sociological Yearbook of Religion in Britain*, 5, pp. 119–136.

Crockford, S. (2021) "What Do Jade Eggs Tell Us About the Category 'Esotericism': Spirituality, Neoliberalism, Secrecy, and Commodities," in Asprem, E. and Strube, J. (eds.) *New Approaches to the Study of Esotericism*. Leiden and Boston: Brill, pp. 201–216.

Faivre, A. (1994) *Access to Western Esotericism*. Albany: State University of New York Press.

Faivre, A. and Hanegraaff, W.J. (eds.) (1998) *Western Esotericism and the Science of Religion*. Leuven: Peeters Publishers.

Farley, H. (2009) *A Cultural History of Tarot: From Entertainment to Esotericism*. London: I.B. Tauris & Co.

Frank, T. (1997) *Conquest of Cool: Business Culture, Counterculture, and the Rise of Hip Consumerism*. Chicago and London: University of Chicago Press.

Goldacre, B. (2008) *Bad Science*. London: HarperCollins, Fourth Estate.

Hammer, O. (2013) "Deconstructing 'Western Esotericism': On Wouter Hanegraaff's Esotericism and the Academy," *Religion*, 43(2), pp. 241–251.

Hanegraaff, W.J. (1995) "Empirical Method in the Study of Esotericism," *Method and Theory in the Study of Religion*, 7(2), pp. 99–129.

Hanegraaff, W.J. (1998) "On the Construction of Esoteric Traditions," in Hanegraaff, W.J. and Faivre, A. (eds.) *Western Esotericism and the Science of Religion*, Leuven: Peeters Publishing, pp. 11–61.

Hanegraaff, W.J. (2001) "Beyond the Yates Paradigm: The Study of Western Esotericism between Counterculture and New Complexity," *Aries*, 1(1), pp. 5–37.

Hanegraaff, W.J. (2005) "Forbidden Knowledge: Anti-Esoteric Polemics and Academic Research," *Aries*, 5(2), pp. 225–254.

Hanegraaff, W.J. (2010) "The Birth of Esotericism from the Spirit of Protestantism," *Aries*, 10(2), pp. 197–216.

Hanegraaff, W.J. (2012) *Esotericism and the Academy: Rejected Knowledge in Western Culture*. Cambridge: Cambridge University Press.

Hedenborg White, M. (2021) "Double Toil and Gender Trouble? Performativity and Femininity in the Cauldron of Esotericism Research," in Asprem, E. and Strube, J. (eds.) *New Approaches to the Study of Esotericism*. Leiden and Boston: Brill, pp. 182–200.

Kahn-Harris, K. (2006) *Extreme Metal: Music and Culture on the Edge*. Oxford and New York: Berg Publishers.

Okropiridze, D. (2021) "Interpretation Reconsidered: The Definitional Progression in the Study of Esotericism as a Case in Point for the Varifocal Theory of Interpretation," in Asprem, E. and Strube, J. (eds.) *New Approaches to the Study of Esotericism*. Leiden and Boston: Brill, pp. 217–240.

Partridge, C. (2014) "Occulture Is Ordinary," in Asprem, E. and Granholm, K. (eds.) *Contemporary Esotericism*, London: Routledge, pp. 113–133.

Pasi, M. (2013) "The Problems of Rejected Knowledge: Thoughts on Wouter Hanegraaff's *Esotericism and the Academy*," *Religion*, 43(2), pp. 201–212.

Robertson, D. (2016) *UFOs, Conspiracy Theories, and the New Age*. London: Bloomsbury Academic.

Saif, L. (2021) "'That I did love the Moor to live with him': Islam in/and the Study of 'Western Esotericism'," in Asprem, E. and Strube, J. (eds.) *New Approaches to the Study of Esotericism*. Leiden and Boston: Brill, pp. 67–87.

Saul, N. (2007) *Gypsies and Orientalism in German Literature and Anthropology of the Long Nineteenth Century*. London: Maney Publishing.

Singh, S. and Ernst, E. (2008) *Trick or Treatment: Alternative Medicine on Trial*. London: Bantam Press.

Stausberg, M. (2013) "What is *it* all about? Some reflections on Wouter Hanegraaff's *Esotericism and the Academy*," *Religion*, 43(2), pp. 219–230.

Strube, J. (2017a) "Revolution, Illuminismus und Theosophie: Eine Genealogie der 'häretischen' Historiographie des frühen fanzösischen Sozialismus und Kommunismus," *Historische Zeitschrift*, 304(1), pp. 50–89.

Strube, J. (2017b) "Occultist Identity Formations between Theosophy and Socialism in *fin-de-siècle* France," *Numen*, 64, pp. 568–595.

Strube, J. (2021) "Towards the Study of Esotericism Without the 'Western': Esotericism from the Perspective of a Global Religious History," in Asprem, E. and Strube, J. (eds.) *New Approaches to the Study of Esotericism*. Leiden and Boston: Brill, pp. 45–66.

The Guardian, 1 April, 2010. "Simon Singh wins libel court battle". URL: https://www.theguardian.com/uk/2010/apr/01/simon-singh-wins-libel-court (accessed Nov 14 2019).

Tiryakian, E. (ed.) (1974) *On the Margin of the Visible: Sociology, the Esoteric, and the Occult*. New York: John Wiley & Sons.

Truzzi, M. (1971) "Definition and Dimensions of the Occult: Towards a Sociological Perspective," *Journal of Popular Culture*, (December 1971), pp. 635–646.

Villalba, M. (2021) "The Occult Among the Aborigines of South America? Some Remarks on Race, Coloniality, and the West in the Study of Esotericism," in Asprem, E. and Strube, J. (eds.) *New Approaches to the Study of Esotericism*. Leiden and Boston: Brill, pp. 88–108.

Webb, J. (1974) *The Occult Underground*. La Salle: Open Court Publishing.

Webb, J. (1976) *The Occult Establishment*. La Salle: Open Court Publishing.

Yates, F. (1964) *Giordano Bruno and the Hermetic Tradition*. London: Routledge & Kegan Paul.

Race and (the Study of) Esotericism

Justine Bakker

The case I wish to make in this essay is simple: race matters in and for the study of esoteric ideas and practice. And how could it not? Esotericisms do not develop in a vacuum, but in particular social, cultural, religious, economic and political contexts. These contexts continue to be marked and shaped by—and in turn inform—what W.E.B. Du Bois so incisively called the "color line."[1] Developed in 1903 in *The Souls of Black Folk* but still poignant, Du Bois coined this phrase to name the visible and invisible lines of demarcation between racial groups. Even as "race is an idea, not a fact," as Nell Irvin Painter (2010, p. ix) famously and concisely put it—and even as racial categories are fluid constructs and not static, fixed identities (Omi and Winant, 1994)—the color line continues to have real-life consequences. This includes explicit forms of racism, like violence and political disenfranchisement, along with implicit racial biases. Examples of such biases are the pervasive inequality in employment, education, health care, and housing, as well as a continued imbalance in the academy when it comes to the study of the history, present, and potential futures of white people and people of color. Racism thus operates in and through systems and structures—and not merely on the level of individual beliefs or actions—that offer advantages for certain racial groups, and disadvantages for others. Racial discrimination comes, moreover, in ever-new forms, and manifests in ever-new ways—in our contemporary moment, such manifestations are often masked or hidden under the guise of the "post-racial" and various forms of "color blindness" (see, among many others, Alexander, 2010; Bonilla-Silva, 2003; Goldberg, 2015). The "color line" is, therefore, neither stable, static nor fixed, nor is it always easily recognizable, nor is its influence always immediately apparent.

There seems to be, then, a rather obvious rationale for *why* perspectives on race matter in and for the study of esotericism. A focus on race will help us to better understand some of the contexts out of which past and present esotericisms emerged, thereby shedding light on why and how certain esotericisms are the way they are. In turn, the study of the intersections of race and esotericism might proffer a new vantage point from where to study processes of

---

1 Du Bois spoke primarily about the United States, but later scholars have expanded this notion as the "global color line" (Marable and Agard-Jones, 2008; see also Wynter, 2003; Sharpe, 2016).

racialization and racial formation.[2] Despite this rationale, until recently race was largely ignored *in* the field of (Western[3]) esotericism. Certainly, scholars have studied the connections between forms of white supremacy and esotericism (see e.g. Gardell, 2003; Goodrick-Clarke, 1985; 2001; Staudenmaier, 2014). Yet, the intersections between esotericisms and less obvious formations of whiteness remain to be investigated. And certainly, the edited volume *Esotericism in African American Religious Experience* (2015) engaged the ways in which African American forms of esotericism wrestle with, resist, or transcend processes of racialization. Yet, the editors of this volume did so explicitly in the context of a new research field, Africana Esoteric Studies, thereby also advancing a necessary critique of the adjective "Western."

And thus, my claim stands: only a handful of texts in (Western) esotericism interrogate the intersections of race and esotericism (Gray, 2019; Knight, 2019; Bakker, 2020). I will turn to the question of why and the implications of this lack towards the end of this essay. However, the bulk of the chapter contributes to efforts that remedy this lacuna by looking at two case studies, both based in the United States. The first engages the phenomenon of what Patrick Polk (2010, p. 26) calls "racialized spirits." I compare the visit of famous Sauk leader Black Hawk at a white séance with that of president Abraham Lincoln at a séance attended solely by black men to ask how constructions of "whiteness," blackness" and "Indianness" are formulated, produced, reinforced, or transcended in and through Spiritualist séances. My second case study tackles the relationship between esotericisms and racialized social location from a different and less obvious vantage point: UFO abduction narratives. In both instances, I make frequent use of secondary literature to demonstrate that although a focus on race certainly is a relatively "new perspective" in the field of (Western) esotericism, it is not foreign to scholarship on esoteric ideas and

---

2 Racialization is a term frequently used, and in various ways. In this essay, I follow Vincent Lloyd (2016, p. 4), who define racialization as the "sets of ideas, institutions, practices and technologies that establish and maintain a racial regime." "Racial formation," first developed by Michael Omi and Howard Winant (1994), refers to the sociohistorical processes by which racial categories are made and unmade, produced and altered, reinforced and destroyed.
3 I use parenthesis when talking about the field of (Western) esotericism to acknowledge recent scholarship that has explicitly called for the dismissal of the adjective "Western" (see Granholm, 2013; Asprem, 2014; Roukema and Kilner-Johnson, 2018; Strube, 2021). In a recent essay, I joined efforts that query and challenge "Western"; however, I also see value in temporarily keeping the adjective, when used in a self-conscious way, to signal, problematize, and study how the adjective, in and for the study of Western esotericism, has functioned as a racialized category (Bakker, 2019).

practice conducted in other fields. My engagement with secondary literature shows, too, that there is not "one" perspective on race; a focus on race may in fact yield very different and sometimes even contradictory interpretations. In my conclusion, I make a case for further methodological and theoretical diversification in the field of (Western) esotericism.

1   Racialized Communication with the Dead

In September 1874, the spirit of Abraham Lincoln (1809–1865) manifested at the séance table of the Cercle Harmonique, a Spiritualist group in New Orleans comprised of black men. The timing, as Emily Suzanne Clark writes, was significant: the city was "on the brink of racial violence" when Lincoln came to "lament" the bloodshed of the city's black inhabitants and "warn" those who advocated white supremacy (2018, p. 161–2). Lincoln often frequented the group and was, as it turns out, not the only famous visitor. From their beginnings in 1858 until their final meeting in 1877, the members of the Cercle Harmonique—of which Henri Louis Rey (1831–1894) was the most prominent—convened on a weekly basis and welcomed a wide variety of spirits. Philosophers Voltaire (1694–1778) and Montesquieu (1689–1755), abolitionist John Brown (1800–1859), confederate leader Robert E. Lee (1807–1870) and even Pocahontas, famous daughter of Native American chief Powhatan (c. 1596–1617) appeared at the men's table to deliver a message of egalitarianism and reform. In Clark's *A Luminous Brotherhood* (2016) we read that the spirits formed a collective that imagined "a more egalitarian United States" (p. 4). In an effort to implement what they called "the Idea"—an "egalitarian republicanism" that Clark summarizes as "humanitarian progress, equality, egalitarianism, brotherhood, and harmony"—the spirits acted as teachers, guiding members of the Cercle Harmonique in their efforts for social reform and opposition to the destructive forces of white supremacy (Clark, 2016, p. 5). There remained, after all, as Clark also notes, an enormous difference between the egalitarian, non-hierarchical world of the spirits, and the racialized, if not racist, material world that formed the immediate surroundings of the Cercle Harmonique.

Almost twenty years earlier, and fifteen hundred miles to the north, the spirit of another famous person showed up at a séance table. Black Hawk (1767–1838) manifested for the first time during a séance in New York conducted by two sisters named Jennie and Annie Lord in 1857. In his lifetime, Black Hawk was an important Sauk leader who resisted white oppression in Illinois and what is now Wisconsin during what is now called the Black Hawk

War of 1832. However, his spirit, which subsequently also manifested through other mediums, most often spread a "benevolent" message that "symbolized a cosmic level of peaceful relationships between Indians and whites" (Troy, 2017, p. 39).[4] Appearing, in particular, in the 1860s and 1870s, "Indian spirits" often spread a message of a "peaceful relationship" and came in the spirit of forgiveness and reconciliation (McGarry, 2008, pp. 78–79; Cox, 2003; p. 198, p. 206–8). Scholars have argued that we cannot understand the presence of "Indian spirits" outside of policies designed to exterminate, segregate, or "civilize" living Native Americans (Cox, 2005; McGarry, 2008; Bennett, 2007; Troy, 2017). "Amongst the vast throngs of American mediums," Emma Hardinge Britten once wrote, "there is scarcely one who has not at some time or other been controlled, and that most beneficially, by Indian Spirits" (1892, p. 289). It is not a stretch, then, to suggest that as living Native Americans "vanished," they came to "haunt" white Spiritualist séances (McGarry, 2008, p. 66; Bennett, 2007, p. 12; Cox 2003, p. 190; cf. Troy, 2007, p. xvii).

Surveying the scholarship of Clark, Troy, McGarry, Bennett, and Cox—who work in fields such as (African) American religion and literary studies and thus, it begs repeating, outside of the field of Western esotericism—it becomes immediately evident that when it comes to communication with the dead, race is often not far away. We can approach the intersections of race and Spiritualism from a variety of vantage points. For instance, we could investigate—as Alex Owen has done so expertly in relation to gender (1989)—the complicated issue of agency (on the part of mediums and/or spirits). In this essay, however, I want to shed a comparative light on how the racialized manifestation of spirits—or lack thereof—in and during the séances of the Cercle Harmonique and selected examples in white American Spiritualism–produces, reinforces, transforms, or transcends racial constructs. The analysis that follows below is, by necessity, incomplete and simplified; what it demonstrates, however, is that Spiritualism has a racialized history that has been investigated in and from other disciplines and should be further interrogated in the field of (Western) esotericism. As will become evident, the members of the Cercle Harmonique and the white Spiritualists I will discuss had very different understandings of the significance and presence of race in the afterlife. What are we to make of these differences? How did race "show up" at the séance table? And

---

4 Although I focus here solely on manifestations of Black Hawk at the séances of late nineteenth-century white Spiritualists, I should note that in black Spiritualist churches, where the spirit of Black Hawk was and is also a frequent visitor, he is generally seen as a symbol of resistance against oppression, subjugation, and domination (Guillory, 2018; Troy, 2017; Wehmeyer, 2010).

what can this tell us about the "color line" in the second half of the nineteenth century?

To begin to answer these questions, I turn to prominent white Spiritualist Benjamin Coleman's *Spiritualism in America*, published in 1861. When Coleman attended a séance conducted by one of the Lord sisters, Black Hawk manifested. The spirit spoke in "broken English," Coleman writes, offering the statements "Me do something else for you" and "How you do, Mr. Coleman" as evidence (Coleman, 1861, p. 11–12). Black Hawk played one of the many instruments standing in the room, a tambourine, which he "jingled" in "the wildest manner" before proceeding to give an "Indian dance" during which, Coleman notes, "the dull heavy bumping and thumping sounds as if feet in moccasins, or Indian slippers, kept excellent time" (p. 11). Coleman's conclusion is jubilant: "the whole exhibition," he writes, "was a most marvellous and convincing proof of the presence of intelligent invisible agencies" (p. 12).

As Robert Cox writes, most white Spiritualists believed that race was maintained in the afterlife because they saw it as one of the strongest parts of one's identity, a "manifestation" of an "interior" state (Cox, 2003, p. 192). Reading Coleman's account, it becomes evident however that it could show up in very specific ways: in the form of racial stereotypes. The séance that Coleman attended was not an exception. As Troy (2017), McGarry (2008), and Bennett (2005; 2007) demonstrate, "Indian spirits" often manifested in highly racialized and stereotypical ways. Even if the majority of white American Spiritualists critiqued US policy as it related to the "Indian question" and lamented the murder of Native Americans in their periodicals, they also engaged in modes of racial stereotyping that suggest a belief in the cultural superiority of white people. Some white American Spiritualists believed, for instance, that "Indian spirits" resided in the lower realms of heaven, imagined as a "happy hunting ground" where they could continue to use their "traditional" customs and tools (ibid., p. 193). This conceptualization of Native American (after)life—and, in particular, that only "Indian spirits" resided here—perpetuates, in turn, racial stereotype and bespeaks that white people saw themselves as more technologically and culturally "advanced." Not only did race transcend death; racial hierarchies did so, too. To complicate matters further, supposed cultural inferiority did not necessarily imply spiritual inferiority, as there were other white Spiritualists, such as Eugene Crowell and Charles Hammond, who conveyed that "Indian spirits" were morally superior and occupied the highest spiritual realm (Cox, 2003, p. 194). Molly McGarry highlights, in turn, that some white Spiritualists saw "Indian spirits" as "powerful spiritual predecessors" that could function as spiritual guides— she notes, too, however, that this reverence of Native American forms of spirituality could easily translate into "unchecked cultural appropriation" (2008, p. 67).

There is considerable debate on how to interpret these stereotypes. For Troy, racial stereotypes were part of, in fact even necessary for, the process of "authenticating": speech patterns, movements, gestures, and dress helped mediums ensure their audience that the spirits they invoked were real (p. xix, 26–30, 65–68). "Mediums," Troy concludes "could not, in essence, break new ground in stereotype construction without first playing upon accepted ones" (p. 7). Cox, however, arrives at a different interpretation. Speaking of "becoming" or "being" "Indian" and utilizing Philip Deloria's well-known concept of "playing Indian," he suggests that "white medium" and "red spirit" seemed to merge, such that the audience "experienced a true interracial fusion, if only vicariously" (2003, p. 203).[5] This "fusion" was accompanied by "signifiers of cultural inferiority," however, implying that these séances involved a "declaration" of white superiority and, upon returning in/to white skin, an "affirmation" of white identity (p. 205). Where Troy sees a necessity, Cox exhibits a more pernicious aspect. Pushing his argument, we may conclude that racialized "others"—in this case "Indian spirits"—emerged and were used in the service of whiteness. Utilizing the spirits of the deceased is, then, an example of what

---

5 The notion of "playing Indian"—which details how whites used constructions of "Indianness" to produce and reinforce a particular "American identity"—offers the opportunity to consider Spiritualism alongside other forms of racialized performance, such as blackface minstrelsy, as Daphne Brooks (2006) and Bridget Bennett (2007) have done. Of course, the concepts of minstrelsy and "playing Indian" invokes the register of performance and spectacle—and, therefore, matters of identification, personification, mimicking—a register that Troy wishes to avoid (2017, p. xxvii). As rationale, Troy offers that mediums believed in "agencies outside of the self;" the framework of performance, she cautions, would necessarily regard all séances and mediums as frauds. This, it seems to me, is an overstatement: conceiving séances as a form of performance does not necessarily refute the veracity of these experiences. Troy, in fact, tacitly acknowledges that séances had a performative aspect when she discusses the presence of "Indian" dress, or costume. Moreover, placing Spiritualist séances in a comparative framework with other racialized performances allows us to see them as part of a wide and diverse set of cultural acts that wrestled with—and reinforced—racialized difference and hierarchy; it allows us to see, too, that "the bodies of spirit mediums," as Brooks writes, operate "as a point of encounter, as an imaginary site of contact and conflict, a frontier on which to locate both 'terror and pleasure'" (2006, p. 27). Brooks takes "terror and pleasure" from Saidiya Hartman's *Scenes of Subjection* (1997), which argues that minstrelsy and the slave auction block were "sites of performance" where black "suffering was transformed into wholesale pleasures" (p. 32). Brooks analysis is incisive. It also demonstrates the need for a larger range of methods and theories in the study of esoteric idea and practice. I return to this towards the end of the essay. I want to thank Adrienne Rooney for encouraging me to think through this issue.

Angela Riley and Kirsten Carpenter call "Indian appropriation" (2016). White American Spiritualism, to be sure, did not escape the long, ongoing history of white people appropriating and using the knowledge, practices, artifacts, identities, and bodies of Native Americans for their own benefit (see, among others, Deloria, 1998). Moreover, the temporal nature of the fusion of "red" and "white" reinscribed racial categories, if not hierarchies (see, on this issue, in particular Brooks, 2006). After all, irrespective of how one interprets these stereotypes, it is certain that "unlike white [spirits], Indian spirits bore the attributes of an entire race. Every spirit Indian was, in a sense, Every-Indian, stripped to the essentials" (Cox, 2003, p. 190; see also Bennett, 2007, p. 99; Troy, 2017, p. 30).

Part of the reason that manifestations of Black Hawk and countless nameless "Indian spirits" often relied on essentialized and racialized cultural representations of Native Americans was that white American Spiritualists interacted to a very limited extent with living Native Americans. Such representations were produced in and reinforced through books written by white authors, such as James Fenimore Cooper's *The Last of the Mohicans* (1826), and numerous plays (Cox, 2003; Troy, 2017). And while not all representations of Native Americans were the same—Troy (2017, p. 34), for instance, notes that the linguistic representation of "Indian spirits" oscillated between "broken English" and "noble speak," both of which hark back to racialized stereotypes of Native American speech and language—the wide diversity in language, culture, and religion among Native Americans was altogether reduced. What emerged and appeared at the séance table was "the white man's Indian" (McGarry, 2008, p. 67).

With the above in mind, we could ask if the spirits of Lincoln, Montesquieu, Voltaire, and Lee who manifested through members of the Cercle Harmonique were stand-ins for "the" white race.[6] We should ask, furthermore, if they appeared in a way that presented or depicted an essentialized conceptualization of whiteness. The answer, unsurprisingly, seems to be no. Abraham Lincoln, who appeared at the séance table because of his prominent position in US society and as a "martyr" for abolition (Clark, 2018), simply manifested as himself. In contrast, Black Hawk—even if he retained some of his unique characteristics in spirit (although as noted above, he advanced a message of reconciliation and peace that was rather distant from the message he espoused

---

6   Or, perhaps, "white races": as Painter (2010, p. ix) argues, Americans have always been convinced of the plurality of "more than one European race," which in and of itself bespeaks a certain privilege afforded to white people that was not afforded to people of color. I return to this below.

when still alive)—also appeared as "Every-Indian." To better understand why, we need to take into account the destructive and centuries-long history of racialization. Racial stereotyping is wrapped up with power; white people have historically controlled the process of racialization (which includes and is reinforced by racial stereotyping). One of the implications is that white people have named and categorized other peoples into racial groups, whereas whiteness itself has remained unnamed and invisible in the larger public domain (Dyer, 1997). As dominant voices and actors in public domains, white people could introduce a host of different representations of white people and whiteness; the more so, indeed, because whereas white people are seen as individuals, racialized minorities are often treated as an undifferentiated, homogeneous group. White spirits did not appear in an essentialized manner, in other words, because a white hegemony in the public and cultural domain prevented them from doing so.

There is some evidence, however, that essentialized representations of Native Americans did reach the Cercle Harmonique: a Native American spirit named Paloah told the group that the "peace pipe and tomahawk," which she regarded as expressions of "barbarism," were now "buried forever" (Clark, 2016, p. 137). Clark observes that this statement "contained a negative view of Native American religion," but in the context of our discussion above, we can also link this to stereotypical representations of Native Americans. This should come as no surprise: black Americans, too, would have had access to representations of the "white man's Indian." Moreover, even though racialized cultural representations also found way to the séance table in New Orleans, there was a significant difference: in spirit, Poloah was part of an "enlightened" and non-hierarchical "spiritual brotherhood" that included members of all racial groups, nationalities and ethnicities. Whereas white American Spiritualists, by and large, believed that race and nation (and racial hierarchies) remained significant and present in the afterlife, the Cercle Harmonique conceived the spirits that visited with them as "raceless." As Clark writes, "the races of material bodies no longer existed in the spirit world" (2016, p. 136). Racial hierarchies had no place in the spirit world—and should, indeed, have no place in the material world either.

We can begin to make sense of these differing treatments of race in the afterlife when we contextualize them within race relations in the United States. The members of the Cercle Harmonique, as Clark presses over and over, were acutely aware of the ways in which racism continued to shape American life. Even though the members of the group came from a "privileged background"—that is, they were free and educated—racial solidarity and racial equality were immediate, visceral concerns. Consider, for instance, that a week and a half after Lincoln's spirit delivered the message with which I opened this section, members of the white supremacist group White League occupied New Orleans—a city that, after the Civil War, witnessed outbursts of racial violence as well as moments of progress—for three days (Clark, 2018, p. 162). As racism continued to segregate the material world, communications with a spiritual, non-hierarchical, egalitarian brotherhood in which race had seemingly ceased to exist helped the Cercle Harmonique to envision a world in which racial hierarchies would be overcome.

The continued and pervasive existence of racial hierarchies had very different implications for white American Spiritualists. In many ways, their push for a more equitable treatment of Native Americans and a "politically non-racial society" was dependent on the racial make-up of the spirits that visited them. After all, it was precisely the fact that these spirits were "Indian" that allowed them to serve as "guides and instructors" in the fight for a more equitable, just society in which Native Americans would become full citizens (Troy, 2017, p. xiii; see also McGarry, 2008, p. 68). In doing so, "Indian spirits" had another function, too: appearing, in particular, in the 1860s and 1870s, they often spread a message of a "peaceful relationship" and/or came in the spirit of forgiveness and reconciliation (McGarry, 2008, pp. 78–79; Cox, 2003, pp. 198, 206–8). And many white American Spiritualists *were* seemingly committed to what we may now call a "post-racial" society. However, that undercurrents of white cultural superiority percolated in their practices, and that they supported policies amounting to assimilation, demonstrates that the "post-racial" is itself racially loaded and highly problematic. Most white American Spiritualists favored the dissolution of individual "tribes" and advocated Anglo-American education (Troy, 2017; McGarry, 2008). Yet, in doing so, as Troy incisively notes, they failed "to realize that instead of establishing a raceless society, they had furthered white hegemony" (Troy, 2017, pp. 147, 149).

In some ways, this blind spot may be the result of the fact that white American Spiritualists remained unaware of the fact that whiteness, too, was a particular, and invented, racialized category. As noted above, since white people had control over the production of racial categories, they could mark others as belonging to a certain race, while inventing themselves as "neutral" or "universal." Whiteness was thereby normative, but simultaneously invisible, unacknowledged, hidden, masked as default, color-free (see Nakayama and Krizek, 1995; Dryer, 1997). This remains commonplace: in fact, the phrase "people of color," although often used, is itself evidence of the continued neutrality of whiteness. In a society marked and demarcated by the color line, whiteness remained a powerful, dominating, yet often unacknowledged and understudied force.

2 Abduction

A century after Black Hawk and Lincoln returned as spirits, in the late summer of 1961, Betty and Barney Hill were on the way back to New Hampshire after a delayed honeymoon in Canada. Driving on a "deserted" road "just south of Lancaster," the couple witnessed something bright in the sky—a star, they initially thought, or a plane, or perhaps a "straying satellite." At some point, it became clear that it was none of these, but a UFO (Fuller, 1966, pp. 6–7). Stepping out of the car and into the field next to the road, Barney saw "at least half a dozen living beings" behind its windows, and immediately "he was certain he was about to be captured" (p. 16). Then, everything went hazy until the Hills were awoken by a beeping sound and realized that they were back in the car, and that Barney was, in fact, driving. Back home, the couple felt "clammy" and "unclean." Barney felt the unexplainable urge to go into the bathroom and examine his "lower abdomen" (pp. 19–20). Upon inspection, the couple realized their shoes were dirty, their watches broken, and Betty's dress ripped. They vowed not to discuss what happened with anyone—and what had, indeed, happened was at that point altogether unclear. However, "uncanny" traces, scary nightmares, and memory gaps compelled Betty, an avid reader of UFO literature, to report it to the National Investigative Committee of Aerial Phenomena (NICAP), in those days the most prominent UFO organization. The NICAP recommended hypnosis, which would become standard procedure in ufology circles.

The Hills' abduction story would become the first reported UFO abduction account in the U.S. The case—which was widely reported by the press, narrated by John Fuller in his bestseller *The Interrupted Journey* (1966), and made into a TV movie (1975)—served as a kind of blueprint for future UFO abduction narratives. It became the "origin story of the genre" (Lepselter, 2016, p. 65). Indeed, although each UFO abduction account is unique, we can also speak of the existence of a "generic narrative" (Luckhurst, 1998, p. 31; see also Bullard, 1989; Smith, 2001). This narrative has continued to evolve, but Betty and Barney Hill first voiced many of its core elements. These include being taken by unknown gray non-human beings and subjected to medical examinations (among which a pregnancy test), the experience of missing time and memory loss, and the eventual "recovery" of this experience in and through hypnosis.

But what does all this have to do with race? Whereas the manifestation of an "Indian spirit" in "moccasins" in and through a white female medium, or the presence of Abraham Lincoln at the séance table of the Cercle Harmonique, provides a very clear and straightforward starting point for thinking through the intersections of race and the esoteric, the Hills' experience—and ufology more generally—offers, at first sight, no such thing. And yet, Barney was black, and Betty was white, at a time when interracial marriages remained illegal in many U.S. states (it became legal across the country in 1967, following the landmark *Loving v. Virginia* U.S. Supreme Court case). In both popular and academic accounts, however, the interracial nature of their relationship has been mostly mentioned as a curious fact, rather than something that was part, perhaps even constitutive, of the abduction experience (Lepselter, 2012, p. 67). However, when it comes to esoteric phenomena, race shows up and comes to matter in both obvious and obscure ways. If we want to uncover and explore in depth how processes of racialization shape and are informed by esoteric ideas and practice, we also need to look beyond the most clear-cut examples. With the help of Susan Lepselter, Christopher Roth, and Stephen Finley, I will make a case here for the significance of race in the Hills' story, and abduction narratives more generally.

Roth (2005, p. 61) takes race seriously when he characterizes the Hills' story as "the suppressed trauma of a mixed-race couple during the civil rights era." Placing their abduction narrative in the context of the history of ufology, Roth sees it as a turning point. Whereas 1950s contactees relied on theosophical ideas "to reerect a toppled racial order"—in particular through their conceptualization of certain extraterrestrials as Aryan—"the Hills story grasps for a position from which white and black Americans can ponder, resolve, and transcend, racial divisions" (p. 61). Race, Roth notes and I concur, has everything to do with it. Consider the following transcript of a hypnosis session, included in Fuller's *Interrupted Journey*, in which Barney tries to describe what the people behind the window of the UFO looked like,

> DOCTOR: What was his face like? What did it make you think of?
> BARNEY: It was round. (Pauses for a moment, then:) I think of-I think of-a red-headed Irishman. I don't know why. (Another pause, then:) l think I know why. Because Irish are usually hostile to Negroes. And when I see a friendly Irish person, I react to him by thinking: I will be friendly. And I think this one that is looking over his shoulder is friendly. (1966, p. 90)

And then, a little further:

> DOCTOR: Oh. Did they have faces like other people. You said one was like a redheaded Irishman.
> BARNEY: (Describing the scene very slowly and carefully.) His eyes were slanted. Oh-his eyes were slanted! But not like a Chinese. (p. 92)

These exchanges thus demonstrate that thinking about extraterrestrials very much involves thinking about bodily difference, and, in a racialized "modern West" thus shapes and is informed by processes of racialization (Roth, 2005, pp. 71–4). I do not claim that race *determines* UFO abduction experiences (neither does Roth, for that matter), but to suggest that race somehow *shaped* these experiences seems rather obvious. Importantly, the first exchange cited above highlights that racial hierarchies and racial discrimination inform Barney's conceptualization of otherness. After all, his identification of the extraterrestrial as reminding him of a "red-headed Irishman" is all wrapped up in (racialized) hostility. Considering this, the fact that Barney, after seeing the beings, immediately felt that he would be captured gains heightened significance. In other words, we should ask how this feeling and his racially-inflected description of the extraterrestrials as a "red-headed Irishman" relate.

Race is constitutive of how we conceptualize extraterrestrials. Science fiction scholars have made this claim often. One of the first and still most famous novels about an alien invasion—H.G. Wells's *War of the Worlds* (1898)—was all about racialized human difference. Writing about an alien invasion from Mars functioned as a fictional outlet for Wells' reflections on the British invasion of Tasmania (Rieder, 2008, p. 5; Kripal, 2017, p. 56). Stories about encounters with extraterrestrials are, as Wells' famous novel also demonstrates, narratives about "us" versus "them" that have the potential to reinscribe if not radicalize the possibility for what Ashon Crawley (2017) and Nahum Chandler (2014) would call "categorical distinctions" that underlie the production of racial categories (see also Rubenstein, 2018). Simultaneously, however, UFO abduction accounts can also transcend these distinctions. Roth (2005, p. 80) calls attention to the fact that in her memoir, Betty Hill conceived the gray beings that abducted her as beings from the future; a future where, ostensibly, racial difference would be transcended, subsumed in all-grey. In "Close Encounters of Diverse Kinds" (2001), a comparative study of UFO abduction accounts and the organization of human difference in and through taxonomy, Jonathan Z. Smith also underscores the greyness of the extraterrestrials to suggest that UFO abduction accounts should be understood as myths that transcend racial categories. The uniformity of alien bodies, Smith writes, is "a striking exaggeration of our commonsense belief (...) that there is an essential core of human sameness" (p. 15). However, Smith too quickly overlooks the extent to which racial categories remain part of UFO abduction accounts, and that abduction accounts also reinscribe racial hierarchies.

If *The Interrupted Journey* is, as Roth also notes, despite itself a book about race, and if this book served as "blueprint" for all future accounts, then we must ask to what extent UFO abduction narratives are, generally, shaped by race. The first thing that stands out, then, is the curious (or perhaps not at all curious) fact that UFO abductions, when perusing academic texts, *seem* a very white phenomenon—and that, again, this whiteness seems largely understudied. In 2001, Brenda Denzler wrote that Barney Hill was one of only four persons of color who has reported a UFO abduction experience (2001, p. 196n79), and Susan Lepselter's ethnographic research in Arizona confirmed the overwhelming whiteness of ufology communities (2012, pp. 76, 156). However, a lack of reports does not necessarily imply that fewer people of color claim to have been abducted by extraterrestrials. It could be that they are less likely to speak openly about such experiences out of fear of further marginalization, or that their accounts are ignored in the Academy or by the U.S. government. Scholarship on UFOs, moreover, largely ignores the history of African American UFO traditions, such as the Nation of Islam (Pasulka, 2019, p. 237; Finley, 2016; Kripal, 2017). Studies of Stephen Finley and others have revealed that black people do, in fact, claim to have been abducted. In addition to Louis Farrakhan, leader of the Nation of Islam (Finley, 2012; Lieb, 1998; Bakker, 2013), we may include Prophet Yahweh, Riley Martin (Finley, 2016), and musicians Sun Ra (Szwed, 2012; Youngquist, 2015) and George Clinton (Finley, 2016).

Like in the study of Spiritualism, whiteness emerges as neutral, normative, and universal in the study of UFO abduction accounts. In a short and unpublished "position paper" on UFOs, Finley asks what we may have missed in our exclusive focus on white people (2015). This is an important question that we can ask of much academic research on esoteric phenomena. Finley notes that although UFOs may very well (also) have "universal" meanings and implications, the abduction accounts that he studies do emphasize the "particularity of race." Listing the various experiences of black people who have engaged extraterrestrials (some of whom are mentioned above), Finley posits the possibility of a deep connection between racialized subjectivity and abduction accounts. His interlocutors, he writes, connect their blackness with that of the universe, and as such reconceptualize blackness as "metaphysical." For these abductees, moreover, "aliens" are not the ultimate "other," but rather "kin." Finley links UFO abduction accounts to the transatlantic slave trade, framing white slavers as an "alien presence" that abducted black "bodies"—at which point, he notes, they in turn became an "alien presence" in the United States. This observation gains heightened significance when we take note of scholarship in black studies that demonstrates that what is at stake in conversations about race and racial difference is not merely a "social construct" or the topic of "identity," but a matter of who is considered to be "fully human" (see among others Fanon, 1952; Moten, 2008; 2013; Sharpe, 2016; Spillers, 1987; Weheliye, 2014; Wynter, 2003; 2015). It is important to keep this in mind when we assess and analyze the intersections between whiteness and (the study of) esotericism, as this underscores just how significant race and processes of racialization are in and to our current social order.

Finley's work helps me to emphasize that although the power to racialize has lain, historically, with white people, people of color have utilized esotericisms to produce new racial formations (for important examples, see Finley, Guillory and Page, 2015; Weisenfeld, 2016). But his provocations prompt, for me, also a question. If there is a link—experientially and epistemologically—between blackness and abduction, then what can we make of the fact that most of the abduction accounts that we have access to are reported by white people? What have we missed by ignoring race in the reports that we do study, in which white people claim to have been abducted? Racial constructs and racial hierarchies inform UFO abduction accounts. They also shape the way they have been studied: the questions asked or ignored, and the frameworks deployed or rejected.

One possibility, voiced by Roger Luckhurst (1998, p. 44) in an article that understands alien abduction narratives as the "science fictionalization of trauma" is that these stories—among many other things—allegorize "the foundation of America," which was built via "the abduction of Africans into slavery." The general tropes of these accounts—abductees are often restrained before they are transported to the space ship, undergo a variety of medical tests (often related to reproduction, such as the harvesting of sperm or eggs), have reported experiences of sexual assault, speak of "missing time," and believe their "hybrid" children to be stolen by aliens—are, to be sure, eerily similar to (although also displaying significant differences from) the experiences of enslaved Africans. Radicalizing Luckhurst's proposal, Adam Roberts suggests that we should understand UFO abduction experiences as a kind of "return of the repressed." With recourse to Freud's theory of repressed memory, he posits the possibility that although the narrative of American progress and success seeks to push "eighteenth and nineteenth century slaving" to the realm of the "political unconsciousness," it resurfaces in alien abduction narratives (2006, p. 106). In so doing, "mainstream America (…) interpolat[es] itself into the victim role" (ibid.).

Susan Lepselter's ethnographic research allows us to make the connections between UFO abduction experiences and America's traumatic past more explicit and tangible. In *The Resonance of Unseen Things* (2016) she jots down the many times that she's heard white people who experienced alien abductions reflect on the fact that to Native Americans, white people would have been an alien presence (p. 67). "We invaded their land," one of them notes—a twenty-first century statement that takes us right back to Wells' late nineteenth-century story. A flyer, handed to Lepselter during a UFO meeting, makes the connections even more clear, if also all the more ambiguous: "Do you have an interest in Native Americans, or maybe some Native American blood? It could be a sign that you've been abducted by aliens" (p. 78). Lepselter does not elaborate on the precise meaning or implication of this specific flyer but it is worth noting that connecting "abduction" by "aliens" with "Native American blood" seems to imagine a particular and rather uncomfortable intimacy or proximity between Native Americans and abduction. For Lepselter, such statements are part of a complex narrative of guilt and desire, appropriation and concern, commodification and interest.

How should we read these links between alien invasion and colonization in the context of our topic at hand? Lepselter writes about a "friend" from the "Hillview UFO Experiencers Group" who moved to Arizona, in part, to "be near Indians." A more charitable reading could thus suggest that one of the "outcomes" of alien abduction narratives is that white people become more interested in past and present Native American life and religion—even if, as Lepselter also makes clear, this interest is commodified and borders on appropriation. Rather than engaging living Native Americans, this informant ended up meeting like-minded white people (2016, p. 75). Here, whiteness recenters itself.

This brings me to another, admittedly more cynical reading. As UFO abduction narratives gain more and more prominence—in the public domain, in writings, in films, on TV—white people essentially replace Native Americans as the prime targets of invasion and abduction. In doing so, the prominence of white UFO abduction accounts trivializes, indeed erases, the traumatic pasts of Native Americans and black Americans, who are doubly displaced when we consider, once more, that their accounts are ignored. Here we see, again, the power of whiteness to not merely present itself as neutral and universal, but also (indeed therefore) to appropriate, claim, and own. This observation gains, in turn, heightened significance when we consider that white rights and demands to property and ownership were often developed and exercised in relation to the (continued) disenfranchisement, displacement, and dehumanization of African Americans and indigenous peoples (see, for example, Harris, 1993; Bhandar, 2018).

3 A Final Note on Method and Theory

The studies discussed in this essay demonstrate that Spiritualism and UFO abduction accounts have a racialized history. When we consider that some of these publications are older than fifteen years, we must conclude that we have known this for quite a while. But this has seemingly not (yet) compelled scholars in the field of (Western) esotericism to embrace race as a critical category of analysis, a fact that becomes particularly curious when we consider that Spiritualism now plays a central role in the "canon" of Western esoteric traditions. We must ask, in other words, why the study of esotericism privileges certain peoples, texts, ideas, themes and perspectives over others, a question that points us to persistent power imbalances, inequalities, and practices of "othering" (see also Bakker, 2020). Part of the reason for this neglect is the overwhelming but unrecognized, unacknowledged, and understudied whiteness of the field (Bakker, 2020; see also Finley, Guillory and Page, 2015). It seems as if most scholars in Western esotericism were (or are) largely unaware that whiteness is a racial category. This has allowed for a situation in which scholarship in the field focuses on white esoteric ideas and practices, yet does not investigate how (constructions of) whiteness shape and operate in (the study of) esoteric ideas and practice. As a result, dominant themes, concepts, and frameworks in the field are structured around what Sylvester Johnson, in a different context, would call a "core of white subjectivity" (2009, p. 160).

With the survey presented above in mind, I want to suggest here a second, if very much intertwined reason for the lack of research on the intersections of race and esotericism: a limited engagement with fields, approaches, discourses and texts in which race is a focal point of analysis. The scholars cited above come from a wide variety of fields: Christopher Roth and Susan Lepselter approach the UFO movement from anthropology; Bridget Bennett operates within the domain of literary, and more specifically, Victorian studies; Molly McGarry and Kathryn Troy are historians; and Emily Suzanne Clark works in American Religion. Yet all display an acute understanding of how race works and operates in American history and society, revealing an implicit (and often explicit) indebtedness to critical race theory. It seems to me possible, if not likely, that their scholarship was overlooked because of a "negative heuristic" (to use Egil Asprem's term, 2014, p. 15) that encouraged a refusal to engage texts with a specific, and theoretical, focus on race. That the field of Western esotericism works with a rather limited set of methods and theories—mainly historical methods and textual analysis—has been remarked by other scholars (Crockford and Asprem, 2018, p. 2; Asprem, 2014, p. 19; Finley, Guillory and Page, 2015a, pp. 1–3). In some cases, scholars even displayed an explicit aversion for "cultural studies" and "critical theory" (e.g. Hanegraaff, 2019; cf. Strube, 2021). And while this narrow methodological scope is certainly changing—consider, for instance, recent special issues on esotericism and cognitive science (in *Aries*) and esotericism and ethnography (in *Corre-*

spondences)—several frameworks and approaches remain understudied and underrepresented, among which frameworks and approaches developed in decolonial, ethnic, black, and whiteness studies (see, for an exception, Gray, 2019).

At the risk of stating the obvious, I posit furthermore that the limited engagement with these approaches in the study of esotericism is, in itself, racialized: working from a privileged position in which whiteness is seen as normative and neutral, if not universal, scholars have not been forced to engage with race, and have not been encouraged to confront that whiteness is a racialized category that demands careful scrutiny. Although whiteness studies first came to Europe in the 1990s, when the field of Western esotericism was still in its infancy, scholars could ignore it because they had not been forced to engage scholarship that thinks critically and carefully about whiteness and race. The overwhelming whiteness of the field and the limited amount of methodologies engaged are connected.

Recent years have witnessed a number of publications of scholars working in the field of (Western) esotericism that do engage race—and more are in the pipeline. It is my hope that these works intensify the much-needed diversification of methods in the field. After all, embracing race as an analytical category in the field of (Western) esotericism demands not only an awareness of the racial diversity of esoteric belief and practice, but also a rigorous and sustained engagement with frameworks developed in fields such as black studies, ethnic studies, whiteness studies, and critical race theory.

Bibliography

Alexander, M. (2010) *The New Jim Crow: Mass Incarceration in the Age of Colorblindness*. New York: The New Press.

Asprem, E. (2014) "Beyond the West: Toward a New Comparativism in the Study of Esotericism," *Correspondences*, 2(1), pp. 3–33.

Bakker, J.M. (2013) "'On the Knowledge of God, Self and Enemy': Secrecy, Concealment, and Revelation in the Nation of Islam," Unpublished MA thesis, University of Amsterdam.

Bakker, J.M. (2020) "Hidden Presence: Race and the History, Construct and Study of Western Esotericism," *Religion*, 50(4), pp. 479–503.

Bennett, B. (2007) *Transatlantic Spiritualism and Nineteenth-Century American Literature*. Manchester: Manchester University Press.

Berry, C. (1876) *Experiences in Spiritualism*. London: James Burns.

Bhandar, B. (2018) *Colonial Lives of Property: Law, Land, and Racial Regimes of Ownership*. Durham: Duke University Press.

Bonilla-Silva, E. (2003) *Racism Without Racists: Color-blind Racism and the Persistence of Racial Inequality in the United States*. Lanham: Rowman & Littlefield.

Brooks, D. (2006) *Bodies in Dissent: Spectacular Performances of Race and Freedom, 1850–1910*. Durham: Duke University Press.

Bullard, T.E. (1989) "UFO Abduction Reports: The Supernatural Kidnap Narrative Returns in Technological Guise," *Journal of American Folklore*, 102, pp. 147–170.

Chandler, N. (2014) *X: The Problem of the Negro as a Problem for Thought*. New York: Fordham University Press.

Clark, E.S (2016) *A Luminous Brotherhood: Afro-Creole Spiritualism in Nineteenth-Century New Orleans*. Chapel Hill: University of North Carolina Press.

Clark, E.S. (2018) "'To Battle for Human Rights': Afro-Creole Spiritualism and Martyrdom," *Journal of Africana Religions*, 6(1), pp. 161–189.

Coleman, B. (1861) *Spiritualism in America*. London: F. Pitman.

Cox, R.S. (2003) *Body and Soul: A Sympathetic History of American Spiritualism*. Charlottesville: University of Virginia Press.

Crawley, A.T. (2017) *Blackpentecostal Breath: The Aesthetics of Possibility*. New York: Fordham University Press.

Crockford, S. and Asprem E. (2018) "Ethnographies of the Esoteric: Introducing Anthropological Methods and Theories to the Study of Contemporary Esotericism," *Correspondences*, 6(1), pp. 1–23.

Denzler, B. (2001) *The Lure of the Edge: Scientific Passions, Religious Beliefs, and the Pursuit of UFOs*. Berkeley: University of California Press.

Du Bois, W.E.B. (1903) *The Souls of Black Folk*. Chicago: A.C. McClurg & Co.

Fanon, F. (1952) *Black Skin/White Masks*. New York: Grove Press.

Ferguson, C. (2012) *Determined Spirits: Eugenics, Heredity and Racial Regeneration in Anglo-American Spiritualist Writing, 1848–1930*. Edinburgh: Edinburgh University Press.

Finley, S.C. (2012) "The Meaning of Mother in Louis Farrakhan's "Mother Wheel": Race, Gender, and Sexuality in the Cosmology of the Nation of Islam's UFO," *Journal of the American Academy of Religion*, 80(2), pp. 434–465.

Finley, S.C. (2015), "UFOs: A Position Paper," presented at "Beyond the Spinning: Shifting the Conversation around the UFO Phenomenon," a symposium sponsored by the Center for Theory and Research, Esalen Institute, at Institute of Noetic Sciences, Petaluma, California, September 11–13, 2015.

Finley, S.C. (2016) "The Supernatural in the African American Experience," in Kripal, J.J. (ed.) *Religion: Super Religion*. New York: Macmillan Reference USA, pp. 231–46.

Finley, S.C., Guillory, M.S., and Page Jr., H.R. (eds.) (2015) *Esotericism in African American Religious Experience: "There is a Mystery*, Leiden: Brill.

Fuller, J.G. (1966; 1967) *The Interrupted Journey: Two Lost Hours 'Aboard a Flying Saucer'*. New York: Dial Press.

Goldberg, D.T. (2015). *Are We All Postracial Yet?* New York: Polity Press.

Goodrick-Clarke, N. (1985) *The Occult Roots of Nazism: Secret Aryan Cults and Their Influence on Nazi Ideology*. New York: New York University Press.

Goodrick-Clarke, N. (2003) *Black Sun: Aryan Cults, Esoteric Nazism and the Politics of Identity*. New York: New York University Press.

Granholm, K. (2013) "Locating the West: Problematizing the Western in Western Esotericism and Occultism," in Bogdan, H. and Djurdjevic G. (eds.) *Occultism in a Global Perspective*. London/New York: Routledge, pp. 17–36.

Gray, B. (2019) "The Traumatic Mysticism of Othered Others: Blackness, Esotericism, and Islam in the Five Percenters," *Correspondences*, 7(1), pp. 201–238.

Guillory, M.S. (2018). *Spiritual and Social Transformation in African American Spiritual Churches*. New York: Routledge.

Hanegraaff, W.J. (2019) "Rejected Knowledge...So You Mean That Esotericists Are the Losers of History?" in Hanegraaff, W.J., Forshaw, P., and Pasi, M. (eds.) *Hermes Explains: Thirty Questions about Western Esotericism. Celebrating the 20-Year Anniversary of the Centre for History of Hermetic Philosophy and Related Currents at the University of Amsterdam*. Amsterdam: Amsterdam University Press, pp. 145–52.

Harris, C. (1993) "Whiteness as Property," *Harvard Law Review*, 106(8), pp. 1707–1791.

Hartman, S. (1997) *Scenes of Subjection: Terror, Slavery and Self-Making in Nineteenth-Century America*. New York: Oxford University Press.

Johnson, S.A. (2009) "Religion Proper and Proper Religion: Arthur Fauset and the Study of African American Religions," in Curtis IV, E.E. and Brune Sigler, D. (eds.) *The New Black Gods: Arthur Huff Fauset and the Study of African American Religions*. Bloomington: Indiana University Press, pp. 145–70.

Knight, M.M. (2019) "'I am Sorry, Mr. White Man, These are Secrets that You are Not Permitted to Learn': The Supreme Wisdom Lessons and Problem Book," *Correspondences*, 7(1), pp. 167–200.

Kripal, J.J. (2017) *Secret Body: Erotic and Esoteric Currents in the History of Religions*. Chicago: University of Chicago Press.

Lepselter, S. (2016) *The Resonance of Unseen Things: Poetics, Power, Captivity, and UFOs in the American Uncanny*. Ann Arbor: University of Michigan Press.

Lieb, M. (1998) *Children of Ezekiel: Aliens, UFOs, the Crisis of Race, and the Advent of End Times*. Durham: Duke University Press.

Lloyd V.W. (2016) "Managing Race, Managing Religion," in Khan, J.S. and Lloyd, V.W. (eds.) *Race and Secularism in America*. New York: Columbia University Press, pp. 1–21.

Luckhurst, R. (1998) "The Science-Fictionalization of Trauma: Remarks on Narratives of Alien Abduction," *Science Fiction Studies*, 25(2), pp. 29–52.

Marable, M. and Agard-Jones, V. (eds.) (2008) *Transnational Blackness: Navigating the Global Color Line*. New York: Palgrave MacMillan.

McGarry, M. (2008) *Ghosts of Futures Past: Spiritualism and the Politics of Nineteenth-Century America*. Berkeley: University of California Press.

Moten, F. (2008) "The Case of Blackness," *Criticism*, 50(2), pp. 177–218.

Moten, F. (2013) "Blackness and Nothingness (Mysticism in the Flesh)," *The South Atlantic Quarterly*, 112(4), pp. 737–80.

Nakayama, T.K. & Krizek, R.L (1995). "Whiteness: A Rhetoric," *Quarterly Journal of Speech*, 81(3), pp. 291–309.

Omi, M. and Winant, H. (1994) *Racial Formation in the United States: From the 1960s to the 1990s*. New York: Routledge.

Owen, A. (1989) *The Darkened Room: Women, Power and Spiritualism in Late Victorian England*. Chicago: Chicago University Press.

Painter, N.I. (2010) *A History of White People*. New York: W.W. Norton & Company.

Pasi, M. (2010) "Oriental Kabbalah and the Parting of West and East in the Early Theosophical Society," in Huss, B., Pasi, M., and Stuckrad, K.v. (eds.) *Kabbalah and Modernity: Interpretations, Transformations, Adaptations*. Leiden/Boston: Brill, pp. 151–66.

Pasulka, D.W. (2019) *American Cosmic: UFOs, Religion, Technology*. Oxford: Oxford University Press.

Polk, P. (2010) "'He Will Remember Me': Anglo-American Spiritualists, Slavery, and the Ghosts of Miscegenation." *Southern Quarterly*, 47(4), pp. 24–42.

Rieder, J. (2008) *Colonialism and the Emergence of Science Fiction*. Middletown: Wesleyan University Press.

Riley, A.R. and Carpenter, K.A. (2016) "Owning Red: A Theory of Indian (Cultural) Apprpriation," *Texas Law Review*, 94, pp. 859–931.

Roberts, A. (2004) *Science Fiction* (Second Edition). London: Routledge.

Roth, C.F. (2005) "Ufology as Anthropology: Race, Extraterrestrials, and the Occult," in Battaglia, D. (ed.) *E.T. Culture: Anthropology in Outer Spaces*. Durham: Duke University Press, pp. 38–93.

Roukema, A. and Kilner-Johnson, A. (2018) "Editorial: Time to Drop the 'Western,'" *Correspondences*, 6(2), pp. 1–7.

Rubenstein, M.-J. (2018) *Pantheologies: Gods, Worlds, Monsters*. New York: Columbia University Press.

Sharpe, C. (2016) *In the Wake: On Blackness and Being*. Durham: Duke University Press.

Silva, D.F.d. (2007) *Toward a Global Idea of Race*. Minneapolis: University of Minnesota Press.

Smith, J.Z. (2001) "Close Encounters of Diverse Kinds," in Muzruchi, S.L. (ed.) *Religion and Cultural Studies*. Princeton: Princeton University Press, pp. 3–21.

Spillers, H.J. (1987) "Mama's Baby, Papa's Maybe: An American Grammar Book," *Diacritics*, 17(2), pp. 64–81.

Staudenmaier, P. (2014) *Between Occultism and Nazism: Anthroposophy and the Politics of Race in the Fascist Era*. Leiden: Brill.

Strube, J. (2021) "Towards the Study of Esotericism without the 'Western'": Esotericism from the Perspective of a Global Religious History," in Asprem, E. and Strube, J. (eds.) *New Approaches to the Study of Esotericism*. Leiden and Boston: Brill, pp. 45–66.

Strube, J. (2016) "Transgressing Boundaries: Social Reform, Theology, and the Demarcations between Science and Religion," *Aries*, 16(1), pp. 1–11.

Szwed, J. (2012) *Space is the Place: The Life and Times of Sun Ra*. New York: Knopf Doubleday Publishing Group.

Troy, K. (2017) *The Specter of the Indian: Race, Gender, and Ghosts in American Seances, 1848–1890*. New York: SUNY Press.

Weheliye, A.G. (2014) *Habeas Viscus: Racializing Assemblages, Biopolitics, and Black Feminist Theories of the Human*. Durham: Duke University Press.

Wehmeyer, S. (2010) "Marching Bones and Invisible Indians: African American Spiritualism in New Orleans, Past and Present," *Southern Quarterly*, 47(4), pp. 43–60.

Weisenfeld, J (2016) *New World A-Coming: Black Religion and Racial Identity During the Great Migration*. New York: New York University Press.

Wynter, S. (2003) "Unsettling the Coloniality of Being/Power/Truth/Freedom: Towards the Human, After Man, Its Overrepresentation—An Argument," *CR: The New Centennial Review*, 3(3), pp. 257–337.

Youngquist, P. (2016) *A Pure Solar World: Sun Ra and the Birth of Afrofuturism*. Austin: University of Texas Press.

"What Can the Whole World Be Hiding?": Exploring *Africana* Esotericisms in the American Soul-Blues Continuum

Hugh R. Page, Jr. and Stephen C. Finley

The essays in *Esotericism in African American Religious Experience: "There is a Mystery"* ... (Finley, Guillory and Page, 2015) inscribe the broad contours for trans-disciplinary examination of esoteric thought and practice in the *Africana* world. Having established the preliminary groundwork for a new field—*Africana* Esoteric Studies (AES)—the stage is set for exploration of the ways in which secrecy, concealment, and selective disclosure of information deemed essential for survival function within an array of African and African-Diasporan settings, particularly those that are part of the Atlantic World (on the nature of this area of cultural exchange, see the now classic treatment of Gilroy, 1993).

As is to be expected, much work remains to be done in articulating the boundaries and teasing out the methodological particularities for this new enterprise. Such must involve, but is certainly not limited to, offering suitably inclusive, yet non-essentialist, parameters for that part of the *Africana milieu* whose esoteric elements are embraced by AES and clarifying the theoretical underpinnings of this trans-disciplinary enterprise. Another has to do with delimiting the relationship of AES to the already established discipline of Western esotericism.

The current essay hopes further to advance this process by examining four issues: (1) by what *criteria* figures are deemed to be either creators or critics of the artifacts and lore constitutive of both Western esotericism and AES; (2) the discursive and experiential *matrices* within which theories of the esoteric have heretofore been articulated; (3) the role that visual and performing artists have played in the creation and promulgation of esoteric cosmologies; and (4) the extent to which more expansive methodological and hermeneutical paradigms may create space for the engagement of persons, movements, and ideational currents often considered peripheral in terms of their relationship to the Western esoteric mainstream. It will also offer an experimental paradigm for thinking about African-American esotericism, grounded in critical and aesthetic engagement of expressive culture.

The essay will utilize as historical touchstones several key *foci* of and contributors to Western esotericism as well as selected artists in the American

© HUGH R. PAGE, JR. AND STEPHEN C. FINLEY, 2021 | DOI:10.1163/9789004446458_010
This is an open access chapter distributed under the terms of the CC BY-NC-ND 4.0 license.

Soul-Blues *continuum* of the late 1960s to the early 1970s. The latter will be featured because of their creation, adaptation, or re-appropriation—during a period of remarkable civic unrest—of disparate sources in the fashioning of *Africana* esotericisms; and their social positioning as *prophetic figures* through which such traditions are disclosed, *gate keepers* hinting at the existence of alternative realities, creators of new *Africana Weltanschauungen*, and grassroots *theorists*. The essay will also use, as an illustrative model, an experimental interpretive method (flash non-fiction) for engaging selected African-American musical artists. Such will include the group Earth, Wind & Fire, the refrain from whose song, "The World's a Masquerade," serves as inspiration for the title of this essay.

This investigation will be suggestive rather than exhaustive in scope. Two of its more important desired outcomes will be a deeper appreciation of: (1) the role that artists play as stewards, creators, and interpreters of *esoterica* in Western esotericism and AES; as well as (2) the ways in which signature artifacts and iconic performances become generators of context–specific *Africana* esoteric worldviews *and* the theories deployed in understanding them.

1   Prolegomenon—Epistemological, Theoretical, and Methodological Contestations

Conversations about "Western esotericism" take one immediately into a fraught realm of contested nomenclature, both complementary and discordant methodologies, and competing notions about both the cultural phenomena being studied and the *Sitze im Leben* in which such work is conducted. The same can be said of recent efforts to interrogate Western esotericism critically and propose alternative approaches for studying esotericism in general. Evidence of such can be clearly seen in Wouter Hanegraaff's article on the history and global scope of esotericism (2015, p. 4). His arguments: in favor of maintaining the designation "Western esotericism" to describe a disparate range of "beliefs, practices, and traditions of knowledge that the Enlightenment has rejected in its own backyard" (p. 86); justifying the use of "Western" in reference to the historically situated epistemological domain in which the study of esotericism unfolds (p. 82); in support of research exploring the global diffusion of European esoteric traditions as well as studies that examine cultural phenomena and lore that "resist discursive language and logical analysis" (p. 87); and cautioning against forcing "traditional beliefs and practices" encountered throughout the world into the "Western category of 'esotericism'" (p. 86) are cogent—in some cases compelling—though not altogether convincing.

One can reasonably take issue with any conceptualization of "Western esotericism" that defines it exclusively in terms of the materialistic and empirical norms of the Enlightenment. If one looks, for example, at the historical life settings of *subaltern* populations subject to acts of colonial violence and repression, tools of resistance were often—by nature and necessity—placed under a veil of secrecy. They became, thereby, part of an esoteric *poetics* and *praxis* of liberation. In an African-American context, this could encompass the symbols emblematic of escape encoded in Black Spirituals, way stations on the Underground Railroad, family recipes, traditions of land-keeping (Gundaker, 1998), or even the *materia medica* from indigenous systems of healing. Such ideas and practices were made necessary by the conditions of existence that made Black life in the United States precarious. Moreover, many other examples of secretly coded esoteric cultural artifacts were produced in African-American esoteric *milieus*, such as the Harlem Renaissance. African-American literary theorist, Jon Woodson, may be the leading scholar on this subject. Woodson has done the most extensive work, tracking and interpreting Harlem Renaissance literature as African-American esoteric interventions into European and American occult texts (Woodson, 1999, pp. 1–28).

Among Woodson's significant works on the subject of African-American esotericism are his book, *To Make a New Race: Gurdjieff, Toomer, and the Harlem Renaissance* (1999) and his chapter in *Esotericism in African American Religious Experience: "There Is a Mystery"...* entitled "The Harlem Renaissance as Esotericism: Black Oragean Modernism" (2014). Woodson contends that much of the literature that has come to represent the Harlem Renaissance was produced by a secret enclave of African-American esoteric intellectuals, led by writer Jean Toomer, but that included Zora Neal Hurston, Melvin Tolson, Nella Larson, Wallace Thurman, George Schuyler, Rudolph Fisher, and many other literary prodigies. These thinkers took European and American esoteric thought such as that of George Ivanovich Gurdjieff and occult leaders who studied his systems or who studied with him, such as Alfred Richard Orage and Pyotr Demianovich Ouspensky, and turned these esoteric systems into something uniquely African-American. In short, they utilized these thought systems—critiquing some of the racial animus that they found within them—and transformed them into something that was not just contemplative but that had to be enacted; they required action, specifically with regard to race and racism. Indeed, while Toomer studied directly with Gurdjieff, the "Black esoteric underground," in the words of Hugh R. Page, Jr., of the Harlem Renaissance transmuted occult thought into revolutionary African-American literature that served to subvert the vicissitudes of racialized existence. This creative alteration of something pre-existing into something that differed qualitatively from its former state, which specifically served the intentions and purposes of African-American life, was one of the hallmarks of Africana culture in the United States. In some cases, African Americans took something that was used in service of their oppression, and flipped it, changing its meaning and function to something used to create new life worlds. Moreover, *Africana* esoteric thought was expansive since it was reflected in many other aspects of the movement, such as in the art of Aaron Douglas and the philosophical musings of Alain Locke.

Most of the aforementioned would not have been part of the "Global Dustbin of Rejected Knowledge" (Hanegraaff, 2015, p. 64), but many of them would have been perceived as implicitly threatening to those in Europe and the Americas whose power and wealth were enhanced by tools of empire building derived in part from Enlightenment science. Here, one could certainly include technologies used to subdue, imprison, transport, and commodify *Africana* bodies. Which is to say, new perspectives and approaches to the study of Western esotericism might well consider the importance of embodiment, which, heretofore, has not taken center stage because the disciplinary method has privileged historiography. The "dustbin of rejected knowledge," then, becomes strictly about excluded ideas (cf. Asprem, 2021). But what then of rejected bodies: people whose identities were created in the very processes of the West that yielded "rejected knowledge?" It is impossible to speak of *Africana* Esoteric Studies without giving serious consideration to the idea of "rejected people" whose knowledge was cast aside precisely because of their embodiment. Their knowledge about the world has been doubly concealed in this context; their "esotericism" has not historically registered as "rejected knowledge" within the discourses and schemes of Western esotericism and the West, more generally, while, at the same time, they have been forced to conceal and reveal selectively their Truths within intellectual and cultural worlds in which African-American "Truth" (capital "T") has been written and intellectualized as an impossibility across discursive and semiotic fields. This is an issue to which Finley, Guillory, and Page make reference in the opening chapter of *Esotericism in African American Religious Experience* (2015). Thus, black bodies were constituted as the esoteric of Western esotericism, the people most rejected in modernity, whose most meaningful ideas were relegated to the "dustbin" of the "dustbin" (cf. also Bakker, 2021).

Because *blackness* is ontologically mapped as *surface*, according to Philosopher George Yancy (2004, p. 9), rather than interiority, whose meaning is disbursed across its skin, black bodies were doubled, perhaps tripled, since to be black was and is already the quintessential rejection. To gloss Fanon's *Black Skin, White Masks* (1967, p. 112), the agential corporeal schema of black embodiment is reduced to and externalized as a racial epidermal schema, and, indeed, as Yancy notes "there is no apparent position of externality from which the black is able to negotiate his identity" (2004, p. 13). That is, within the West's discursive schemes and racial structures, blackness is ontologically frozen as inferior and mute, thereby rendering black critical thought unintelligible and illogical in Western intellectual frames of reference. This is why the maintenance of the category "Western" and all its historical and racial significations amounts to an epistemic consolidation of power that determines what knowledge is legitimate and what is not, what is apprehended and what remains obscured, and what is pure transcendence and what is externalized as immanence.

To this end, questions can be raised about Hanegraaff's methodologically grounded rationale for maintaining the use of the term "Western" to identify the intellectual domain in which so-called "rejected knowledge" (2015, p. 66) is engaged (cf. Strube, 2021). The same is true of his notion that esoteric *realia* are only made known to us "as specific products of Western culture" (p. 82). Ways of seeing, hearing, and knowing discarded by the West—and other epistemic discourses of empowerment created within the *Africana* (i.e., African and African-Diasporan) World—have often been curated according to canons and passed on *via* an assortment of media, some of which are *hybrid* and others that are neither European nor Western. Furthermore, those ideas and artifacts judged to be esoteric according to specifically African-American criteria are often understood as part of a legacy from an actual, imagined, or longed-for homeland, rather than as the fruit of cultural production in the West.

Tracey Hucks' *Yoruba Traditions & African American Religious Nationalism* (2012) is most insightful here. This notion of a *homeland*, which animates many of the sources and *realia* that are used by and constitute *Africana* Esoteric Traditions (AETs) are not insignificant, and Hucks engages in a methodologically rich approach, which includes ethnography (necessary, since AETs often have no archive for historiography), to uncover and make sense of what *Africana* religions such as African-American or "African Diasporic" Yoruba religions are doing. Hucks also gives attention to religious groups like the Nation of Islam, whose ideas and practices have been greatly misunderstood in popular discourses. What she argues is that *Africana* religions' longing for a homeland is much more symbolic than political in the sense that such longings have religious rather than decidedly political intentions. To this end, such religious communities are not interested in becoming nation-states. Their quests for imagined or symbolic homelands have much more to do with experiences of displacement and otherness; these are communities that have been violated, marginalized, and separated from their actual and mythological origins. Thus,

Africana religions re-imagine beginnings in service of new epistemologies and ontologies that would (re-)authenticate their humanity in a hostile world that often denied it.

Re-authentication is important for Hucks. While the site of religion allowed African Americans to create new realities, knowledge, and identities, these served—not as new *per se*—but as "reconnections" to cosmologies and mythologies that signified some original state of being that transcended their racialized existences in which the meanings of their bodies were formulated by others and thrust back at them *as them*. This could only result in an experience of alienation from their own bodies, which their own autonomous truth, to borrow a term from Charles H. Long, would not allow them to recognize *as themselves*, but rather as the products of a racist and racializing western project. Re-imagining a homeland, thus, was a creative project of transcendence that afforded new ontologies and epistemologies in a world where there was no intimacy of knowledge *of* African-Americans, only a concretizing and distancing knowledge *about* them. African-Americans, then, were able to create new systems of knowledge, appropriating multiple sources including those that were discarded and abandoned in the West.

Regarding analysis of knowledge abandoned in the wake of the Enlightenment and diffused worldwide, such is crucial. One example would be the spread and reception of various forms of Freemasonry among African Americans beginning in the late eighteenth and early nineteenth centuries, including Prince Hall Freemasonry (Page, 2003). Furthermore, the embrace and adaptation of European esoteric traditions (e.g., Rosicrucian, Elus Cohens, and Martinist) in West African and Caribbean contexts offers opportunities to assess how such traditions were preserved and/or brought into conversation with philosophies and cosmologies indigenous to these regions.

Hanegraaff's caution to avoid "terminological imperialism" (2015, p. 86) is well taken. Imposing *etic* categories on phenomena for which *emic* taxonomies are available (if, at times, not readily accessible) is a danger in ethnographic description and comparison. Equally problematic, however, is the tendency toward claiming exclusive ownership of terms like esotericism, culture, religion, etc., by one or more academic disciplines; or insisting that research on them conform to an established set of methodological conventions or engage a specific body of secondary literature. For example, Hanegraaff objects to the way that the co-editors of *Esotericism in African American Religious Experience* define esotericism and what he considers their failure to engage, "twenty years of theoretical debate" (2015, p. 61n22). However, just as he provides his own definition of esotericism and selects those with whom he will be in conversation about its essential features—i.e., E.B. Tylor, Lucien Lévy-Bruhl, Carl

Jung, Richard Wilhelm, and Antoine Faivre (2015, pp. 71–80)—do the aforementioned co-editors not have the right to define terms, establish methods, and determine those with whom they will engage in discussion? Moreover, the extent to which sustained and nuanced theoretical debate has been a cornerstone of Western esotericism to date is open to question. Paul Lawrence Dunbar, Zora Neale Hurston, Houston Baker, Kevin Young, and Helena Andrews—to name just a few—introduce us to a rich nomenclature of secrecy and hiddenness within *Africana* life in the North American Diaspora. Such includes Dunbar's nuanced understanding of masking,[1] Hurston's interpretation of lying (see, for example, Hurston, 1990), Baker's notion of being "trained" (1984, pp. 8, 10), Young's conception of the "hiding tradition" (2012, p. 23), and Andrews' definition of "reserve" (2012, p. 37).

Moreover, Hanegraaff's contention that those luminaries studying beliefs that ran counter to Enlightenment thought did not hold that such traditions were confined to the West is worthy of note (2015, p. 70). However, the list of those he identifies as contributors to this scholarly conversation is somewhat narrow (e.g., Waite, Baumann, Magee, Otto, Granholm, Asprem, Strube, Godwin, Pasi, Partridge, Said, etc.) and excludes, for example, those paving the way for the establishment of AES. He also corrects his own prior assumption about the racial homogeneity of those involved in esoteric activities (p. 60n21), given perspectives presented in the anthology edited by Finley, Guillory, and Page (2015).

2   Toward a New Paradigm

One wonders about the potential of context-specific and historically framed methodologies focusing on esotericism(s) in the *Africana* world: interventions that use as starting points artifacts and ideas derived from African and African-Diasporan life settings. Approaches of this kind can proceed from locally derived definitions of the esoteric and situate the concept within disparate *Africana* imaginaries; focus attention on those that create and/or curate esoteric lore from *Africana* and other cultural spaces; and offer readings (or, to use a concept from the work of Charles Long, "significations"; 1986, pp. 1–9) of the esoteric within and beyond *Africana* settings.

---

[1] See his poem, "We Wear the Mask"—https://www.poetryfoundation.org/poems/44203/we-wear-the-mask (accessed July 29, 2020).

The balance of this essay will be dedicated to one such experimental "signification," creative and critical in orientation, and an assessment of the potential impact of such interventions for the study of esotericism. Utilizing "flash non-fiction" (FNF), complemented by the second-person narration utilized to great effect by Claudia Rankine in *Citizen: An American Lyric* (2014), we offer a partial theoretical map for the esoteric topography of African-American music from the late 1960s and early 1970s. Miller and Paola (2012, p. 110) describe FNF as a concise (1,000 words or less), lyrical, imaginative, targeted, and evocative narrative centering on a single theme or image. We proceed from the assumption that on occasion, esoteric realities are perhaps best explored through esoteric genres.

3 Not the Way It Is, but the Way "It Tiz ...": An Africana Esoteric Signification

"Playlist" is one of many words in the twenty-first century *lexicon* you find endlessly fascinating. It conjures moments of cognitive dissonance. What have "play" and "list" to do with each other? Where is the supposed relationship to music? One might well "play" a song, or even read an album's inventory of "cuts." Listening, however, is an altogether different experience.

How far you've come from 45s, LPs, reel-to-reel recorders, 8-track players, and cassette tapes, some of which you still own and enjoy. You are neither an anachronism nor a Luddite. Neither are you a hoarder. You've come to appreciate the power—the *àshe*, as it were (Thompson, 1984, p. 5)—in old things. Even before you learned who he was, you've known that Amiri Baraka was right about African-American music containing the narrative of Black history (Jones, 1963, p. viii). Knowing that keeps you from discarding those vestiges of the Analog Era, on which ancestors and elders recorded our stories and encoded our secrets. You gather originals and re-mastered versions from *Bob's Blues and Jazz Mart* and other sanctuaries that traffic in the remnants of *Africana* culture (Reich, 2016). You mine the digital catalogues of *iMusic* and *Pandora* for albums and songs no longer easily accessible on other media. You return to them time and again, each encounter bringing with it new realizations. Each engagement reveals hidden truths to you, especially when you are capable of setting aside the "respectability politics" that once characterized Black creative expression as dangerous; and the Gospel as the only authoritative truth. You take Ben Harper's advice and "listen close to what you see" (1997). You heed James Blood Ulmer's admonition to "use the concept of the Blues to feel" your "way around" (2011). You "build" against convention like

Erykah Badu in, "On and On" (1997), and trust that those with "ears to hear" (Deuteronomy 29:4; Mark 4:9—New Revised Standard Version of the Bible) will understand the "method to your madness," as some of the "old folk" say. It's fine if they don't get it. An old warning—"Tell some, keep some, you'll always have some"—has a chastening effect when you consider bringing those things that have kept us alive into the academy for intellectual dissection. The tradition keepers sensed that some things should *never* be shared.

"Back in the day," there was so much you didn't understand. Some knowledge was dangerous: so much so that it was only selectively disclosed to Black youth. *Not knowing* kept you from misreading the secrets "grown folk" talked about when they thought you weren't listening; or even from being killed. As you enter the generation of Black tradition keepers, you wonder about the seemingly boundless depths of their knowledge? In fact, you're still learning. Certain lore is only now being passed on to you. The good thing is that the community of those with interests like your own is growing and that the sharing of truths once hidden comes by means of the internet, articles, and books rather than *via* word-of-mouth alone. You marvel at the things revealed. You're "blown away" by their implications for understanding the Black World and the place underground ways of knowing occupy in it.

You realize that "La, la, la, la, la, la, la, la, la" meant much more than "I love you" (1968); that Thomas Bell and William Hart were strategically trafficking in "wordlessness"; and that Hart's falsetto vocals on Delfonics' songs were conjuring "Elsewhere."[2] You can detect the not-so-subtle critiques of Black consumerism and conjure culture in the lyrics of the Temptations' "I Can't Get Next to You" (1969) and their topographical mapping of *numinous* revelatory *loci* beyond the doors of the Black Church in "Psychedelic Shack" (1970). You hear in the words of Undisputed Truth's "Smiling Faces Sometimes" (1969) poignant reservations about emotional masking and "reserve" (Andrews, 2012). You wonder about the deeper meanings that accrue to the teleological journey and final destination envisioned in the Staples Singers' "I'll Take You There" (1972) and are inspired to explore the relationship between mainstream epistemologies and esoteric ways of knowing by Earth, Wind & Fire's "The World's a Masquerade" (1973). You wonder about the odd inter-textual discussion about Black life brokered by Blue Magic's performance of "Sideshow" (1974), the lyrics for which were co-authored by Robert Rivkin, Lisa Coleman, and Wendy Malvoin—none of whom are of African descent, but all of whom were members of the late Prince Rogers Nelson's backup band, "The Revolution."

---

2   On falsetto, elsewhere, and wordlessness, see Young (2012, pp. 52–53, 259–261). Young is, in a real sense, the esoteric *docent* through which these realizations were disclosed.

•••

You have a surprising sense of *ennui*. A Black world saturated with secrets—some hidden virtually in plain sight and at times unknown even to Black *mystagogues* themselves—exists. Why has it taken so long to see, acknowledge, value, collect, and study them? Yours is a fetishized body in colonized space. Such activities are *messy*. They require you to embrace your hybrid identity as *Africana* elder, citizen of the Western academy, and *provocateur*; to challenge certain disciplinary orthodoxies; and even to blur the boundaries between scholarship and resistance. The *poetics* and potential outcomes of such acts are dangerous. This is one of those realities you've come to accept as normal. As the elders often say, "It be's like that" (on the meaning of which, see Major, 1994, p. 252). Or, as your contemporaries say, that's just "the way 'it tiz.'"

4   AES—toward a Scholarship of Resistance

There has long been a tendency to view academic writing and scholarly performance as functions that were "hermetically sealed" (pun intended) from other realms of creative human endeavor, and to ascribe authority for development of the tools for meta-critical analysis to theoreticians purportedly situated at a safe distance from (and beyond the influence of) the phenomena they study. Approaches of this kind permit rather facile distinctions to be made between practitioners and scholars, broadly defined. They also lead to the relationship between power, privilege, and the construction of knowledge being insufficiently queried. This has potentially disastrous consequences for appreciating the complexity of some figures in the history of Western esotericism—e.g., Hildegard von Bingen, Louis Claude de Saint-Martin, and Jakob Böhme—whose *oeuvres* defy singular categorization. It is equally problematic for understanding the formative influences on and contributions of individuals such as Paschal Beverly Randolph and Pamela Colman Smith, whose ideas can be productively viewed through the intersecting perspectives of Western esotericism and AES. It is completely untenable for de-colonial methodologies that take into consideration the social locations and biographies of researchers, expand the circle of interlocutors and topics engaged, and take seriously what might be termed "grassroots theorizing" about the nature of reality (cf. Villalba, 2021).

The FNF piece above narrates one de-colonial journey of AES discovery. Central to it are a number of ethical issues, such as: what occurs when scholars within the *Africana* world use as starting points for their work tangible artifacts, ideas, taxonomies, and descriptive language from their immediate surroundings; factors contributing to the concealment of *Africana* epistemologies and their selective disclosure in academic settings; the utility of literary and performative *genres*—like FNF—in descriptive, analytical, and interpretive interventions that increase our understanding of various *Africana* esotericisms; and the important place that non-traditional conversation partners—e.g., community elders, tradition keepers, poets, musicians, etc.—occupy as creators, collectors, and curators of secret lore, particularly on the American side of the Black Atlantic.

AES creates space for this kind of work, which holds great promise for understanding the local histories and traditions governing the concealment and selective disclosure of cultural traditions and practices. The seven songs from the Soul-Blues continuum constituting touchstones for this essay provide evidence of a rich conversation about the particularities of African-American survival in the late 1960s and early 1970s and navigating a fraught social landscape in which all things Black were considered as radical expressions of alterity in the West.

This essay—and the experimental FNF foray therein—is, in a manner of speaking, an effort to *re-signify* scholarship in AES as a radically self-conscious and emancipatory enterprise in which the cultural *realia* of the colonized are subject to a non-exploitative subaltern "gaze." Here, one thinks immediately of the role that songwriters and lyricists such as Thomas Bell, William Hart, Norman Whitfield, Sr., Norman Whitfield, Jr., Barrett Strong, Alvertis Bell, and Clarence "Skip" Scarborough—whose works were engaged directly in the aforementioned FNF piece—played in this process. It is, by intent, non-totalizing and partially obfuscating. Unlike projects such as the *Dictionary of Gnosis and Western Esotericism* (Hanegraaff et al., 2005), it in no way purports to be "comprehensive" (ibid., p. vii). Instead, keeping in mind the implicit dangers associated with academic disclosure, it compels readers to search for and engage persons, concepts, and themes considered, by and large, absent from or tangential to Western esotericism. Our hope is that this essay will further establish inclusive parameters for creative interventions that shed light on the varieties of esotericism in the *Africana* world.

Bibliography

Songs Referred to in This Study
"La La Means I Love You" · Performed by "The Delphonics" · Songwriters—Thomas Bell & William Hart (1968)

"I Can't Get Next to You" · Performed by "The Temptations" · Songwriters—Strong, Whitfield, and Whitfield (1969)

"Psychedelic Shack" · Performed by "The Temptations" · Songwriters—Strong, Whitfield, & Whitfield, Jr. (1970)

"Smiling Faces Sometimes" · Performed by "The Undisputed Truth" · Songwriters—Strong & Whitfield (1971)

"I'll Take You There" · Performed by "The Staples Singers" · Songwriter—Alvertis Bell (1972)

"The World's a Masquerade" · Performed by "Earth, Wind & Fire" · Songwriter—Clarence "Skip" Scarborough (1973)

"Sideshow" · Performed by "Blue Magic" · Songwriters—Robert Rivkin, Lisa Coleman, and Wendy Malvoin (1974)

References

Andrews, H. (2012) "Reserve," in Walker, R. (ed.) *Black Cool: One Thousand Streams of Blackness*. Berkeley, CA: Soft Skull Press, pp. 29–38.

Asprem, E. (2021) "Rejected Knowledge Reconsidered: Some Methodological Notes on Esotericism and Marginality," in Asprem, E. and Strube, J. (eds.) *New Approaches to the Study of Esotericism*. Leiden and Boston: Brill, pp. 127–146.

Badu, E. (1997) *Baduizm*. New York, NY: Universal Records.

Baker, H., Jr., (1984) *Blues, Ideology, and Afro-American Literature*. Chicago, IL: University of Chicago Press.

Bakker, J.M. (2021) "Race and (the Study of) Esotericism," in Asprem, E. and Strube, J. (eds.) *New Approaches to the Study of Esotericism*. Leiden and Boston: Brill, pp. 147–167.

Blue Magic (1974) "Sideshow," *Blue Magic*. New York, NY: Atco.

Delfonics (1968) "La-La-Means I Love You," *Philadelphia, PA*. Philly Groove Records.

Earth, Wind & Fire 1973, "The World's a Masquerade," *Head to the Sky*. New York, NY: Columbia Records.

Fanon, F. (1967) *Black Skin, White Masks*. New York, NY: Grove Press.

Finley, S., Guillory, M., and Page, H.R., Jr. (eds.) (2015) *Esotericism in African American Religious Experience: "There is a Mystery"* … Leiden: E.J. Brill.

Gilroy, P. (1993) *The Black Atlantic: Modernity and Double Consciousness*. Cambridge, MA: Harvard University Press.

Gundaker, G. (ed.) (1998) *Keep Your Head to the Sky: Interpreting African American Home Ground*. Charlottesville, VA: University Press of Virginia.

Hanegraaff, W.J. (2015) "The Globalization of Esotericism," *Correspondences*, 3, pp. 55–91.

Hanegraaff, W.J., Faivre, A., Broek, R.v.d., and Brach, J.-P. (eds.) (2005) *Dictionary of Gnosis and Western Esotericism*. Leiden/Boston: E.J. Brill.

Harper, B. (1997) "Jah Work," *The Will to Live*. Virgin Records America, Inc.

Hucks, T.E. (2012) *Yoruba Traditions & African American Religious Nationalism*. Albuquerque, NM: University of New Mexico Press.

Hurston, Z.N. (1990) *Mules and Men*. Reprint of 1935 edn. New York: HarperPerennial.

Jones, L. (1963) *Blues People: The Negro Experience in America and the Music that Developed from It*. New York, NY: Morrow.

Long, C. (1986) *Significations: Signs, Symbols, and Images in the Interpretation of Religion*. Minneapolis: Fortress Press.

Major, C. (1994) *Juba to Jive: A Dictionary of African-American Slang*. New York, NY: Penguin.

Miller, B. and S. Paola. (2012) *Tell it Slant: Creating, Refining, and Publishing Creative Nonfiction*. 2nd ed. New York: McGraw Hill.

Page, H.R., Jr. (2003) "A Case Study in Eighteenth-Century Afrodiasporan Biblical Hermeneutics and Historiography: The Masonic Charges of Prince Hall," in Bailey, R.C. (ed.) *Yet With A Steady Beat: Contemporary U.S. Afrocentric Biblical Interpretation Semeia Studies*. Atlanta: Society of Biblical Literature, pp. 103–122.

Rankine, C. (2014) *Citizen: An American Lyric*. Minneapolis, MN: Graywolf.

Reich, H. (2016) "Jazz Record Mart's Bob Koester Celebrates 84th Birthday and a New Store," *Chicago Tribune*(November 1, 2016), https://www.chicagotribune.com/entertainment/music/howard-reich/ct-jazz-mart-bob-koester-record-store-ent-1102-2016 1101-column.html. Available at: https://www.chicagotribune.com/entertainment/music/howard-reich/ct-jazz-mart-bob-koester-record-store-ent-1102-20161101-column.html (Accessed July 29, 2020).

Strube, J. (2021) "Towards the Study of Esotericism without the 'Western'": Esotericism from the Perspective of a Global Religious History," in Asprem, E. and Strube, J. (eds.) *New Approaches to the Study of Esotericism*. Leiden and Boston: Brill, pp. 45–66.

Temptations (1969) "I Can't Get Next to You," Detroit, MI: Hitsville USA.

Temptations (1970) *Psychedelic Shack*. Motown Records.

The Staples Singers (1972) *I'll Take You There*. Memphis, TN: Stax Records.

Thompson, R.F. (1984) *Flash of the Spirit: African and Afro-American Art and Philosophy*. 1st Vintage Books edn. New York, NY: Vintage Books.

Ulmer, J.B. (2011) There is Power in the Blues. *Greatest Blues Hits*. Hyena.

Undisputed Truth (1969) "Smiling Faces," Detroit, MI: Motown.

Villalba, M. (2021) "The Occult Among the Aborigines of South America? Some Remarks on Race, Coloniality, and the West in the Study of Esotericism," in Asprem, E. and Strube, J. (eds.) *New Approaches to the Study of Esotericism*. Leiden and Boston: Brill, pp. 88–108.

Woodson, J. (1999) *To Make a New Race: Gurdjieff, Toomer, and the Harlem Renaissance*. Jackson, MS: University of Mississippi Press.

Woodson, J. (2014) "The Harlem Renaissance as Esotericism: Black Oragean Modernism," in Finley, S., Guillory, M.S. and Page, H.R., Jr. (eds.) *Esotericism in African American Religious Experience: "There is a Mystery"* ... Leiden: E.J. Brill, pp. 102–122.

Yancy, G. (ed.) (2004) *What White Looks Like: African American Philosophers on the Whiteness Question*. New York, NY and London, UK: Routledge.

Young, K. (2012) *The Grey Album*. Minneapolis, MN: Graywolf.

Double Toil and Gender Trouble? Performativity and Femininity in the Cauldron of Esotericism Research

Manon Hedenborg White

"Double, double toil and trouble; / Fire burn and cauldron bubble." Thus chant the three potion-brewing witches ominously in Shakespeare's *Macbeth* (4.1.10–38). The witch's cauldron is a fitting starting point for an exploration of (Western) esotericism, gender, and femininity. Boiling and brewing, poisoning and stewing, have gendered connotations, evoking the labor of house chores—socially coded as feminine—and the historically misogynistic stereotype of the witch that has been subject to feminist reworkings in modern esotericism and Paganism (Hanegraaff, 2002). The witches' song—and the stirring of a proverbial pot or cauldron—conjures the idea of trouble. Analytically, *troubling* or causing trouble can mean challenging taken-for-granted categories—surface and core, dominance and subjugation, female and male. The queer associations of the term "trouble" are epitomized by Judith Butler's paradigmatic work of queer theory, *Gender Trouble* (1999).

The late 1960s witnessed the emergence of women's studies or women's history as a distinct academic domain, with feminist scholars bringing attention to the obscuration of women's historical contributions to culture and society. Over time, this corrective focus on women gave way to analyses of masculinity *and* femininity as socially constructed. As highlighted by Joan W. Scott (1986), the growing preference for the term "gender" over that of "women's studies" in academia reflects an understanding that neither women's nor men's social experiences happen in isolation. Simone de Beauvoir's (1987, p. 267) famous declaration that "[o]ne is not born, but rather becomes, a woman" epitomizes the view that what is perceived as feminine and masculine is socially constructed, rather than the outward manifestations of some natural, gendered essence. A distinction between physical sex and social gender allowed feminist scholars to theorize the roles and expectations attached to masculinity and femininity as separate from the supposedly "natural" bodies they were projected onto. From the 1990s on, postmodern and poststructuralist interventions have challenged this division, with scholars of queer theory—a paradigm emerging from the intersection of gender and gay and lesbian studies—highlighting the link between the construction of sex, gender, and sexuality. The term queer is often used to indicate configurations of gender and sexuality that displace het-

© MANON HEDENBORG WHITE, 2021 | DOI:10.1163/9789004446458_011
This is an open access chapter distributed under the terms of the CC BY-NC-ND 4.0 license.

erosexuality and/or binary gender, or dominant concepts thereof (cf. Warner, 1993). Gender and queer studies scholars question the idea of a natural and deterministic link between (con)genital morphology, social roles, and desire, believing that concepts such as masculinity and femininity, heterosexuality and homosexuality, are to some extent socially constructed and historically variant. However, they disagree on many points, some of which will be highlighted herein. Thus, while the present article will stir the proverbial cauldron with particular theoretical precepts, the study of gender in esotericism does not require fealty to specific theoretical frameworks.

Recent decades have witnessed the publication of a number of works addressing issues of gender in esotericism (e.g. Braude, 1989; Owen, 1989; Kraft, 1999; Dixon, 2001; Owen, 2004; Snoek and Heidle, 2008; Ferguson, 2012; Lowry, 2017; Hedenborg White, 2020). Several of these studies have focused on esoteric movements—especially around the *fin-de-siècle*—with a large female presence, such as Spiritualism and Theosophy, exploring how these movements functioned as forums for alternative views on gender. Much remains to be done—not least in terms of interrogating how esotericism as an object, and the scholarly study thereof, is demarcated (cf. Johnston, 2014; 2015). Given the historical marginalization of women and femininity from hegemonic institutions of knowledge production, the notion of esotericism as "rejected knowledge" (Hanegraaff, 2012) could productively be engaged from perspectives of gender. Discussing Spiritualism, Elizabeth Lowry (2017, p. xxvii) links Hanegraaff's historical analysis of the academy's "ostentatious performance of skepticism" towards esotericism with a feminist-historiographic endeavor to recover and take seriously women's experiences. The association of the slippery category of magic with women, the working classes, gendered and sexual deviance, and various racialized "Others" (cf. Styers, 2004, pp. 14–18; Bogdan, 2012, p. 2) is also fertile ground for future research. Simultaneously, the idea of esotericism as "rejected knowledge" is complicated by the fact that esotericisms have sometimes replicated foundational discourses of Western modernity, such as (white) European supremacy or masculine rationality (cf. Bakker, 2019; Asprem, 2021).

Rather than venture into this meta-conceptual discussion or review the state of research, this article will zoom in on a particular material: instances of modern esoteric ritual drawn from the religion Thelema, founded in 1904 by the British occultist Aleister Crowley (1875–1947). I have conducted historical and ethnographic research on Thelema since 2012 (for details, see Hedenborg White, 2013; 2020, pp. 8–10). Herein, I will analyze experiences of Crowley's Gnostic Mass, written in 1913, and three rituals oriented toward the Thelemic goddess Babalon that were scripted from the 1990s on. All four rituals contain elements likely to be familiar to students and scholars of esotericism—recitation of historical esoteric texts, visualization, vibration of divine names, banishing, invocation, the tracing of shapes in the air, symbolic correspondences, and references to the kabbalistic Tree of Life. Crucially, they also entail performances of femininity (see subsequent section) that relate to hegemonic gender logics in complex ways. These gendered aspects are, arguably, neither inconsequential nor superficial, but are integral to the rituals' social function and (perceived) transformative power. Aided by gender and queer theoretical frameworks, it is possible to disentangle some aspects of esotericism that may otherwise be overlooked, contributing to a fuller understanding of esoteric worldviews and practices, and the inscription and challenging of power relations therein.

1 Theoretical Framework: The Performance of Femininity

My analysis herein will draw on two central concepts: *performativity* and *femininity*. Judith Butler has challenged the distinction between biological sex and sociocultural gender. Not contesting the fact of bodily difference, Butler argues that the mapping of a myriad of bodily differences onto an incommensurable, yet complementary, sexual binary is a social construction (e.g. Butler, 1993, pp. 10–11, 66–67). Understandings of biological sexual difference are culturally produced and entangled with social expectations, and thus it is problematic to speak of a pre-discursive, sexed body onto which social gender is then projected. Instead, understandings of biological sex are historically situated and culturally variant.

Butler views gender as performative. Her notion of performativity is inspired by the philosopher of language J.L. Austin's distinction between constative and performative language. Simply put, constative utterances can be verified as true or false (i.e., "the sky is blue"), while performative utterances are such that their very pronouncement changes social reality (i.e., "I now pronounce you husband and wife," "I promise you that...") (e.g. Butler, 1993, pp. 10–11, 243–246). Butler's concept of performative gender thus means that there is no essential gendered identity that structures behavior—instead, people are gendered through continuous repetition of behaviors that suggest an underlying gendered essence. In other words, gender is something one *does*, rather than something one is or has (see also West and Zimmerman, 1987). This does not imply that gender is a "choice," in the sense that one may choose one's shoes. Rather, gender is continuously reproduced via imitation of a limited number of culturally intelligible ways of "doing gender," and this process is intimately linked to the construction of selfhood. Gender is relational—notions of masculinity acquire meaning in relation to notions of femininity, and so on (e.g. Butler, 1999, pp. 33–43, 142). Being gendered thus means part of that which constitutes one's identity is situated outside of oneself (Butler, 2004, p. 19). However, the performative nature of gender means that it is possible to destabilize hegemonic gender logics by doing gender in creative ways that scramble or stretch the existing categories (Butler, 1999, p. 43).

Though approaches to gender as performative can be used to elucidate esoteric practices in numerous ways, this article will especially highlight performances of femininity. Anthropologist and gender studies scholar Ulrika Dahl notes that femininity "has had a bit of a bad reputation in feminist theory; far too often tied to phenomena feminism seeks to eliminate; subordination, sexualisation, objectification, commodification, vulnerability, and so on" (Dahl, 2016, p. 7). Illustratively, American legal scholar and radical feminist theorist Catharine MacKinnon (1982, p. 531) argued in the 1980s that femininity, as a social ideal of womanhood, means "[sexual] attractiveness to men ... sexual availability on male terms." MacKinnon claimed that "what defines woman as such is what turns men on," and her equation of femininity with attractiveness to the male gaze is representative of much radical feminist theorization on femininity. Drawing on a Foucauldian analysis of power and discipline, Sandra Bartky (1988) has argued that bodily practices such as dieting and feminine fashion styles produce a body that is docile, object-like, and vulnerable to attack. In Bartky's (pp. 146–147) view, women must discard femininity if they are to gain equality. Similarly, according to Susan Brownmiller (1985, p. 81), investment in "feminine fashion" means being "obsessively involved in inconsequential details on a serious basis." In Brownmiller's (1985, p. 86) words, feminine styles of dress are inherently uncomfortable, as "practicality is a masculine virtue," and being "truly feminine is to accept the handicap of restraint and restriction, and to ... adore it."

MacKinnon, Bartky, Brownmiller and similar theorists share an understanding of femininity and its associated bodily styles as a debilitating mask, which women can and should discard. During the 1980s "sex wars"—intra-feminist disputes surrounding sexuality—radical feminists extended their critique of femininity to lesbian femmes. The term "femme" (sometimes spelled *fam*) originated in 1940s working-class lesbian bar culture, where it denoted a "feminine" lesbian who desires a "masculine" lesbian or butch (cf. Lapovsky Kennedy and Davis, 1993). Many radical feminists accused femmes of replicating a heterosexist standard of feminine beauty (e.g. Jeffreys, 1987). Radical feminists were also critical of pornography and BDSM, viewing these as heightened forms of patriarchal sexual violence (e.g. Linden et al., 1982). Femmes responded to radical feminist critiques by arguing that their deliberate and often exaggerated femininity did not replicate heterosexist standards, instead constituting a brazen form of gender subversion that flouted the conventions of heterosexual, feminine respectability (e.g. Duggan and McHugh, 1996). Simultaneously, sex radical feminists critiqued the tendencies toward sexual prescriptivism among radical feminists, calling for an analysis of feminine sexuality that accounts both for "pleasure and danger," power and resistance (e.g. Vance, 1992).

The assumption that femininity is always structured by and performed for a male gaze fails to take seriously queer feminine desire. The radical feminist critiques of femininity also disregarded the fact that not all who are (seen as) feminine are women. Crucially, what is viewed as appropriately feminine is not only defined in relation to maleness or masculinity, but through numerous intersections of power including race, sexuality, ability, and social class. In other words, white, heterosexual, binary gender-conforming, able-bodied, and upper- or middle-class femininity is privileged in relation to other varieties. Any social system may contain multiple femininities that differ in status, and which relate to each other as well as to masculinity. As highlighted by "effeminate" gay men, trans women, femmes, drag queens, and "bad girls," it is possible to be perceived as excessively, insufficiently, or wrongly feminine without for that sake being seen as masculine. Finally, the view of femininity as a restrictive yet disposable mask presupposes that emancipation entails departure into neutral (or masculine) modes of being. This is a tenuous assumption, as the construction of selfhood is entangled with gender, and conceptions of androgyny and gender neutrality similarly hinge on culturally specific ideas of masculinity and femininity.

Within this article, femininities will be seen as symbolic constructions tied to clusters of characteristics and behaviors that are perceived as womanly (cf. Schippers, 2007), and which are neither exclusively heterosexual nor only inhabitable by women. Femininity does not simply emanate from or conceal some supposedly "authentic" version of womanhood, but is performatively produced and enacted in historically, culturally, and contextually variant ways. Following scholars of queer femininities such as Ulrika Dahl (e.g. 2010; 2016; 2017) and Hannah McCann (2018), I am skeptical of assumptions that particular iterations of femininity (such as femme, or the ritual roles analyzed below) are inherently more emancipatory simply on the grounds of being intentional or deliberate. Concurrently, I will consider femininities as positionalities that entail both agency and being acted upon (cf. Butler, 2014). Elizabeth Lowry has highlighted this potential of femininities with regard to nineteenth-century Spiritualist mediums. Female Spiritualists negotiated the space between the idealized cult of "True Womanhood"—represented by the pious, chaste, and domestic woman—and the brazen and often stigmatized "New Woman." Instead, they drew on the ideal of "Real Womanhood"—a frequently overlooked model of femininity occupying a sort of middle ground and which emphasized practicality, strength, and courage (Lowry, 2017, pp. x–xx).

It will be assumed herein that gendered attributes (such as dress or adornment) are neither inherently oppressive nor liberating. Instead, they will be seen as linked both to regimes of power and the possibility of resistance theretoward. Particular behaviors or bodily styles may connote femininity in one particular context and not another. In the context of late-modern, North American and European culture, for example, high heels, lace lingerie, emphasized makeup, and long hair—especially in combination—are part of a socially constructed feminine aesthetic. As will become evident below, these attributes are recognizable to esotericists who utilize them partly because of their broader cultural connotations. However, these attributes also gain particular meaning in some Thelemic ritual contexts. As will be discussed in the subsequent section, nakedness—seemingly divested of the gendered cultural attributes of dress—also communicates a specific femininity with particular assumptions attached to it in the context of the Gnostic Mass.

2 'Bare and Rejoicing': The Naked Priestess of the Gnostic Mass

In 1904, Aleister Crowley received what he perceived as a divinely inspired text, later given the title *Liber AL vel Legis* (abbreviated *Liber AL*), and colloquially known as *The Book of the Law*. Divided into three chapters attributed, respectively, to the goddess Nuit, the god Hadit, and the god Ra-Hoor-Khuit, this text proclaims: "Do what thou wilt shall be the whole of the Law" (*AL* I:40). In 1912, Crowley was made head of the British branch of the initiatory fraternity Ordo Templi Orientis (OTO). He proceeded to reshape OTO's degree structure and rituals in accordance with Thelema, penning the so-called Gnostic Catholic Mass for the order in 1913. Though structurally similar to the Tridentine Mass, Crowley's ritual celebrates the Thelemic cosmology. According to Crowley, the Gnostic Mass communicates the central mystery of OTO, generally held to be a particular formulation of sexual magic. From 1914, Crowley systematically explored sexual magic with a plethora of female and male partners (see e.g. Crowley, 1972, pp. 1–82).

The Gnostic Mass is conducted by a priest and priestess, aided by a deacon and two "children." A cursory and selective outline (which does not account for the roles of deacon or children) follows: the priestess, dressed in "white, blue, and gold" and bearing a sword from a "red girdle," enters the temple and raises the priest from his "tomb." Crowley's instructions for the priestess's dress leave room for variations. It is common for her to wear a blue robe, dress, or tunic, but cut, length, and fabric vary, as do—to a greater extent—hair, makeup, jewelry or lack thereof. The priest, wearing a white tunic and carrying a lance, proclaims: "I am a man among men." The priestess purifies and consecrates him with instruments representing the four elements. She robes and crowns him, proclaiming his ascension from mortal man to "priest of the sun." The priest aids the priestess onto a high altar, purifying and consecrating her before drawing a veil to conceal her. He invokes the goddess Nuit while the priestess disrobes completely. She delivers her own address, drawn from the first chapter of *Liber AL*, attributed to Nuit. As explanation for the priestess's nudity, Crowley quotes from the same chapter, which states that the priestess should stand "bare and rejoicing" whilst calling to her celebrants (*AL* 1:62). Having delivered her invocation, the priestess can choose to re-robe or remain naked, while the priest invokes the divine masculine (as Hadit). The priest then opens the veil revealing the priestess to the congregation, and priest and priestess jointly consecrate the Eucharist. They enact the "Mystic Marriage" (a symbolic sexual union) by lowering the priest's lance into a wine-filled grail, after which the priest—followed by the rest of the congregation—consumes the Eucharist, proclaiming: "There is no part of me that is not of the gods" (Crowley, 2007, pp. 247–270).

Conducted under the auspices of Ecclesia Gnostica Catholica (EGC), the ecclesiastical arm of OTO, the Gnostic Mass is celebrated hundreds of times annually across the globe. Since 2012, I have observed approximately 40 performances of the Gnostic Mass, mostly in the United States. I have also conducted semi-structured interviews and countless informal conversations with priests and priestesses of EGC. These exchanges have revealed a variety of interpretations and local variations, including how priestesses choose to present themselves as the veil opens. For instance, some priestesses who elect to remain disrobed retain adornments such as jewelry or body art. Others re-robe only partly, or don underwear in significant colors. The priestess's nakedness is often interpreted as symbolic of her identification with Nuit, traditionally represented as a naked woman stretching across the sky (inspired by the iconography of the Egyptian sky-goddess Nut). This is unsurprising, given how the mass script draws on the chapter of *Liber AL* attributed to this deity. However, the nakedness of the priestess is ascribed multiple and contradictory meanings within the Thelemic milieu. Many contemporary Thelemites have told me that the priestess's disrobing—whether or not she re-robes before reappearing before the congregation—both marks and contributes to her transformation into goddess. This parallels how the male officiant's robing and crowning at the hands of the priestess marks and effects his transformation from "man" to "priest."

The priestess's and priest's dress changes as understood by the Thelemites I have spoken to are performative—altering social relations within the ritual space by contributing to the clergy members' (perceived) transition into divine embodiments. The social reality of the mass is gendered—as the priest transforms into the masculine divine, the priestess becomes representative of an aspect of the feminine divine and the attributes that are ascribed thereto in this specific context. Importantly, it is common for Thelemites to associate Nuit with receptivity and openness, in contrast to the perceived activity of the masculine principle (Hedenborg White, 2013, p. 107). While many Thelemites reflect critically on the idea of femininity as receptive (see Hedenborg White, 2020, pp. 211–215), the nakedness of the priestess may contribute to the idea of feminine nudity and receptivity as intertwined. Sophie, a longtime EGC priestess stated of her experience of appearing on the altar in the mass: "You're vulnerable every way you can be. You're energetically wide open" (quoted in Hedenborg White, 2020, p. 213). This highlights how the femininity of the priestess-as-Nuit can be associated with "traditionally" feminine attributes such as vulnerability.

Contemporary Thelemites' reflections on the Gnostic Mass illustrate that the meaning of esoteric ritual is neither fixed nor determined by authorial intent. Instead, the meaning of ritual is continuously negotiated, and broader tendencies and perceptions among practitioners may impact attitudes towards ritual practice. While a dearth of large-scale, quantitative studies renders it difficult to generalize about contemporary Thelemites' values, Anglo-American Thelemites are seemingly more likely than average to support non-normative gendered and sexual modalities (cf. Hedenborg White, 2020, pp. 197–198). My research suggests feminism and the LGBTQ movement have impacted the landscape of contemporary Thelema (at least in the US) from the 1990s onwards, coinciding with an increase in attempts to promote the voices of female Thelemites (e.g., separatist discussion groups, podcasts, and publications) as well as critical emic discussion of gender and magic in relation to trans and queer experience (cf. Hedenborg White, 2020, pp. 195–202). This has implications for the performance of femininity in the Gnostic Mass. The OTO's United States Grand Lodge (the largest and most bureaucratized national grand lodge) stipulates that the priestess should be a woman and the priest a man in "public" (i.e., open to non-initiates) mass celebrations. Alterations are permitted in "private," initiates-only masses. Transgender clergy may perform the mass publicly in the clerical role corresponding to the gender with which they most closely identify (cf. Hedenborg White, 2013). Non-binary/genderqueer individuals have the option of performing the mass in the role corresponding to their birth-assigned gender (or as deacon or "child"). While opinions diverge regarding these conventions, the ongoing discussions and the explicit use of language denoting trans and genderqueer/non-binary experience in OTO policies attests to the impact of LGBTQ discourses on the Anglo-American Thelemic landscape.

Increasing Thelemic engagement with feminist ideas has coincided with varying responses to the priestess's nudity. Several female Thelemites to whom I have spoken were critical of the fact that the priestess is naked while the other ritual officers and congregation are clothed, questioning whether this reduces women to objects of male sexual enjoyment. This reflects feminist concerns with sexual objectification as a form of gendered oppression, as exemplified by the radical feminist critiques cited above. I have also spoken to EGC priestesses who attest to having, on one or several occasions, felt objectified by male members of the congregation.

Emic responses to this critique are varied, sometimes citing a combination of magical, pragmatic, and social rationales. For instance, one EGC priestess I interviewed stated that the priest could conceivably also appear naked, but that symbolic accuracy would require him to maintain an erection throughout the ceremony (after the priestess "awakens" him from his tomb), and that this would be difficult for many males to accomplish in front of an audience. Thus, the priest is robed and the erect lance is used to symbolize the awakened masculine principle. I have also interviewed numerous EGC priestesses who attribute emancipatory (even feminist) potential to the mass. They describe the experience of appearing naked on the altar as liberating and suggest that the naked priestess—far from objectified—challenges misogynistic perceptions of women's bodies and sexuality as deficient or impure. As Amy, a long-time EGC priestess told me: "How do we convince people that the female body isn't really dirty and gross? Well, we can talk about it all day, or a couple times a month we can put a naked female body on the altar and have everybody kneel" (quoted in Hedenborg White, 2020, p. 231). Similarly, Thelemic author Brandy Williams (2009) suggests that the mass can challenge misogynistic perceptions of femininity by showing women as direct representatives of divinity. These interpretations dovetail with sex radical feminist arguments that link female emancipation to sexual liberation.

The point here is not to deduce who is right, but rather to highlight that something as seemingly simple as a naked body is anything but. The priestess's disrobing is not just a stripping of the gendered cultural attributes of dress that uncovers a "natural" naked body, revealing a femininity that exists irrespective of cultural conventions. Instead, the act can be understood as an instance of gender performativity: it shifts the priestess's body from one iteration of femininity (that of priestess) and materializes a different one (that of goddess), both of which are perceived and experienced as sacred in their particular context. This iteration of femininity is not autonomous of dominant gender logics, as evinced by the critical voices questioning whether the naked priestess is objectified. As seen above, the priestess is also associated with conventionally feminine characteristics such as receptivity and vulnerability. Nonetheless, while the sequence is scripted, it is never replicated identically, and there is the possibility for individual creativity. The nudity of the priestess may be read as a challenge to notions of women's value as contingent on sexual modesty, or binary oppositions of masculinity/spirit and femininity/matter. Either way, esotericists interpret the naked priestess of Nuit not only in relation to esoteric teaching, but also in relation to logics of gender in society more broadly, sometimes reading the nakedness of the priestess as a statement *about* gender—as providing a particular vision of femininity may engender both feelings of emancipation and sacredness, or politically informed skepticism.

3   Scarlet Harlots: Femininity and the Goddess Babalon in Ritual

A central focus for my research on Thelema and gender has been historical and contemporary interpretations of the Thelemic goddess Babalon. Babalon is based on Crowley's favorable reinterpretation of the biblical Whore of Babylon (Rev. 17) and is associated with liberated feminine sexuality and the mystical formula of ecstatic union with all. Crowley in his descriptions of Babalon and the related figure of Scarlet Woman, conceived as Babalon's earthly emissary, emphasized many of the same characteristics as her biblical prototype: promiscuous sexuality, eroticized feminine attire, and worldly power (e.g. Crowley, 1974, pp. 261–282; 1998, *AL* III:43–45). Crowley upheld these traits as indexical of Babalon's sacredness, positioning her as a counter-image to *fin-de-siècle* ideals of femininity as chaste, nurturing, and passive. By conceptualizing Babalon as symbolic of the soteriological ideal of ego destruction and union with all, Crowley also positioned the goddess—and the feminized mode of being she is associated with—as an ideal for all seekers (cf. Hedenborg White, 2020, pp. 43–46, 66–70).

Over the twentieth- and twenty-first centuries, numerous esoteric practitioners have continued to interpret Babalon, sometimes with a critical eye to Crowley's writings on this symbol and the role of the Scarlet Woman. Whereas

Crowley appears mainly to have viewed the Scarlet Woman as a role available to women who played particular roles in his life and initiation, a number of later esotericists (many of them female) have stressed that women can and should claim the role for themselves, independently of any partner (male or otherwise). This is also the case in two of the below rituals. Especially from the 1990s onward, the goddess has frequently been construed in emic discourse as a challenge to limited concepts of femininity, and as an image of feminine power beyond misogynistic tropes (Hedenborg White, 2020).

In this section, I will analyze the performance of femininity in three Babalon rituals, relayed to me second-hand in written or oral format.[1] The first ritual "Procession of Babalon," written by Aisha Qadisha (1996), was performed during the 1996 Thelemic Women's Symposium—one of several initiatives undertaken in recent decades to promote female Thelemites' voices. A collective ritual, it presents a succession of three historical epochs associated with different approaches to the divine feminine, who is embodied by three women ritual practitioners as the Semitic goddess Astarte, the Virgin Mary, and Babalon. The cultural meanings ascribed to these figures are conveyed through clothing, posture, and speech. Astarte wears a "loose, flowing robe or gown in ancient style." She states that women's bodies and sexuality were held as sacred in pagan antiquity. The Virgin Mary is dressed in a "blue and white gown … with halo," her eyes lowered in shame. She speaks instead of female sexual repression under Christianity. In stark contrast, Babalon wears a red wig and a red bra and garter with high heels and stockings. Triumphantly, she heralds the social and sexual liberation of women, addressing the (female) ritual participants as her daughters and calling them to carry themselves victoriously, "laugh[ing] and danc[ing] as the dying god crumbles," their laughter being as "the cackle of harlots in a house of fornication." The juxtaposition of Astarte's "ancient style" get-up and Mary's modest attire with Babalon's unabashedly ultrafeminine and eroticized outfit can be interpreted as a challenge to the notion of feminine value as contingent on modesty, reclaiming the negatively stereotyped femininity of "harlot" as indexical of power, sacredness, and sexual freedom.

The second ritual was described to me by Freyja, a female Thelemite and feminist. Freyja conducted the ritual with her male romantic partner James. While James was dressed inconspicuously in black, Freyja donned a low-cut red dress and eye-catching gold jewelry, applying red lipstick and dark eye

---

[1] I have analyzed these rituals in greater detail elsewhere, see Hedenborg White, 2020, pp. 291–320.

makeup—heavier, she observed, than she would ordinarily use. She stated that she donned this ultrafeminine attire as she associates this "look" with Babalon. Given her aim to embody a goddess associated with unabashed feminine sexuality, she believed it would be helpful to encourage James's desire for her. However, Freyja noted that she has worn similar attire when invoking Babalon alone, feeling it is pleasing to the goddess. This evinces that Freyja's dress and adornment was not only aimed to attract a male partner (though it was partly the reason). Practicality was also a concern—having scripted a dance sequence into the ritual, Freyja opted against high heels. After a series of preparatory invocations—Crowley's "Star Ruby" and "Liber V vel Reguli" rituals—James purified and consecrated Freyja in a manner similar to that of the priest and priestess in the Gnostic Mass. The couple took turns reciting texts pertaining to Babalon, mostly derived from Crowley's *oeuvre*. Freyja proceeded to dance ecstatically, while James recited a passage from Crowley's "Liber Samekh" that mentions Babalon (Crowley, 1994, p. 509) as a mantra. Afterward, James removed Freyja's clothing, bound her hands, and administered 156 (derived from the *gematria* value of the name Babalon) blows to her back with a whip, while Freyja used Babalon's seal—a seven-pointed star inscribed with her name first printed in Crowley's *The Book of Lies* (1912)—as a meditative focus. The couple shared a sacramental glass of red wine, had sex, and meditated silently before concluding.

The third ritual was designed by esoteric author Soror Syrinx. Syrinx has written several introductory manuals for esotericists (principally women, though she writes her rituals can be utilized by all) who are interested in the role of Scarlet Woman. She frequently critiques sexism in society and stresses the importance of female emancipation, articulating the figure of the Scarlet Woman as a challenge to narrow stereotypes of femininity. The ritual of interest here is one of solitary adoration, through which Syrinx writes that a female magician can begin to identify herself with Babalon before engaging in partnered sexual magic. Syrinx instructs her reader to design an altar with meaningful items such as a seal of Babalon and the "Lust" card of the Thoth Tarot deck—co-created by Crowley and the artist Frieda Lady Harris (1877–1962)—which is associated with Babalon (Crowley and Harris, 1974, pp. 92–95). She is then to don "fine apparel, red or purple," to use makeup creatively, painting her lips "ruby," and her eyes "a heavenly azure," and to cover herself with "glittering jewels." She then suggests visualizing oneself as Babalon while indulging in luxurious fruits, sweets, and wine in order to encourage a sensual and ecstatic state of mind. The ritual culminates in a guided meditation through which the practitioner envisions herself as adrift in a great womb before being reborn as Babalon. After this, Syrinx suggests engaging in a creative pursuit such as writing, painting, playing an instrument, or dancing (Syrinx, 2014, pp. 72–74).

The aim of the above exposition has been to indicate how some contemporary esotericists use a feminine aesthetic of dress, jewelry, and makeup to inhabit and communicate the Thelemic goddess Babalon in ritual. We may regard these women esotericists' actions as instances of performative gender, both drawing on and (re)producing particular iterations of femininity—associated with sexual assertiveness (but also submissiveness), aestheticized excess, and sensual pleasure—as subculturally meaningful. While a review of a greater range of rituals would produce a more complex image, representativity has not been the objective here. Instead, this overview will serve as the basis for a critical analysis of femininity, exemplifying the broader importance of gender perspectives for the study of esotericism.

4   Agency and Vulnerability: Gender and Contradiction in Esoteric Ritual

Why does a ritual practitioner strip naked, don high heels or red lingerie, apply pronounced makeup or allow herself to be bound and whipped for the purposes of esoteric ritual? Read through the radical feminist critiques of femininity outlined in the section on theoretical frameworks, these practices may appear simply as fetishization of female subjugation. However, these actions take place in a religious milieu that has been influenced by feminist thought, and several of the abovementioned female ritual creators and participants articulate these practices as part of an endeavor to redefine femininity in emancipatory ways. Following Dahl, McCann, and other theorists who have suggested femininities as positionalities that entail both vulnerability and agency, I find it too simplistic to read these ritual practices as examples of female sexual objectification for the benefit of a male gaze. No men were present for Syrinx's or Qadisha's rituals—the latter of which emphasizes embodied, sensual relationality between women. While Freyja's ritual involved a male participant, Freyja formulates her relationship with Babalon in terms of both identification and queerly feminine desire.

The notion that the frequently less "practical" nature of contemporary feminine aesthetic styles univocally indicates submissive social status also fails under historical scrutiny. Disregard for practicality is not a universally male prerogative but has often been a privilege of the wealthy and protected, regardless of gender. For contemporary masculine aesthetic styles, practicality does not correlate in simplistic fashion with social status—as exemplified by the preference for (or expectation of) suits in many high-status professions and social milieus. Concurrently, "impractical" feminine fashion has frequently been a marker of class and racial privilege (Skeggs, 2001). While practicality and function may be prioritized in esotericists' selection of ritual gear—as highlighted by Freyja's opting against high heels—they are not always prime concerns for either men or women. Instead, ritual implements and garb may be selected for purposes of symbolic accuracy or magical significance (cf. Owen, 2004, pp. 74–75). Similarly, femininity is performed through nakedness or particular clothing in the above-discussed rituals (partly) for reasons of magical significance—female nakedness connotes Nuit, redness and eroticized attire connotes Babalon, challenging negative stereotypes of assertive female sexuality by rendering it emblematic of divine status. These examples showcase how gender performativity functions as a "material citational practice" (cf. Dahl, 2009, p. 56) that acquires meaning and cultural salience in relation to other performances of gender.

As seen in the above-discussed rituals, femininity is performed as both uplifted and vulnerable (as in the case of the Gnostic Mass priestess), assertive and partially restricted. Significantly, Freyja's ritual includes literal physical restriction in the form of bondage, which—especially combined with flagellation—evokes associations to BDSM. This is not uncommon in contemporary esoteric and Pagan milieus, where discourses on "sacred kink" have garnered increased attention in recent years (cf. Mueller, 2017). So, should we see this aspect of Freyja's ritual as a fetishization of feminine submission, signifying—to quote Susan Brownmiller—the association of femininity with "the handicap of restriction"? Once again, I find this potential reading reductive and dismissive of practitioners' own interpretations and the complex ways in which sexual agency may be structured in BDSM and which cannot solely be reduced to stereotypical gender dynamics (cf. e.g. Rubin, 1984; Carlström, 2016).

Nonetheless, reading Freyja's eroticized submission solely as liberal, empowered non-compliance with hegemonic gender norms reproduces a reductive dichotomy of activity and passivity that does not account for how all gendered performances entail both agency and the potential for being acted upon (cf. Butler, 2014; Dahl, 2017). The responses of some female Thelemites to whom I have spoken indicate how ritual practices are not enacted in a social vacuum—neither the priestess nor anyone else can control the responses of others present. Some mass congregants may look at the naked priestess only as a source erotic stimulation, without awareness of the possible religious connotations. In other cases, a certain critical, feminist gaze renders a hypothetical, objectifying male gaze implicitly present whether or not there are men in the room. The rituals discussed in this article position femininities as the site of interface between humanity and divinity, while also associating femininity, variously, with receptivity, vulnerability, and (possibly) sexual availability. These are linkages many feminists have sought to deconstruct, but which are also, arguably, foundational to relationality. This is a source of productive tension, as reading these characteristics as solely passive or oppressive risks reproducing the very logics one wishes to challenge. As such, an interrogation of gender, performativity, and esotericism must consider the marginalization of women, gender-nonconforming individuals, and sexual minorities (in society and sometimes in esotericism), while taking seriously these same groups' subjective experiences of esoteric practices as transformative.

I do not suggest these ritual performances of femininity are inherently more subversive than normative, "everyday" femininity simply because they are scripted or deliberate. Such an assumption underestimates the agency of "mainstream" femininities while overestimating the connection between intentionality and subversivity (cf. Dahl, 2010; Walker, 2012). Helpfully, McCann (2018, p. 6) suggests considering feminine appearance and embodiment as having the potential to produce "*affects* that might work in various directions." Such affects may include unease at the stigma that follows being read by others as feminine, but also comfort at social acceptance, or forms of pleasure and relationality that transcend self-objectification. Similarly, the performances of femininities in the above-discussed rituals generate complex and contradictory affective responses. Reading femininity in these rituals as structured solely by hegemonic gender logics, or as completely autonomous of them, overlooks the complex ways these rituals are alternately perceived as empowering, controversial, or pleasurable.

In this chapter, I have slipped feminist theorization into the proverbial cauldron of esotericism studies not only to understand the rituals discussed herein, but in the hopes that the resulting brew may say something about the complexities of femininity—and gender—more broadly. While the subject matter may appear a narrow case study, I propose that the conclusions drawn have broader applicability. Specifically, they showcase how the construction and reconstruction of gender can be a vital dimension of esoteric practice and its development over time. Self-transformation is a common goal of contemporary esotericists (cf. Mayer, 2009; Granholm, 2014, pp. 134–138, 158–159). Historical and contemporary esotericism provides several examples of how this ideal may be formulated and experienced in gendered terms, such as female Spiritualists' endeavors to redefine femininity in the public sphere (Owen, 1989; Lowry, 2017); the construction of interiorized androgyny and/or hermaphroditism as an initiatory aim among nineteenth- and early-twentieth century esotericists (Owen, 2004, pp. 109–111; Strube, 2016, pp. 62–63); right-wing philosopher Julius Evola's insistence on a "'masculine' renunciation" (quoted in Hakl, 2018, p. 153); and present-day male adherents of the goddess movement seeking to redefine masculinity in more open ways (Green, 2012). If we only focus on, for instance, how esoteric practice is structured using elements of historical source texts or building on tropes such as correspondences or panentheistic worldviews, without paying attention to gender, we may disregard vital aspects of the social function and meaning of esoteric beliefs, practices, and organization.

Finally, esoteric ritual may provide a fruitful vantage point from which to analyze how all bodies are performatively materialized via selective use (or non-use) of particular aesthetic styles and attributes. The embodied performance of gender cannot be understood simply as operating on a spectrum from functional/practical masculinity to decorative/restrictive femininity. Rather, all forms of bodily adornment replicate and respond to cultural codes and symbols in ways that may both re-inscribe and challenge hierarchies of gender, class, race, religion, sexuality, and other markers of social positionality. While theories of gender and femininity doubtlessly have the potential to stir the cauldron of esotericism studies, esotericism as an object of study offers productive conceptual trouble to the broader study of gender, illustrating how performances of gender are complex and contradictory, having the potential to effect contradictory experiences of politically informed skepticism, sexual arousal, restraint, and sacredness.

Bibliography

Asprem, E. (2021) "Rejected Knowledge Reconsidered: Some Methodological Notes on Esotericism and Marginality," in Asprem, E. and Strube, J. (eds.) *New Approaches to the Study of Esotericism*. Leiden and Boston: Brill, pp. 127–146.

Bakker, J.M. (2019) "Hidden Presence: Race and/in the History, Construct, and Study of Western Esotericism," *Religion*. [Online] DOI: 10.1080/0048721X.2019.1642262.

Bartky, B. (1988) "Foucault, Femininity and the Modernization of Patriarchal Power," in Diamond, I. and Quinby. L. (eds.) *Feminism and Foucault: Reflections on Resistance*. Boston: Northeastern University Press, pp. 61–86.

Bogdan, H. (2012) "Introduction: Modern Western Magic," *Aries*, 12(1), pp. 1–16.

Braude, A. (1989) *Radical Spirits: Spiritualism and Women's Rights in Nineteenth-Century America*. Boston, Mass.: Beacon Press.

Brownmiller, S. (1985) *Femininity*. New York: Ballantine Books.

Butler, J. (1993) *Bodies that Matter: On the Discursive Limits of "Sex."* New York: Routledge.
Butler, J. (1999) *Gender Trouble: Feminism and the Subversion of Identity*. New York: Routledge.
Butler, J. (2004) *Undoing Gender*. New York; London: Routledge.
Butler, J. (2014) "Rethinking Vulnerability and Resistance," *Instituto Franklin*. Accessed July 29, 2020. https://www.institutofranklin.net/sites/default/files/files/Rethinking%20Vulnerability%20and%20Resistance%20Judith%20Butler.pdf.
Carlström, C. (2016) *BDSM: Paradoxernas praktik*. Malmö: Malmö University.
Crowley, A. (1972) *The Magical Record of the Beast 666. The Diaries of Aleister Crowley 1914–1920*. Symonds, J. and Grant, K. (eds.) London: Duckworth.
Crowley, A. (1974) *The Magical and Philosophical Commentaries to the Book of the Law*. Symonds, J. and Grant, K. (eds.). Montreal: 93 Publishing.
Crowley, A. (1998) *The Vision and the Voice: With Commentary and Other Papers: The Equinox, Volume IV Number II*. Beta, H. (ed.). York Beach, ME: Samuel Weiser.
Crowley, A. (2004) *The Book of the Law: Liber AL vel Legis: With a Facsimile of the Manuscript as Received by Aleister and Rose Edith Crowley on April 8, 9, 10, 1904 E.v. Centennial Edition*. York Beach, ME: Red Wheel/Weiser.
Crowley, A. (2007) "Liber XV: Ecclesiæ Gnosticæ Catholicæ Canon Missæ," in Crowley, A., *The Blue Equinox: The Equinox Vol. III No. 1*. San Francisco: Red Wheel/Weiser, pp. 247–270.
Crowley, A. and Harris, F. (1972) *The Book of Thoth: Short Essay on the Tarot of the Egyptians, Being the Equinox, Vol. III, No. 5*. York Beach, ME: S. Weiser.
Dahl, U. (2009) "(Re)Figuring Femme Fashion," *Lambda Nordica*, 2–3, pp. 43–77.
Dahl, U. (2010) "Notes on Femme-inist Agency," in Jónasdóttir, A.G., Bryson, V., and Jones, K.B. (eds.) *Sexuality, Gender, and Power: Intersectional and Transnational Perspectives*. New York: Routledge, pp. 172–188.
Dahl, U. (2016) "Queering Femininity," *Lambda Nordica*, 21(1–2), pp. 7–20.
Dahl, U. (2017) "Femmebodiment: Notes on Queer Feminine Shapes of Vulnerability," *Feminist Theory*, 18(1), pp. 35–53.
De Beauvoir, S. (1984) *The Second Sex*. Harmondsworth: Penguin Books.
Dixon, J. (2001) *Divine Feminine: Theosophy and Feminism in England*. Baltimore: Johns Hopkins University Press.
Duggan, L. and McHugh, K. (1996) "A Fem(me)inist Manifesto," *Women & Performance: A Journal of Feminist Theory*, 8(2), 153–159.
Ferguson, C. (2012) *Determined Spirits: Eugenics, Heredity and Racial Regeneration in Anglo-American Spiritualist Writing, 1848–1930*. Edinburgh: Edinburgh University Press.
Granholm, K. (2014) *Dark Enlightenment: The Historical, Sociological, and Discursive Contexts of Contemporary Esoteric Magic*. Leiden; Boston: Brill.

Green, D. (2012) "What Men Want? Initial Thoughts on the Male Goddess Movement," *Religion and Gender*, 2(2), pp. 305–327.

Hakl, H.T. (2018) "Deification as a Core Theme in Julius Evola's Esoteric Works," *Correspondences*, 6(2), pp. 145–171.

Hanegraaff, W.J. (2002) "From the Devil's Gateway to the Goddess Within: The Image of the Witch in Neopaganism," in Kloppenborg, R. and W.J. Hanegraaff (eds.) *Female Stereotypes in Religious Traditions*. Leiden: Brill, pp. 295–312.

Hanegraaff, W.J. (2012) *Esotericism and the Academy. Rejected Knowledge in Western Culture*. Cambridge: Cambridge University Press.

Hedenborg White, M. (2013) "To Him the Winged Secret Flame, to Her the Stooping Starlight," *Pomegranate*, 15(1–2), pp. 102–121.

Hedenborg White, M. (2020) *The Eloquent Blood: The Goddess Babalon and the Construction of Femininities in Western Esotericism*. New York: Oxford University Press.

Jeffreys, S. (1987) "Butch and Femme: Now and Then," *Gossip*, 5, pp. 65–95.

Johnston, J. (2014) "A Deliciously Troubling Duo: Gender and Esotericism," in Asprem, E. and Granholm, K. (eds.) *Contemporary Esotericism*. Abingdon, Oxon.: Routledge, pp. 410–425.

Johnston, J. (2015) "Gender and the Occult," in Partridge, C. (ed.) *The Occult World*. Abingdon, Oxon.: Routledge, pp. 681–691.

Kaczynski, R. (2010) *Perdurabo: The Life of Aleister Crowley*. 2nd ed. Berkeley, CA: North Atlantic Books.

Kraft, S-E. (1999) *The Sex Problem: Political Aspects of Gender Discourse in the Theosophical Society 1875–1930*. PhD Diss., University of Bergen.

Lapovsky Kennedy, E., and M.D. Davis. (1993) *Boots of Leather, Slippers of Gold: The History of a Lesbian Community*. New York; London: Routledge.

Linden, R.R., Pagano, D.R., Russell, D.E.H., and Star, S.L. (1982) *Against Sadomasochism: A Radical Feminist Analysis*. East Palo Alto: Frog in the Well.

Lowry, E.S. (2017) *Invisible Hosts: Performing the Nineteenth-Century Spirit Medium's Autobiography*. Albany: SUNY Press.

MacKinnon, C.A. (1982) "Feminism, Marxism, Method, and the State: An Agenda for Theory," *Signs*, 7(3), pp. 515–544.

Mayer, G. (2009) "Magicians of the Twenty-First Century: An Attempt at Dimensioning the Magician's Personality," *Magic, Ritual, and Witchcraft*, 4(2), pp. 176–206.

McCann, H. (2018) *Queering Femininity: Sexuality, Feminism, and the Politics of Presentation*. London: Routledge.

Mueller, M. (2017) "If All Acts of Love and Pleasure Are Her Rituals, What about BDSM? Feminist Culture Wars in Contemporary Paganism," *Theology and Sexuality*," 24(2), pp. 1–14.

Owen, A. (1989) *The Darkened Room: Women, Power and Spiritualism in Late Victorian England*. London: Virago.

Owen, A. (2004) *A Place of Enchantment: British Occultism and the Cult of the Modern*. Chicago: University of Chicago Press.

Qadisha, A. (1996) "Procession of Babalon: The Evolution of the Goddess through the Aeons," *Sexmagick.com*. Accessed January 15, 2017 [https://web-beta.archive.org].

Rubin, G. (1984) "Thinking Sex: Notes for a Radical Theory of the Politics of Sexuality," in Vance, C.S. (ed.) *Pleasure and Danger: Exploring Female Sexuality*, pp. 267–321. Boston: Routledge and Kegan.

Schippers, M. (2007) "Recovering the Feminine Other: Masculinity, Femininity, and Gender Hegemony," *Theory and Society*, 36(1), pp. 85–102.

Scott, Joan W. (1986) "Gender: A Useful Category of Historical Analysis," *The American Historical Review*, 91(5), pp. 1053–1075.

Skeggs, B. (2001) "The Toilet Paper: Femininity, Class and Mis-Recognition," *Women's Studies International Forum*, 24(3/4), pp. 295–307.

Snoek, J.A.M. and Heidle, A. (2008) *Women's Agency and Rituals in Mixed and Female Masonic Orders*. Leiden: Brill.

Soror Syrinx (2014) *Traversing the Scarlet Path*. N.p.: America Star Books.

Strube, J. (2016) "The 'Baphomet' of Eliphas Lévi: Its Meaning and Historical Context," *Correspondences*, 4, pp. 37–79.

Styers, R. (2004) *Making Magic: Religion, Magic, and Science in the Modern World*. New York: Oxford University Press.

Vance, C.S. (ed.) (1992) *Pleasure and Danger: Exploring Female Sexuality*. London: Pandora Press.

Walker, L. (2012) "The Future of Femme: Notes on Femininity, Aging and Gender Theory," *Sexualities*, 15(7), pp. 795–814.

Warner, M. (ed.) (1993) *Fear of a Queer Planet. Queer Politics and Social Theory*. Minneapolis: University of Minnesota Press.

West, C. and Zimmerman, D. (1987) "Doing Gender," *Gender and Society*, 1(2), pp. 125–151.

Williams, B. (2009) "Feminist Thelema," in *Beauty and Strength: Proceedings of the Sixth Biennial National Ordo Templi Orientis Conference*. Riverside, CA: Ordo Templi Orientis.

What Do Jade Eggs Tell Us about the Category "Esotericism"? Spirituality, Neoliberalism, Secrecy, and Commodities

Susannah Crockford

While the literature on esoteric texts from antiquity through to the contemporary era is growing, there has been comparatively little written so far about material objects in esotericism and the economic conditions in which they are embedded. The products of contemporary spirituality are a starting point in this chapter, used to interrogate characterizations of the "commodification" of spirituality in neoliberalism, and the consequences this has for definitions of the category "esotericism." Focusing on scholarly arguments that esotericism is characterized by secrecy and rejected knowledge, I question how this applies in the context of global spirituality. Sociological theories of secrecy suggest how secrecy operates to enhance elite claims to power and elevated status. In the context of neoliberalism, claims to secrecy can be leveraged to make substantial profits. Previous definitions of esotericism have occluded this aspect of spirituality because they have failed to reckon with the power relations and economic relations in the field. By examining the material products through which contemporary esotericism has been commodified, the elitism inherent in the category is made overt.

1   An Introduction to Wellness, Goop-Style

Wellness products may seem to have little to do with esotericism at first glance, yet they are marketed with claims to secrecy and knowledge rejected by medical and scientific establishments. An emblematic example is the jade egg promulgated and–briefly–sold by the lifestyle company, Goop. The company was founded by the American actor and entrepreneur, Gwyneth Paltrow, and purveys a range of luxury clothing items, furniture, and wellness products online and through an email newsletter, as well as through a select number of boutiques in expensive locations in New York, Los Angeles, London, Toronto, and New England. There is a subsection "spirituality" on the website under the category "wellness," with an "ancient modality" tag for certain items. One such item was the jade egg, also available in rose quartz. The eggs were first recommended by one of Goop's "featured experts" (habitually representatives of alternative or naturopathic medicine), Shiva Rose. Rose called the jade eggs "the strictly guarded secret of Chinese royalty in antiquity," used by queens and concubines to help their relationships with emperors.[1] Through harnessing the power of energy work and crystal healing, and through insertion in the vagina, the egg would clear the energy of the wearer, providing a spiritual cleanse. It would also strengthen the muscles and increase the sensitivity of the vagina, cultivating sexual energy, intensifying femininity, invigorating life force, and clearing *qi* pathways. The specific type of crystal used was nephrite jade, to which Rose attributed the ability to take away negative energy. It was a substance with great spiritual power in "many traditions." Shiva Rose offered an "incredible, secret practice that benefited everybody," that was used in "Chinese temples" but kept secret for "eons" by the Chinese royal family.

The eggs were soon made available for purchase on the Goop website, advertised with the extra benefit of hormone balancing.[2] The reaction from Goop's consumers was swift: the eggs sold out within days. The reaction from the medical and legal establishments followed at a slower pace, with a lawsuit for false advertising and making medical claims without a license launched, eventually rendering a $145,000 fine and the eggs' withdrawal from sale by Goop.[3] They are still available from other merchants, and Goop's own doctors

---

1 The article originally appeared as "Better sex: jade eggs for your yoni," *Goop*, https://goop.com/wellness/sexual-heidh/better-sex-jade-eggs-for-your-yoni/ but has since been removed from the website. At the time of writing it is still available via the WayBackMachine, url: https://web.archive.org/web/20190718173851/https://goop.com/wellness/sexual-heidh/better-sex-jade-eggs-for-your-yoni/.
2 They remain advertised but not available to buy here https://shop.goop.com/shop/products/jade-egg.
3 The lawsuit and settlement were reported widely in the media at the time. See Julia Belluz, "Let's call Gwyneth Paltrow's jade eggs for vaginas what they are: Goopshit," *Vox* 25 January 2017, https://www.vox.com/policy-and-politics/2017/1/23/14352904/gwyneth-paltrow-jade-eggs; Julia Belluz, "Goop was fined $145,000 for its claims about jade eggs for vaginas. It's still selling them," *Vox* 6 September 2018, https://www.vox.com/2018/9/6/17826924/goop-yoni-egg-gwyneth-paltrow-settlement; Kristine Phillips, "No, Gwyneth Paltrow, women should not put jade eggs in their vaginas, gynecologist says," *Washington Post* 22 January 2017, https://www.washingtonpost.com/news/to-your-health/wp/2017/01/22/no-gwyneth-paltrow-women-should-not-put-jade-eggs-in-their-vaginas-gynecologist-says/
American gynaecologist and medical blogger, Jen Gunter, wrote against the use of jade eggs from a medical perspective, "Dear Gwyneth Paltrow, I'm a GYN and your vaginal jade eggs are a bad idea," 17 January 2017, https://drjengunter.com/2017/01/17/dear-gwyneth-paltrow-im-a-gyn-and-your-vaginal-jade-eggs-are-a-bad-idea/ Gunter argued that the hormone balancing claim is biologically impossible, "Gwyneth Paltrow and GOOP still want you to put a jade egg in your vagina. It's still a bad idea," 11 May 2017 https://drjengunter.com/2017/05/11/gwyneth-paltrows-jade-eggs-again/, she calls believing

wrote about jade eggs defending their business as standing up for marginalized women and their chronic health problems by providing information without judgment.[4] In the parlance of conspiracy theory, they were "just asking questions."[5]

The message of Goop is that there is a way to perfect oneself. By using the right products, it is possible to curate the perfect neoliberal self: energized, tight, fashionable, radiant, glowing.[6] It does, however, require plenty of money to access this route to perfection, as Goop sells primarily luxury fashion and accessories. The jade eggs were sold for $66 a piece. Goop has grown from a free email newsletter to a $250 million business, part of the $4.2 trillion global wellness industry.[7] Goop is not alone in offering a series of products, opaque in purpose and complexity, invoking grand visions of personal enhancement. The wellness industry both fuels and profits from the idea that physical beauty is proof of inner righteousness as well as health. Those perfect on the outside are assumed to be equally perfect inside. In a capitalist society, those that are able to afford this level of purchasable perfection are the wealthiest. There is, therefore, a strong vein of classism and elitism running through not only Goop but the ideology of wellness that informs the industry.

---

in the efficacy of jade a form of believing in magic. Gunter also searched online archives of Chinese antiquities and found no evidence of jade eggs used by the royal family, Elfy Scott, "No Goop, jade vaginal eggs are probably not a 'strictly-guarded secret' from Ancient China," *Buzzfeed News* 30 October 2018, https://www.buzzfeed.com/elfyscott/a-researcher-looked-at-5000-jade-objects-to-prove-vagina.

4 "Uncensored: A word from our contributing doctors," *Goop*, https://goop.com/wellness/health/uncensored-a-word-from-our-doctors/.
5 Interestingly, Alex Jones, host of *Infowars* and talk radio DJ infamous for spreading conspiracy theories, also sells wellness products and supplements similar to those available from Goop, and the majority of the company's profits seem to derive from this source despite being more well known for the sensationalist content on their website. Seth Brown, "Alex Jones's media empire is a machine built to sell snake-oil diet supplements," *New York Magazine* 4 May 2017, http://nymag.com/intelligencer/2017/05/how-does-alex-jones-make-money.html. On conspiracy theories and their relationship to New Age see Robertson 2016.
6 For a first person account of using Goop's products see Amanda Mill, "I gooped myself," *The Atlantic* 26 August 2019, https://www.theatlantic.com/health/archive/2019/08/what-goop-really-sells-women/596773/.
7 The market value estimate is from the annual report of the Global Wellness Institute, https://globalwellnessinstitute.org/press-room/statistics-and-facts/; On the growth of Goop as a business see Taffy Brodesser-Akner, "How Goop's haters made Gwyneth Paltrow's company worth $250 Million," *New York Times Magazine* 25 July 2018, https://www.nytimes.com/2018/07/25/magazine/big-business-gwyneth-paltrow-wellness.html and Olga Khazan, "The baffling rise of Goop," *The Atlantic* 12 September 2017, https://www.theatlantic.com/health/archive/2017/09/goop-popularity/539064/.

Wellness is an unregulated industry that capitalizes on people's desperation and insecurities, offering them cures for all ills and imperfections at high prices. Yet there is more to it than that, as wellness is the latest iteration of what has been known for some time as naturopathic or alternative medicine. The idea that Western biomedicine does not have the answer to every health problem is neither new nor particularly problematic (Baer, 2001). Naturopathic medicine is part of a wider current with many metaphysical, spiritual, and religious associations, informed by New Thought which emerged in America in the nineteenth century (Albanese, 2006, p. 395–421). It fits within the broad field of contemporary religious practice that is variously called the New Age Movement, New Age spirituality, or alternative spiritualities (Sutcliffe, 2002; Heelas, 1996; 2008; Heelas et al., 2005; Hanegraaff, 1996; Campion, 2016; Pike, 2004; Melton, 2007; Hammer, 2004, 2005; Partridge, 2004). Having studied this field for the past ten years, and completed two years of ethnographic fieldwork in the "New Age Mecca" Sedona, I prefer to simply use the term spirituality.[8] Healing modalities involving crystals, energy work, multiple vaguely referenced "ancient" or "indigenous" traditions were a vibrant and easily visible part of the spiritual scene in Sedona, and the wider networks of spirituality that stretch globally. Many benefits, spiritual and physical, were claimed, some of which were unverifiable, but which nonetheless seemed to help people even if the scientific basis was scant.

Jade eggs with *qi* boosting power would be seen as part of the range of acceptable and accepted claims in this milieu. Crystals, in particular, proliferated as part of healing practices, with different crystals attributed various properties such as clearing negative energy, enhancing meditative practice, or realigning chakras (see also Bartolini et al., 2013; Kyle, 1995). What any particular crystal did was an open, protean value, with the general assumption being that they had many special qualities and so any specific attribute was often left to personal interpretation and experience. One of my interlocutors in Sedona told me that she used one of her oblong crystals as a vibrator, since it was much better for the flow of her sexual energy than plastic. Within this milieu, jade eggs would not be cast out for being risible and dangerous, as they were in the media, legal courts, and medical opinion.

---

8 "New Age Mecca" is from Ivakhiv 2001, p. 147; for a substantive discussion of spirituality in Sedona and a working definition of spirituality, see Crockford 2017, 2018, 2019; on the term "spirituality" as a recent cultural category for what was once called New Age, see Huss 2014.

2   Healing, Inc.: Neoliberalism and Spirituality

Yet what does the alliance, embodied in jade eggs, between alternative healing modalities and the high-priced wellness retail industry indicate? The concurrence of the emergence of spirituality with the expansion of neoliberal capitalism has been noted by scholars (Huss, 2014; Redden, 2016; Heelas, 2008, p. 151–164; Possamai, 2003; LoRusso, 2017). Both emerged in North America and Western Europe during the 1970s to 1980s, sprouting up from the same socioeconomic context. The term "neoliberalism" is often used in as much of a vague, woolly, and diffuse way as spirituality is; however, a number of authors have given the term specificity. Loïc Wacquant (2009) set out a clear definition of neoliberalism as a specific set of policies that have been enacted by, or imposed on, governments globally. Deregulation, financialization, the expansion of mass incarceration, and the cultural trope of individual responsibility all characterized neoliberalism in Wacquant's account of the inequities this system caused, with the poor continually impinged, exploited, and incarcerated for the benefit of the wealthy. David Harvey (2005) sought to link neoliberalism to a specific state formation, and highlighted privatization, financialization, and deregulation as the economic policies that such states pursued. Aihwa Ong (2006) focused on neoliberalism as a form of governmentality, a network of power relations that created unequal access to freedom of movement, with capital and some types of citizen able to move freely, and others restricted behind borders.

Spirituality shares certain structural features with those outlined by political economic analyses of neoliberalism. It is a deregulated religion, with no central authority or creed or scripture determining orthodoxy and no priestly caste enforcing it. It is privatized–based on personal interior experience and beholden upon persons to determine for themselves–and part of the wider trend that José Casanova (1994) has named the privatization of religion. Financialization is the conversion of anything into capital: everything is for sale on the free market. Spirituality has been likened to a marketplace of religion (Redden, 2005), where beliefs and practices from any cultural or historical source are available for use and then resale to support spiritual practitioners who lack a supporting congregation or institutional body to pay for them as specialists. The cultural trope of individualism is very strong in spirituality also, where the route to spiritual development is considered to be up to the individual to discern and follow, and all other ties, including jobs, family, and homes can be forsaken in the pursuit of enlightenment.

There is one further value of neoliberalism to be considered, namely that of transparency. The neoliberal ideal is transparent governance (Mahmud, 2013,

p. 190). Freely available, reliable information about public and private business is seen as necessary for the functioning of the free market, to which all other ideals are subservient. Yet conspiracy and secrecy remain rife within neoliberal governance zones, despite supranational bodies like the International Monetary Fund enforcing transparency through anti-corruption requirements in exchange for debts and loans (Sanders and West, 2003, pp. 7–10). The dialectic of secrecy and transparency, concealment and revelation is another thread running through spirituality, one which connects it to the long history of currents that have been named esotericism.

3   Spirituality as Esotericism

To what extent spirituality is a form of esotericism, and whether this is a useful framing, depends of course on how esotericism is defined. In an early theorization of esotericism, Antoine Faivre drew an explicit boundary between esotericism proper and New Age, which he considered the province of studies of New Religious Movements (1994, p. 17). Wouter Hanegraaff defined what he called New Age religion as a form of secularized esotericism, because unlike previous currents of esotericism its "popular western culture criticism" emerged in a secularized rather than enchanted worldview (1996, pp. 520–521). Olav Hammer (2004, pp. 76–77) located New Age as the latest in a historical current of esoteric positions, and provided a useful nine point characterization of it. The work of Hanegraaff and Hammer brought spirituality into esotericism research in a way that Faivre initially avoided.

At which point we have arrived at the core issue: what is esotericism anyway? Much of the work of what Hanegraaff labels the second generation of esotericism studies has been to overturn the religionist paradigms that went before (Hanegraaff, 2016, p. 167). In this mostly historically focused research, esotericism has tended to be defined in oppositional terms, as a "counter" to mainstream knowledge or discourse. In what is perhaps currently the most widely used definition of esotericism, it is a form of rejected knowledge that formed part of how modern identity has been constructed; indeed the "polemical Other of modernity" (Hanegraaff, 2012, p. 374). It is an alternative that remains attractive to those wishing to reject the dominant rationalism of the Enlightenment, for example as Romanticism took as positive what the Enlightenment saw as negative. This is, naturally, a simplification, but the binary of mainstream/alternative reoccurs throughout current definitions of esotericism, as with Hanegraaff's labelling of spirituality as a form of popular western culture criticism. This defines spirituality, which he called "New Age religion," as first of all popular, with which Hanegraaff seems to mean something like a mass as opposed to elite phenomenon, or perhaps more simply that many people seem to like it. Secondly, it is "western"—although the boundaries of this historical-geographical-cultural construction remain unclear, since Hanegraaff uses the term in an under-calibrated way (cf. Strube, 2021). Finally, it is as a form of criticism–New Age is against whatever is dominant, mainstream, or supported by epistemic authorities. At the same time, Hanegraaff accepts that the label "esoteric" has become, in contemporary esotericism, a "desired commodity" (2012, p. 360). As discussed in more detail in Egil Asprem's chapter in this volume, this points to the power of being "alternative" or "rejected," that claiming out-group status can be valuable in some contexts.

The idea that what they are selling has been rejected by the dominant, mainstream powers that be was creatively deployed in the marketing of the jade egg, and in Goop's response to the backlash by said powers. The company's staff doctors claimed to be simply providing information, and countered that doctors and lawyers who complained about the lack of empirical basis of that information were marginalizing women and their choices. There is, as Asprem (2021) also suggests, ambiguous politics layered beneath adopting positions of rejected or alternative knowledge. What is the mainstream here? The medical and legal authorities objecting to crystals as a healing modality? Or the multimillion-dollar valued corporation run by a movie star? I set up this opposition intentionally–what is mainstream and what is rejected, what is dominant and what is alternative, what is orthodox and what is esoteric–is neither an obvious nor a neutral categorization. It is also not a stable or fixed position. The boundaries of mainstream/alternative shift and are contingent on the historical period and cultural context. Much like the term "western," esotericism is a politically and economically mediated category and scholars have to deal with these implications.

Claims to being marginalized or rejected by an ambiguously identified mainstream or dominant position are a common component in discourses of secrecy. The secret of the jade egg was kept by the elites for "eons," and now that secret can be revealed–even if "they" do not want you to know about it. Secrecy grants a form of social power. Hugh Urban (2001) employs the sociological works of Georg Simmel (1950, pp. 307–315) and Pierre Bourdieu (1984) to call secrecy an adornment that can grant forms of capital. In the formation of Scottish Rite Freemasonry in post-Civil War America–a period of intense social change, economic growth, industrialization, and urbanization–the secrecy of the clubs helped white middle-class European-descended Protestant males maintain their status. Lodges were conservative, elitist, and respectable, enabling the maintenance of socioeconomic power through the exclusion of others. What went on at the clubs was not nearly so important as who was and who was not allowed in.

Urban argues that the prevalence of secrecy warrants a theoretical shift in the scholarly approach to esotericism because the content of the secret is often unknowable, or once known, not permissible to transmit to the uninitiated, something he calls the "double bind" of secrecy (1998, p. 212). Identifying another period of upheaval and transition in colonial Bengal, Urban suggests the Kartābhajās, a group in the Vaiṣṇava-Sahajiyā Tantric tradition, gained new forms of power, status, prestige, and identity through secrecy. An elaborate ritual language that seemed nonsensical to the uninitiated allowed the group to imply that they held powerful and valuable secrets. Although the comparison is inexact–unlike American Freemasons the Kartābhajās were low caste and denied economic and symbolic wealth in Indian society both before and during British colonial rule–in both contexts secret societies allowed for the development of social and economic capital through membership. Urban's comparative approach articulates two different kinds of secrecy dynamic: a social function that builds cohesion and elevates the status of a group and a rhetoric of secrecy attached to content both when it is unknowable and well known. Delineating some structural features of secrecy grants the potential to use it as a concept for identifying esotericism across different geographical and historical contexts.

The significance of secrecy, for Urban, is how it operates to grant value to certain forms of knowledge, so that possession of secret knowledge is beneficial in social and political terms to the bearer. A similar position is adopted by Kocku von Stuckrad, who argues that esotericism is a discourse characterized by secrecy and structured by a dialectic of concealment and revelation (2010, p. 243). Secrecy grants social capital, in Bourdieu's sense, because it grants a superior position on the field through knowing something which cannot be shared freely. It is elitist, superior and exclusive, and can also be translated into economic capital. When speaking of the jade egg, this approach seems to fit the claims to a certain extent: buying it is a way of buying in to the secret it embodies and it is only available to those that can afford it. But here a neoliberal economist could argue that it is therefore "freely" available because it is available on the free market, and all citizens in the marketplace are free to sell their labor in exchange for a wage that they can spend on consumer objects as they wish. Jade eggs are not limited to a specific sector of the population nor do they require initiation into a certain organization. It is a commodity.

4 Secrecy, Concealment, and Jade Eggs

When thinking through the dialectic of concealment and revelation that both von Stuckrad and Urban emphasize, what does the jade egg reveal? It is the object of revelation, a secret concealed by Chinese royalty to be disclosed by Shiva Rose through the medium of Goop. The actions required to learn of its content are reading the Goop website and paying money in its webstore. It is marketed to consumers, but not all consumers equally. It is aimed at affluent, anglophone women (the webstore is in English even when set to deliver in Germany or Italy). The market is women who are likely to be older, post-childbirth, and concerned with their social status as well as their physical, sexual and emotional health. Buying the jade egg is not simply a case of purchasing a product. It also buys into the idea, backed by a holistic worldview and claims to secret, ancient knowledge, that such an object is efficacious.

As some scholars have noted (e.g. Hanegraaff, 2016, pp. 163–164), secrecy is not unique to esotericism. This, however, does not mean that secrecy should be excluded as a defining characteristic of the category. The status of being rejected or polemically marginalized is not the sole preserve of esoteric currents, either. Arguably, there are far more systemic marginalizations (along the lines of gender, race, class…) that went into the constitution of "western modernity." What marks esotericism is perhaps the conjunction of the two: a current that clouds itself in obscurity and at the same time has been rejected or marginalized by what is perceived as a more dominant cultural force. Secrecy operates as a basis around which social groups form, mitigating harm through veiling authorship of controversial texts or enrollment in socially questionable clubs (Debenport, 2019). It has been a tenet in social scientific treatments of secrecy, since Simmel, that it is not the content of the secret but its context and functions that matter. This is not to disregard the content, but to acknowledge, as Urban does, that it may be unknowable or untransmittable, and moreover, to understand that the power of the secret in society depends on the conditions of its production and its authorship.[9]

With the specificity of context, secrecy creates value, and its possession excludes outsiders and includes insiders (Jones, 2014, pp. 54–55). It is this dy-

---

9 To illustrate with an example: If I told you that a woman in her sixties living in New York State deleted thousands of old emails, you would rightly treat the disclosure of this secret with the banality it warrants. With the context that this specific woman was Hillary Rodham Clinton, former senator and presidential candidate, and the disclosure occurred three days prior to the US presidential election in 2016, coming from the mouth of the FBI director, this secret gains the power to shift the course of global geopolitical events.

namic, I argue, that is fundamental to esotericism, and what makes the category inherently elitist. Secrets need to be performed in public to be powerful, they must be known to exist. They are concealed to most, disclosed to only a chosen few, and there is power–and capital–in being one of the chosen. Initiatory secrets in particular have a sense of spectacle, being known by many yet only few have the authority to disclose their content–a form of "public secret" (Taussig, 1999). This is illustrated by Lilith Mahmud's (2013) ethnography of Freemasonry in contemporary Italy. Despite being "profane," meaning not initiated into a Masonic lodge and therefore not allowed to know of the content of their rites, Mahmud found that her Masonic interlocutors were happy to discuss their rites and practices after developing friendships with her. The content of lodge rituals was indeed long known to the public because they had been exposed by disgruntled former members and through the media. Even so, Mahmud was not focused on the content of the secret rituals but on how the members of lodges she came to know leveraged their elite positions and relationships to negotiate their status in a society that had become hostile to right wing secret societies. Her characterization of Masonic knowledge production illuminates the production of knowledge in esotericism more widely: "The secret was always in front of our eyes, but it is only in hindsight that we can understand it" (2013, p. 201).

Secrecy as a marker of group identity has been observed by anthropologists in initiatory rituals cross-culturally (Stewart and Strathern, 2014, p. 79). The exegesis of such rituals may not mean the same to specialists and ordinary participants, and certain aspects can be revealed to some but hidden to others. Tanya Luhrmann (1989) applies the anthropological lens to ritual magic in England, remarking that it gave the middle-class professionals a way to better handle their emotions and behavior. The effects of the rituals had a psychological benefit, even if magic could not be scientifically verified. It granted a sense of control over events, elevating the practitioner to a privileged position even if only in their own estimation. This is close to the argument Goop's doctors made in favor of the jade egg. It was not an argument of verifiability in a scientific sense but of psychological and emotional efficacy: putting women in control of their bodies through an object they found useful, even if experts scoffed.

But why should middle-class practitioners of ritual magic, or middle-class practitioners of crystal healing, strive for a sense of control and power? A sense of exclusion can be met with a reassertion of value through inclusion in an alternate group. A woman who feels her symptoms or feelings are not countenanced by conventional medicine can turn to naturopathic medicine. Anxiety increased in neoliberal economies as the middle class shrank. As economic inequality was exacerbated through neoliberal policies that shifted more of the wealth to ever smaller proportions of the population, and real wages remained stagnant, middle class status became harder to maintain (Harvey, 2005, pp. 35–38). Casualization of contracts increased insecurity, as withdrawal of social provision snipped the safety net of welfare states, making the consequences of downward social mobility more devastating. Under neoliberalism, those who manage to remain middle class have much to be anxious about, and material reasons to desire power and control over their lives. Spirituality then becomes a way out of one status, perceived as slipping or failing, through claiming a different status.

The doubleness of secrecy as both known and unknown enhances the value of an alternative status or group membership. This is exemplified by the book, *The Secret* (2006). Despite its name, it is one of the most well-known and best-selling books in English language publishing in the last thirty years, now in its tenth edition. It promises a secret of great value: that you, the individual, are in control of your own reality. This is one of the core tenets of spirituality more widely: each person creates their own reality. *The Secret* offers New Thought-inspired affirmations as a way of manifesting abundance, meaning prosperity, money, good health, whatever one values as worth creating. This is a religious formulation of the cultural trope of individual responsibility in neoliberalism. The poor are responsible and also deserving of their poverty, and the wealthy earn their riches. This abnegates the influence of social structure to the extent that it exacerbates class politics. Secrecy is indeed an important strand of class politics. Obscuring what occurs among, how to act in, or move into higher classes, enables elites to exacerbate divisions among the working and middle classes. The working classes suspect that there are secret cabals making decisions they are not privy to and that do not benefit their interests (Sanders and West, 2003, pp. 11–12).

Secrecy and concealment provide not only the sense of control over one's own self, they also offer a route to control others through demarcation of in-groups and out-groups. As Urban suggests for both post-Civil War America and colonial Bengal, secrecy and membership of secret groups can offer a means to hold onto socioeconomic status, or claim it when it is denied. There is an important aspect of esotericism that is about power, and more specifically attempts to attain, maintain or retain elite status. Secrecy is part of how elitism is produced, this is Simmel's power of the secret. In secret societies, the point is to claim there is a secret, not to reveal the secret nor to keep its very existence hidden. The existence of the secret needs to be revealed, but its content limited to the initiated. The power is in having it and claiming that most other people do not know it, and are therefore inferior because of this lack of knowledge. Who is keeping the secret and for what reason? What group can be formed around the secret? What is the cost of access to the secret? These are important questions to ask of any esoteric currents.

Yet such questions are often left unasked, or relegated to the status of discourse. The academic study of esotericism, coming as it does from intellectual history, all too often revolves around texts of white Western European male authors, a canon that excludes even as it makes claims to being excluded (Bakker, 2019). Defining esotericism as only rejected, hidden, or secret knowledge, without examining what such claims *do*–socially, economic, politically–obscures the implied power relations. Scholars then run the risk of defining esotericism as practitioners of esotericism would want to be defined, as if they really did have a secret. Certain esoteric currents may be rejected but perhaps what is more important, in socioeconomic and political terms, is that they are not universally rejected. A group or form of knowledge or practice that is rejected by some, but not by others, gives those who adopt it a new way of defining their identity. Through joining a secret group, members are acquiring social and economic capital, in contrast to and often antagonism with those that might or do reject them. Spirituality is not rejected by many, but it is rejected by some and that enhances its reputation to those to whom it appeals. The internal differentiation of marginalized groups or discourses creates social hierarchies, an example of "credibility mobility" (Asprem, forthcoming, pp. 22–25).

5 Commodities and Commodification of Spirituality, a Brief Conclusion

Spirituality and its overt and obvious links to neoliberalism lead to it being cast aside as "commodified," devalued as trivial or insignificant because it incorporates consumerism (Redden, 2016). Commodification of religion has been treated with a certain suspicion in historical studies, yet the exchange of commodities for profit has played a role in many different types of religion historically and cross-culturally. Esotericism studies tend towards a certain idealism, or at least, an elevation of ideas and the texts that encode them over objects, commodities, and material conditions. This is partly because the materiality of esotericism is harder to find in historical sources, texts, and so on. Yet objects can enact the same strategy of secrecy as esoteric texts–this is a powerful object, its power is secret, only the initiated elite may access it. Spirituality is replete with objects imbued with special properties, such as crystals, that can be sold and are expected to be sold. It is also possible to construct a whole spiritual path around buying and selling and meditating with crystals. Their flow as commodities does not cancel out their spiritual value. Esotericism looks different when looking at it ethnographically, sociologically, at people living and enacting it now, as opposed to sifting through textual sources (Crockford and Asprem, 2018).

It is much easier to see the elitism of esotericism in the exchange of commodities that also grant spiritual power–it is overt. The most spiritually potent crystals are often the most expensive ones, such as crystal skulls which are sold for thousands of dollars. It is also easier to see the emptiness of the secret. There is often an aura of authenticity that cloaks historical sources, particularly the more ancient ones. But a jade egg can be bought and tested, the value dependent on the ascription of its purchaser more obvious, and its claims to efficacy can be subject to legal challenges. The self-affirming nature of much of spirituality means that it does not matter so much if its objects are efficacious, it matters if people buy it, talk about it, and use it. The secrecy makes them feel like it is worth trying: get in on the secret, into the club, become one of the insiders, the initiated, the elect.

Esotericism as a system of knowledge production has a particular history, and the claims to knowledge are based on the origin of that knowledge being in some way concealed from most eyes–hidden, rejected, secret, and so on. The definitions of the category of esotericism need to be pushed further, to examine the social and economic positions and power relations involved. Who rejects it and who does not? Who benefits from adopting a secret tradition? What does the secret do, in other words? A secret is a way of creating value, and value has no essence, no content, no subjectivity. Value is a magical power, the process of assigning something from nothing (Graeber, 2011, p. 246). This must be hidden, made secret, or else its facade will fall, like the Wizard of Oz. Esotericism is an inherently elitist system of knowledge production, intended for the few, the initiated, the elect, with the power and knowledge to glimpse what must be hidden. But in the end, the secret is that there is no secret.

Bibliography

Albanese, C.L. (2006) *A Republic of Mind and Spirit: A Cultural History of American Metaphysical Religion*. New Haven: Yale University Press.

Asprem, E. (2021) "Rejected Knowledge Reconsidered: Some Methodological Notes on Esotericism and Marginality," in Asprem, E. and Strube, J. (eds.) *New Approaches to the Study of Esotericism*. Leiden and Boston: Brill, pp. 127–146.

Asprem, E. (forthcoming) "On the Social Organisation of Rejected Knowledge: Re-assessing the Sociology of the Occult," in Hedenborg White, M. and Rudbøg, T.

(eds.) *Western Esotericism and Deviance: Proceedings of the Sixth International Conference of the European Society for the Study of Western Esotericism*. Leiden: Brill, pp. 1–36 [Author's pre-print].

Baer, H.A. (2001) "The Sociopolitical Status of U.S. Naturopathy at the Dawn of the 21st Century," *Medical Anthropology Quarterly*, 15(3), pp. 329–346. [Online] DOI: 10.1525/maq.2001.15.3.329.

Bakker, J.M. (2019) "Hidden Presence: Race and/in the History, Construct, and Study of Western Esotericism," *Religion*, pp. 1–25. [Online] DOI: 10.1080/0048721X.2019.1642262.

Bartolini, N. et al. (2013) "Psychics, Crystals, Candles and Cauldrons: Alternative Spiritualities and the Question of Their Esoteric Economies," *Social & Cultural Geography*, 14(4), pp. 367–388.

Bourdieu, P. (1984) *Distinction: A Social Critique of the Judgement of Taste*. London: Routledge.

Byrne, R. (2006) *The Secret*. New York: Atria Books/Beyond Worlds.

Campion, N. (2016) *The New Age in the Modern West: Counterculture, Utopia and Prophecy from the Late Eighteenth Century to the Present Day*. London: Bloomsbury Academic.

Casanova, J. (1994) *Public Religions in the Modern World*. Chicago: University of Chicago Press.

Crockford, S. (2017) *After the American Dream: The Political Economy of Spirituality in Northern Arizona*. Unpublished PhD thesis. London School of Economics and Political Sciences.

Crockford, S. (2018) "A Mercury Retrograde Kind of Day: Exploring Astrology in Contemporary New Age Spirituality and American Social Life," *Correspondences*, 6(1), pp. 47–75 [Online].

Crockford, S. (2019) "Becoming a Being of Pure Consciousness: Fasting and New Age Spirituality," *Nova Religio*, 23(1), pp. 38–59.

Crockford, S. and Asprem, E. (2018) "Ethnographies of the Esoteric: Introducing Anthropological Methods and Theories to the Study of Contemporary Esotericism," *Correspondences*, 6(1), pp. 1–23 [Online].

Debenport, E. (2019) "What is Secrecy and How Can We Understand Its Relation to Social Facts?," *American Anthropologist*, 121(1), pp. 201–204.

Faivre, A. (1994) *Access to Western Esotericism*. Albany: State University of New York Press.

Graeber, D. (2011) *Debt: The First 5,000 Years*. New York: Melville House.

Hammer, O. (2004) *Claiming Knowledge: Strategies of Epistemology from Theosophy to the New Age*. Leiden: Brill.

Hammer, O. (2005) "New Age and the Discursive Construction of Community," *Journal of Alternative Spiritualities and New Age Studies*, 1, pp. 111–127.

Hanegraaff, W.J. (1996) *New Age Religion and Western Culture: Esotericism in the Mirror of Secular Thought*. Leiden: Brill.

Hanegraaff, W.J. (2012) *Esotericism and the Academy: Rejected Knowledge in Western Culture*. Cambridge: Cambridge University Press.

Hanegraaff, W.J. (2016) "Esotericism Theorized: Major Trends and Approaches to the Study of Esotericism," in DeConick, A. (ed.) *Religion: Secret Religion*. New York: Macmillan, pp. 155–170.

Harvey, D. (2005) *A Brief History of Neoliberalism*. Oxford: Oxford University Press.

Heelas, P. (1996) *The New Age Movement: The Celebration of the Self and the Sacralization of Modernity*. Oxford: Blackwell.

Heelas, P. (2008) *Spiritualities of Life: New Age Romanticism and Consumptive Capitalism*. Oxford: Blackwell.

Heelas, P. et al. (2005) *The spiritual revolution: why religion is giving way to spirituality*. Oxford: Wiley-Blackwell.

Huss, B. (2014) "Spirituality: The Emergence of a New Cultural Category and Its Challenge to the Religious and the Secular," *Journal of Contemporary Religion*, 29(1), pp. 47–60.

Ivakhiv, A. (2001) *Claiming Sacred Ground: Pilgrims and Politics at Glastonbury and Sedona*. Bloomington: Indiana University Press.

Jones, G.M. (2014) "Secrecy," *Annual Review of Anthropology*, 43(1), pp. 53–69.

Kyle, R.G. (1995) *The New Age Movement in American Culture*. Lanham: University Press of America.

LoRusso, J.D. (2017) *Spirituality, Corporate Culture, and American Business: The Neoliberal Ethic and the Spirit of Global Capital*. London: Bloomsbury Academic.

Luhrmann, T.M. (1989) "The Magic of Secrecy," *Ethos*, 17(2), pp. 131–165.

Mahmud, L. (2013) "The Profane Ethnographer: Fieldwork with a Secretive Organisation," in Garsten, C. and Nyqvist, A. (eds) *Organisational Anthropology: Doing Ethnography in and among Complex Organisations*. London: Pluto Press, pp. 189–207.

Melton, J.G. (2007) "Beyond Millenialism: The New Age Transformed," in Kemp, D. and Lewis, J.R. (eds) *Handbook of new age*. Leiden: Brill, pp. 77–101.

Ong, A. (2006) *Neoliberalism as Exception: Mutations in Citizenship and Sovereignty*. Durham: Duke University Press.

Partridge, C. (2004) *Re-Enchantment of the West: Alternative Spiritualities, Sacralisation, Popular Culture and Occulture*. London: T&T Clark.

Pike, S.M. (2004) *New Age and Neopagan Religions in America*. New York: Columbia University Press.

Possamai, A. (2003) "Alternative Spiritualities and the Cultural Logic of Late Capitalism," *Culture and Religion*, 4(1), pp. 31–43.

Redden, G. (2005) "The New Age: Towards a Market Model," *Journal of Contemporary Religion*, 20(2), pp. 231–246.

Redden, G. (2016) "Revisiting the Spiritual Supermarket: Does the Commodification of Spirituality Necessarily Devalue It?," *Culture and Religion*, 17(2), pp. 231–249.

Robertson, D.G. (2016) *UFOs, Conspiracy Theories and the New Age: Millennial Conspiracism*. London: Bloomsbury.

Sanders, T. and West, H.G. (2003) "Power Revealed and Concealed in the New World Order," in West, H.G. and Sanders, T. (eds.) *Transparency and Conspiracy: Ethnographies of Suspicion in the New World Order*. Durham: Duke University Press, pp. 1–37.

Simmel, G. (1950) *The Sociology of Georg Simmel*. Translated by K.H. Wolff. Glencoe: The Free Press.

Stewart, P.J. and Strathern, A. (2014) *Ritual: Key Concepts in Religion*. London: Bloomsbury Academic.

Strube, J. (2021) "Towards the Study of Esotericism without the 'Western'": Esotericism from the Perspective of a Global Religious History," in Asprem, E. and Strube, J. (eds.) *New Approaches to the Study of Esotericism*, Leiden and Boston: Brill, pp. 45–66.

Sutcliffe, S. (2002) *Children of the New Age: A History of Spiritual Practices*. London: Routledge.

Taussig, M.T. (1999) *Defacement: Public Secrecy and the Labor of the Negative*. Stanford: Stanford University Press.

Urban, H.B. (1998) "The Torment of Secrecy: Ethical and Epistemological Problems in the Study of Esoteric Traditions," *History of Religions*, 37(3), pp. 209–248.

Urban, H.B. (2001) "The Adornment of Silence: Secrecy and Symbolic Power in American Freemasonry," *Journal of Religion & Society*, 3, pp. 1–29.

Von Stuckrad, K. (2010) "Secrecy as Social Capital," in Kilcher, A.B. (ed.) *Constructing Tradition: Means and Myths of Transmission in Western Esotericism*. Leiden: Brill, pp. 239–253.

Wacquant, L.J.D. (2009) *Punishing the Poor: The Neoliberal Government of Social Insecurity*. Durham: Duke University Press.

Interpretation Reconsidered: The Definitional Progression in the Study of Esotericism as a Case in Point for the Varifocal Theory of Interpretation

Dimitry Okropiridze

This chapter sets out to explore and resolve a philosophical problem, which is at the core of each and every act of interpretation, no matter the subject. Scholarship on esotericism will serve as a case study for the conundrum of opposing interpretations, which—regardless of the intellectual effort—cannot be squared due to their incommensurability and cannot be applied adequately due to their individual necessity. Once the simultaneous incommensurability and individual necessity of the interpretational directionalities in question is understood, a philosophically coherent outline of their side-by-side application emerges, helping the study of esotericism—and by extension the study of any given entity—to a clearer and broader comprehension of the respective subject of inquiry.

The first segment starts out with the definitional progression in the study of esotericism, by selecting the approaches advanced by Antoine Faivre, Wouter Hanegraaff, Michael Bergunder, and Egil Asprem. The argument made here consists in the observation that interpretations of esotericism fall into two categories; one assumes that our interpretation results from esotericism *showing itself* to the interpreter while the other suggests that our interpretations are *socially negotiated projections*. The second segment argues that these two fundamental modes of interpretation can be thought of as fundamentally irreconcilable directionalities of interpretation. The implication is that the incommensurability at the core of the interpretational endeavor must be understood philosophically in order to arrive at a clear understanding of esotericism. The third segment explores the rationale behind the simultaneously incommensurable and individually necessary directionalities of interpretation, emphasizing the need to reject attempts of forcibly synthesizing both approaches as the fusion of one with the other is logically impossible, leading to contradictions and a fragmentary appreciation of the interpreted subject. The fourth segment provides a philosophically reflected theory of interpretation, which refrains from a hierarchical ordering of the two incommensurable directionalities, allowing for an analysis of esotericism that continuously oscillates between one and the other option, in order to arrive at an optimal understanding of the subject. The fifth and last segment summarizes the argument and offers a perspective on the broader application of the established theory of interpretation.

1 The Definitional Progression in the Study of Esotericism[1]

The quest for the ontological substance of esotericism amidst the epistemological uncertainties of history took place through the assumption that signifiers (i.e., entities that *indicate* meaning) such as "esotericism" possessed epistemologically accessible signifieds (i.e., the *expressed* sense): whatever esotericism was, would show itself to the interpreter, once closely examined. Even scholars acknowledging the semantic fluidity of esotericism's signified expected to find specific and enumerable qualities belonging to the phenomenon in question. In his unambiguously titled monograph *Access to Western Esotericism* (1994) the pioneering scholar Antoine Faivre cautioned against essentialist assumptions about esotericism:

> Above all, we do not want to start with what "esotericism" would be "in itself," we doubt that such a thing exists. Nor is it even a domain in the sense we would use in speaking of the domain of painting, philosophy, or chemistry. Rather than a specific genre, it [i.e., esotericism, D.O.] is a form of thought, the nature of which we have to try and capture on the basis of the currents which exemplify it. (Faivre, 1994, p. 4)

A philosophically informed glance at Faivre's displacement of esotericism from a "thing in itself" to a "form of thought" reveals it to be a distinction without a difference,[2] since Faivre did precisely what he set out to avoid: laying claim to the ontology (i.e., the "nature") of esotericism (i.e., "a form of

---

1 As it is impossible to discuss the entirety of approaches to esotericism on these pages, a number of prominent articulations are selected, in order to set up the ensuing philosophical argument. This does not suggest that the selected approaches can provide a definitive summary of the many academic perspectives on esotericism. Nor does it imply that the approaches discussed here should be reduced to the presented and analyzed material, as the perspective of the authors has continued to evolve throughout their scholarship. This chapter deliberately drops the term "Western" from the often-used notion of "Western esotericism," following the argument advanced by Julian Strube, 2021.

2 Given the (post)Kantian notions of "thing in itself" and "form of thought," Faivre's displacement can be read as an attempt to de-ontologize esotericism and render it an epistemological framework, thereby echoing the narrativizing and discursive approaches. However, as will be argued here, there is no such thing in human interpretation as epistemology without ontological implications and vice versa. Moreover, one does not have priority over the

thought"). This presupposition of an observer-independent reality "out there," making itself epistemologically available to the interpreter, becomes even more apparent in Faivre's emphasis that through the careful study of the material pertaining to esotericism "[...] we see harmonies and contrasts appear before us" (Faivre, 1994, p. 3). Faivre structured said harmonies and contrasts by attributing to them more or less fixed terminological associations—e.g., gnosis, theosophy, secrecy, occultism, Hermeticism (Faivre, 1994, pp. 19–35)—and debating esotericism in terms of socio-historical (e.g., antiquity, the Middle Ages, the Renaissance etc.) contexts (Faivre, 1994).

The post-Faivre development of an ever more nuanced history of esotericism, tended to move away from essentializing esotericism, instead aiming at narrativizing definitions (i.e., looking at esotericism as appearing in and shaped through linguistic/textual practices). Wouter Hanegraaff suggested that the discourse on "ancient wisdom" in the Renaissance brought about a grand narrative, challenging long-established ideas about the relation between "philosophy and theology, or rationality and revelation" (2012, p. 6). Hanegraaff went on to point out that:

> this grand narrative of "ancient wisdom" survived as a widespread but officially discredited countercurrent at odds with mainstream intellectual thought. It has been accepted or implied, in one version or another, by most of the authors and practitioners studied under the umbrella of Western esotericism, up to the present; but, interestingly, it has also strongly influenced the thinking even of the most important modern scholars who have shaped and developed that field. (2012, pp. 6–7)

If, as Hanegraaff seems to imply here, esotericism should be regarded not as a self-sufficient ontological entity, but as a historical web of linguistic/textual negotiations debating the relation between "philosophy and theology, or rationality and revelation", the ontological status of the negotiated subjects (i.e., philosophy, theology/rationality, revelation) must be clarified. On the one hand, Hanegraaff's reifying usage of these signifiers suggests that they can be regarded as self-sufficient ontological entities offering themselves to be "figured out" through various narratives (e.g., "this grand narrative of 'ancient wisdom'" vs. "mainstream intellectual thought"). On the other hand, Hanegraaff's theoretical practice (i.e., his lack of essentialist definitions and the

---

other, since what is epistemological implies an ontology and what is ontological requires epistemology.

tendency to treat every subject as a narrative) suggests that philosophy and theology/rationality and revelation are equally to be seen as narratives, which would render esotericism a negotiated narrative *about* negotiated narratives. Consequently, the narrativizing approach leaves the scholar with the study of competing stories, excluding us from studying reality outside of its emergence in the socio-historically dominant paradigm (Kuhn, 1962); not esotericism, but the discursive formation of what esotericism *came to mean* and *continues to become* would then constitute our subject of inquiry. Although this line of thought would constitute a coherent and significant departure from the essentialist impetus visible in Faivre, Hanegraaff is reluctant to deny the agency of his source materials:

> In other words, I am not interested in selecting from my materials only the supposedly "esoteric elements" (whatever those might be) but in studying the full complexity of sources that can be seen as falling under the umbrella of "Western esotericism." Yet another way of saying this is that I want to begin with an attitude of *listening* to whatever my sources want to tell me, rather than an attitude of *telling* them what they can and cannot talk about. (Hanegraaff, 2013, p. 255)

Here, Hanegraaff reveals a crucial inconsistency: on the one hand, he rejects an essentialist understanding of esotericism ("supposedly 'esoteric elements'"), which suggests a narrative character of what is deemed to belong to esotericism. On the other hand, he trusts his sources to inform him about the elements "falling under the umbrella of 'Western esotericism,'" thereby making his way back to an essentialist notion.

The displacement emerging from Faivre's to Hanegraaff's understanding of esotericism—i.e., the fragmentary shift from the hope for the ontology of esotericism to make itself epistemologically available to the assumption of the epistemological manufacturing of esotericism's ontology—was taken to the next level by the poststructuralist variety of the linguistic turn: the latter declared any articulation about any given entity based on the presupposed "essence" of said entity to be the product of historically and geographically contingent meaning negotiations, rather than descriptions of an extra-discursive reality (Foucault, 1977). Consequently, Michael Bergunder has opted to regard "esotericism" as a discursive entity, the processuality of which can be traced in time and space. Bergunder argued with strong recourse to the philosophy and political thought of Ernesto Laclau that the formation of a more or less stable signified attached to the signifier "esotericism"—e.g., Faivre's placing of esotericism in gnosis, theosophy, and secrecy—takes place through articulatory chains emphasizing equivalence (i.e., similarity among elements) and difference (i.e., dissimilarity between elements) (Bergunder, 2010, pp. 20–22). Following the semiotic understanding of Laclau (2005), the given discursive environment can be regarded as the social context in which "esotericism" is understood to be *present in* elements p, q, r—for instance in "gnosis," "theosophy," "secrecy"—and *absent from* x, y, z—for instance, "scientific materialism," "religious fundamentalism," "institutionalized religion."[3] Through asymmetric, i.e., hegemony-aspiring processes of negotiation with competing individuals, collectives, and institutions and always temporary "winners" and "losers" of the negotiated outcome, the signified—e.g., the accepted notion of "esotericism"—is established, subverted, and re-established in an ever-conflictual field of rivaling ascriptions (Bergunder, 2010, pp. 20–22). Hinting at the thoroughly, if not exclusively historicizing dimension of scholarship implied by the discursive approach, Bergunder suggested highlighting the role of hegemonic constellations for the formations of esotericism:

> esotericism can be understood as a general term of identification in the form of an empty signifier, which is articulated and reproduced by means of a discourse community and in different fields of discourse. In this sense, esotericism is a historical phenomenon and is to be understood neither as nominalistic nor idealistic, but as a contingent nodal point or rather as the fixing of a contentious power discourse. (2010, p. 26)

While it seems plausible to regard esotericism as a "term of identification," Bergunder's approach begs the question as to how to regard (and whether to trust) his own theoretical tools. After all, terms such as "discourse," "empty signifier," and "power" might be terms of identification of their own, which would make them "the fixing of a contentious power discourse" in their own right. But in that case, Bergunder would be basing his approach to esotericism on something just as discursive and unstable as esotericism itself. If, on the other hand, "discourse," "empty signifiers," and "power" are located beyond the discursive ambit, it is unclear how their ontological status can be substantiated by the discursive approach itself, which must, according to its own presupposition, regard claims to truth as the result of contingent socio-historical negotiations.

Looking back at the progression from Faivre to Hanegraaff to Bergunder, three effects have originated as a result of the repositioning from the attempt

---

3 The significatory examples given for x, y, z as the chain constituting "non-esotericism" are my own suggestions, based on the discursive gravitation surrounding the signifier "esotericism." Cf. Hanegraaff, 2012.

to directly access esotericism's ontology to the view of historically changing epistemologies as "production sites" of esotericism. First, the object of study has ceased to be defined by the respective scholar's fiat and/or informed by hegemonic interpretations, often of orientalist and theological provenance, making the latter part and parcel of the critical analysis of esotericism's history as a subset of genealogical approaches (King, 1999; Masuzawa, 2005; McCutcheon, 1997). Second, the now fully semanticized subject of investigation has been thoroughly dematerialized and disembodied: material and somatic elements historically associated with esotericism such as altered states of consciousness, the immersion into archetypal mythologies, and alchemical practices (Hanegraaff, 2012), have been cut back to their emergence as entities *within* discourse. Third, the rejection of an extra-discursive ontology and its replacement with the epistemology of discourse has effectively reified poststructuralist linguistics as the sole locus of a philosophically idealist ontology (i.e., the notion that discourse generates reality and does not reflect it),[4] denying or at the very least ignoring the independent legitimacy of scholarship stemming from the natural sciences (which suggest that scientific discourse describes reality rather than creating it) (cf. Boyer, 2001).

As a response to the definitional progression in the study of esotericism leading from the search for esotericism's signified to the historical tracing of its signification, Egil Asprem (2016) has suggested the *building block approach* as an integration of differing perspectives. Asprem employs the cognitive science of religion as a theoretical framework, which enables the scholar to study the (often scholarly) ascriptions to esotericism—e.g., "the production and dissemination of 'special knowledge'" (Asprem, 2016, p. 159)—in a research process that employs "constructionist and naturalistic methods" (ibid., p. 162).

First, ascriptions to esotericism (seen as a "complex cultural concept"; ibid., p. 160) are identified and disassembled on the level of discourse, where the socially produced semantic constructions of esotericism are analyzed:

> These include theological and worldview positions that deny a strict separation of god and world (e.g., cosmotheism, panentheism), notions of an ageless wisdom that can be comprehended with special hermeneutic strategies, and epistemological attitudes emphasizing radical experiential knowledge (e.g., "gnosis"). (ibid., 167)

---

4 The poststructuralist connection to idealist philosophy is visible in the reception of the (post-)Kantian privileging of epistemology as the basis for philosophizing, acting as a "watchdog" against unwanted ontological intrusions. Cf. Bergunder, 2010.

Second, the cognitive building blocks pertaining to the practices (e.g., alchemy, astrology, divination, etc.), which are discursively negotiated *as esotericism*, are broken down to their lower level features, accessible to the cognitive study of religion. For instance, Asprem distinguishes two types of building blocks for the cluster of ascriptions in which esotericism appears as a form of thought or mentality:

> *universal cognitive dispositions* and dispositions of *personality and individual difference*–which are, moreover, developed, calibrated, and combined in various ways through what we might call *learning dispositions*. (2016, p. 177)

In a last step, the building blocks associated with the discourse on esotericism are dialectically synthesized with the latter:

> Finally, the constructive *reassembly* stage is where we develop new theory and design research programs that reconnect the lower levels with the cultural and set up new comparisons between formations. Reassembling the complex, socially embedded wholes from a set of building blocks, then, does *not* guarantee a return to the old labels and categorizations with which we originally set out. (ibid., p. 162)

In Asprem's theory the vertical integration between lower and higher levels of ontology ought to be consistent and allow for explanatory pluralism according to the level of analysis (e.g., historical) without contradicting analysis on other levels (e.g., biological). At the same time the comparison taking place through a horizontal integration should enable intellectual exchange with neighboring disciplines (e.g., intellectual history, history of science, art history) working on the same or on similar levels of resolution but focusing on different aspects on a shared continuum (Asprem, 2016, p. 179).

In contrast to the previous definitional progression spanning from Faivre to Hanegraaff and to Bergunder, Asprem's approach is acutely aware of the tension between the creative power of epistemology (i.e., discourse producing reality) and the forceful creativity of ontology (i.e., materiality showing itself to be real). Asprem does not buy into any posits either promising direct access to the "essence" of esotericism or constructing a taxonomic scaffold from contingently available sources (2016, pp. 158–159). Nor does he ignore the world outside of discourse as an ontologically lower (i.e., developmentally foundational) level with human culture supervening on the evolutionary antecedent material and the embodied properties of the building blocks that light up in the ontologically higher (i.e., developmentally succeeding) level of discursive interaction, where the meaning of esotericism is negotiated (ibid., p. 161). Instead, Asprem argues for a reconstruction of the cognitive building blocks (e.g., universal cognitive dispositions), which are not identical to the docking discourse (e.g., esotericism), but will nevertheless inform the researcher about the relationship between the extra- and intra-discursive processes.

To rephrase this development with a more formal focus on the subject of esotericism: a thesis of ontological access ("we know esotericism to be x"/"we know esotericism to be constituted by x, y, z") (Faivre, 1994; Hanegraaff, 2012), has been countered by its antithesis of epistemological limitation ("we can only ever know 'esotericism' to be interpreted as x, y, z") (Bergunder, 2010), whereupon both have been sublated in the hierarchical system of the building blocks approach ("whatever the interpretation of the signifier 'esotericism,' we can scale it down to the point where we can know its constituent components and reassemble it from there") (Asprem, 2016).

2 The Antinomy of Interpretation

Despite the apparent elegance of the definitional progression with an encompassing theoretical framework at its presumed synthesis of ontological and epistemological deliberations, the issue of interpreting esotericism—indeed, the issue of interpretation as such—is more complicated. Once we take a closer look at the basic axioms underlying each and every interpretational endeavor, an uncomfortable paradox makes itself felt, which will henceforth be referred to as the *antinomy of interpretation*. As we shall see in a moment, this incompatibility between two self-sufficient principles—already indicated in the juxtaposition of essentialist vs. discursive approaches, with Hanegraaff's narrativizing approach uncomfortably aiming in both directions—cannot be resolved through a dialectic argument (i.e., by combining "constructionist" and "naturalistic" analyses within a hierarchical framework) (Asprem, 2016, p. 162), since such synthesizing attempts reproduce the very binary which they set out to overcome. Instead, the conundrum at hand must be understood philosophically in order to be dealt with on a practical level, where radically divergent interpretations—e.g., of esotericism—will have to be acknowledged side by side as contributions to an eclectic understanding of our scholarly subject that cannot possibly be regarded as a "whole" because there is no unifying interpretation, but only conflicting accounts that can nevertheless be understood as philosophically necessary juxtapositions.

Broadly speaking, the essentialist approach to esotericism relies on the scholar's relatively unconstrained interpretation (i.e., our epistemology) of available sources, in which historical entities manifest, entering discourse from a non-discourse outside (i.e., their ontology), while the discursive approach claims that interpretation of esotericism (i.e., its ontology) is thoroughly determined by contingent linguistic negotiations (i.e., our epistemology). Asprem's building blocks approach, in turn, attempts to combine both interpretational directions. On the one hand, it implies that discourses generate and sediment the meaning of esotericism (ontology) by dint of their persuasive gravitation (epistemology). On the other hand, it claims to retrieve the cognitive foundations (ontology) of practices, which are discursively linked to esotericism, employing the empirical inquiry of the cognitive science of religion (epistemology).

What we see here are two basic directionalities of interpretation, which I will refer to as *vectors*.[5] In the first case, esotericism is excavated and carved out from time and space (i.e., from different moments, geographical locations and social contexts in history leading up to the present) in which "it" exists in the form of potent narratives, materialities, and practices that present themselves to the interpreter. This vector will be referred to as *onto-epistemological*, since in this directionality of interpretation the ontology of esotericism informs the interpreter's epistemology. For instance, we can observe the onto-epistemological vector in Faivre's understanding of esotericism as "a form of thought, the nature of which we have to try and capture on the basis of the currents which exemplify it" (Faivre, 1994, p. 4). Despite the necessity of the scholar to actively look into the sources "containing" esotericism, esotericism itself is presupposed (contrary to Faivre's own claim) as an entity, which makes itself noticeable through its manifestation in sources. In the second case, esotericism is *generated throughout* history, where linguistic (re-)negotiations attribute themselves to it. Regardless of the scholar's invested circumspection, whatever will eventually appear on the radar, will be a construct of the applied search filter. This vector will be referred to as *epistemo-ontological*, since the interpreter's epistemology of esotericism informs its ontology. For instance, we can observe the epistemo-ontological vector in Bergunder's understanding of esotericism as a "general term of identification" (2010, p. 26), which Bergunder regards as a "contingent nodal point or rather as the fixing of a contentious power discourse" (ibid., p. 26) in need of historicization.

---

5   For the purposes of this chapter, the usage of the term "vector" is limited to the directionality in the space of interpretation and does *not* claim any mathematical implementation, although a further development based on set theory appears to be a feasible endeavor.

The Antinomy of Interpretation

	Esotericism Within Discourse	Esotericism Outside of Discourse
Onto-Epistemological Vector	point of manifestation	**point of origin**
Epistemo-Ontological Vector	**point of origin**	point of projection

SCHEMATIC 1

In sum, this means that the onto-epistemological vector of interpretation allows us to see esotericism as an extra-discursive entity, *manifesting* within discourse while the epistemo-ontological vector of interpretation allows us to see esotericism as a discursive formation being *projected* to an assumed outside of discourse (schematic 1).

The inherent antinomy between the two vectors of interpretation and its consequences for the study of esotericism becomes evident once we closely examine the outlined definitional progression and spell out some of the intrinsic philosophical consequences for the various approaches to the study of esotericism. Bergunder's initial point of criticism was directed at the essentialist approach, which operates via the onto-epistemological vector and performs a readout of the available data on esotericism—i.e., ascertaining that esotericism *is* gnosis, theosophy, secrecy, or maintaining that it *does* gravitate around the themes of philosophy, science, and religion (Faivre, 1994). We can now interpret Bergunder's intervention as an application of the epistemo-ontological vector, which suggests that an ostensible readout of data—i.e., gnosis, theosophy, secrecy—is a socially negotiated projection to an assumed discursive outside, *not* a manifestation of an outside within discourse. The negation of this extra-discursive potentiality is identical with the negation of the onto-epistemological vector, which promises precisely the type of access—i.e., an understanding what esotericism "is" outside of its fluctuating social construction—which Bergunder's approach renders impossible. While Faivre and Bergunder can be allocated to one specific interpretational directionality, Hanegraaff's narrativizing approach seems to represent an intermediate step between Faivre and Bergunder, displaying the incommensurability between both directionalities of interpretation. Attempting to ride both vectors simultaneously, Hanegraaff suggests that esotericism is a narrative (epistemo-ontology), while also implying that the sources debating philosophy, theology/rationality, revelation can inform the scholar about the nature of esotericism (onto-epistemology) (Hanegraaff, 2012, pp. 6–7; Hanegraaff, 2013, p. 255). Asprem's building blocks approach, making use of the cognitive study of religion as a gateway to studying esotericism, is then the attempt to consciously work with both vectors by allocating them to different operational spheres. This synthesizing attempt is visible in Asprem's (2016) lower and higher levels of analysis—e.g., the biology of religious experience/the cultural construction of religious experience—which are integrated through the vertical (i.e., hierarchical) and horizontal (i.e., interdisciplinary) axes.

The crucial problem with the entire definitional progression in the study of esotericism—and, in fact, with any comparable definitional progression—is the varying inability to address and clarify the basic axioms of interpretation, which are directly linked to the two interpretative directionalities. The relationship between the onto-epistemological and the epistemo-ontological vectors can be clarified through four propositions, the first two of which describe the *antinomy of interpretation*:

- Proposition 1: If esotericism exists as a self-sufficient entity outside of discourse manifesting within discourse (e.g., the neural structures of the human brain generating communicable perceptions of non-material worlds),[6] then its contingent (i.e., culturally negotiated) interpretations will not affect its essential extradiscursive features (e.g., the impact of neurotransmitters on the perception of non-material worlds).
- Proposition 2: If esotericism exists within discourse (i.e., as culturally negotiated interpretations concerning experiences of non-material worlds) and is merely being projected onto a presumed outside of discourse (e.g., attributing contingent meaning to neurotransmitters), this outside will have no say whatsoever in what esotericism *is within discourse* and will therefore have no meaning pertaining to the study of esotericism.

---

6 Note that evolutionary theory is only one possible element of many onto-epistemological interpretations, since the different theories are defined by the vectors, not vice versa.

These propositions, which correspond with the onto-epistemological and the epistemo-ontological vectors, are incommensurable. We can either accept that the outside of discourse determines the inside of discourse *or* maintain that the inside of discourse determines the outside of discourse—both cases can be plausibly argued and have engaged philosophical thinking throughout the centuries as well as the present (Meillassoux, 2008).

To be clear, the argument here is not that either interpretational directionality is correct or mistaken; rather we cannot use both vectors in the same interpretive act. If we interpret esotericism onto-epistemologically (e.g., as hardwired predispositions to see supernatural beings), it will manifest in discourse *as esotericism* no matter what signifiers (e.g., "gnosis," "theosophy," "secrecy," "occultism," "Hermeticism") discourse uses for the signified. If we interpret esotericism epistemo-ontologically (e.g., the vision of supernatural beings as a historically contested ascription to evolutionary mechanisms), the signified will not tell us anything about itself, because we are assuming it to be the contingent product of discourse.

The antinomy of interpretation is perhaps most plainly visible in Asprem's attempt of synthesizing both vectors. Asprem relies on an evolutionary paradigm (i.e., on the onto-epistemological vector) within which human biology (i.e., onto-epistemological) and culture (i.e., epistemo-ontological) are hierarchically connected (Asprem, 2016, pp. 160–161). The trouble with this hierarchy, however, consists in the intrinsic function of the epistemo-ontological vector to call into question the very existence of an evolutionary process as an extradiscursive reality. As Asprem himself writes with regards to the building blocks: they are conceptual tools that help us see how complex composites might work—not a route to "foundations," "essences," or "rock bottom" (2016, p. 161).

But if this were to be the case, we would have to find a reason to choose one conceptual tool over another. The mere speculation as to how "composites might work" flows in the direction of the epistemo-ontological vector, the onto-epistemological vector cannot but lead the interpreter to "'foundations,' 'essences,' or 'rock bottom.'" Logically speaking, then, Asprem has no choice but to consolidate his theory onto-epistemologically, since a thorough consideration of the epistemo-ontological vector would suggest that evolution itself is but *a* contingent theory, projecting itself to an outside of discourse, which, in turn, would be unable to manifest on the inside.

This observation suggests that approaches operating with one or the other vector can function well for themselves but will inevitably lead to contradictions if confronted with each other, as has been demonstrated up to this point.

3   The Principle of Bivectoral Necessity

So far, two points have been argued. First, the two vectors of interpretation—i.e., onto-epistemological and epistemo-ontological—have been derived from the definitional progression in the study of esotericism. Second, their incommensurable character has been discussed as the *antinomy of interpretation*. And yet, it remains far from obvious, in what sense these vectors exist in the first place and how their incommensurability can be squared with their individually meaningful performance. After all, interpreting esotericism as a sedimented societal ascription appears equally plausible to interpreting it as a discourse emerging from the potentiality of the human nervous system. There is ample evidence for the hegemonic character of meaning negotiations, taking place throughout human history and retroactively portraying themselves as inevitable and "natural" (Butler, 1993). Put more formally, the very act of interpretation requires the projection of a signified by the interpreter onto a signifier, since the signified is attributed *to* a signifier *by* an interpreter (i.e., *we* make the connection between our research in neuroscience and the esoteric narratives, materialities, and practices of our research subjects). However, an equally plausible case can be made for the unfolding of esoteric narratives, materialities, and practices as a consequence of the biopsycho-social mechanics we refer to as "human culture" (Boyer, 2001). Put more formally, we have to "take" the signified from the signifier, precisely because it is "given" (e.g., the religious experience of individuals offers an understanding of itself through research in neuroscience done by the interpreter). Once the respective epistemo-ontological and onto-epistemological presuppositions (i.e., contingent semantics/evolutionary constraints) are accepted, *uni*vectoral interpretation delivers sensible information about our subject of study (e.g., esotericism as a projection of discourse vs. esotericism as a manifestation of the human psyche) while excluding the reverse directionality.

A clarification of both unanswered questions (in what sense do the vectors exist and how can their incommensurability be squared with their individual functioning) can be provided by what will be referred to as the *principle of bivectoral necessity*, described in the third and fourth proposition pertaining to the basic axioms of interpretation. Assuming the existence of an interpreter and an interpreted, two incommensurable functions of interpretation will take place:

– Proposition 3: Some*thing* will be interpreted via a signified which emerges from a signifier (e.g., practices directed at the knowledge-acquisition of non-material worlds show themselves to the interpreter *as such*).

– Proposition 4: The interpreter will interpret *some*thing by attributing a signifier with a signified (e.g., the interpreter projects "esotericism" onto a set of practices directed at the knowledge-acquisition of non-material worlds). As should be evident by now, both propositions correspond with the onto-epistemological and the epistemo-ontological vectors and are therefore incommensurable. However, they are simultaneously logically necessary *in themselves* as unifocal directionalities, since they and only they make interpretation possible. We can make sense of the *principle of bivectoral necessity* by imagining the situation through the metaphorical use of Schroedinger's famous cat, which is presumed to be simultaneously dead and alive in its box (due to an installed mechanism, killing the cat with a 50% probability) until the box is opened and the cat is observed (Gribbin, 1984). Let us presume that we want to know *what a cat is*, never having seen one and only being informed that a cat is in the box. Once interpretation takes place, we will have one and only one of two and only two possible outcomes. The repetition of the experiment will bring about an even distribution of two outcomes, helping us to arrive at the conclusion that the cat exists in two states. These two states, however, will have no middle ground between them, there will be no continuum connecting the living and dead cat—the interpretations will be literally incommensurable but equally necessary, in order to arrive at a description of what is interpreted.

Put together, the underlying logic for the *principle of bivectoral necessity*—i.e., the necessity of onto-epistemological and epistemo-ontological directionalities of interpretation—and the *antinomy of interpretation*—i.e., the incommensurability of the two fundamental interpretational directionalities—constitute a set of counterintuitive, yet indispensable assumptions. It might, in fact, be possible to explain both principles semiotically by borrowing from and significantly adapting Ernesto Laclau's theory of signification (Laclau, 2005), which was used by Bergunder as the basis for his exclusively epistemo-ontological approach (Bergunder, 2010). In this re-interpretation of Laclau,[7] the semiotic logic of equivalence states that signifier and signified share common (i.e., equivalential) ground, since they would otherwise not be understandable as two distinct, yet connected elements in a shared context (e.g., the materiality from which neurotransmitters and experiential narratives of non-material worlds emerge as causally connected entities). Onto-epistemologically speaking, the evolved materiality of neurotransmitters is the signified which manifests in the signifier of experiential narratives of non-material worlds. This implies that the onto-epistemological directionality of

---

7   For a concise understanding of Laclau's epistemo-ontological semiotics, cf. Laclau, 2005.

interpretation takes the equivalence between the seemingly different signified (molecular structures) and signifier (language) to be their point of origin rather than the result of a projection (i.e., neurotransmitters and experiential narratives of non-material worlds originate from a common evolved material foundation with neurotransmitters at the lower level and experiential narratives at the upper level).

The logics of difference states that the signifier and the signified are not identical, since they would otherwise not be understandable in a shared context as two connected, yet distinct (i.e., differential) elements (e.g., experiential narratives of non-material worlds and neurotransmitters are linked through discourse). Epistemo-ontologically speaking, neurotransmitters are the signifier while experiential narratives of non-material worlds would be the signified being impressed into the signifier. This implies that the epistemo-ontological directionality of interpretation takes the equivalential context of differing elements to be the result of a projection rather than the point of origin. From this we can deduce that the onto-epistemological vector is operating on the assumption that equivalence manifests differential elements, which are nevertheless causally linked to the lower level, while the epistemo-ontological vector is operating on the assumption that differential elements are projected into equivalence, reversing the causality.

What this all means in more prosaic terms is this: the onto-epistemological vector is active when equivalence bifurcates into difference (neurotransmitters and experiential narratives of non-material worlds) by dint of its own potentiality (e.g., evolved materiality). The epistemo-ontological vector is active when difference (e.g., neurotransmitters and experiential narratives of non-material worlds) contracts to equivalence (e.g., materiality) through a discursive intervention (schematic 2).[8] But what is it that happens *before* interpretation takes place? The answer, which brings back the analogous use of Schroedinger's cat, is that we cannot possibly know, because it is only when interpretation takes place that we have access to whatever is interpreted. A possible speculation would be to think of the pre-interpreted state as a superposition of signifier and signified in a state of pure potential, leaping from their superposition to the respective starting and ending points of the two vectors, once interpretation takes place and the logics of difference and equiv-

---

[8] Framed in this way, the mind/matter dichotomy can be seen as the ultimate polarity at the respective starting and ending points of the onto-epistemological and epistemo-ontological vectors. Stretching this line of thought even further, matter and mind could be regarded as the impossible, yet necessary complements of Being that emerge in each and every act of interpretation.

The Principle of Bivectoral Necessity

	Signifier/Signified	Interpretation
Onto-Epistemological Vector	Equivalence < Difference	e.g. evolution affords the connection between neurotransmitters and experiential narratives of non-material worlds
Epistemo-Ontological Vector	Difference > Equivalence	e.g. experiential narratives of non-material worlds and neurotransmitters are linked through discourse

SCHEMATIC 2

alence take over. What we *can* say with more certainty, however, is how to bring about the two possible states of interpretation, since we are able to consciously employ the onto-epistemological and epistemo-ontological vectors. This implies that all interpretable entities (again, there is little we can say about uninterpreted entities) can be forced to show themselves through their onto-epistemological and epistemo-ontological components, resulting in incommensurable yet necessarily correct interpretations that cannot be synthesized but must be acknowledged as equally sensible.

4 The Varifocal Theory of Interpretation

If we accept the *antinomy of interpretation*, which has been rendered plausible through the *principle of bivectoral necessity*, we must ask ourselves two questions: first, why should the study of esotericism—or the study of any subject for that matter—not simply proceed with its already existing approaches? Second, how can our insight into the opposed directionalities of interpretation contribute to an alternative take on the object of inquiry, integrating elements from the definitional progression in the study of esotericism?

To tackle the first question: if it is indeed the case that two and only two directionalities of interpretation exist and can be applied to esotericism and that they are antinomic as well as necessary, using only one vector of interpretation by definition neglects information offered by the other vector. We have seen, however, that the unconscious oscillation between both vectors will lead to intractable contradictions. This was the case with Faivre, who first claimed that there was no such thing as "esotericism in itself" (epistemo-ontologically) before arguing the opposite by suggesting that esotericism had indeed a nature showing through the study of the source material (implying an onto-epistemological vector) (Faivre, 1994, p. 4). This was the case with Hanegraaff, who started out with the assumption that esotericism emerged as a narrative about ancient wisdom, while simultaneously suggesting that his sources could inform him about esotericism (2012, pp. 6–7; 2013, p. 255). This was the case with Bergunder, who approached esotericism as a negotiated term of identification (epistemo-ontological) without however, granting the same critical privilege to his theoretical toolset consisting of terms such as "discourse," "empty signifier," and "power," which, in turn, appeared to be the foundation of reality (implying an onto-epistemological vector) (2010, p. 26).

In contrast to the aforementioned approaches, Asprem (2016) attempts to consciously work with both vectors by incorporating "naturalistic" and "constructionist" methods. In this way, he aims to integrate research on esotericism along a vertical as well as a horizontal axis and allow for the coexistence of similar as well as dissimilar research paradigms on the continuum of the scientific and scholarly disciplines. However, Asprem's approach reaches an insurmountable obstacle with the *antinomy of interpretation*, which re-inscribes itself into Asprem's integrative endeavor, once the epistemo-ontological vector is activated: while the horizontal axis allows for the coexistence of *uni*vectoral approaches (e.g., intellectual history, history of science, art history/medicine, neuroscience, psychology), the vertical axis promises a hierarchical integration of onto-epistemological and epistemo-ontological interpretations, a promise it can only deliver by subordinating one vector under another (i.e., epistemo-ontological under onto-epistemological). The repressed *antinomy of interpretation* returns forcefully due to the *principle of bivectoral necessity*, once the underlying evolutionary theory, which is the indispensable onto-epistemological foundation for the building blocks approach, is analyzed epistemo-ontologically and deciphered as a contingent product of negotiations for interpretative hegemony, masking itself as self-evidently objective (Hull, 2005). To fully answer the first question: we should *not* simply proceed with the already existing approaches to esotericism, because none of them are capable of dealing with the *antinomy of interpretation* and the *principle of bivectoral necessity*, which, in turn, are able to explain the contradictions of interpretation.

This reflection allows us to tackle the second question: if it is indeed the case that two and only two directionalities of interpretation exist and can be applied to esotericism and that they are antinomic as well as necessary, we ought to accomplish, not a linear hierarchical, but an *oscillatory side-by-side integration* of both vectors in order to acquire the fullest possible interpretation of our subject. This excludes the option of using only one vector, but also disables us from trying to subordinate both vectors in one interpretive approach because the other vector will inevitably "cannibalize" our interpretive foundation, either because we produce contradictions (e.g., Faivre, Hanegraaff, Bergunder), or because we realize that no matter how sophisticated our theory, contradictions remain unresolved (e.g., Asprem). The only remaining option, then, is *not* to synthesize the vectors, while allowing numerous interpretations to flow both ways. What is interpreted in this fashion will invariably be eclectic, since adding the interpretations available through the onto-epistemological and the epistemo-ontological vectors will result in separate but complementary interpretations, which cannot be summed up but must be understood as equally valid contributions to an eclectic totality. As with Schroedinger's cat, which can be dead *or* alive without any intermediate state, esotericism will be interpreted as onto-epistemological *or* epistemo-ontological. What this rather uncomfortable suggestion implies is that our interpretations of esotericism (e.g., esotericism as the result of evolutionary processes vs. the evolutionary predisposition to sense superhuman entities as a discursive fixation) will have to stand next to each other on truly equal footing without merging into one single explanatory framework.

What *can* act as an encompassing theoretical structure, explaining, *not what esotericism is, but why it will inevitably be interpreted through two vectors*, is a theory of sensemaking emerging from the *antinomy of interpretation* and the *principle of bivectoral necessity*. This *Varifocal Theory of Interpretation* posits that an interpretation adequately showing the eclectic interpretive outcome of any given research subject (i.e., presenting through the onto-epistemological and the epistemo-ontological vector) needs to apply a set of varifocal (i.e., bifocal) lenses between which the interpreter will have to switch back and forth in order to gain an in-depth understanding of esotericism (schematic 3).

Since no single theory can simultaneously peak through both lens sections, the oscillatory employment of several approaches along the transdisciplinary spectrum between the natural sciences, the social sciences, and the humanities is in order, each of which have traditionally employed both vectors with a binary tendency (i.e., with the natural sciences often choosing the onto-epistemological route, the humanities regularly opting for the epistemo-ontological route and the social sciences employing one or the other, depend-

Varifocal Interpretation

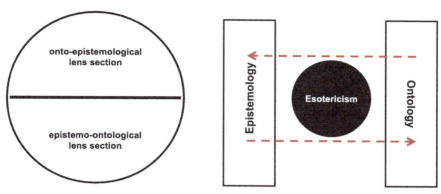

SCHEMATIC 3

ing on their inclination towards semantic or mathematical models). In direct contrast to the usage of different approaches found in the definitional progression in the study of esotericism, this endeavor has to be constantly and consistently aware of the *antinomy of interpretation* and the *principle of bivectoral necessity*.

A varifocal interpretation of esotericism will therefore proceed by continuously alternating between both vectors. On the one hand, Asprem's leaning towards an evolutionary perspective as the foundation for human perception could function as a starting point and theoretical umbrella for neighboring theories that operate exclusively through the onto-epistemological analysis of esotericism. The lower-level components structuring onto-epistemological interpretation could then be thoroughly analyzed as

> relatively simple and stable concepts that are grounded in evolved mental architecture and embodied interactions with the environment. Examples include the bodily based, domain-general schemata studied by cognitive linguistics (e.g., part-whole, path, CONTAINMENT) and concepts such as ACTION, CAUSE, INTENTION, or EVENT that are presumably grounded in evolved, domain-specific learning systems and hence recognizable across cultures. (Asprem, 2016, pp. 160–161)

From this point onwards, an onto-epistemological analysis could fully embrace the *intra*vectoral spectrum of disciplines, analyzing esotericism as a bio-psycho-socially evolved set of narratives, materialities, and practices. Various (sub)disciplines based on the premises of evolutionary theory and the methods of inferential statistics—sociobiology, evolutionary psychology, neuroscience, psycholinguistics, etc.—could then make their contributions as to why, when, where, and how esotericism has emerged in the complex interactions between human individuals, collectives, and institutions (Downes, 2011; Grinde, 1998; McNamara, 2009).

On the other hand, Bergunder's discursive approach could function as a starting point and theoretical umbrella for neighboring theories which operate exclusively through the epistemo-ontological study of esotericism. The negotiatory practices gravitating around the signifier "esotericism" could then be thoroughly analyzed on the *intra*vectoral spectrum. Epistemo-ontologically operating concepts from (sub)disciplines such as the study of religion, sociology, cultural theory, semiotics etc. could augment and enlarge the notion of esotericism as an empty signifier prone to contingent fixations (Barker, 2001; Bourdieu, 1993; Chandler, 2017; Wijsen, 2013). Bergunder himself has introduced an additional theoretical tool, arguing for Pierre Bourdieu's sociological concept of the *field*, which suggests a differentiation of articulatory discursive spaces and could help to situate esotericism within a variety of intersecting societal fields (Bourdieu, 1993):

> Thus, there are academic, journalistic, literary, religious and political fields of discourse etc., which can be differentiated [...].[9] Applying this to esotericism, it could be said that the reproduction of esotericism's empty signifier takes place through the articulation of a discursive community in different discourse fields. Esotericism as an identity positioning has its place in a religious discourse field. However, the articulation of equivalence chains and their reproduction takes place also in other discourse fields. [...] [A]cademics can be esotericists or journalists can be anti-esotericists etc. (Bergunder, 2010, p. 25)

While Bergunder is clearly limiting his approach epistemo-ontologically, Asprem's attempt to synthesize both vectors is subdued by the *antinomy of interpretation*, leading Asprem to privilege the onto-epistemological vector due to his hierarchical subordination of discourse to the evolved materiality of

---

9 Note how Bergunder rhetorically inhibits even the possibility of an onto-epistemological vector in the missed-out lines: "Surely nothing can be said against this proposal, so long as the field concept does not contain any hidden category of order that exhibit an outer discursive reference. Fields of discourse must themselves emerge in the discursive articulation" (2010, p. 25).

human cognition. It might, however, be possible to reformulate the building blocks approach as *varifocal* in order to avoid the philosophical conundrum at hand. If Asprem should choose to adopt the *Varifocal Theory of Interpretation*, he would have to resist the temptation to generate a hierarchical connection of the two vectors, instead, accepting the principle of bivectoral necessity and letting both vectors oscillate with their interpretational directionalities untouched by each other.

5 In Sum

This chapter has made the point that the definitional progression in the study of esotericism from Faivre to Hanegraaff to Bergunder and to Asprem—despite resembling a dialectical movement—has ultimately been unable to bring about a theoretical clarification and synthesis of interpretive approaches to esotericism. This conundrum was explained through the *antinomy of interpretation* (schematic 1) and the *principle of bivectoral necessity* (schematic 2) as the two elements governing each and every interpretational enterprise. As a counterproposal, a varifocal understanding of esotericism has been suggested, oscillating between the onto-epistemological and the epistemo-ontological vectors without attempting to generate a hierarchy between the two interpretational directionalities. This move allows us to access the always eclectic interpretational outcome predicted by the *antinomy of interpretation* (schematic 3).[10] Moreover, the *principle of bivectoral necessity* explains why—despite our inability to synthesize the onto-epistemological and the epistemo-ontological vectors—we cannot but employ both interpretative directionalities, even though our usage should be careful not to subsume one approach under the other in order to avoid the contradictions running through the definitional progression in the study of esotericism as well as the entire history of interpretation itself.

---

10 To quickly counter the possible allegation of promoting a reactionary return to some 'long overcome' cartesian dichotomy: arguing that the onto-epistemological and the epistemo-ontological vectors are incommensurable *does indeed* block a merged interpretative access to esotericism as a materially potent entity *and* esotericism as a discursively inscribed notion. Although this concept is arguably hard to take and in need of further philosophical explanation and empirical application, I have attempted to demonstrate its logical structure and empirically observability, shining a new light on the longstanding conflict between academic disciplines spread between the two vectors. Cf. Ashman and Barringer, 2001.

What, then, would a discipline or academic field admitting to the *Varifocal Theory of Interpretation* look like? Needless to say, the varifocal approach is not limited to any subject of interest, since the general presuppositions of the onto-epistemological and epistemo-ontological vectors apply for the process of interpretation itself. However, disciplines used to operate with one vector or the other would have to significantly expand their theoretical and methodological scope in order to conduct varifocal analysis. This is why Bergunder's sole focus on the poststructuralist tradition with its epistemo-ontological interpretations cannot be employed towards a varifocal analysis, while Asprem's usage of the cognitive science of religion in addition to discourse theory (or vice versa!) can be reformulated as a varifocal analysis of esotericism.

The ultimate benefit of the *Varifocal Theory of Interpretation* lies not in a grand unifying system, but in rejecting the impossible unification of incommensurable directionalities, which are nevertheless equally accepted. Although this might seem to be a rather dull suggestion in light of the theoretical effort which has been employed to arrive at this conclusion, the implications are far from trivial. Academic disciplines with the *Varifocal Theory of Interpretation* at their heart would be relieved from the burden to persistently partake in shadowboxing with opposing academic viewpoints (if the opposition is due to the *antinomy of interpretation*). They could, instead, focus on the full scope and abundance of both interpretational directionalities. This might also have a significant effect on highly politicized subjects of interpretation. After all, poststructuralist deconstruction has been used to constantly question the legitimacy of scientific findings (e.g., the onto-epistemological interpretation of sex and gender as essentially binary) while the reduction of human behavior to evolved material constraints has continued to dismiss the legitimacy of individually queering identity-articulations (e.g., gender and sex as purely performative acts) (Ashman and Barringer, 2001). Allowing for both interpretive directionalities would imply an acceptance of this fundamental paradox, which we cannot dissolve, no matter how convincing our *uni*vectoral arguments might be. It would force us out of the echo-chambers created around our favorite interpretational route and compel us to acknowledge, rather than ignore, suppress, or fight the opposing avenue. It would enable us to fully appreciate the scope and depth of scientific and scholarly understanding tilting to one vector or the other, without constantly attempting to subvert incommensurable interpretations. This oscillating movement between the two vectors rightly feels like the alternation between two entirely different worlds. These worlds, however, are all we have in interpretation. It is therefore our choice to remain partial foreigners or become questing commuters.

Bibliography

Ashman, K.M.B. and Barringer, P. (eds.) (2001) *After the Science Wars*. London and New York: Routledge.

Asprem, E. (2016) "Reverse-Engineering 'Esotericism': How to Prepare a Complex Cultural Concept for the Cognitive Science of Religion," *Religion*, 46, pp. 158–185.

Barker, C. and Dariusz, D. (2001) *Cultural Studies and Discourse Analysis: A Dialogue on Language and Identity*. London: SAGE.

Bergunder, M. (2010) "What is Esotericism? Cultural Studies Approaches and the Problems of Definition in Religious Studies," *Method and Theory in the Study of Religion*, 22, pp. 9–36.

Bourdieu, P. (1993) *The Field of Cultural Production*. New York: Columbia University Press.

Boyer, P. (2001) *Religion Explained: The Evolutionary Origins of Religious Thought*. New York: Basic Books.

Butler, J. (1993) *Bodies that Matter: On the Discursive Limits of "Sex."* New York and London: Routledge.

Chandler, D. (2017) *Semiotics: The Basics*. London and New York: Routledge.

Downes, W. (2011) *Language and Religion: A Journey into the Human Mind*. Cambridge: Cambridge University Press.

Faivre, A. (1994) *Access to Western Esotericism*. New York: State University of New York Press.

Foucault, M. (1977) "Nietzsche, Genealogy, History," in Bouchard, D.F. (ed.) *Language, Counter-Memory, Practice*. Ithaca: Cornell University Press.

Gribbin, J. (1984) *In Search of Schrödinger's Cat*. Toronto: Bantam Books.

Grinde, B. (1998) "The Biology of Religion: A Darwinian Gospel," *Journal of Social and Evolutionary Systems*, 21, pp. 19–28.

Hanegraaff, W.J. (2012) *Esotericism and the Academy: Rejected Knowledge in Western Culture*. Cambridge: Cambridge University Press.

Hanegraaff, W.J. (2013) "The Power of Ideas: Esotericism, Historicism, and the Limits of Discourse," *Religion*, 43, pp. 252–273.

Hull, D.L. (2005) "Deconstructing Darwin: Evolutionary Theory in Context," *Journal of the History of Biology*, 38, pp. 137–152.

King, R. (1999) *Orientalism and Religion: Postcolonial Theory, India and "the Mystic East."* London and New York: Routledge.

Kuhn, T.S. (1962) *The Structure of Scientific Revolutions*. Chicago and London: University of Chicago Press.

Laclau, E. (2005) *On Populist Reason*. London and New York: Verso.

Masuzawa, T. (2005) *The Invention of World Religions: Or, How European Universalism Was Preserved in the Language of Pluralism*. Chicago and London: The University of Chicago Press.

McCutcheon, R.T. (1997) *Manufacturing Religion: The Discourse on Sui Generis Religion and the Politics of Nostalgia*. New York and Oxford: Oxford University Press.

McNamara, P. (2009) *The Neuroscience of Religious Experience*. Cambridge: Cambridge University Press.

Meillassoux, Q. (2008) *After Finitude*. London and New York: Continuum.

Strube, J. (2021) "Towards the Study of Esotericism without the 'Western'": Esotericism from the Perspective of a Global Religious History," in Asprem, E. and Strube, J. (eds.) *New Approaches to the Study of Esotericism*. Leiden and Boston: Brill, pp. 45–66.

Wijsen, F. (2013) "Editorial: Discourse analysis in religious studies," *Religion*, 43, pp. 1–3.

Afterword: Outlines of a New Roadmap

Egil Asprem and Julian Strube

We opened this volume by observing that esotericism scholars' scope is undergoing a phase of geographical, cultural, and demographic expansion. With these developments comes the need for theoretical and methodological reflection. As scholars are now once again inquiring about esotericism in a global context—not as part of a phenomenological comparative program, but as a critical historical undertaking—it has become clear that some of the field's core assumptions and key terminology must be rethought. The chapters of this book have demonstrated this need in a number of different ways, and put theoretical tools and existing scholarly literatures on the table that would help the field succeed at the task.

If there is one central assumption that rises above all others, due to its centrality to the field and the way its consequences make themselves felt on a number of different issues, it is the Eurocentrism embedded in the notion that esotericism is specifically "Western." Chapters in this book have drawn on a number of scholarly literatures that critique this issue in different but compatible ways, notably postcolonial studies and global history (Strube, 2021), decolonial approaches (Villalba, 2021, Page and Finley, 2021), and critical race and whiteness studies (Bakker, 2021). The chapters demonstrate that, contrary to some polemical framing that has now become fashionable even in the field of esotericism, these approaches are not out on an iconoclastic mission to demolish Western civilization and denigrate its values: they are about doing historical and social-scientific work in a theoretically and methodologically more substantiated way. This means taking into account the complexities and contingencies, the ambiguities and contradictions, and the ruptures and continuities of the historical developments that have shaped not only understandings of "Western civilization," but of "esotericism" as well. Decades of scholarship have demonstrated how diffusionist assumptions about the unilateral spread of Western knowledge have obstructed our understanding of such complexities and still play a crucial part in present-day scholarly and political polemics.

What we have called the "diffusionist reaction" to global approaches in the study of esotericism is exemplary not only of the neglect but also of the outright misrepresentation of such insights, and also illustrate a lack of (self-)reflection on the positionality of those who, today, carry out historical or social-scientific research on esotericism. In this sense, we hold that the structural analysis of biases and power inequalities that is of major concern for postcolonial, (global) historical, or critical-theoretical approaches are tools that will ultimately equip us to uncover sources, voices, historical relationships, and entanglements that we had ignored—not because they weren't there, but because we were systematically looking the other way. The consequences of engaging these frameworks seriously and thereby challenging the field's Eurocentrism when we start studying esotericism around the world are that the "Western" moniker should be dropped, along with the diffusionist representations that come with it and that have so far dominated attempts to study esotericism outside its imagined occidental homeland.

Why is this important? The key reason, discussed in several chapters of this book, has to do with a basic concept of historical analysis and interpretation: *agency*. This notion signifies the capabilities of historical actors to shape history, which is conditioned and structured by their individual embedment in complex historical contexts. The diffusionist frameworks have, as we think is now well demonstrated, led to a selective and distortive attribution of agency to historical actors. It has essentially meant following the activities of the Western, often European, usually white and mostly male actors already well-known to esotericism scholars, and prioritizing their creative activities and contributions even when these contributions are clearly negotiated in non-European contexts—to the occlusion of non-white, non-Western actors. The effect is a self-sustaining and circular line of scholarship, which cannot fail to reproduce its own assumptions because it only selects sources capable of confirming them. Put differently, the critical approaches introduced in this book are a remedy against the field's persistent confirmation or "myside" bias.

The paradigmatic example, as discussed by Strube (2021) and Cantú (2021), is the activities of occultists in India, such as the Theosophical Society and various occultist engagements with yoga, but we have seen the same logic applied to South America, the entire Islamic world, and the descendants of the Atlantic slave triangle's displaced bodies. Reclaiming and making space for subaltern voices, then, must be a major project for a global study of esotericism. While most chapters have focused on the theoretical prerequisites for this project, it bears emphasizing that the realization of the project must above all be a revision in *methodology*: giving space for subaltern voices requires selecting different sorts of material, reading different languages, and perhaps even embracing alternative modes of scholarly representation, as was argued and effectively illustrated by Finley and Page's flash non-fiction exercise as part of their recovery of *Africana* esoteric discourse through the lyrics and material culture of soul and blues music.

The issues of agency, subaltern voices, selection of sources, and scholarly representations of the same are not only relevant for the discussion of esotericism globally; they also bear on the question of an *historical* expansion of the field, and its relationship with other fields and disciplines. The study of esotericism holds enormous potential for entering dialogue with, significantly enrich, and even transform the perspectives of other fields of study. It is able to demonstrate the outstanding but notoriously neglected importance of currents such as Theosophy or occultism, not only in terms of historical relevance but also in light of theoretical and methodological approaches and concepts. Esoteric contexts often function like a burning glass for controversially debated issues such as agency, colonialism, racism, gender, or "appropriation" and "authenticity." This is not least because of esotericism's constant tendency to defy modern categorizations (e.g. the religion-science-magic triad; high and low culture; the political right-left spectrum), a fact which indeed has been a major contribution of the field as a whole. The concentrated study of how esotericism is entangled with debates of colonialism, gender, racism, etc. offers instructive insights into the often ambivalent *negotiations and performances of identities*, not only in light of broader political or cultural trends, but also, as Hedenborg White has demonstrated in her chapter (2021), of gender, sex, and sexuality.

The scholarship that formed the basis of the various chapters of this volume is concerned with unraveling such intricacies. That does not mean "eagerly deconstructing Western culture," but explaining how "it" was subject to constant renegotiations and transformations, in which esotericism played a crucial and still under-studied part. In this sense, the study of esotericism should also complicate both the ideas of a unilateral spread of some knowledge from the West to the East and the unilateral "appropriation" of other knowledge from the East by the West. These ideas do not only mark predominant approaches within the study of esotericism, but also more extreme postcolonial views on the colonial context as exclusively determined by oppression, exploitation, and cultural incommensurability. From both angles, the agency of "non-hegemonic" actors is historiographically obscured. At a time when such issues are the subject of prominent academic and socio-political debates, the study of esotericism could make a significant and valuable contribution on the basis of a revised and substantiated toolkit that would break the self-referential circle, complicate ongoing polemics, and attract the attention of other scholars and institutions.

To this end, it is imperative to rethink the categories at work within the study of esotericism, including its conceptualization as a dustbin of rejected knowledge. As Burns (2021) has demonstrated, esotericism scholars often operate with categories that are ahistorically projected on earlier source material, without sufficiently engaging with the expertise of the fields of study dedicated to them. Not only does this contribute to the self-isolation and self-marginalization of the field because of a lack of interdisciplinary dialogue and scholarly rigor; it also perpetuates the historiographical marginalization of its *subjects*, which, as Asprem (2021) points out, often enough were anything but marginal or rejected. One crucial step to counter these perceptions is a methodological focus on the *reception history* of historical subjects, the fruitfulness of which becomes evident in Burns' treatment of "gnosis." Such an approach harmonizes well with the *genealogy* proposed by Strube, in demonstrating how historical narratives and polemics have shaped and often distorted the perception of historical sources and their contexts up to the present day. While a call for "strictly historical" approaches and an awareness of the polemical and/or retrospective construction of esotericism *as* rejected knowledge are by no means absent from earlier scholarship, Burns' chapter further underlines that such calls have not always been consistently and thoroughly carried out. These shortcomings also reveal themselves in the neglect of Islamicate contexts examined by Saif, which ironically shaped much of the historical material—such as Hermetism—that is often considered an integral part of "Western" esotericism. When we further consider that there are more texts dedicated to Hermes in Arabic than in any other language (van Bladel, 2009), it becomes all the more reasonable to decenter the particularly European and Christian reception that has been given pride of place so far, and present it instead as just one among many receptions of Hermetic writings.

The study of esotericism as rejected knowledge also carries great potential for contributing to broader discussions in the humanities if it is done right. As Asprem argued in his chapter, doing it right would mean scrapping the inflated version of the thesis, which risks amounting to hyperbolic statements about the field as the ultimate victim of hegemonic knowledge systems, while at the same time contradicting the likely results of in-depth analyses of rejection processes, marginalization, and distributions of power—or worse, making such analyses impossible. By contrast, the strict version of the rejected knowledge model has a lot to offer to broader understandings of modernity, and especially the impact of the Reformation and the Enlightenment on the formation of a modern "historical *a priori*" or tacit knowledge of what counts as acceptable claims. In particular, this aspect of esotericism has much to gain from integrating with a broader sociology of knowledge and related perspectives, whether in the history of religion, science, or medicine. To begin with, this is, as Asprem noted, because the stigmatization of knowledge systems or particular knowledge claims can happen in many different ways and for different reasons—from explicit rejection by specific authorities, to shifts in orientation by knowledge users and producers resulting in forgetfulness and replacement, to the ignoring of low-prestige knowledge not considered worthy of attention in the first place.

Moreover, the study of modern and contemporary esotericism offers excellent opportunities to study the complex *effects* and diverging *motivations behind* the production of esoteric ideas and practices as being somehow marginal or even subversive. As Asprem also highlighted, such status seems in fact to be an integral component of what makes esotericism attractive as an "alternative" to "official" positions, whether in the domains of religion, arts, politics, medicine, worldviews, or "lifestyles." Crockford's chapter (2021) further illustrated how this aspect troubles the view of esoteric rejected knowledge as the essential "underdog," divested of "Establishment" power, by showing how the rhetoric of being rejected, marginal, oppositional and, moreover, *secret*, is used successfully in marketing purposes by the wellness industry. The thrust of Asprem's and Crockford's arguments is that a critical reappraisal of how rejected knowledge narratives are constructed leads us to consider the agency of those who are either "rejected" by others, claim such status for themselves, or gravitate towards that which has already been construed as marginal. Further studies along these lines can contribute a lot to our understanding of more general processes of exclusion and opposition, which seems crucial at a time when anti-Establishment rhetoric is a potent political force in the world.

Conceptualizing "Esotericism" for a New Generation

The focus of this book has been on how we can responsibly and fruitfully expand the perimeters of the study of esotericism. The responses to this question—and the particular recommendations to drop the Western demarcation, avoid diffusionist models, readjust our foci on (historical) actors, and rethink the rejected knowledge thesis—inevitably brings us back to the question of how esotericism ought to be defined. We can hear the worries of some readers that there will be nothing left of the field once the reflection is done, or that a global approach on non-diffusionist terms leaves us with a concept so diluted that it signifies anything and nothing, anywhere and nowhere. Let us in conclusion address this worry by showing that, to the contrary, we have a lot left to work with, and clear directions for a plurality of different research projects where esotericism can be operationalized on lucid and sound foundations.

As Okropiridze (2021) argued in his philosophy-inflected contribution on the definitional progression in the field, there is currently an unresolved tension between definitions that claim to be grounded in the way things are (what he calls the onto-epistemological directionality) and approaches that hold esotericism to be a human (scholarly or otherwise) projection onto reality (historical, social, psychological or otherwise; what he calls the epistemo-ontological directionality). In the first camp he singles out Faivre's definition as the gold standard, while elements of it are also found in Hanegraaff's empiricist project of letting sources speak for themselves and in Asprem's cognitivist project of studying the mental and evolutionary building blocks of practices deemed esoteric. In the second camp he singles out Bergunder's approach to esotericism as an "empty signifier" that temporarily fixes contentious power discourses in concrete historical contexts as the clearest example, while again also finding elements of it in Hanegraaff's insistence that esotericism emerged as a narrative construct shaped in polemical discourses, and Asprem's insistence that the cognitive building blocks are not building blocks *of* esotericism (constituting and defining it), but rather of individual practices that are *labelled* such in various discursive formations (and yet differently in other formations).

Okropiridze's conclusion is worth noting, for it offers consolation to those who worry that scholars will have nothing left to work with following theoretical interventions of the type offered in this book, or that the field will be dominated by "deconstructions." To the contrary, Okropiridze argues that *neither* the "deconstructionist" *nor* the "inductivist-realist" side of the spectrum can succeed on their own, because the nature of interpretation requires both that there is some*thing* revealing itself to be interpreted (the onto-epistemic, or realist presupposition) and that *some*thing is singled out for interpretation by the scholar (the epistemo-ontological, or "deconstructionist" presupposition). Since Okropiridze thinks this conundrum *cannot* be solved, his prescription is that we must allow for differing approaches and, indeed, definitions, to work side by side in the field—on the condition that each research program self-reflectively acknowledges their limitation, restrains any ambition for dominance, and listens attentively to what other projects built on different assumptions are achieving.

In that spirit, let us now return to the definition question as it looks in light of the chapters of this book. While the definition debate has not been at the forefront, we have seen several strategies deployed throughout the book, notably a consistent genealogical approach based on Bergunder (Strube), and stipulative, heuristic definitions singling out specific understudied subfields, such as "ancient (Mediterranean) esoteric traditions" (Burns) and "Africana esoteric studies" (Page and Finley). These approaches work in opposing directionalities, to use Okropiridze's terminology, but can, as we will show, still fruitfully speak to one another.

AFTERWORD: OUTLINES OF A NEW ROADMAP

The first thing to make clear is what is and is not entailed by the genealogical approach that Strube suggests as the basis for a global history of esotericism. First of all, while it is true that it dismisses the possibility of simply uncovering a set of sources out there that can be made to speak for "esotericism," it does not follow that we thereby lose access to our sources, that esotericism doesn't "really exist," or that *anything* could be made into esotericism on the scholar's whim. What the approach leaves us with in terms of defining a field of study is in fact very precise and empirically accessible: starting with the existence of the term itself, it points us to the discourses in which it is articulated, by real flesh-and-blood people, along with the contexts in which they live and act, and asks us to pay attention to the meaning-making processes and negotiations over the term's significance *in those contexts* and *to those people*. Working our way backwards, we land in the nineteenth century as the crucial period in which meanings of esotericism are enunciated, connected with ancient wisdom traditions, initiations, secrecy, magical power, tantra, mesmeric trance and somnambulism, hidden Tibetan masters, yoga, gnosis, perennial truth, astral travel, and all the rest. As Strube demonstrates, this genealogical foundation then requires us to decenter the particular voices we have been used to prioritize and analyse the entire discourse on the esoteric/esotericism where, e.g., South Asian individuals and organizations, as well as rank-and-file Indian members of the Theosophical Society are given equal attention, and their own local motivations, background knowledge, and pre-Theosophical horizon of meaning are explored for how they actively shaped the negotiations that ensued. A crucial insight resulting from this perspective is that the meanings of notions such as esotericism, occultism, or Theosophy were anything but fixed and subject to constant controversial negotiations—they were *not* ready-made "Western concepts" that could be exported into the rest of the world. Quite the contrary, they were shaped within global exchanges. As Cantú demonstrated with regards to the study of yoga, this tracking of existing local traditions, practices, and meanings has already turned up lots of empirical evidence that causes significant problems for the narrative of Western occultists simply "appropriating" an authentic yoga and adapting it to comply with "essentially Western" ideas. Instead we see genuine entanglements of pre-existing Indian and European traditions that mutually influence each other.

Some might object that a genealogical approach will run into problems if it wants to push further back in history to times before there was a discourse on "esotericism" (because the term was not yet coined). For such an expansion to succeed, it will usually be necessary to invent analytic concepts for heuristic purposes, or to follow other "empty signifiers" (such as "gnosis," "kabbalah," or "magic") that made it into the temporary fixing of "esotericism." In fact, the genealogical approach does already provide us with crucial insights that must be taken into account if we are to stipulate definitions to be deployed backwards in history. It is also well equipped to conceptualize responsible comparative projects, as it consistently works through the contextualization of historical sources (Bergunder, 2016). For example, it is already clear that, while "esotericism" as such is empty, the connections that the term fixed in nineteenth-century discourses tended to draw on a number of rather specific ideas, particularly when narratives of tradition were invented. As is well known, Jacques Matter was first to define the term in French as denoting the elitist secrecy that he associated with Gnosis and ancient Gnosticism—significantly influenced when doing so by existing Illuminist currents in France that combined initiatory societies with magical and theurgic practice, divination, and oracles. In the German context, the noun *Esoterismus* was first used in discussions about Pythagoreanism and their apparent secret societies, while it soon also came to be used in the context of Freemasonry, across the continent as well as in English (Neugebauer-Wölk, 2010). It bears emphasizing that the earliest authors who used such vocabulary did so in the context of orientalist studies and, like Matter, linked Gnostic doctrines to common civilizational roots in "India" and "the East" from the very beginning (Strube, forthcoming; cf. 2016b, pp. 115–121 and passim). Among the occultists, invocations of esotericism or "esoteric tradition" would seldom fail to reference the Gnostics, kabbalists, mystery cults, Hermes Trismegistus, Pythagoras, Plato, the Neoplatonists, the Knights Templars, the Cathars, the Rosicrucians, the alchemists, and so forth. It did not take occultists long, then, to embark on journeys to "the East" on their quests for the origins of the ancient wisdom supposedly handed down by these traditions. A genealogical perspective offers explanations of this circumstance on the basis of historical source material and investigates how and why historical actors identified and compared "esoteric traditions" across the globe.

Such a perspective also helps to understand the emergence of such (invented) traditions. Esoteric narratives and ideas emerged and were shaped in all sorts of different contexts and for different reasons: as Strube has shown elsewhere (2016a), the first occultists did it in the very specific contexts of French pre-Marxist "utopian socialism" and neo-Catholicism—and emphatically not in the context of an actually existing tradition where these systems were passed down in an unbroken chain that can simply be studied historically. Yet, the meanings and connections that such enunciations assembled provide us with a framework for further, necessarily more fragmented, historical studies along the lines of reception history. It is precisely through such a lens that the study of esotericism could demonstrate the relevance of its subjects, and thus its own relevance: orientalist studies, historical-critical Bible studies, socialism, and the most influential Catholic movements at a given time were anything but rejected or marginal. A consistent pursuit of such a research program could thus not only yield crucial insights into historical and social-scientific material; it also could help other scholars understand the history of their subjects, for instance by demonstrating the relevance of esotericism within the history of socialism. It could also help them understand the history of their disciplines: even a cursory look at Indological scholarship or studies focusing on late antiquity, for instance, will reveal an abundance of "esoteric" vocabulary.

This is also where we can see how Burns' suggestions complement the genealogical approach, which starts by stipulating "ancient (Mediterranean) esoteric traditions," which is to cover religious and philosophical traditions in the ancient world centrally concerned with an "esoteric" dynamic of hiding and revealing higher truths usually held to be ineffable, whether we find these in Neoplatonic theurgic traditions, Gnostic apocalyptic texts, or the Enochic literature of Jewish apocalypses. Having defined this area of interest, Burns suggests we can fruitfully build our way through history, not by tracing "surviving traditions" from antiquity, but through a reception-historical approach in which the memory of and references to such texts, whether in existing manuscripts or fragmentary reconstructions, have constantly been reinterpreted and reimagined over the first millennium, into the European Renaissance and down to our own days. Eventually, then, these two approaches meet in the fixing of discourses on "esotericism"—the crucial point is that while these discourses retroactively point out the direction for us of what's relevant to study, the critical reflection on how those connections were fixed should enable us to resist simply reproducing, for instance, nineteenth century historical narratives. Any ancient sources we end up studying, then, are not sources "of" esotericism (strictly speaking invented in the eighteenth and nineteenth centuries), even though their *reception history* and their later entanglements eventually contributed to the formation of "esotericism" as an empirically available historical subject matter in the modern colonial period.

Along the way, scholars get plenty of opportunities to study the social roles of secrecy and initiation, the construction of tradition, the production and contestation of knowledge, and rejection and exclusion practices—as well as the shifting ways in which this material is connected with political, economic, and religious power. Not least due to the oppositional and non-hegemonic status that is often ascribed to esotericism by practitioners, their critics and opponents, or scholars studying them, this material holds huge potential for analyses of social practices and socio-political issues. Several chapters in this volume have highlighted this potential with regard to sexuality, gender, and race. It is in light of such examples that the study of esotericism can make significant contributions, not only to research on historical subjects but also on how they inform and shape present-day developments.

All of this should suffice to illustrate that there is a vast continent of material left to study with such conceptualizations of "esotericism." While it does not lead to an "anything goes" attitude, it does open up the field in very significant ways. For example, Burns' reception-historical approach could equally validly be applied in the South Indian context, as indeed Cantú does in his chapter, or in the context of South and Latin America, as indicated by Villalba, and obviously too in the Islamic world, as Saif argues. Rather than escalating into a diffuse or even neo-perennialist historiography, or attempting to write a "universal" or "planetary" history of esotericism, the decentered and global approaches suggested in this volume form solid foundations for strictly historical, consistent, and theoretically substantiated research. Equipped with such a roadmap, we invite scholars of esotericism as well as outside observers to explore the expanding horizon of our field and secure not only its internal solidification, but also its establishment within academia at large.

Bibliography

Asprem, E. (2021) "Rejected Knowledge Reconsidered: Some Methodological Notes on Esotericism and Marginality," in Asprem, E. and Strube, J. (eds.) *New Approaches to the Study of Esotericism*. Leiden and Boston: Brill, pp. 127–146.

Bakker, J.M. (2021) "Race and (the Study of) Esotericism," in Asprem, E. and Strube, J. (eds.) *New Approaches to the Study of Esotericism*. Leiden and Boston: Brill, pp. 147–167.

Bergunder, M. (2016) "Comparison in the Maelstrom of Historicity: A Postcolonial Perspective on Comparative Religion," in Schmidt-Leukel, P. and Nehring, A. (eds.) *Interreligious Comparisons in Religious Studies and Theology*. London/New York: Bloomsbury Academic, pp. 34–52.

Bladel, K.v. (2009) *The Arabic Hermes: From Pagan Sage to Prophet of Science*. Oxford: Oxford University Press.

Burns, D. (2021) "Receptions of Revelations: A Future for the Study of Esotericism and Antiquity," in Asprem, E. and Strube, J. (eds.) *New Approaches to the Study of Esotericism*. Leiden and Boston: Brill, pp. 20–44.

Cantú, K. (2021) "'Don't Take Any Wooden Nickles': Western Esotericism, Yoga, and the Discourse of Authenticity," in Asprem, E. and Strube, J. (eds.) *New Approaches to the Study of Esotericism*. Leiden and Boston: Brill, pp. 109–126.

Crockford, S. (2021) "What Do Jade Eggs Tell Us about 'Esotericism'? Spirituality, Neoliberalism, Secrecy, and Commodities," in Asprem, E. and Strube, J. (eds.) *New Approaches to the Study of Esotericism*. Leiden and Boston: Brill, pp. 201–216.

Hedenborg White, M. (2021) "Double Toil and Gender Trouble? Performativity and Femininity in the Cauldron of Esotericism Research," in Asprem, E. and Strube, J. (eds.) *New Approaches to the Study of Esotericism*. Leiden and Boston: Brill, pp. 182–200.

Neugebauer-Wölk, M. (2010) "Der Esoteriker und die Esoterik: Wie das Esoterische im 18. Jahrhundert zum Begriff wird und seinen Weg in die Moderne findet," *Aries*, 10(2), pp. 217–231.

Okropiridze, D. (2021) "Interpretation Reconsidered: The Definitional Progression in the Study of Esotericism as a Case in Point for the Varifocal Theory of Interpretation," in Asprem, E. and Strube, J. (eds.) *New Approaches to the Study of Esotericism*. Leiden and Boston: Brill, pp. 217–240.

Page, H.R. Jr. and Finley, S.C. (2021) "'What Can the Whole World Be Hiding?' Exploring *Africana* Esotericisms in the American Soul–Blues Continuum," in Asprem, E. and Strube, J. (eds.) *New Approaches to the Study of Esotericism*. Leiden and Boston: Brill, pp. 168–181.

Saif, L. (2021) "'That I Did Love the Moore to Live with Him': Islam in/and the Study of 'Western Esotericism,'" in Asprem, E. and Strube, J. (eds.) *New Approaches to the Study of Esotericism*. Leiden and Boston: Brill, pp. 67–87.

Strube, J. (2016a) "Socialist Religion and the Emergence of Occultism: A Genealogical Approach to Socialism and Secularization in 19th-Century France," *Religion*, 46(3), pp. 359–388.

Strube, J. (2016b) *Sozialismus, Katholizismus und Okkultismus im Frankreich des 19. Jahrhunderts: Die Genealogie der Schriften von Eliphas Lévi*. Berlin/Boston: De Gruyter.

Strube, J. (2021) "Towards the Study of Esotericism without the 'Western'": Esotericism from the Perspective of a Global Religious History," in Asprem, E. and Strube, J. (eds.) *New Approaches to the Study of Esotericism*. Leiden and Boston: Brill, pp. 45–66.

Strube, J. (forthcoming) *Tantra in the Context of a Global Religious History* (working title).

Villalba, M. (2021) "The Occult Among the Aborigines of South America? Some Remarks on Race, Coloniality, and the West in the Study of Esotericism," in Asprem, E. and Strube, J. (eds.) *New Approaches to the Study of Esotericism*. Leiden and Boston: Brill, pp. 88–108.

Index

agency   4, 9–10, 55, 57, 59, 67, 70, 110, 117, 150, 186, 194–196, 242–243, 245
Africa   68, 69–70, 94, 96, 97, 98–99, 101
African American/African Americans
   in the study of "Western esotericism"   12–13, 148, 150, 168–169, 171–174
   See also racism
   See also slavery
Africana Esoteric Studies (AES)   12–13, 148, 168–174, 174–175, 178, 242, 246
Alexandria, (school of)   20n2, 28–31, 33, 34, 36
antiquity   20–38, 192, 202, 219, 249
Apocrypha   36–37, 38
appropriation   11, 51, 67, 75, 90, 93, 94, 99, 101, 113, 114, 118–119, 122, 151–152, 152–153, 161, 169, 173, 243, 247
Asia   1, 2–3, 11, 50, 52, 53, 68–70, 93, 97, 98–99, 110, 117, 121, 247
authenticity   3–4, 11, 52, 76, 109–123, 141, 152, 172–173, 186, 213, 243, 247
Babalon   183–184, 191–195
bāṭiniyya
   See Islamic esotericism
Bible   9, 24–25, 35–36, 69–70, 98, 175–176, 191, 248–249
blackness   148, 159–160, 171–172
Buddhism   35, 59, 68, 76, 109, 111
canon   4, 5, 6, 12, 37, 54, 75–76, 81, 94–95, 127–128, 132, 134, 138, 162, 172, 212
Cercle Harmonique   149–150, 153–155, 156–157
chakras   112–113, 121, 204
colonialism, colonial   3, 6–7, 10–11, 55, 56, 57, 58, 59, 60, 70–71, 73–74, 76, 80, 88–89, 91, 92–93, 94, 95–98, 100, 101, 104–105, 110, 113, 115–116, 117–118, 120, 121–122, 170, 208, 211, 243, 249
coloniality   97–98, 104
   See also decolonial approaches
   See also postcolonial approaches
commodification, commodities   13–14, 114, 161, 171, 185, 201, 207, 208, 212–213
conspiracy theory   136–137, 203, 206
Corbinophilia and Corbinophobia   81

Corpus Hermeticum   22
critical race studies   12, 142, 162–163, 241
cultic milieu   25, 140–141
decolonial approaches   10, 89, 96, 97–98, 104, 142, 162–163, 177–178, 241
   See also postcolonial approaches
diachronic perspectives   58, 61
Dictionary of Gnosis and Western Esotericism   3, 94, 178
diffusionism   3, 9, 45–46, 52–55, 57, 58, 60, 88, 93–97, 169, 241–242, 245
East/Eastern   10, 25–28, 48–49, 59, 67–73, 75, 77, 82, 93, 98, 103–104, 109–111, 114–118, 243, 248
elected marginality   132, 140–141
Enlightenment, the   72, 78–80, 91, 95–96, 98, 112, 130, 133, 135, 169–171, 173–174, 206, 244
   See also Post-Enlightenment
entanglement/entangled history   47, 49, 53, 55, 58, 60, 60–61, 67, 68, 80, 81, 184, 186, 241–242, 243, 247, 249
esotericism
   Western esotericism as polemical concept   46, 47–49, 61–62
   See also Africana Esoteric Studies
   See also Eurocentrism
   See also gender
   See also global approaches
   See also Islam
   See also race
   See also rejected knowledge
   See also West/Western
Eurocentrism   58, 60, 88–89, 93–97, 98, 103–104, 242
   See also diffusionism
extraterrestrials   157–159
femininity   13, 182–197
feminism   1, 141, 182–183, 185–186, 189–190, 192, 194, 195–196
gender   8, 13, 55, 100, 101, 131, 140, 142, 150, 182–197, 209, 238, 243, 249–250
   See also femininity
   See also queer
   See also sexuality

genealogy   37, 59, 60, 67, 92, 99–100, 110, 112, 118, 133, 134, 222, 244, 246–249
global approaches   1, 3–4, 7, 9–10, 13–14, 45–62, 67, 78–82, 88–89, 95, 103–105, 147, 169, 171, 201, 203–204, 205, 241–243, 245, 247, 250
global religious history   9–10, 46, 59–62
gnosis   9, 20, 21, 25–26, 28, 29–38, 77, 132, 219, 220–221, 222, 226, 228, 244, 247–248
  See also ʿirfān
Gnostic Mass   183–184, 187–190, 193, 195
gnosticism   8, 20–22, 25, 29–38, 129, 130, 248
Grand Polemical Narrative   11, 28, 55, 130–131, 134
Harlem Renaissance   170–171
Hermetica   27, 32–33
Hermetism   8, 20, 37–38, 59, 129, 244
Hinduism   59, 68, 76, 111, 113, 118–119
hybridity   57, 113, 172
identity politics   4, 55, 60, 61–62, 113, 131
Illuminationism   25, 75
incommensurability   14, 184, 217, 227, 228, 229–230, 232, 237, 238, 243
ʿirfān   77
  See also gnosis
Islam   1, 3, 10, 29, 38, 48, 52, 67–82, 100, 111, 114, 159, 172, 244
Islamic esotericism   1, 3, 10, 67, 75–78, 80, 81
Islamic World   3, 71, 81, 242, 250
late antiquity   8, 22–25, 28, 29–30, 93, 98, 249
Latin America   52, 54, 88–105, 250
magic   7, 15, 20, 21, 22, 24, 29, 30, 36, 37, 55, 72, 100, 101–102, 115, 120–121, 130, 135, 138, 139, 183, 187, 189, 190, 193, 195, 203n3, 210, 213, 243, 247, 248
maps   69, 70, 98
Martinism   89, 101, 102–103, 173
masculinity   182–186, 191, 196–197
modernity   15, 20, 25, 30, 46, 51, 56–58, 60, 70, 78–81, 88–89, 93–95, 96–98, 98–99, 100, 103, 104, 110n1, 111–112, 113, 117, 118, 121, 127–128, 171, 183, 206, 209, 244
music
  American Soul and Blues   13, 168–169, 175–176, 178, 242
Nag Hammadi Codices   21, 30–31, 33, 37

Nation of Islam   159, 172
Native Americans   12, 149–155, 160–161
neoliberalism   13–14, 201, 203, 205–206, 208, 210–211
Neoplatonism   20–21, 22, 25, 28–29, 34, 37–38, 80, 129, 248, 249
New Age   5, 37, 80, 81, 136, 203n5, 204, 206–207
occidentalism   74n1, 91, 99, 110–111
occultism   3, 5, 6, 7, 9, 10–11, 22, 28, 30, 33, 48, 49–50, 51, 52, 61, 71, 80, 88, 96–97, 101–102, 104, 109–110, 111–114, 116–118, 121, 122, 128, 136, 141, 142, 183, 219, 228, 242–243, 247–248
Orientalism   10, 51, 52, 55, 67, 71, 72, 73, 74, 76, 98–99, 109, 110–111, 114–117, 222, 248
  See also Positive Orientalism
positionality   61, 79, 197, 241
Positive Orientalism   10, 51, 52, 74
  See also Orientalism
  See also Platonic Orientalism
Other/Othering   14, 29–30, 56–57, 68, 71, 82, 98, 104, 131, 136, 162
Paracelsism   21, 129, 134
Perennialism   2, 10, 27, 49, 67, 71, 74, 74, 133, 250
performativity   13, 184, 190–191, 195–196
philosophia perennis   25, 33, 71, 72
  See also perennialism
philosophy   21, 24, 25, 28–29, 31, 32n7, 35, 37–38, 72, 73, 75, 81, 89, 92–93, 95, 119–121, 122, 129–130, 132, 133, 138, 218, 219–221, 222n4, 226–227, 245–246
Platonic Orientalism   9, 10, 20, 21, 25–29, 32, 33, 36, 72–74, 132n2
Platonism   20–31, 33–35
postcolonial approaches   46–47, 49, 51, 53, 56–57, 59, 60, 73n1, 97, 122, 142, 241, 243
  See also decolonial approaches
Post-Enlightenment   4, 78–80, 111–112, 128, 135
Postmodernism   7, 45–46, 55–56, 137, 142, 182
poststructuralism   57, 59, 182, 220, 222, 238
Pseudepigrapha   36–37, 38
queer   1, 13, 182–183, 184, 186, 189–190, 194, 238

race   12, 69–70, 88–89, 92–93, 96–97, 99–102, 104, 113, 147–163, 170–174, 186, 195, 197, 209
   and/in Spiritualism   149–155
   and/in UFO abduction narratives   156–161
   in the study of esotericism   4, 8, 10, 11–13, 55, 99–101, 104, 142, 147–163, 183, 241, 249–250
racism   10, 12, 55, 100, 147, 149, 161, 170, 173, 243
rationality/rationalism   56, 70, 75, 77, 78–82, 93, 96–97, 183, 206, 219–220, 227
reception-history   9, 20–22, 28–31, 33, 35–38, 61, 118, 244, 248–250
rejected knowledge   1, 5–6, 7, 8, 11, 12–14, 20, 47, 52, 55, 61, 95, 96, 127–143, 169, 171–172, 183, 201, 206–207, 209, 212, 213, 243–245, 248–249
   inflated and restricted model   11, 127, 130–132, 136–137, 143, 244
   See also rejected people
rejected people   12–13, 171
   See also Africana Esoteric Studies
   See also race
Renaissance   8–9, 20, 22, 31, 33, 36, 37, 54, 72, 80–81, 88–89, 90, 92–93, 94, 95, 98, 99, 111–112, 127, 128, 170, 219, 249
revelation   9, 20–21, 24–25, 26, 28, 32, 33, 35–38, 72–73, 92, 100, 176, 206, 208–209, 219–220, 227
Rosicrucianism   5, 59, 129, 173, 248
Scandinavia   1, 2–3, 69, 94
séances   148, 149–155, 156–157
secrecy   1–2, 9, 20, 23, 36, 168, 170, 174, 201, 206, 207–213, 219, 220–221, 226, 228, 247–248, 249
self-marginalization   6–8, 11, 61–62, 132, 142–143
sexuality   13, 182–183, 185–186, 190, 191–193, 195, 197, 243, 249–250

slavery   97, 152n5, 159, 160, 242
sociology of the occult   128, 139–140
Spiritualism   7, 12, 61, 80, 148–155, 159, 161–162, 183, 186–187, 196–197
spirituality   24, 32–35, 77, 136–137, 201, 204–208, 211–213
Sufism (*taṣawwuf*)   67, 71, 74, 76–78, 109
tantra   61n2, 114–115, 116, 122, 208, 247
Templars   5, 114, 248
Thelema   13, 109, 183, 187–195
theology   22, 26, 35, 36, 37, 59, 80, 133, 219–220, 222, 227
Theosophical Society/Theosophy   4, 7, 34, 48–49, 50–51, 54–55, 61, 71, 74, 110, 115–116, 121, 136, 183, 242, 243, 247
theosophy   34, 48–49, 129, 219, 220–221, 226, 228
theurgy   8, 20, 22, 24–25, 28, 29, 72, 248, 249
Traditionalism   67, 71, 74, 76–77, 81, 117, 136, 137
translocalization   110, 122
UFO abductions   148, 156–161
   See also African Americans
   See also Native Americans
   See also race *and* racism
wellness industry   13–14, 135, 201–205, 245
West/Western   2–6, 8–10, 12, 15, 29, 31, 37, 45–62, 67–82, 88–89, 91–96, 98–100, 103–104, 109–110, 112–117, 119–123, 130–131, 134, 148, 158, 169, 171–174, 177–178, 183, 204–207, 209, 212, 218, 241–243, 245, 247
white supremacy   12, 148–149, 155
whiteness   4, 12, 148, 152–155, 159
   and the study of esotericism   148–149, 159–160, 162
   constructs of   148, 155
   studies   12, 163, 241
yoga   11, 109–123, 242, 247
Zoroaster/Zoroastrianism   68, 72, 77, 100, 111

Printed in the United States
By Bookmasters